Texts in Computer Science

Editors
David Gries
Fred B. Schneider

Joseph Migga Kizza

Ethical and Social Issues
in the Information Age

Prof. Joseph Migga Kizza
Department of Computer Science and Engineering
University of Tennessee
Chattanooga, TN
USA
joseph-kizza@utc.edu

Series Editors:
David Gries
Department of Computer Science
Cornell University
Ithaca, NY
USA

Fred B. Schneider
Department of Computer Science
Cornell University
Ithaca, NY
USA

ISBN 978-1-84996-037-3   e-ISBN 978-1-84996-038-0
DOI 10.1007/978-1-84996-038-0
Springer London Dordrecht Heidelberg New York

British Library Cataloguing in Publication Data
A catalogue record for this book is available from the British Library

Library of Congress Control Number: 2010920467

Printed on acid-free paper

Springer is part of Springer Science+Business Media (www.springer.com)

Preface to the Fourth Edition

The frequency of new editions of this book is indicative of the rapid and tremendous changes in the fields of computer and information sciences. First published in 1995, the book has rapidly gone through three editions already and now we are in the fourth. Over this period, we have become more dependent on computer and telecommunication technology than ever before and computer technology has become ubiquitous. Since I started writing on social computing, I have been advocating a time when we, as individuals and as nations, will become totally dependent on computing technology. That time is almost on us. Evidence of this is embodied in the rapid convergence of telecommunication, broadcasting, and computing devices; the miniaturization of these devices; and the ever increasing storage capacity, speed of computation, and ease of use. These qualities have been a big pulling force sucking in millions of new users every day, sometimes even those unwilling. Other appealing features of these devices are the increasing number of applications, *apps*, as they are increasingly becoming known, and being wireless and easily portable. Whether small or big, these new gizmos have become the centerpiece of an individual's social and economic activities and the main access point for all information. Individuals aside, computing technology has also become the engine that drives the nations' strategic and security infrastructures that control power grids, gas and oil storage facilities, transportation, and all forms of national communication, including emergency services. These developments have elevated cyberspace to be the most crucial economic and security domains of nations.

US President Barack Obama has classified cyberspace security and cyber threat as one of the most serious economic and national security challenges the United States is facing as a nation.[1] He, in particular, classified the country's computer networks to be the national security priority. What led to this has been a consistent and growing problem of cyber threats. In 2007 alone, the Pentagon reported nearly 44,000 incidents of malicious cyber activities carried out by foreign militaries, intelligence agencies, and individual hackers.

In April 2009, the US government admitted, after reports, that the nation's power grid is vulnerable to cyber attack, following reports that it has been infiltrated by foreign spies. According to reports, there is a pretty strong consensus in the security

---

[1]"US 'concerned' over cyber threat". http://news.bbc.co.uk/2/hi/americas/8126668.stm

v

community that the SCADA (*Supervisory Control And Data Acquisition*), an industrial control system that is used to monitor and control industrial, infrastructure, or facility-based processes, has not kept pace with the rest of the industry; it needs, if not total replacement, at least a detailed update to keep abreast of rapid changes in technology. According to the *Wall Street Journal*, the intruders had not sought to damage the power grid or any other key infrastructure so far, but suggested that they could change their approach in the event of a crisis or war. The motives behind these potential attacks are undoubtedly military, economic, and political.[2] There are almost similar stories with other countries.

The rising trend in cyber attacks, many of them with lightening speed, affecting millions of computers worldwide and in the process causing a loss of billions of dollars to individuals and businesses, may be an indication of how unprepared we are to handle such attacks not only now but also in the future. It may also be a mark of the poor state of our cyberspace security policies and the lack of will to implement these policies and develop protocols and build facilities that will diminish the effects of these menacing activities if not eliminating them altogether.

It is encouraging though to hear that at last governments have started to act. For example, the US government has started to take all aspects of cyber crime very seriously and the department of defense (DoD) has formed an entire cyber command to handle online threats to the country. The United Kingdom (UK) has also launched a cyber defense program and both countries are in possession of and are building more effective cyber warfare capabilities. They are not the only one. This is not limited to the United States and the United Kingdom alone; a number of other countries including China and Russia are also building their own capabilities. There is a growing realization that the next big war may probably be fought in cyberspace. One hopes, though, that as these governments prepare defensive stances, they also take steps to protect the individual citizens.

As we look for such defensive strategies, the technological race is picking up speed with new technologies that make our efforts and existing technologies on which these strategies based obsolete in shorter and shorter periods. All these illustrate the speed at which the computing environment is changing and demonstrate a need for continuous review of our defensive strategies and more importantly a need for a strong ethical framework in our computer, information and engineering science education. This has been the focus of this book and remains so in this edition.

What Is New in This Edition

There has been considerable changes in the contents of the book to bring it in line with the new developments we discussed above. In almost every chapter, new content has been added and we have eliminated what looked as outdated materials.

---

[2] Maggie Shiels. "Spies 'infiltrate US power grid'".
Thursday, 9 April 2009 http://news.bbc.co.uk/2/hi/technology/7990997.stm

Since content in some chapters had not changed since the first edition, this was an opportunity to bring all chapter contents up to date. In addition to new chapter contents, chapter objectives have been added to streamline chapter content to give it a telescoping view for the student to look forward to. I also wanted to make the reading of chapters more interactive by including, sporadically, **Issues for Discussion**, a series of thought-provoking questions and statements. These are intended to ignite students' interest beyond the entrance scenarios that open up the book chapters and start classroom discussions.

Chapter Overview

The book is divided into 14 chapters as follows:

Chapter 1—History of Computing (New) gives an overview of the history of computing science in hardware, software, and networking, covering pre-historic (prior to 1946) computing devices and computing pioneers since the *Abacus*. It also discusses the development of computer crimes and the current social and ethical environment. Further, computer ethics is defined, and a need to study computer ethics is emphasized.

Chapter 2—Morality and the Law defines and examines personal and public morality, identifying assumptions and value the law, looking at both conventional and natural law, and the intertwining of morality and the law. It, together with Chapter 3, gives the reader the philosophical framework needed for the remainder of the book.

Chapter 3—Ethics and Ethical Analysis (New) builds upon Chapter 2 in setting up the philosophical framework and analysis tools for the book discussing moral theories and problems in ethical relativism. Based on these and in light of the rapid advances in technology, the chapter discusses the moral and ethical premises and their corresponding values in the changing technology arena.

Chapter 4—Ethics and the Professions (changed) examines the changing nature of the professions and how they cope with the impact of technology on their fields. An ethical framework for decision making is developed. Professional and ethical responsibilities based on community values and the law are also discussed. And social issues including harassment and discrimination are thoroughly covered.

Chapter 5—Anonymity, Security, Privacy and Civil Liberties surveys the traditional ethical issues of privacy, security, anonymity and analyzes how these issues are affected by computer technology. Information gathering, databasing, and civil liberties are also discussed.

Chapter 6—Intellectual Property Rights and Computer Technology discusses the foundations of intellectual property rights and how computer technology has influenced and changed the traditional issues of property rights, in particular intellectual property rights.

Chapter 7—Social Context of Computing considers the three main social issues in computing namely, the digital divide, workplace issues like employee monitoring, and health risks, and how these issues are changing with the changing computer technology.

Chapter 8—Software Issues: Risks and Liabilities revisits property rights, responsibility, and accountability with a focus on computer software. The risks and liabilities associated with software and risk assessment are also discussed.

Chapters 9—Computer Crimes surveys the history and examples of computer crimes, their types, costs on society, and strategies of detection and prevention.

Chapter 10—New Frontiers for Ethical Consideration: Artificial Intelligence, Cyberspace, and Virtual Reality discusses the new frontiers of ethics: virtual reality, artificial intelligence, and the Internet, and how these new frontiers are affecting the traditional ethical and social issues.

Chapter 11—Cyberspace and Cyberethics and Social Networking (New) discusses the new realities of global computer networks, the intertwining of global economies, monopolies and their economic implications, globalization, emerging issues like global ethics, culture, and the development of the lingua franca for the Internet. It also focuses the discussion on the new realities of social networking.

Chapter 12—Computer Networks and Online Crimes begins by presenting the core basics of computer networks for those readers who have never taken a course in computer networks. Then the chapter discusses the major online crimes and ends by a discussion of techniques and technologies in use to mitigate these crimes.

Chapter 13—Computer Crime Investigations discusses what constitutes digital evidence, the collection and analysis of digital evidence, chain of custody, the writing of the report, and the possible appearance in court as an expert witness.

Chapter 14—Biometrics starts by discussing the different techniques in access control. Biometric technologies and techniques are then introduced to be contrasted with the other known techniques. Several biometrics and biometric technologies are discussed.

Audience

The book satisfies the new **Computer Science curriculum 2008: An Interim Revision of CS 2001**, which includes updates of the **CS2001 Computer/Science Curricula for undergraduates: Social and Professional Issues/(SP)**. This new curriculum is intended for computer science, information science, and software engineering students. Students in related disciplines like computer information and information management systems, and library sciences will also find this book informative.

It is also good for anyone interested in knowing how ethical and social issues like privacy, civil liberties, security, anonymity, and workplace issues like harassment and discrimination are affecting the new computerized environment.

In addition, anybody interested in reading about computer networking, social networking, information security, and privacy will also find the book very helpful.

Acknowledgments

I appreciate all the help I received from colleagues who offered ideas, criticism, sometimes harsh, and suggestions from anonymous reviewers over the years. Special thanks to my dear wife, Dr. Immaculate Kizza, who offered a considerable amount of help in proofreading, constructive ideas, and wonderful support.

Chattanooga, TN, USA   Joseph Migga Kizza

Contents

Chapter 1
History of Computing

Learning Objectives

After reading this chapter, the reader should be able to:

1. Learn about the contributions of several pioneers in the computing field.
2. Compare life before and after the advent of personal computers and the Internet.
3. Identify significant continuing trends in the history of the computing field.

1.1 Historical Development of Computing and Information Technology

1.1.1 Before AD 1900

From time immemorial, human beings have been trying to make their lives easy and worth living through the invention of gadgets. The invention of the computer and, therefore, the history of computing have taken the same track. The timeline of the development of computing stretches back like the recorded history of humanity itself.

Besides tools that make life easier, human beings have always been fascinated with numbers. So it should be no surprise that the first utility tools recorded in history dealt with numbers. For example, it is believed that the first prime numbers recorded on animal bones and rocks—the only available and durable storage devices of the time— were done between 20000 BC and 30000 BC [1]. By 1800 BC, the first place-value number system was in place. To help merchants who were trading goods to quickly calculate goods bought and sold, and also gains and losses, there was a need to develop a device to do the mathematics quickly. This led to the invention of the abacus, the device many believe was the mother of the digital computer as we know it today, between 1000 BC and 500 BC. Without performing actual calculations, the abacus helps the person using it to keep track of the calculated results he or she has done mentally. Zero and negative numbers were first used between 300 BC and 500 AD.

The period between 1500 and 1900 saw a surge of activity in the development of computing devices. Many of these developments were driven by the commerce of the time. In 1500, the computing community got a boost when Leonardo da Vinci

J.M. Kizza, *Ethical and Social Issues in the Information Age*, Texts in Computer Science, DOI 10.1007/978-1-84996-038-0_1, © Springer-Verlag London Limited 2010

invented a mechanical calculator. This was followed by the invention of the slide rule in 1621. Leonardo da Vinci's mechanical calculator was followed by Wilhelm Schichard's mechanical calculator in 1625 and by Blaise Pascal's arithmetic machine 15 years later.

The major breakthrough in speed came in 1800 with the invention of the punched card by Joseph-Marie Jacquard, a French silk weaver [1]. Jacquard's punched card revolutionized computing in the sense that it quickly spread to other fields where it was used not only to speed up computation but also to store information.

The period after 1830 was an exciting one in the history of computing because during this period there were successive history-making inventions starting with Charles Babbage's analytical engine in 1830 and George and Edward Schutz's difference engine. Within a decade, these were followed by one of the milestone inventions in computing and mathematics—George Boole's development of Boolean algebra. The invention of Boolean algebra opened up the fields of mathematics, engineering, and computing to the new frontiers in logic, where the possibilities were boundless.

Sir Charles Wheatstone's invention of the paper tape to store information in 1857 created new excitement in the computing community of the time. With paper tape, huge amounts of data could be fed into the computing device and similar quantities could also be stored. This invention brought computing to a new level and into a new era.

From mid-1850s through the turn of the century, computing made a broad progress with various inventions including the invention of the logic machine by William Stanley Jovons in 1869, the invention of the first keyboard by Sholes around 1874, and the rectangular logic diagrams by Allan Marquand in 1881. Starting around 1890, a burst of major inventions similar to those of 1850s started all over again. In 1886, Charles Pierce first linked Boolean algebra to circuits based on switches, a major breakthrough in mathematics, engineering, and computing science. In 1890, John Venn created the Venn diagrams now used extensively in switching algebras in both hardware and software development. Finally, in 1890, Herman Hollerith invented the tabulating machine. Hollerith's invention utilized Jacquard's punched card to read the presence or absence of holes. The data read were to be collated using an automatic electrical tabulating machine with a large number of clocklike counters that summed up and accumulated the results in a number of selected categories.

1.1.2   After AD 1900

The inventions before AD 1900 were all crucial building blocks of the computing industry. The period created a child, but the child did not grow until the second period of development that started around the turn of the twentieth century. The century began with a major milestone in the computing history—the invention of the vacuum tube by John Ambrose Fleming. This was a major development in computing as the vacuum tube played a major role in computing for the next half century. All digital computers in the first half century ran on vacuum tubes. The next 20 years saw the development of computing with a variety of inventions including the invention of the triode by Lee de Forest in 1906. However, another major milestone invention was to be recorded during this period, although it was not to come into full use for some time. The year 1926 saw the invention of the first semiconductor transistor, which would come to dominate the computing industry from that point forward.

Many smaller and less significant inventions were made during the next 10 years that included the complex number calculator by George Robert Stibitz in 1937. That same year also saw another key advance in the history of computing. The invention of the Turing machine by Alan Turing in 1937 was as revolutionary as it was exciting. Turing, an English mathematician, showed by the invention of an abstract computer that some problems do not lend themselves to algorithmic representations, and therefore are not computable. This was a major development in computing. Turing was 7 years later to work on the design of COLOSSUS, one of the first working programmable digital computers.

Two years after Turing, in 1939, the world saw the first digital computer developed by John Vincent Atanasoff, a lecturer at Iowa State College (now University). Atanasoff's computer was the first special-purpose electronic digital computer. Working with his graduate assistant Clifford Berry, Atanasoff designed a device that utilized capacitors to store electronic charge to represent Boolean numbers 0 and 1 to be used by the machine in calculations, a major breakthrough in computing history [1]. Both input and output data were on punched cards, and Atanasoff's magic was in creating a storage representation for intermediate data in the machine as it is used by the digital machine for calculations before it is output on the punched cards and tape. There is doubt, however, whether Atanasoff's model ever worked. Around the same time Atanasoff and Berry were working on their model in 1939, Howard Aiken, a graduate of Harvard University, was developing the first large-scale automatic digital computer. Aiken's computer came to be known as the Harvard Mark I (also known as IBM automatic sequencer calculator – ASC) [1].

The following decade saw the development of an actual working model of the digital computer as we know it today. In 1943, Alan Turing, working as a cryptographer, constructed the COLOSSUS, considered by many as the world's earliest working programmable electronic digital computer. The COLOSSUS, designed to break the German ENIGMA code, used about 1,800 vacuum tubes to execute a variety of routines.

Around the time that COLOSSUS was being developed by Turing, the team of John William Mauchly and J. Presper Eckert, Jr., was working at the University of Pennsylvania to develop another vacuum tube-based general-purpose electronic digital computer. Their model, named *electronic numerical integrator and computer* (ENIAC) was 10 ft high, weighed 30 t, occupied 1,000 ft^2, and used about 70,000 resistors, 10,000 capacitors, 6,000 switches, and 18,000 vacuum tubes [1,2]. After ENIAC went into use, the team encountered a number of problems, the main one being that it did not have an internal memory because it was hard-wired and was consistently programmed by switches and diodes. This problem had to be worked on for the next model.

From 1944 through 1952, the team developed a new computer called the *electronic discrete variable automatic computer* (EDVAC). This is believed to be the first truly general-purpose digital computer. EDVAC was a stored-program computer with internal read-write memory to store program instructions. The stored program concept gave the device the capability to branch the program under execution to alternative instruction sequences elsewhere in the stored program. When it was completed in 1956, EDVAC was still a carousel machine with 4,000 vacuum tubes and 10,000 crystal diodes.

Although most of these activities were taking place in the United States, there were other efforts in other countries. For example, around the time EDVAC was being developed, an experiment was being conducted at the University of Manchester in the United Kingdom, also based on the stored program concept. By 1948, the Manchester team had produced a machine working with 32 words of memory and a five-instruction set. Also in England, at Cambridge University, the *electronic delay storage automatic calculator*, EDSAC, was produced in 1949. In 1948, the *universal automatic computer*, UNIVAC I, became the first commercially available computer.

From that point, the general-purpose computer took on a momentum of its own. It became bigger and more powerful. Companies sprang up both in the United States and Europe to manufacture these wonder machines. Among the leaders were International Business Machines (IBM), Honeywell, and Control Data Corporation (CDC) in America, and International Computers Limited (ICL) in England. These companies and a number of others, built what came to be known as the *mainframe*, a huge computer that consisted of a 4–5 ft by 8 ft tape drive, a huge control processing unit, a huge printer, several huge fixed disks, a large card reader, and a paper punch. These components usually filled a large room or two. Because these computers were big, expensive, and difficult to use, computer users could only use them through an operator. The operator fed jobs to the computer via a card or tape reader. The jobs were submitted to the card reader as decks of punched cards. Because these computers were big, expensive, and, as we have seen, difficult to use, only large companies and institutions were able to use them.

Around the mid- to late 1960s, a movement to make computers less expensive and more affordable started gathering momentum. This movement led to a number of developments. First, it led to the manufacture of a less expensive and smaller computer—the medium-range computer commonly referred to as a *minicomputer*. Second, it started a mode of computing that later led to networking. This was time-sharing, where one computer could be used by a number of users who would remotely connect on to the mainframe. Third, and most important, between 1971 and 1976 it led to a milestone in the history of computing: the development of the first microprocessor. A microprocessor is an integrated circuit with many transistors on a single board. Before the birth of the microprocessor, computer technology had developed to a point that vacuum tubes and diodes were no longer used. Computers were constructed from thousands of transistors. The demand for more powerful computers necessitated the development of computers with many thousands of transistors. But it was not possible at the time to simply pack in more transistors and create a working, more powerful computer. A way forward had to be found.

1.1.3 The Development of the Microprocessor

That way was found by Ted Hoff. Hoff designed the world's first microprocessor, the 4004. The fours in 4004, indicated that the device had a four-bit data path. The 4004 microprocessor was a four-chip system consisting of 256-byte ROM, a 32-bit RAM, 4-bit data path, and 10-bit shift register. It used 2,300 transistors to execute 60,000 operations per second, a top speed at the time [3]. The development of the first microprocessor caught the world off guard. Even Biscom, the company that had commissioned Hoff, did not understand the potential of the 4004. So they requested him to design the 12-chip set they had originally wanted him to design [3].

In 1972, Intel introduced the 8008, an 8-bit microprocessor based on the 4004. The 8008 used 3,300 transistors and was the first microprocessor to use a compiler, a system program that interprets user inputs into machine code and machine code to system outputs understandable by the user. The 8008 supported the compiler called PL/M. Both the 4004 and the 8008 were specific application microprocessors. The truly general-purpose microprocessor came out in 1974. It was the 8080, an 8-bit device with 4,500 transistors, performing an astonishing 200,000 operations per second. From 1974 forward, the development of microprocessors exploded as companies like Motorola developed the 6800 in 1974, MOS Technology developed the 6502 in 1975, and Zilog developed the Z80 in 1976. Since then, many new companies have sprung up and the speed, density of transistors, and functionality of microprocessors has been on the rise.

1.1.4 Historical Development of Computer Software and the Personal Computer (PC)

Up until the mid-1970s, the development of computing science was led by hardware. Computers were first designed, and then software was designed to fit the hardware. The development of software to run the computers was in the hands of the companies that designed the hardware. The break from this routine came from two fronts: in 1976, the Apple I and Apple II microcomputers were unveiled, and in 1981, IBM joined the PC wars. These two developments started a new industry, the personal computing industry. Perhaps the PC industry would not be the way it is today were it not the development of the personal computer operating system (OS). It involved three players: IBM; Gary Kildall, the developer of CP/M, the PC operating system many believe to be the first PC operating system; and Bill Gates, the developer of the disk operating system (DOS). The story behind these players, part legend, is the story of the beginning of the PC. The legend has it that when IBM developed the personal computer based on Intel's 8088 microprocessor, in 1981, it needed an operating system. It is alleged that IBM approached Both Kidall and Gates. However, Kidall was out flying and failed to attend to IBM's request before Gates did [2,4]. Gates developed the first DOS and a version of the BASIC programming language for IBM, and the rest is history.

Two dominant brands of chips for the first PCs were Intel and Motorola. The IBM/DOS combination, which later led to the Windows brand, gained over Apple's Motorola-based model because of Intel's policy of backward compatibility—that is, developing new products based on the previous versions—which Apple never embraced. Microsoft took the lead over other software developers by creating an operating system and application software for both standards. It has since then gained an overwhelming dominance of the marketplace.

1.2 Development of the Internet

The Internet, a global network of computers, owes its development to the invention of four technologies: telegraph, telephone, radio, and computers. History has it that the Internet originated from the early work of J.C.R. Licklider of the Massachusetts Institute of Technology (MIT) on "galactic networks." Licklider conceptualized a global interconnected set of computers with communication channels between them through which programs and data could be accessed quickly by any computer from any computer [5,6]. This networking concept envisioned by Licklider would support communication between network nodes using a concept of packets instead of circuits, thus enabling computers to talk to one another.

Licklider left MIT to head the computer research program at the Department of Defense's Defense Advanced Research Projects Agency (DARPA) in 1962. A year before, at MIT, researcher Leonard Kleinrock had written what is believed to be the first published work on packet switching theory [5]. This work created the momentum for the concept of a packet-switching network. However, it was not the only work on the concept. There were two additional independent projects on this same topic—that of Donald Davies and Roger Scantleberg at the British National Laboratory (BNL)—which later was credited with coining the term "packet," and that of Paul Baran at RAND. In 1965, Lawrence Roberts at MIT, who had been collaborating with Licklider, and Thomas M. Roberts connected the TX-2 computer in Boston to the Q-32 computer in Los Angeles with a low-speed dial-up telephone line. This test experiment created the first working wide area network (WAN). This experiment opened up the doors to all computer network communications as it is known today.

In 1966, Roberts left MIT for DARPA to develop the computer network concept, publishing the first plan for ARPANET in 1967 [5,7]. In 1968, a go-ahead was given by DARPA for the development of the packet switches called interface message processors (IMP). As the team, led by Frank Heart and including Bob Kahn, developed the IMP, a team consisting of Roberts and Howard Frank designed the network topology and economics. The network measurement system was created by Kleinrock and his team [5,7]. The work of these teams led to the testing of the first IMP at UCLA in 1969, connected to a second node at the Stanford Research Institute (SRI). After these tests, more nodes were added to ARPANET and by the end of 1969 four nodes formed the ARPANET [5]. From this point on the Internet started to grow. However, more work was needed to incorporate the host-to-host protocol into ARPANET. The first host-to-host protocol, called network control protocol (NCP), was developed by the Network Working Group (NWG) in 1970. But NCP did not have "the ability to address networks further downstream than a destination IMP on the ARPANET" [5,7]. Kahn then developed what later became the Transmission Control Protocol/Internet Protocol (TCP/IP). The first day of January in 1983 was the transition day from NCP to TCP/IP. By this time, ARPANET was being used by a significant number of users both in the military and nonmilitary.

As the number of nodes increased, more universities joined the exclusive club, and ARPANET became not only a research facilitator, but also a free, federally funded postal system of electronic mail. In 1984, the US National Science Foundation (NSF) joined ARPANET in starting its own network, code named NSFNET. NSFNET set a new pace in nodes, bandwidth, speed, and upgrades. This NSF-funded network brought the Internet within the reach of many universities throughout the country, as well as around the world, which would not otherwise have been able to afford the costs, and many government agencies joined in. At this point, other countries and regions were establishing their own networks.

With so much success and fanfare, ARPANET ceased to exist in 1989. As the number of nodes on the Internet climbed into hundreds of thousands worldwide, the role of sponsoring agencies like ARPA and NSF became more and more marginalized. Eventually, in 1994, NSF also ceased its support of the Internet. The Internet by now needed no helping hand since it had assumed a momentum of its own.

1.3 Development of the World Wide Web

The World Wide Web, as we know it today, had its humble beginning in concepts contained in Tim Berners-Lee's 1989 proposal to physicists calling for comments. Berners-Lee, a physicist-researcher at the European High-Energy Particle Physics lab—the Conseil Europeenne pour la Recherché Nucleaire (CERN), Switzerland—wrote the proposal called *HyperText and CERN*, to enable collaboration between physicists and other researchers in the high-energy physics research community. Three new technologies were incorporated. They were: (1) HyperText Markup Language (HTML) based on hypertext concepts, to be used to write web documents; (2) HyperText Transfer Protocol (HTTP), a protocol to be used to transmit web pages between hosts; and (3) a web browser client software program to receive and interpret data and display results. His proposal also included a very important concept for the user interface. This browser-supported interface was based on the concept that it would be consistent across all types of computer platforms to enable users to access information from any computer. The line-mode interface was developed and named at CERN in late 1989. It came to be known as the World Wide Web or *WWW* [6]. By 1991, the concept developed only 2 years earlier was put into practice on a limited network at CERN. From the central computer at CERN with only a few web pages, the number of servers started to grow from the only one at CERN in 1991, to 50 worldwide by 1992, to 720,000 by 1999, and to over 24 million by 2001 [6].

In the United States, in 1993, Marc Andreesen, a student at the University of Illinois at Urbana-Champaign, and his team, while working for the National Center for Supercomputing Applications (NCSA), developed another graphic user interface browser they named *Mosaic*. The graphic user interface (GUI) popularized the user and fueled the growth of the World Wide Web to bring it to the point where it is today.

1.4 The Emergence of Social and Ethical Problems in Computing

1.4.1 The Emergence of Computer Crimes

The known history of computer crimes is not as old as computing is. One can perhaps say that the history of computer crimes started with the invention of the computer virus. Thinking along these lines, therefore, we will track the development of the computer virus. The term *virus* is a Latin word which means poison. For generations, even before the birth of modern medicine, the term had remained mostly in medical circles, meaning a foreign agent injecting itself in a living body, feeding on it to grow and multiply. As it reproduces itself in the new environment, it spreads throughout the victim's body, slowly disabling the body's natural resistance to foreign objects, weakening the body's ability to perform needed life functions, and eventually causing serious, sometimes fatal, effects to the body.

A computer virus, defined as a self-propagating computer program designed to alter or destroy a computer system resource, follows almost the same pattern, but instead of using the living body, it uses software to attach itself, grow, reproduce, and spread in the new environment. As it spreads in the new environment, it attacks major system resources that include the surrogate software itself, data, and sometimes hardware weakening the capacity of these resources to perform the needed functions. Eventually, it brings the system down.

The word "virus" was first assigned a nonbiological meaning in the 1972 science fiction stories about the G.O.D. machine, which were compiled in the book *When*

Harly Was One by David Gerrod (Ballantine Books, New York, 1972). In the book, according to Karen Forchat, the term was first used to describe a piece of unwanted computer code [8]. Later association of the term with a real-world computer program was made by Fred Cohen, then a graduate student at the University of Southern California. Cohen first presented his ideas to a graduate seminar class on information security in 1983. His seminar advisor, Len Adleman, was the first to assign the term "virus" to Cohen's concept. During his student days at the University of Southern California, Cohen did more theoretical research and practical experiments regarding viral-type programs. As part of these experiments, Cohen wrote five programs, actually viruses, to run on a VAX 11/750 running Unix—not to alter or destroy any computer resources, but for class demonstration. During the demonstration, each virus obtained full control of the system within an hour [8].

From that simple beginning, computer viruses, and hence computer crimes, have been on the rise. Table 1.1 shows the explosive growth of reported incidents of cyber attacks, most of which are virus attacks. To many, the growth of the Internet, together with massive news coverage of virus incidents, have caused an explosion of all types of computer viruses [9].

1.4.2 The Present Status: An Uneasy Cyberspace

As the level of computer crimes increases on the one hand and our reliance and dependence on computer and telecommunications technology increases on the

Table 1.1 Number of attack incidents reported to CERT (1988–2001, third quarter) – Update Table

Year	Incidents
1988	6
1989	132
1990	252
1991	406
1992	773
1993	1,334
1994	2,340
1995	2,412
1996	2,573
1997	2,134
1998	3,734
1999	9,859
2000	21,756
2001 (Q1–Q3)	34,754

Carnegie Mellon University, Software Engineering Institute (http://www.cert. org/stats/cert_stats.html#incidents" http://www.cert.org/stats/cert_stats. html#incidents)

other, we are becoming more and more susceptible and exposed to cyberspace evils and insecurity. In addition, all critical components of the national infrastructure such as telecommunication, electrical power grids, gas and oil storage, water supply systems, banking and finance, transportation, and emergency services that include medical, police, fire, and rescue—all of which are connected to cyberspace in some form—are becoming unreliable and vulnerable as well. This makes cyberspace an important security concern not only to those in government and those charged with the security of the nation, but to all of us, for our personal individual security and well-being, because the potential for a cyberspace attack, a kind of "cyber Pearl Harbor," is high.

If the recent trend in cyber attacks is any indication, we are in for an avalanche of cyber vandalism as society becomes more dependent on computer networks and as more people jump on the cyber train. The rate of cyber vandalism, both reported and unreported, is on the rise. This rise is an indication of the poor state of our cyberspace security and the vulnerability of all cyberspace resources. Yet there are no signs on the horizon to indicate a slowdown in these acts. Indeed, all predictions are that they are likely to continue because of the following reasons [10]:

- Cyberspace infrastructure and communication protocols are inherently weak.
- The average user in cyberspace has very limited knowledge of the computer network infrastructure, its weaknesses and gapping loopholes.
- Society, as a whole, is increasingly becoming irreversibly dependent on an infrastructure and technology that it does not fully understand.
- There are no long-term, let alone immediate, plans or mechanisms in place to better educate the public.
- There is a high degree of complacency in a society that still accords a "Wiz Kid" status to cyberspace vandals.
- The only known and practiced remedies are patching loopholes after an attack has occurred.
- The price of this escalating problem is not yet known.
- Reporting is voluntary and haphazard.
- The nation has yet to understand the seriousness of cyber vandalism.

If we as a society are concerned about individual as well as collective security, privacy, and civil liberties, we need to start finding solutions. A good national cyberspace security policy is needed to [10]:

(i) Make everyone aware of the vulnerability and consequences of a cyberspace attack on their well-being.
(ii) Ensure that everyone is well equipped to safely deal with a cyber attack in this technology-driven and fast-changing society.
(iii) Help put in place a set of mechanisms to detect, prevent, and handle any cyber attack, and
(iv) Devise a legal and regulatory framework to handle cyberspace's social consequences.

1.5 The Case for Computer Ethics Education

1.5.1 What Is Computer Ethics?

According to James H. Moore, who is believed to have first coined the phrase "computer ethics," computer ethics is the analysis of the nature and social impact of computer technology and the corresponding formulation and justification of policies for the ethical use of such technology [11]. Moore's definition focuses on the human actions that are routed in computer technology or influenced by computer technology. In other words, it is an analysis of the values of human actions influenced by computer technology. Computer influence on human actions is widespread throughout the decision-making process preceding an action. In the previous sections of this chapter, we discussed the many problems we are facing today as a result of computer technology. We are looking for a way to deal with these problems, probably through education. So the definition of computer ethics, as outlined by Moore, gives us a starting point on this long journey.

1.5.2 Why You Should Study Computer Ethics

Moore's contention is that the central task of computer ethics in decision-making processes that involve computer technology should be to "determine what should be done" whenever there is a policy vacuum. Moore first observed that there are times when policy vacuums are created in the decision-making processes, especially those that involve processes in which computer technology is "essentially involved."

It is difficult to fully explain the cause of these vacuums, but one can say that they are mainly caused by the "confusion" between the known policies and what is presented. Moore tries to explain these muddles by a software example. As we will see in Chapter 6, software can either be a product in which case patent laws apply, or it can be a service where no intellectual property laws apply. The multiplicity of choices like this, presented to a decision maker by computer technology, can result in policy vacuums. Several other factors contribute to the creation of these muddles. It is likely that computer users, especially computer professionals, may be unprepared to deal effectively with the ethical issues that arise in their places of work and everywhere else computers and computer-related technology is used.

So, naturally, one would come to the conclusion that since we cannot stop computer technology that causes these muddles, we need a plan of action that will work with the changing computing technology and at the same time deal with the ethical issues that do arise. We need computer ethics education. There are two schools of thought on this subject. One school believes in the study of computer ethics as remedial moral education. The other school believes in computer ethics education not as a moral education but as a field worthy of study in its own right. But for it to exist as a separate independent field of study, there must be a unique domain for computer ethics distinct from the domain for moral education, distinct even from the domains of other kinds of professional and applied ethics [12]. In his paper "Is Computer Ethics Unique?" Walter Maner explains the existence of the two schools with two views that:

(i) Certain ethical issues are so transformed by the use of computers that they deserve to be studied on their own, in their radically altered form.

(ii) The involvement of computers in human conduct can create entirely new ethical issues, unique to computing, that do not surface in other areas.

According to Maner there are six levels of justifications for the two views, the first two for the first school and the last four for the second school [12]:

(i) We should study computer ethics because doing so will make us behave like responsible professionals.

(ii) We should study computer ethics because doing so will teach us how to avoid computer abuse and catastrophes.

(iii) We should study computer ethics because the advance of computing technology will continue to create temporary policy vacuums.

(iv) We should study computer ethics because the use of computing permanently transforms certain ethical issues to the degree that their alterations require independent study.

(v) We should study computer ethics because the use of computing technology creates, and will continue to create, novel ethical issues that require special study.

(vi) We should study computer ethics because the set of novel and transformed issues is large enough and coherent enough to define a new field.

Whatever school one falls in, there is enough justification to study computer ethics.

Exercises

1. Discuss two reasons why it is good to study computer ethics.
2. Walter Maner believes that computer ethics education should not be given purely as a remedial moral education. Do you agree? Discuss.
3. Give support to the argument that computer ethics must be taken as a remedial moral course.
4. Computer ethics education taken as a remedial education does not provide an adequate rationale. Discuss.
5. Discuss each of Walter Maner's six levels of justification for the study of computer ethics.
6. Write a chronology of the history of computers listing the milestones in a timeline.
7. List and discuss the major categories of computers based on processing powers.
8. Discuss three reasons that led to the development of PCs.
9. What government agencies underwrote the development of the Internet? Why did this support stop? Was it good for the Internet?
10. How is the Internet governed today? Discuss the governing structure.
11. What is Mosaic? When was it developed and by whom? Why is not popular today?

References

1. "A History of Computers." http://www.maxmon.com/timeline.html
2. Robert J. Baron and Lee Heigbie. *Computer Architecture.* Addison-Wesley, Reading, MA, 1992.

3. "The First Microprocessor." http://www.maxmon.com/timeline.html
4. "A Short History of PCs." http://www.highwaysgds.net/pchist.html
5. Barry M. Leina, Vinton G. Cerf, David D. Clerk, Robert E. Kahn, Leonard Kleinrock, Daniel C. Lynch, Jon Postal, Larry G. Roberts, and Stephen Wolf. "A Short History of the Internet." http://www.isoc.org/internet/history/brief.html
6. Cherly Gribble. "History of the Web Beginning at CERN." *Hitmill*, Jan. 18, 2001.
7. Joseph M. Kizza. Civilizing the Internet: Global Concerns and Efforts Towards Regulation. McFarland, 1998, Jefferson, NC.
8. Karen Forch. Computer Security Management. Boyd & Fraser, 1994, Danvers, MA.
9. Carnegie Mellon University, Software Engineering Institute. http://www.cert.org/stats/cert_stats.html#incidents
10. Joseph M. Kizza. *Computer Network Security and Cyber Ethics*. McFarland, 2001, Jefferson, NC.
11. Terrell W. Bynum. (Ed.) *Computers & Ethics*. Basil Blackwell, 1985, New York.
12. Walter Maner. "Is Computer Ethics Unique?" *Science and Engineering Ethics*, volume 2, number 2 (April, 1996), pp. 137–154. See http://www.cableol.co.uk/opragen/

Chapter 2
Morality and the Law

Maybe...

J.M. Kizza, *Ethical and Social Issues in the Information Age*, Texts in Computer Science, DOI 10.1007/978-1-84996-038-0_2, © Springer-Verlag London Limited 2010

Learning Objectives

After reading this chapter, the reader should be able to:

1. Learn to make sound moral reasoning.
2. Learn about moral values and ideals in a person's life.
3. Learn about the relationship between morality and religion.
4. Distinguish between morality and etiquette, law, and professional code of conduct.
5. Learn what it means to have moral principles, the nature of conscience, and the relationship between morality and self-interest.
6. Learn the values and ideals in a person's life.

Scenario 1
With Stem Cell Research We Can Grow Just About Anything Human!

The parliament of the Republic of Kazini passed legislation, and the president signed into law, authorizing its citizens and scientists working on Kazini territory to carry out stem cell research to the best extent possible only limited by the physical resources. Scientists in Kazini have spearheaded such research and have made major breakthroughs in recent years.

Stem cells abound in bodies, but as human bodies age, the number of these cells and their potential and functions start to diminish as well. Embryonic stem cells that are found in the early stages of the body's development have the ability to divide indefinitely in culture and can therefore, at least in the laboratory, develop into virtually any cell type in the body.

The scientists in Kazini and their counterparts from around the world believe in the great benefits of stem cell research, especially embryonic stem cells. Many newspapers and scientific journals, not only in Kazini but also from other countries, have written stories of limitless benefits, the most immediate being the replacement of insulin-producing cells in the pancreas, damaged muscle cells, and dead nerve cells due to strokes, spinal injury, and degenerative diseases that include Alzheimer's and Parkinson's. It may also lead to the development and replacement of liver cells destroyed by a hepatitis and other liver diseases.

Dr. Don Rogan, a brilliant young scientist, is the director of Kazini Clinical Research Laboratory, the leading research nerve center in Kazini. Rogan is convinced that the legislature's action is morally wrong. However, his Laboratory has been chosen for funding and his dedicated scientists and staff are excited by the legislature's actions. They had lobbied hard for the passage of the bill. Now they see a ray of hope for millions of people not only on Kazini but also around the world. Rogan is facing a personal problem.

Discussion Questions

1. *What options does Rogan have?*
2. *If you were Dr. Rogan, what would you do?*
3. *Is Dr. Rogan bound by the legislation?*

2.1 Introduction

Whether you believe in a supreme being or you are an atheist, you acknowledge the existence of human life because you are alive. You are alive because someone nurtured you and protected you from all adversities. Whoever did so followed a set of rules of conduct that kept both of you alive. Such shared rules, written or not, play a vital role in all human existence.

Human beings do not live randomly. We follow a script—a life script. In that script are hundreds of subscripts we follow both for survival (e.g., eating and sleeping) and for specific tasks. For example, when you meet a stranger, you follow a subscript different from the one you follow when you meet a long-held friend. If you are hungry, the subscript you follow is different from the one you use to overcome anger. Within each subscript are variations we introduce to suit the situation. For example, when meeting an old friend, some people cry and others jump up and down, but both responses remain within the same subscript of meeting an old friend. The most important purpose of all these subscripts is human life, our own as well as others.

Believing in human life implies that we also believe life has a purpose. And because no one wants to live a life of pain, every human being believes in happiness as a purpose for life. To be happy, we need those conditions that create happiness, namely life, liberty, and property. Each condition is embodied in each of the three basic human survival subscripts: morality, ethics, and law. In this chapter, we discuss morality and law, and in Chapter 3 we discuss ethics.

2.2 Morality

Morality is a set of rules for right conduct, a system used to modify and regulate our behavior. It is a quality system in human acts by which we judge them right or wrong, good or bad. This system creates moral persons who possess virtues like love for others, compassion, and a desire for justice; thus it builds character traits in people. In particular, morality is a survival subscript we follow in our day-to-day living. According to Wikipedia [1], morality has three deferent definitions:

- A descriptive definition according to which morality means a set of rules (code) of conduct that governs human behavior in matters of right and wrong. An example of the descriptive usage could be "common conceptions of morality have changed significantly over time."
- A normative and universal definition which is more prescriptive and refers to an ideal code of conduct that would be observed by all rational people, under specified conditions. An example is a moral value judgment such as "murder is immoral."
- A definition of morality that is synonymous with ethics. Ethics is the systematic philosophical study of the moral domain. We will define and discuss ethics in the coming chapter.

In each one of these definitions, morality concerns itself with a set of shared rules, principles, and duties, independent from religion, applicable to all in a group or society, and having no reference to the will or power of any one individual whatever his or her status in that group or society. Although moral values are generally shared values in a society, the degree of sharing these values varies greatly. We may agree more on values like truth, justice, and loyalty than on others. To paraphrase Shakespeare, life is but a stage on which there is continuous acting from the subscript of morality. Every time we interact in a society or group, we act the moral subscript that was developed by that society or group for its members over time.

Because morality is territorial and culturally based, as long as we live in a society we are bound to live within that society's guidelines. The actions of individuals in a society only have moral values if taken within the context of this very society and the culture of the individual. A number of factors influence the context of morality, including time and place.

2.2.1 Moral Theories

If morality is a set of shared values among people in a specific society, why do we have to worry about justifying those values to people who are not members of that society? In other words, why do we need moral theories? What do moral theories have to do with the moral subscript? If you write a script for a play, you want both the audience and the cast to understand the message of the play. If you can find a way to help them get that message and believe it, then you have put credibility in the script. This is where moral theories come in. According to MacDonnell, moral theories "seek to introduce a degree of rationality and rigor into our moral deliberations" [1]. They give our deliberations plausibility and help us to better understand those values and the contradictions therein. Because many philosophers and others use the words *moral* and *ethical* synonymously, we delay the discussion of moral theories until we discuss ethics.

2.2.2 Moral Decision Making

Every human action results from a decision process. Because every human action follows a subscript, the decision-making process follows a subscript as well. A decision is morally good if the result from it is good. A good moral decision embodies nearly all moral theories and usually takes into consideration the following:

1. All the facts surrounding the situation, taking into account the interests of all parties involved, and
2. The moral principles involved and how they will affect all others involved

Combining 1 and 2 implies there must be reasoning and impartiality in any moral decision. Moral and ethical theorists have outlined four ways of ensuring reason and impartiality in moral decision making:

1. The use of rational intuition of moral principles, which helps us perceive moral principles such as the notion of justice and deciding what is good.
2. The use of reason to determine the best way to achieve the highest moral good.

3. The ability to distinguish between primary and secondary moral principles. Primary moral principles are more general; secondary principles are more specific and are generally deduced from the primary ones.
4. The rational calculation of the consequences of our actions. The calculation should tell us whether the action is good or bad depending on the consequences [2].

Nearly all moral theories embody one or more of these themes.

2.2.3 Moral Codes

The *Internet Encyclopedia of Philosophy* defines moral codes as rules or norms within a group for what is proper behavior for the members of that group [2]. The norm itself is a rule, standard, or measure for us to compare something else whose qualities we doubt. Moral codes are often complex definitions of right and wrong that are based upon well-defined group's value systems.

In a way, moral codes are shared behavioral patterns of a group. These patterns have been with us since the beginnings of human civilization and have evolved mainly for the survival of the group or society. Societies and cultures survive and thrive because of the moral code they are observing. History has shown failures of societies and cultures like the once mighty civilizations and great empires of the Babylonians, the Romans, and the Byzantines probably because their code failed to cope with the changing times.

Although different cultures have different codes, and we have established that morality is relative to time, there have been some timeless and culture-free (moral) codes that have been nearly universally observed. Such codes include this partial list created by the astronomer Carl Sagan [3]:

1. *The Golden Rule*: "Do unto others as you would have them do unto you."
2. *The Silver Rule*: "Do not do unto others what you would not have them do unto you." Great men like Mahatma Gandhi followed this rule almost to the letter.
3. *The Bronze Rule*: "Repay kindness with kindness." This rule is widely observed because of its many varying interpretations. Some people "carrot-and-stick" rule. However you interpret it, it seems to support the vendetta syndrome.
4. *The Iron Rule*: "Do unto others as you like, before they do it unto you." This rule, if followed by a leader, can create dictatorships. It seems to say, "He who is on the floor cannot make rules" or "Do it if you can get away with it."
5. *The Tin Rule*: "Pay homage to those above you and intimidate those below you." This is what many call the bully rule.
6. *The Nepotism Rule*: "Give precedence in all things to close relatives, and do as you like to others." This rule legitimizes corruption.

Because most of these rules seem vindictive, corruptible, dictatorial, and abusive, Sagan proposes the following as what seems to be a good culture-free and timeless universal set of moral codes:

1. Be friendly at first meeting.
2. Do no envy.
3. Be generous; forgive your enemy if he or she forgives you.
4. Be neither a tyrant nor a patsy.
5. Retaliate proportionately to an intentional injury (within the constraints of the rule of the law).
6. Make your behavior fair (although not perfectly) clear and consistent.

Other timeless, culture-free, but less widely practiced and less universally accepted codes are those observed by small groups of people with similar interests (e.g., religious and Professional groups). Examples of such moral codes include the Native American Ten Commandments, the Jewish and Christian Ten Commandments, and the Unix Users Group Ten Commandments as outlined here:

2.2.3.1 Native American Ten Commandments [4]

1. Treat the Earth and all that dwell thereon with respect.
2. Remain close to the Great Spirit.
3. Show great respect for your fellow beings.
4. Work together for the benefit of all Mankind.
5. Give assistance and kindness wherever needed.
6. Do what you know to be right.
7. Look after the well being of mind and body.
8. Dedicate a share of your efforts to the greater good.
9. Be truthful and honest at all times.
10. Take full responsibility for your actions.

2.2.3.2 The Christian Ten Commandments [5]

1. I, the Lord, am your God. You shall not have any other gods besides Me.
2. You shall not take the name of the Lord, your God, in vain.
3. Remember to keep holy the Sabbath day.
4. Honor your father and your mother.
5. You shall not kill.
6. You shall not commit adultery.
7. You shall not steal.
8. You shall not bear false witness against your neighbor.
9. You shall not covet your neighbor's wife.
10. You shall not covet anything that belongs to your neighbor.

2.2.3.3 Unix Users Group Ten Commandments (The Manual, Ex. 20, Verses 1–21) [6]

And lo did Unix[1] speak these words upon the reboot:

1. Thou shalt use no other operating system than Unix.
2. Thou shalt not make unto thee a false operating system. Thou shalt not program them for I am the Unix and a jealous O/S.
3. Thou shalt not take the mark of trade of Unix in vain, or thou shalt be sued.
4. Remember thy password, and keep it secret.
5. Honour thy parent shell, for if it should die, thou shalt not live long (unless thou hast dissociated thyself).
6. Thou shalt not kill (l)-9 any process, for surely they shalt becometh zombies or defunct.
7. Thou shalt not commit hacking, else thou shalt eat quiche.
8. Thou shalt not use other users' data, for thou shalt be referred to the Data Protection Act, 1984, and sued (again).
9. Thou shalt not create Trojan horses, worms, viruses, or other foul beasts of false programming.
10. Thou shalt not rm -rf thy neighbour's $HOME, nor covet his disk space allocation, nor his workstation account.

The purpose of moral codes in a society is to exert control over actions of members of the group resulting from emotions. Observance of moral codes in most societies is almost involuntary because members grow up with these codes, so they tend to follow them without questioning. In some societies, observance is enforced through superstition and in others it is done through folklore and customs. In Chapter 4, we show that professions need to have codes for their members to adhere to in order for them to be ethical and moral in their day-to-day professional activities.

2.2.4 Moral Standards

Amoral standard is a moral norm, a standard to which we compare human actions to determine their goodness or badness. This standard guides and enforces policy. Morality is a system that, in addition to setting standards of virtuous conduct for people, also consists of mechanisms to self-regulate through enforcement of the moral code and self-judge through guilt, which is an internal discomfort resulting from disappointment in self-mediated conscience.

---

[1]Let Unix be a trademark of AT&T.

2.2.5 *Guilt and Conscience*

Moral guilt is a result of self-judging and punishing oneself for not living up to the moral standards set for oneself or for the group. If individuals judge that they have not done "good" according to moral standards, they can activate the guilt response, which usually makes them feel bad, hide their actions from both self and others, and find a fitting punishment for themselves, sometimes a very severe punishment. This internal judgment system is brought about because human beings have no sure way of telling whether an action is good or bad based independently on their own "standards." Individual standards are usually judged based on group standards. So individuals judge themselves based on group standards, and self-judgment comes into play whenever one's actions fall short of the group's standards.

The problem with guilt is that it can be cumulative. If individuals commit acts repetitively that they judge to be below moral standards, they tend to become more and more withdrawn. This isolation often leads individuals to become more comfortable with the guilt. As they become comfortable living with the guilt, their previous actions, which were previously judged below standards, begin to look not so bad after all. Individuals become more and more complacent about the guilt and begin to look at the whole moral system as amoral.

Guilt can be eased by encouraging people to focus on the intentions behind the actions. Sometimes the intentions may be good but the resulting action is bad. In such a case the individual should not feel so guilty about the action. Besides looking for intentions of actions, one should also have the will and ability to forgive oneself. Self-forgiveness limits the cumulative nature of guilt and hence helps an individual to keep within the group.

Our moral code, and many times the law, lay out the general principles that we *ought* not do or that because it is wrong to do it. The law also tells us not to do this or that because it is illegal to do so. However, both systems do not specifically tell us whether a particular human action just committed is an immoral or illegal act. The link must be done by the individual—a self-realization. It is this individual inner judgment to tell us that the act is right or wrong, lawful or unlawful, that we call our *conscience*. Additionally, conscience is the capacity and ability to judge our actions ourselves based on what we set as our moral standards. The word *conscience* comes from a Latin word *conscientia*, which means *knowing with*. It is an "inner voice" telling us what we do or not do. This kind of self-judgment is based on the responsibility and control we have over our actions. Conscience is motivated by good feelings within us such as pride, compassion, empathy, love, and personal identification. Conscience evolves as individuals grow. The childhood conscience is far different from the adult conscience because of our perception of evil that evolves with age. The benefits of conscience are that the actions done with good conscience, even if they end up being bad, do not make one guilty of the actions.

Fr. Fagothey [11] writes that conscience applies to three things:

1. The intellect as a faculty for forming judgments about right and wrong individual acts
2. The process of reasoning that the intellect goes through to reach such judgment and

3. The judgment itself, which is the conclusion of this reasoning process

We have seen in this section that morality does not belong to any individual, nor does it belong to any society or group of people. Thus, it cannot be localized. However, those parts of the moral code that can be localized become law.

2.2.6 Morality and Religion

Religion, unlike morality, draws a lot from the divine. Most religious belief systems include or are built around the idea of divine will and divine judgment. However, many of these systems usually correspond to a moral code of conduct, and because of this, many religions claim that religion and morality are intimately connected.

2.2.6.1 Issues for Discussion

In Roman Catholicism, morality derives from God because God created man and nature and that the ultimate sanction for immorality is the loss of a relationship with God. How does your religion relate to the morality of your society?
How do both Atheism and Pantheism relate to morality ?
What values are essential for a person that would allow him/her to starve rather than to steal?

2.3 Law

According to *Webster's Dictionary*, law is a rule of conduct or an action recognized by custom or decreed by a formal enactment, community, or group [7]. Black states that law is an art we can create and model, and contemporary critics define law as an instrument of exercising power [8].

Bryan Bourn combines both these definitions of law and describes it as both an art and an instrument for exercising power [8]. He bases his definition on the fact that law on many occasions strives forcefully to create something desirable without following a precise and exact process or formula that can be reproduced (thus the art component). Fr. Fagothey defines laws as a rule and measure of actions directing them to proper ends. It obliges us to make our conduct conform to the norm of morality. He goes on to divide law into two types:

1. Physical law, which directs nonfree irrational beings to uniform action toward their ends by inner necessity of their nature, that is, imposing physical necessity
2. Moral law or natural law, which directs free rational beings toward their ends by imposing obligations on the free will—thus imposing moral necessity

However one defines law, whether as a rule, an injunction, an art, or an exercise of power, there is always a component of force that must be obeyed with the purpose of creating something desirable for the community that the law is intended to serve. This goal is achieved through the reign of equal justice for all in the community. We tend to obey two types of laws: the natural and the conventional.

2.3.1 The Natural Law

Natural law is an unwritten but universal law. It is a theory that an eternal, absolute moral law can be discovered by reason and is derivable from reason. It is distinct from the law of nature, applies to all rational creatures, exists independently of human preferences and inclinations, and is applied cross-culturally. According to James Donald [9], natural law "follows from the nature of man and the world, and consists of rights like the right to self-defense and the right to individual property. So naturally it is 'higher' than any other conventional law enacted by a human authority like a government because no conventional law has jurisdiction over natural law." Natural law has been known since the time of Plato and Aristotle (ca. 500 BC) but has its clear formulation and definition in the writings of Thomas Aquinas, a thirteenth-century philosopher and theologian [1].

Natural law is the anchor of our rights of self-preservation, liberty, and property. Before organized human societies, humans existed because of natural law. It secured the environment in those human settlements for those activities that sustain life, beginning with hunting and progressing through business and commerce. Even today, there are human societies that exist without conventional law. Present-day examples include those states like Somalia that have collapsed because of political strife. People in these states, even in the absence of a central governing authority and a functioning legal system, are still living their lives, many of them happily. Although they may not enjoy all the pleasures of life, they have a way of protecting life, liberty, and personal property. Ironically, there are even states that supposedly live with organized authorities like government yet have no rule of conventional law; they are surviving on natural law.

The existence of natural law has been debated for centuries. In fact, there are many who do not believe in natural law and are always advocating the supremacy of conventional law. Thomas Hobbes, the famous English philosopher argued that the nature of man is not such that one could deduce natural law from it, that the natural law so deduced does not place any significant limits on the powers of civil law, and that social order is a creation of state power [1].

2.3.2 Conventional Law

Conventional law is a system created by and for human beings usually in public deliberations like a council of elders or representatives in national legislatures. It derives from that part of the moral code which is enforceable and varies from society to society and from culture to culture. Although history and experience have shown that natural law has been used as the basis for some conventional laws and there are examples such as the English Magna Carta and the US Constitution and Bill of Rights, judgment is not based on natural law [9,10]. In day-to-day judgment, decisions are based on facts and the matching of facts to words, not on natural law.

Conventional law takes two forms: (1) declarative, which simply restates what the natural law declares, such as forbidding murder, theft, etc. and (2) determinative, which fixes ways of acting in accordance with natural law, such as in contracts, taxes, traffic, and other types of laws. Conventional law has a long history of evolution from natural law. Some of the outstanding examples are [11]:

1. *Law of nature.* Originating from the Roman *jus gentium*. The Romans developed *jus gentium* from a mosaic of nations that formed the Roman Empire. *Jus gentium* was a common factor of all laws of all nations in the empire. When the empire collapsed, the resulting states developed this *law of nations* into the modern European legal system.
2. *English common law.* It is a result of centuries of unwritten precedents and decisions of common courts, statutes, and acts of the English Parliament.

The English common law gave birth to the modern English and American law.

2.3.3 The Purpose of Law

Both conventional and natural laws exist to protect the life, liberty, and property of the group covered by these laws. According to Fr. Fagothey [11], laws are needed because:

1. The ignorant need instruction and control by the wise
2. Earthly penalties are required for the safety of society
3. Concerted action demands teamwork and leadership
4. Society must meet changed conditions harmoniously

2.3.4   The Penal Code

Laws are always useless unless there is a right to punish and an enforcement mechanism is in place. The penal code is a system of set rules prescribing punishment for unlawful acts. In a way, the penal code is that enforcement mechanism. The punishment system consists of three functions [11]:

1. *Retributive*—by paying back the criminal for the crime committed, re-establishing the equal balance of justice and re-asserting the authority.
2. *Corrective*—by trying to improve the offender; in other words, rehabilitating the offender back into society.
3. *Deterrent*—by trying to prevent similar actions in the future by the offender, and indeed the offender community, that is, forewarning the offender community by the state, which is the law maker.

The enforcement is different in criminal and civil cases. In criminal cases, the punishment may lead to denial of certain individual rights for a period of time. The period of incarceration depends on the nature and types of violations. In civil cases, punishments are usually damage awards to those whose rights were infringed upon.

2.4   Morality and the Law

Conventional laws of a society are determined by the moral beliefs of that society. Many people disagree with this statement. In fact, there are two views. The proponents of natural law believe that conventional laws are valid if they meet certain standards of morality, whereas opponents of natural law, usually referred to as legal positivists, do not believe in the validity of conventional laws based on morality [11]. Whatever your camp, both morality and the legal system serve the purpose of keeping society stable and secure. They are both used in making judgments about people's actions and such judgments are justifiable by reason. Although morality and the law seem to have a common purpose and the means to achieve the stated purpose, the implementation of these means to achieve the purpose is different. The following are some of the major differences:

1. *The process of making codes and laws*: Laws are enacted by authorities like councils of elders and assemblies of the people's representatives. Moral codes, however, are developed not by one central authority but by all members of a society, over a period of time, from experiences and reason.
2. *Enforcement*: Laws are enforced by the authority that enacted them or representatives of that authority like judges and courts, and security forces like the police. However, morality is not enforceable by courts, nor is it enforceable by any

authorized security force. There is no moral or ethical court to judge moral wrongdoers. For example, no one can impose penalties for not obeying the Ten Commandments.

3. *Nature of punishments*: Unlawful acts are punishable by penalties that depend on type, nature, and civility of the action. If it is criminal, it may result in incarceration and if it is civil, it may result in payment of damages. However, if the act is judged to be immoral, the judgment is usually based on the individual's perception of that society's morality, and the penalties imposed are also individually based.

4. *Conflict resolution*: Laws are used to resolve interpersonal conflicts in a society. However, morality is mostly used to harmonize intrapersonal conflicts.

5. *Types of judgment*: Morality passes judgment on a person's intentions and character based on what is in your heart. Although courts do not always ignore a person's intention or state of mind, the law cannot normally govern what is in the person's heart.

Because of these differences, it is correct to say that in any society not all laws are based on the morality of that society. Because morality is a higher and superior system, there is only a small area where the two overlap, and there are many times when the two conflict. Let us look at examples. In February 1997 came the startling news of the results of a bold genetic engineering experiment. The Roslin Institute in Edinburgh, Scotland, reported that a team of researchers led by embryologist Dr. Ian Wilmut had successfully cloned two identical sheep. Wilmut's team beat the odds predicted by researchers around the world by taking a mammary cell from an adult sheep, preparing its DNA to be accepted by the egg from another sheep, moving the egg's own DNA, and replacing it with the DNA from the adult sheep by fusing the egg with the adult cell. The fused egg began to grow normally to form an embryo, which scientists then implanted into another sheep, and that sheep later gave birth to a cloned lamb they named Dolly.

Although the experiment was done purely for animal reproduction, many scientists saw the potential for drug manufacturing and replacing human parts. Animals could be used to produce pharmacologically useful proteins for manufacturing drugs, literally making animals serve as drug factories. Animal clones could also be used to "manufacture" animal parts with human characteristics that could later be used in human transplants.

The cloning experiment created substantial legal, ethical, and moral problems. In many countries, it is not illegal to clone human beings, but because of the potential for abuse, such countries are already scrambling to enact laws that will make such an act illegal. Moral and ethical issues also need to be addressed. For example, what will prevent an unethical scientist from cloning a person he or she loves or a person to experiment on, and what will stop governments strapped by lack of labor from cloning thousands of their best living human beings who have exhibited extraordinary intelligence or skills?

In the rush to create ourselves, we may end up creating monsters that could destroy us because although the physical characteristics of clones will be similar, behavior characteristics will be as unpredictable as ours! Wilmut acknowledges the potential for misuse of this scientific breakthrough [10]. It is a daunting moral dilemma for which the society must come up with solutions.

Imagine seeing someone drowning and calling desperately for help and you simply look on and enjoy the show. Your action is not only repugnant, but immoral and depending on whether the laws of deliberate indifference apply to you, your action may not even be illegal. In another example, authorities in some societies fight teen violence by imposing a night curfew on the teens. In such societies, it is illegal for teens to venture out after curfew hours, although it is not immoral. Another good illustrative example is free speech. Consider a situation that occurred on a college campus in which a list of male students, posted by a group of female students led by a faculty member, warned that those male students were potential rapists. Such an act is repugnant, yet it is legal to post such a list. Consider also the trade in pornographic images both in print and on the Internet. These images not only degrade the men, women, and children depicted; they also contribute to other related crimes such as rape. Yet in most cases, trading in such images is legal.

These examples illustrate that even though both morality and conventional law are integral parts of human life, they do not cover the same domains. There are hundreds of similar cases where the legal system, although protecting civil liberties, unintentionally obscures morality.

2.4.1 Issues for Discussion

Name a few of what you consider to be unjust laws and sometimes injustice legal systems that imprisons innocent people.

2.5 Morality, Etiquettes and Manners

Etiquette refers to a code of behavior, a set of norms of correct conduct expected by society, group, or social class. It is a general expected social behavior. These rules of the code or the set of norms is usually unwritten, but aspects of which may reflect an underlying moral code.

Manners are unenforced standards of conduct or cultural norms that show that an individual is "refined" and "cultured" with a society or group. These norms e codify or set a standard for human behavior. However, unlike laws which also codify human behavior, manners just like morality have no formal system for punishing transgressions, other than social disapproval.

2.5.1 Issues for Discussion

Lapses in etiquettes occur when least expected. The consequences of which may vary depending on the audience. Discuss these consequences and how etiquettes are related to the moral code of the group.

Discuss your own situations that involved such lapses. What does society expect from the offending individual?

Exercises

1. How do morality and law relate to each other?
2. What is moral relativism?
3. What is the connection between law and art?
4. Why is reasoning so important in morality?
5. Is morality evolutionary or revolutionary? Discuss.
6. Happiness is human. Discuss.
7. What is the role of education in moral behavior?
8. Show how and why the following rules are culture-free:
   (i) The Golden Rule
   (ii) The Bronze Rule
   (iii) The Iron Rule
9. If you were charged with creating a "new" human society, what moral code would you design and why?
10. We tend to live a moral script everyday. Reflect on what is in your script.
11. Morality is time sensitive. Discuss.
12. Study the Native American Ten Commandments and the Christian Ten Commandments. Without comparing them, discuss the common thread between them.
13. How does guilt help to shape our moral journey?
14. Discuss the interplay between guilt and conscious.
15. What roles does conscious play in decision making?
16. Natural law is universal. Discuss.
17. What is the law of nature? Discuss why it is different from natural law?
18. What role does each one of the following play in our lives?
   (i) Conventional law
   (ii) Natural law
   (iii) Law of nature
19. Can there be a common morality? Why or why not?
20. Is common morality possible in cyberspace?
21. Discuss the possibility of common morality in the age of globalization.
22. What is the effect of globalization on morality?

References

1. MacDonnel, C. "Moral Decision Making: An Analysis." http://www.ethics.ubc.ca/-chrismac/moral.decision.html

2. "Moral Relativism." *Internet Encyclopedia of Philosophy.* http://www.utm.edu/research/iep/ni/m-ration.html
3. Sagan, Carl. "A New Way to Think About Rules to Live By." *Parade Magazine*, November 28, 1993, p. 12.
4. "The Native American Ten Commandments." http://www.indians.org/prayer/ten.html
5. "The Christian Ten Commandments." http://www.avenue.com/v/ktheten.html
6. "The Unix Ten Commandments." http://www.pipex.net/people/jasonh/command.html
7. Kauffman, Liz. (ed). *Webster's Dictionary.* Boyne City, MI: Harbor House, 1989.
8. Bourn, Bryan. "Law as Art (with apologies to Charles Black)." http://www.usinternet.com/bdbourn/black.html
9. Donald, James. "Natural Law and Natural Rights." http://catalog.com/jamesd/rights.html
10. Kalota, Gina. "Scientists Report First Cloning Ever for Adult Mammal." *New York Times*, February 23, 1997, sec. 1, p. 1. http://search.nytimes.com/search/daily/bin/fastweb? search/
11. Fr. Austin Fagothey. *Right and Reason*, Second Edition. Tan Books and Publishers, Rockford, IL, 1959.

Further Readings

12. "Conclusion: Words, Not Laws, Should Be the Weapons." *The Ethical Spectacle*, November 1995. http://www.spectacle.org/1995/concl.html
13. Edel, A., Elizabeth Flower, and Finarr O'Connor. *Morality, Philosophy, and Practice: Historical and Contemporary Readings and Studies*, Third Edition. Random House, New York, 1989.
14. Johnson, D.G. Computer Ethics, Second Edition. Prentice Hall, Englewood Cliffs, NJ, 1994.
15. Kizza, J.M. (ed.). Social and Ethical Effects of the Computer Revolution. McFarland, Jefferson, NC, 1996.
16. Macer, D.R.J. *Bioethics for the People by the People.* Eubios Ethics Institute, Christchurch, New Zealand, 1994, pp. 74–91. http://bio.tsukuba.ac.jp/-macer/BFPSE.html
17. "Objective Morality." http://www.percep.demon.co.uk/morality.html
18. Shepard, John, Micheal G. Goldsby, and Virginia W. Gerde. "Teaching Business Ethics Through Literature." The Online Journal of Ethics. http://condor.depaul.edu/ethics/gerde.html

Chapter 3
Ethics and Ethical Analysis[1,2]

[1]Source: Chattanooga Time/Free Press—Sunday Jan 2, 2000 section H4.
[2]Source: Chattanooga Time/Free Press—Sunday Jan 2, 2000 section H4.

Learning Objectives

After reading this chapter, the reader should be able to:

1. Analyze an argument to identify premises and conclusion.
2. Illustrate the use of ethical argument.
3. Detect basic logical fallacies in an argument.
4. Identify stakeholders in an issue and our obligations to them.
5. Articulate the ethical tradeoffs in a technical decision.
6. Evaluate the professional codes of ethics from the ACM and other organizations.

Scenario 2
Should We Clone Humans?

Professor John Wesley is a brilliant scientist with an enviable track record of medical successes. In the last 5 years, he has carried out a dozen high-risk medical operations successfully and has become a must-have on talk shows. He is a sought-after speaker on medical matters, and he is gifted on all reasonable subjects. He has led pioneering research in cloning and has been contemplating cloning some human replacement parts, if he can only get a human experience to give him a convincing push.

Mrs. Joan Kaggwa is a well-known and successful entrepreneur, a wonderful wife, and a philanthropist. She is a president of several local and national charity organizations. She sits on the boards of several national and international corporations. For the last 21 years of her marriage, she has worked hard for her family and community. Two years ago, however, her only son, a young man nearing his 18th birthday, was killed in an automobile accident. He was the apple of his parents' eyes. The family was devastated by the death.

For a while now, Mrs. Kaggwa has been following the cloning stories that have appeared on television and in the newspapers, but without seriously giving them much thought until the day of her son's death. Then, with her assistance, and to the annoyance of her husband, the family agreed to keep their son's body with Infinite Life Corporation, a company that keeps human frozen bodies in liquid nitrogen for years. Mrs. Kaggwa hoped that someday science would bring her son back. Her prayers were answered, at least according to her, one Sunday morning when she was going through the Sunday paper just before church. A small article caught her eye. The article was about a planned cloning experiment by a young scientist. During the following 2 weeks, Joan made calls that led her and her husband to the waiting room of Professor Wesley to discuss the cloning of their beloved, but dead, son.

Discussion Questions

1. *Are there justifiable reasons that lead people to clone their loved ones?*
2. *Is Mrs. Kaggwa justified in wanting to clone her son?*
3. *Do you think the Kaggwas' son, if successfully cloned, will be the same as the dead son? Why or why not?*
4. *What compelling reasons can Professor Wesley give to justify cloning the Kaggwas' son?*
5. *Do you subscribe to such reasoning?*
6. *What are the pros and cons of human cloning?*
7. *Animal cloning is now routine. Why has there been no organized opposition to it?*

3.1 Traditional Definition

Fr. Austin Fagothey in Right and Reason [5] traces the origins of ethics from the Greeks. He observes that the Greeks' desire and curiosity to learn about themselves, the human life, and society led to the examination of all human conducts, a part of philosophy called ethics. Ethics is, therefore, a study of right and wrong in human conduct. Ethics can also be defined as a theoretical examination of morality and as an equivalent of the "theory of morals." Other philosophers have defined ethics in a variety of ways.

Robert C. Solomon in Morality and the Good Life [1] gives a traditional philosophical definition of ethics as a set of "theories of value, virtue, or of right (valuable) action." Johnson elaborates on Solomon's definition by defining ethics as a set of theories "that provide general rules or principles to be used in making moral decisions and, unlike ordinary intuitions, provides a justification for those rules" [2]. The word "ethics" comes from an ancient Greek word eché [1], which means character. Every human society, whether civilized or primitive, practices ethics because every society attaches a value on an individual's actions, on a continuum of good to bad, right to wrong, according to where that individual's actions fall within the domain of that society's rules and canons.

Ethics helps us not only in distinguishing between right and wrong but also in knowing why and on what grounds our judgment of human actions is justified. Ethics, therefore, is a field of inquiry whose subject is human actions, collectively called human conduct, which are performed consciously, willfully, and for which one can be held responsible. According to Fr. Fagothey [5], such acts must have knowledge that signifies the presence of a motive, volunteeriness to signify that it is willed, and freedom to signify the presence of free choice to act or not to act.

The purpose of ethics is to interpret human conduct, acknowledging and distinguishing between right and wrong. The interpretation is done based on a system. This system, according to Fr. Fagothey, uses a process of argumentation consisting of a mixture of inductions and deductions. In most cases, these arguments are based on historical schools of thought called ethical theories. There are different kinds of ethical theories, and within each theory there may be different versions of that theory.

3.2 Ethical Theories

For centuries, in different societies, human actions have been judged good or bad, right or wrong, based on theories or systems of justice developed, tested, revised, and debated by philosophers and/or elders in that society. Such theories are commonly known as ethical theories. Codes of ethics have then been drawn up based on these ethical theories. The processes of reasoning, explanation, and justification used in ethics are based on these theories. There are many ethical theories, but we consider only a few that are most widely discussed and used, namely consequentialism, deontology, human nature, relativism, hedonism, and emotivism.

3.2.1 Consequentialism

In consequentialism ethical theory, human actions are judged good or bad, right or wrong, depending on the results of such actions—a desirable result denotes a good action and vice versa. There are three commonly discussed types of consequentialism theory:

1. *Egoism*: This theory puts an individual's interests and happiness above everything else. With egoism, any action is good as long as it maximizes an individual's overall happiness. There are two kinds of egoism: ethical egoism, which states how people ought to behave as they pursue their own interests, and psychological egoism, which describes how people actually behave. For example, if a family wanted to be happier, an ethical egoism theorist would prescribe to each family member how he or she ought to behave to achieve individual happiness first before considering the happiness of the family. A psychological egoism theorist, however, would describe how each individual family member should actually behaveto achieve his or her happiness and hence the happiness of the family as a whole.

2. *Utilitarianism*: Unlike egoism, this theory puts a group's interest and happiness above those of an individual, for the good of many. Thus, an action is good if it benefits the maximum number of people. Among the forms of utilitarianism are the following:

   - Act utilitarianism: Tells one to consider seriously the consequences of all actions before choosing the one with the best overall advantage, happiness in this case, for the maximum number of people [3].
   - Rule utilitarianism: Tells one to obey those rules that bring the maximum happiness to the greatest number of people. Rule utilitarianism maintains that a behavioral code or rule is good if the consequences of adopting that rule are favorable to the greatest number of people [3].

3. *Altruism*: In altruism an action is right if the consequences of that action are favorable to all except the actor.

3.2.2 Deontology

The theory of deontological reason does not concern itself with the consequences of the action but rather with the will of the action. An action is good or bad depending on the will inherent in it. According to deontological theory, an act is considered good if the individual committing it had a good reason to do so. This theory has a duty attached to it. In fact, the word "deontology" comes from two Greek words, deon meaning duty, and logos meaning science [2]. For example, we know that killing is bad, but if an armed intruder enters your house and you kill him or her, your action is good, according to deontologists. You did it because you had a duty to protect your family and property.

3.2.3 Human Nature

This theory considers human beings as endowed with all faculties and capabilities to live in happiness. We are supposed to discover and then develop those capabilities. In turn, those capabilities become a benchmark for our actions, and our actions are then gauged and judged on how much they measure up to those capabilities. According to the famous Greek philosopher Aristotle, an individual committing an evil action is lacking in some capabilities.

3.2.4 Relativism

This theory is negatively formulated, denying the existence of universal moral norms. It takes right and wrong to be relative to society, culture, or the individual. Relativism also states that moral norms are not fixed in time.

3.2.5 Hedonism

Hedonism is one of the oldest ethical theories. It claims that pleasure is the only good thing in human life, the end of life as the highest good. A hedonist acts only for maximum pleasure and whatever he or she does, it is done to maximize pleasure or minimize pain. There are two types of hedonism: psychological hedonism, which claims that in fact what people seek in their everyday actions is pleasure, and ethical hedonism, which claims that people ought to seek pleasure, and that pleasure is the moral good. Modern hedonists use the word pleasure to mean happiness.

3.2.6 Emotivism

This theory maintains that ethical statements are neither true nor false and cannot be proven; they are really only statements about how someone feels [3]. Philosophers use these theories as engines to help them to understand and justify human actions. Although over the years and in different places changing values have been attached to human actions, these ethical theories have remained relatively unchanged. This means that although ethics as a discipline is evolving, ethical reasoning has relatively remained the same. In other words, Aristotle and Plato's reasoning to explain and justify human actions is still valid, although the premises surrounding human actions are changing with time and with every new technology.

The process of ethical reasoning takes several steps, which we refer to as layers of reasoning, before one can justify to someone else the goodness or badness, rightness or wrongness, of one's action. For example, if someone wants to convince you to own a concealed gun, he or she needs to explain to you and justify why it is good to have a concealed gun. In such an exercise, the person may start by explaining to you that we are living in difficult times and that no one is safe. You may then ask why no one is safe, to which the person might reply that there are many bad people out there in possession of high-powered guns waiting to fire them for various and very often unbelievable reasons. So owning a gun will level the playing field. Then you may ask why owning a gun levels the playing field, to which the answer would be that because if the bad guys suspect that you own one just like theirs, they will think twice before they attack you. You may further ask why this is so; the answer may be that if they attack you, they themselves can get killed in the action. Therefore, because of this fear you are not likely to be attacked. Hence owning a gun may save your life and enable you to continue pursuing the ultimate concept of the good life: happiness.

On the other hand, to convince somebody not to own a concealed gun again needs a plausible explanation and several layers of reasoning to demonstrate why owning a gun is bad. Why is it a bad thing, you would ask, and the answer would be because bad guys will always get guns. And if they do, the possibility of everyone having a concealed gun may make those bad guys trigger happy to get you before you get them. It also evokes the image of the Wild West filled with gun-toting people daring everyone to get a kick out of what may be a boring life. You would then ask why is this situation dangerous if none fires? The reply might be because it creates a potential situation in which innocent people may get hurt and therefore an unhappy situation is created, denying people happiness and the good life. The explanation and reasoning process can go on and on for several more layers before one is convinced that owning a gun is good or bad. The act of owning a gun is a human act that can be judged as either good or bad, right or wrong, depending on the moral and ethical principles used.

The spectrum of human actions on which ethical judgments can be based is wide ranging, from simple traditional and easy-to-understand actions like killing and stealing, to complex and abstract ones like hacking, cellular telephone scanning, and subliminal human brain alterations. On one side of this spectrum, the inputs have straight output value judgments of right and wrong or good and evil. The other end of the spectrum, however, has inputs that cannot be easily mapped into the same output value judgments of good and bad or right and evil. It is at this side of the input spectrum that most new human actions created as a result of computer technology are found. It is at this end, therefore, that we need an updated definition of ethics—a functional definition.

3.3 Functional Definition of Ethics

Let $A = \{a_1, a_2, a_3,..., a_n\}$ be a collection of identifiable objects, a_i, $i = 1, 2, \ldots, n$. We call this collection a set. A function f defined on set A is a rule that takes elements of A and assigns them values into another set R, called the range of the function. The set A is the domain of f. We represent the function f as $f{:}A \rightarrow R$. A function defined on two sets A and B takes pairs (a, b) of elements $a \in A$ and $b \in B$ and assigns to each pair a value r in the range set R. For example, let $A = \{a1, a2, a3\}$ and $B = \{b1, b2\}$. Then $f(A, B) \rightarrow C$ is a mapping $f(a_i, b_j) = r_k$ for all $a_i \in A$, $b_j \in B$, and $r_k \in C$ where $r_k = a_j * b_j$ for some operation * defined on elements of A and B.

An example of a function like f would be the mixing of two colors. Suppose A is a can of blue paint and B is a can of yellow paint. Let f be the process of mixing these two colors from both cans. After mixing the contents or some of the contents of can A with those of can B, the resulting mixture is the green color put in can C.

Let us use this model to construct a functional definition of ethics. Let the set A be the set of all possible human actions on which it is possible to pass a value judgment. For example, if you think of an artwork, the human actions on it could be an array of things like lifting it, hiding it, stealing it, and many others. So define $A = \{a_1, a_2, a_3, \ldots \}$. Let the second set B consist of many ethical or moral theories such as the ones we have discussed in the previous sections. So B could contain theories like egoism, act utilitarianism, and others. Define $B = \{b_1, b_2, b_3, \ldots \}$. Finally, let R, the third set, be the set of all possible value judgments on the human actions in A based on the ethical theories in B. The function f maps each pair (a, b) of elements, with $a \in A$ and $b \in B$ to a binary value in R. The first set is the set of input parameters. The inputs are human actions on which it is possible to pass a judgment. The second set consists of the ethical theories discussed earlier, like consequentialism, deontology, and human nature. The third set R = {RIGHT or WRONG, GOOD or BAD}, the range of the function f on the two sets A and B, is the value set. Now define a function f on a pair of elements (a, b) with $a \in A$ and $b \in B$ to produce an element $r \in R$ as $f{:}\ (a, b) \rightarrow r$. We call this function the ethics decision function. Recalling our earlier discussion of ethics, function f represents a sequence of explanations and reasoning on the elements of sets A and B. The elements of R have two values: 1 for GOOD or RIGHT and 0 for WRONG or BAD.

Because the power of reasoning associates to each pair of elements (a, b), with a in A and b in B, a binary value equivalent to good, bad, right, or wrong using the set B of ethical theories, we represent this function as follows:

$$f(a,b) \rightarrow \begin{cases} 1\{\text{"right","or"good"}\} \\ \hline 0\{\text{"bad","or"wrong"}\} \end{cases}$$

for all $a \in A$ and $b \in B$

What is the relationship between this function, f, and the human mind? If you reflect on it you will see that the human mind seems to employ a similar function in making ethical and moral judgments. Notice that the human mind associates an integer value 0 or 1 to all human actions it perceives through sight, smell, touch, and hearing. Let us use an example to explain this. Suppose you see somebody breaking into a church. Chances are you are going to like or dislike that action. If you like it, you associate the "like" value to an integer 1 and if you dislike it, you again associate this "dislike" value to an integer value 0. We tend to associate these two integer values to everything our mind perceives.

In making your decision whether or not you liked the action of the person who broke into the church, you probably based your "judgment" of this action on how that action registers in one of the moral and ethical theories. If it does, and it will always fall in at least one of the theories, then you will associate a weight depending on the hierarchy of reasoning you go through to justify right or wrong. Let us use this new functional model of ethics to get a glimpse into the prospects of ethics in the future. Advances in computer technology can greatly influence this model. An explanation is in order. The presence of computer technology creates multitudes of possibilities for every human action and greatly enhances and expands the input set A. The expansion of set A is likely to bring fuzziness to our traditional definition of ethics. Thus, there is a need to expand our definitions of ethics to meet the constantly changing technology-driven landscape of human actions.

3.4 Ethical Reasoning and Decision Making

Both reasoning and logic are important elements in daily human interactions. Reasoning is a human cognitive process of looking for ways to generate or affirm a proposition. Cognitive processes are mental functions or activities that are grouped based on *experience, interpretation, foreseeing, ordering, analyzing, valuing, and making connections*. Logic on the other hand, based on the Greek meaning, is the tool for distinguishing between truth and falseness. Human beings, on a daily basis, engage in reasoning and logic to achieve the desire results from a problem or an issue. Both reasoning and logic are important in decision making.

Each day we make hundreds of decisions from what we will wear to what side of bed to sleep on. When making these everyday decisions, many people tend to rely on a variety of biases and heuristics as they do their reasoning. This kind of reasoning based on intuition unfortunately leads to wrong and ethical decisions. Ethical reasoning is integrating ethical principles in the reasoning process. Each day we are faced with a variety of ethical or moral decisions ranging from simple ones like to liar about a spouse's choice of dressing to hard ones like contributing to an abortion campaign.

Ethical decision making is the process of making a decision with decision that results in a least number of conflicts. Such process involves the decision maker to [6]:

- Recognize the inherent ethical conflicts through comprehension, appreciation, and evaluation of all ethical dimensions of problem
- Knowing the parties involved
- Being aware of alternatives
- Demonstrating knowledge of ethical practices
- Understand how the decision will be implemented and who will be affected
- Understand and comprehend the impact of the decision of the parties involved

3.4.1 A Framework for Ethical Decision Making

There are different elements that make a good framework for an ethical decision. The most common of these that must be in a good framework are:

- Recognize inherent ethical conflicts through comprehension, appreciation, and evaluation of all ethical dimensions of problem
- Understanding the problem and the facts of the problem
- Knowing the parties involved
- Being aware of alternatives
- Demonstrating knowledge of ethical practices
- Understand how the decision will be implemented and who will be affected
- Understanding the impact the decision will have on the parties affected
- Understand and comprehend the impact of the decision of the parties involved

Taking these elements of the framework into consideration when making a decision lessens the number of conflicts and the severity of the impact resulting from the decision.

3.4.2 Making and Evaluating Ethical Arguments

In real life, especially in professional life, or in whatever we do, we are going to be faced with an ethical problem for which we need to seek solutions. Many real-life problems have systematic structures on which the search for a solution is based. For example, mathematical problems have rules called algorithms to follow. Many other real-life problems can be modeled in such a way that an algorithm can always be found, or in such cases where no mathematical formula can be used, empirical models can be used. Ethical problems are not like problems in a structured environment, where there are rules to follow. The main question is how to find solutions to ethical problems. We find solutions to ethical problems through a process, or series of steps, which often leads to an ethically justified resolution of the problem. This is a process of ethical reasoning that we discussed in Chapter 3. Ethical reasoning either brings a resolution to an ethical problem or, at worst, helps to deepen our understanding of the ethical problem which may eventually lead to the resolution of the problem at a future date. As we pointed out in Chapter 3, the process of ethical reasoning involves a set of layers of reasoning.

The process of ethical reasoning and ethical problem resolution can be likened to the process of software engineering. As in software engineering, the process goes through a number of stages with specific facts and responsibilities before a genuine solution to the problem is found. Before a resolution is embarked on, there must be a clear understanding of the problem. A clear picture of the relevant facts or specifications must be developed. A good description of these facts is then written down and guided by these facts; a set of layers of reasoning is entered into. Although the initial description of the problem is crucial, it should not be the last. As the reasoning process develops, the initial description could be revised and expanded, which may bring more understanding of the problem and may lead to the revision of our reasoning layers as further steps in the reasoning process are added or removed as additional information comes in.

The process of ethical reasoning must avail the decision maker with a safe or valid alternative from a multitude of alternatives presented by the ethical problems. This safe alternative is the way out of the ethical muddles presented by the ethical problem. As the process of reasoning progresses, the following information will start to emerge [9]:

(i) Information to confirm whether the problem is really an ethical problem or not
(ii) Information on whether further description of the facts can add anything to the resolution process of the problem
(iii) Information to identify the key ethical theories, principles, and values that fit the safe alternatives being pursued
(iv) Information on the strength and validity of the ethical theory chosen and whether there are possible conflicts in the ethical theories, principles, and values with the reasoning processes and facts

When a final decision has been made, an evaluation of that decision is needed.

The goal of evaluating an ethical argument is to make sure that each of the alternatives being considered is "weighted" against all others using the facts at hand developed earlier, and, in some cases, based on anticipated outcomes to our decisions. In so doing, we determine which alternative is best based on sound reasoning. Two outcomes are possible: one, we pick the best alternative, in which case our reasoning showed more validity of the facts of the problem than all other alternatives. Two, we may find that we are unable to come out with a winning alternative. In this case, it means that there is no convincing reasoning in any one of the two or more deadlocking alternatives. This may require any one of the following: the addition of more layers of reasoning, addition of new facts, or replacement of ethical theories and principles in the argument. In either of the two cases, however, justification of the choice of alternatives is based on examining all of the reasons given for all the alternatives. A thorough examination of our reasoning is based on the criticism of the ethical reasoning used for each alternative. There are several critical strategies used to achieve a good examination of the reasoning process including whether the reasoning used was [16]:

(i) Based on factual assumptions that are actually false or unsupported by good evidence. If assumptions are false or unsupported by any evidence, the reasons that make use of them are suspect and carry little weight, if any, or
(ii) Valid. A reasoning is valid if its premises are true. Then the conclusion is also very probably true

3.5 Codes of Ethics

The main domains in which ethics is defined are governed by a particular and definitive regiment of rules called "codes of ethics." These rules, guidelines, canons, advisories, or whatever you want to call them, are usually followed by members of the respective domains. Depending on the domain, ethical codes can take any of the following forms:

1. Principles, which may act as guidelines, references, or bases for some document
2. Public policies, which may include aspects of acceptable behavior, norms, and practices of a society or group
3. Codes of conduct, which may include ethical principles
4. Legal instruments, which enforce good conduct through courts

Although the use of codes of ethics is still limited to professions and high-visibility institutions and businesses, there is a growing movement toward widespread use. The wording, content, and target of many codes differ greatly. Some codes are written purposely for the public; others are targeting employees, and yet others are for professionals only. Reproduced here is the ACM Code of Professional Conduct.[3]

Association of Computing Machinery (ACM) Code of Ethics and Professional Conduct

On October 16, 1992, ACM's Executive Council voted to adopt a revised Code of Ethics. The following imperatives and explanatory guidelines were proposed to supplement the Code as contained in the new ACM Bylaw 17.

Preamble
Commitment to ethical professional conduct is expected of every member (voting members, associate members, and student members) of the Association for Computing Machinery (ACM). This Code, consisting of 24 imperatives formulated as statements of personal responsibility, identifies the elements of such a commitment. It contains many, but not all, issues professionals are likely to face. Section 1 outlines fundamental ethical considerations, while Section 2 addresses additional,

---

[3]© 1993 Association of Computing Machinery, Inc.

more specific considerations of professional conduct. Statements in Section 3 pertain more specifically to individuals who have a leadership role, whether in the work place or in a volunteer capacity, for example with organizations such as ACM. Principles involving compliance with this Code are given in Section 4. The Code is supplemented by a set of Guidelines, which provide explanation to assist members in dealing with the various issues contained in the Code. It is expected that the guidelines will be changed more frequently than the Code.

The Code and its supplemented Guidelines are intended to serve as a basis for ethical decision making in the conduct of professional work. Second, they may serve as a basis for judging the merit of a formal complaint pertaining to violation of professional ethical standards.

It should be noted that although computing is not mentioned in the moral imperatives section, the Code is connected with how these fundamental imperatives apply to one's conduct as a computing professional. These imperatives are expressed in a general form to emphasize that ethical principles which apply to computer ethics are derived from more general ethical principles. It is understood that some words and phrases in a code of ethics are subject to varying interpretations, and that any ethical principle may conflict with other ethical principles in specific situations. Questions related to ethical conflicts can best be answered by thoughtful consideration of fundamental principles, rather than reliance on detailed regulations.

1. GENERAL MORAL IMPERATIVES
   As an ACM member I will...
   1.1 Contribute to society and human well-being.
   1.2 Avoid harm to others.
   1.3 Be honest and trustworthy.
   1.4 Be fair and take action not to discriminate.
   1.5 Honor property rights including copyrights and patents.
   1.6 Give proper credit for intellectual property.
   1.7 Respect the privacy of others.
   1.8 Honor confidentiality.

2. MORE SPECIFIC PROFESSIONAL RESPONSIBILITIES
   As an ACM computing professional I will...
   2.1 Strive to achieve the highest quality, effectiveness, and dignity in both the process and products of professional work.
   2.2 Acquire and maintain professional competence.
   2.3 Know and respect existing laws pertaining to professional work.
   2.4 Accept and provide appropriate professional review.
   2.5 Give comprehensive and thorough evaluations of computer systems and their impacts including analysis of possible risks.
   2.6 Honor contracts, agreements, and assigned responsibilities.
   2.7 Improve public understanding of computing and its consequences.
   2.8 Access computing and communication resources only when authorized to do so.

3. ORGANIZATIONAL LEADERSHIP IMPERATIVES

As an ACM member and an organizational leader, I will...

3.1 Articulate social responsibilities of members of an organizational unit and encourage full acceptance of those responsibilities.

3.2 Manage personnel and resources to design and build information systems that enhance the quality of working life.

3.3 Acknowledge and support proper and authorized uses of an organization's computing and communications resources.

3.4 Ensure that users and those who will be affected by a system have their needs clearly articulated during the assessment and design of requirements; later the system must be validated to meet requirements.

3.5 Articulate and support policies that protect the dignity of users and others affected by a computing system.

3.6 Create opportunities for members of the organization to learn the principles and limitations of computer systems.

4. COMPLIANCE WITH THE CODE

As an ACM member, I will...

4.1 Uphold and promote the principles of this Code.

4.2 Treat violations of this code as inconsistent with membership in the ACM. GUIDELINES

1. GENERAL MORAL IMPERATIVES

As an ACM member I will...

1.1 Contribute to society and human well-being.

This principle concerning the quality of life of all people affirms an obligation to protect fundamental human rights and to respect the diversity of all cultures. An essential aim of computing professionals is to minimize negative consequences of computing systems, including threats to health and safety. When designing or implementing systems, computing professionals must attempt to ensure that the products of their efforts will be used in socially responsible ways, will meet social needs, and will avoid harmful effects to health and welfare.

In addition to a safe social environment, human well-being includes a safe natural environment. Therefore, computing professionals who design and develop systems must be alert to, and make others aware of, any potential damage to the local or global environment.

1.2 Avoid harm to others.

"Harm" means injury or negative consequences, such as undesirable loss of information, loss of property, property damage, or unwanted environmental impacts. This principle prohibits use of computing technology in ways that result in harm to any of the following: users, the general public, employees, and employers. Harmful actions include intentional destruction or modification of files and programs leading to serious loss of resources or unnecessary expenditure of human resources such as the time and effort required to purge systems of computer viruses.

Well-intended actions, including those that accomplish assigned duties, may lead to harm unexpectedly. In such an event the responsible person or persons are obligated to undo or mitigate the negative consequences as much as possible. One way to avoid unintentional harm is to carefully consider potential impacts on all those affected by decisions made during design and implementation. To minimize the possibility of indirectly harming others, computing professionals must minimize malfunctions by following generally accepted standards for system design and testing. Furthermore, it is often necessary to assess the social consequences of systems to project the likelihood of any serious harm to others. If system features are misrepresented to users, co-workers, or supervisors, the individual computing professional is responsible for any resulting injury.

In the work environment the computing professional has the additional obligation to report any signs of system dangers that might result in serious personal or social damage. If one's superiors do not act to curtail or mitigate such dangers, it may be necessary to "blow the whistle" to help correct the problem or reduce the risk. However, capricious or misguided reporting of violations can, itself, be harmful. Before reporting violations, all relevant aspects of the incident must be thoroughly assessed. In particular, the assessment of risk and responsibility must be credible. It is suggested that advice be sought from other computing professionals. (See principle 2.5 regarding thorough evaluations.)

1.3 Be honest and trustworthy.

Honesty is an essential component of trust. Without trust an organization cannot function effectively. The honest computing professional will not make deliberately false or deceptive claims about a system or system design, but will instead provide full disclosure of all pertinent system limitations and problems. A computer professional has a duty to be honest about his or her own qualifications, and about any circumstances that might lead to conflicts of interest.

Membership in volunteer organizations such as ACM may at times place individuals in situations where their statements or actions could be interpreted as carrying the weight of a larger group of professionals. An ACM member will exercise care to not misrepresent ACM or positions and policies of ACM or any ACM units.

1.4 Be fair and take action not to discriminate.

The values of equality, tolerance, respect for others, and the principles of equal justice govern this imperative. Discrimination on the basis of race, sex, religion, age, disability, national origin, or other such factors is an explicit violation of ACM policy and will not be tolerated. Inequities between different groups of people may result from the use or misuse of information and technology. In a fair society, all individuals would have equal opportunity to participate in, or benefit from, the use of computer resources regardless of race, sex, religion, age, disability, national origin, or other such similar factors.

However, these ideals do not justify unauthorized use of computer resources nor do they provide an adequate basis for violation of any other ethical imperatives of this code.

1.5 Honor property rights including copyrights and patents.

Violation of copyrights, patents, trade secrets, and the terms of license agreements is prohibited by law in most circumstances. Even when software is not so protected, such violations are contrary to professional behavior. Copies of software should be made only with proper authorization. Unauthorized duplication of materials must not be condoned.

1.6 Give proper credit for intellectual property.

Computing professionals are obligated to protect the integrity of intellectual property. Specifically, one must not take credit for other's ideas or work, even in cases where the work has not been explicitly protected, for example by copyright or patent.

1.7 Respect the privacy of others.

Computing and communication technology enables the collection and exchange of personal information on a scale unprecedented in the history of civilization. Thus there is increased potential for violating the privacy of individuals and groups. It is the responsibility of professionals to maintain the privacy and integrity of data describing individuals. This includes taking precautions to ensure the accuracy of data, as well as protecting it from unauthorized access or accidental disclosure to inappropriate individuals. Furthermore, procedures must be established to allow individuals to review their records and correct inaccuracies.

This imperative implies that only the necessary amount of personal information be collected in a system, that retention and disposal periods for that information be clearly defined and enforced, and that personal information gathered for a specific purpose not be used for other purposes without consent of the individual(s). These principles apply to electronic communications, including electronic mail, and prohibit procedures that capture or monitor electronic user data, including messages, without the permission of users or bona fide authorization related to system operation and maintenance. User data observed during the normal duties of system operation and maintenance must be treated with strictest confidentiality, except in cases where it is evidence for the violation of law, organizational regulations, or this Code. In these cases, the nature or contents of that information must be disclosed only to proper authorities. (See 1.9.)

1.8 Honor confidentiality.

The principle of honesty extends to 'issues of confidentiality of information whenever one has made an explicit promise to honor confidentiality or, implicitly, when private information not directly related to the performance of one's duties becomes available. The ethical concern is to respect all obligations of confidentiality to employers, clients, and users unless discharged from such obligations by requirements of the law or other principles of this Code.

2. MORE SPECIFIC PROFESSIONAL RESPONSIBILITIES

As an ACM computing professional I will . . .

*2.1 Strive to achieve the h*ighest quality, effectiveness, and dignity in both the process and products of professional work.

Excellence is perhaps the most important obligation of a professional. The computing professional must strive to achieve quality and to be cognizant of the serious negative consequences that may result from poor quality in a system.

2.2 Acquire and maintain professional competence.

Excellence depends on individuals who take responsibility for acquiring and maintaining professional competence. A professional must participate in setting standards for appropriate levels of competence, and strive to achieve those standards. Upgrading technical knowledge and competence can be achieved in several ways—doing independent study, attending seminars, conferences, or courses—and being involved in professional organizations.

2.3 Know and respect existing laws pertaining to professional work.

ACM members must obey existing local, state, provincial, national, and international laws unless there is a compelling ethical basis not to do so. Policies and procedures of the organizations in which one participates must also be obeyed. But compliance must be balanced with the recognition that sometimes existing laws and rules may be immoral or inappropriate and, therefore, must be challenged. Violation of a law or regulation may be ethical when that law or rule has inadequate moral basis or when it conflicts with another law judged to be more important. If one decides to violate a law or rule because it is viewed as unethical, or for any other reason, one must fully accept responsibility for one's actions and for the consequences.

2.4 Accept and provide appropriate professional review.

Quality professional work, especially in the computing profession, depends on professional reviewing and critiquing. Whenever appropriate, individual members should seek and utilize peer review as well as provide critical review of the work of others.

2.5 Give comprehensive and thorough evaluations of computer systems and their impacts, including analysis of possible risks.

Computer professionals must strive to be perceptive, thorough, and objective when evaluating, recommending, and presenting system descriptions and alternatives. Computer professionals are in a position of special trust, and therefore have a special responsibility to provide objective, credible evaluations to employers, clients, users, and the public. When providing evaluations the professional must also identify any relevant conflicts of interest, as stated in imperative 1.3. As noted in the discussion of principle 1.2 on avoiding harm, any signs of danger from systems must be reported to those who have opportunity and/or responsibility to resolve them. See the guidelines for imperative 1.2 for more details concerning harm, including the reporting of professional violations.

2.6 Honor contracts, agreements, and assigned responsibilities.

Honoring one's commitments is a matter of integrity and honesty. For the computer professional this includes ensuring that system elements perform as intended. Also, when one contracts for work with another party, one has an obligation to keep that party properly informed about progress toward completing that work. A computing professional has a responsibility to request a change in any assignment that he or she feels cannot be completed as defined. Only after serious consideration and with full disclosure of risks and concerns to the employer or client, should one accept the assignment. The major underlying principle here is the obligation to accept personal accountability for professional work. On some occasions other ethical principles may take greater priority. A judgment that a specific assignment should not be performed may not be accepted. Having clearly identified one's concerns and reasons for that judgment, but failing to procure a change in that assignment, one may yet be obligated, by contract or by law, to proceed as directed. The computing professional's ethical judgment should be the final guide in deciding whether or not to proceed. Regardless of the decision, one must accept the responsibility for the consequences. However, performing assignments against one's own judgment does not relieve the professional of responsibility for any negative consequences.

2.7 *Improve public understanding of* computing and its consequences.

Computing professionals have a responsibility to share technical knowledge with the public by encouraging understanding of computing, including the impacts of computer systems and their limitations. This imperative implies an obligation to counter any false views related to computing.

2.8 Access computing and communication resources only when authorized to do so.

Theft or destruction of tangible and electronic property is prohibited by imperative 1.2: "Avoid harm to others." Trespassing and unauthorized use of a computer or communication system is addressed by this imperative. Trespassing includes accessing communication networks and computer systems, or accounts and/or files associated with those systems, without explicit authorization to do so. Individuals and organizations have the right to restrict access to their systems so long as they do not violate the discrimination principle (see 1.4). No one should enter or use another's computing system, software, or data files without permission. One must always have appropriate approval before using system resources, including .rm57 communication ports, file space, other system peripherals, and computer time.

3. ORGANIZATIONAL LEADERSHIP IMPERATIVES

As an ACM member and an organizational leader, I will...

3.1 Articulate social responsibilities of members of an organizational unit and encourage full acceptance of those responsibilities.

Because organizations of all kinds have impacts on the public, they must accept responsibilities to society. Organizational procedures and attitudes oriented toward quality and the welfare of society will reduce harm to members of the public, thereby serving public interest and fulfilling social responsibility. Therefore, organizational leaders must encourage full participation in meeting social responsibilities as well as quality performance.

3.2 Manage personnel and resources to design and build information systems that enhance the quality of working life.

Organizational leaders are responsible for ensuring that computer systems enhance, not degrade, the quality of working life. When implementing a computer system, organizations must consider the personal and professional development, physical safety, and human dignity of all workers. Appropriate human–computer ergonomic standards should be considered in system design and in the workplace.

3.3 Acknowledge and support proper and authorized uses of an organization's computing and communications resources.

Because computer systems can become tools to harm as well as to benefit an organization, the leadership has the responsibility to clearly define appropriate and inappropriate uses of organizational computing resources. While the number and scope of such rules should be minimal, they should be fully enforced when established.

3.4 Ensure that users and those who will be affected by a system have their needs clearly articulated during the assessment and design of requirements.

Later the system must be validated to meet requirements. Current system users, potential users, and other persons whose lives may be affected by a system must have their needs assessed and incorporated in the statement of requirements. System validation should ensure compliance with those requirements.

3.5 Articulate and support policies that protect the dignity of users and others affected by a computing system.

Designing or implementing systems that deliberately or inadvertently demean individuals or groups is ethically unacceptable. Computer professionals who are in decision-making positions should verify that systems are designed and implemented to protect personal privacy and enhance personal dignity.

3.6 Create opportunities for members of the organization to learn the principles and limitations of computer systems.

This complements the imperative on public understanding (2.7). Educational opportunities are essential to facilitate optimal participation of all organizational members. Opportunities must be available to all members to help them improve their knowledge and skills in computing, including courses that familiarize them with the consequences and limitations of particular types of systems. In particular, professionals must be made aware of the dangers of building systems around oversimplified models, the improbability of anticipating and designing for every possible operating condition, and other issues related to the complexity of this profession.

4. COMPLIANCE WITH THE CODE

As an ACM member I will...

4.1 Uphold and promote the principles of this code.

The future of the computing profession depends on both technical and ethical excellence. Not only is it important for ACM computing professionals to adhere to the principles expressed in this Code, each member should encourage and support adherence by other members.

4.2 Treat violations of this code as inconsistent with membership in the ACM. Adherence of professionals to a code of ethics is largely a voluntary matter. However, if a member does not follow this code by engaging in gross misconduct, ACM may be terminated. This Code and the supplemental Guidelines were developed by the Task Force for the Revision of the ACM Code of Ethics and Professional Conduct: Ronald E. Anderson, Chair, Gerald Engel, Donald Gotterbarn, Grace C. Hertlein, Alex Hoffman, Bruce Jawer, Deborah G. Johnson, Doris K. Lidtke, Joyce Currie Little, Dianne Martin, Donn B. Parker, Judith A. Perrolle, and Richard S. Rosenberg. The Task Force was organized by ACMISIGCAS and funding was provided by the ACM SIG Discretionary Fund. This Code and the supplemental Guidelines were adopted by the ACM Council on October 16, 1992.

3.5.1 Objectives of Codes of Ethics

Different domains and groups of people formulate different codes of ethics, but they all have among them the following objectives:

1. Disciplinary: By instilling discipline, the group or profession ensures professionalism and integrity of its members.
2. Advisory: The codes are usually a good source of tips to members and offer advice and guidance in areas where there are fuzzy moral issues.
3. Educational: Ethical codes are good educational tools for members of the domain, especially the new ones who have to learn the do's and don'ts of the new profession. These codes are also a good source of renewal for the older members needing to refresh and polish their possibly waning morals.
4. Inspirational: Besides being disciplinary, advisory, and educational, the codes should also carry subliminal messages to those using them to inspire them to be "good."
5. Publicity: One way for professions to create a good clientele is to show that they have a strong code of ethics and, therefore, their members are committed to basic values and are responsible.

3.6 Reflections on Computer Ethics

3.6.1 New Wine in an Old Bottle

We have so far defined computer ethics as a subset of set A in the functional definition of ethics. We next elaborate on this by pointing out some likely differences
between the set A in the traditional definition and set A in the functional definition,
which now includes computer ethics. Although the overall picture remains the
same, there are differences in the overall implementation of the models because of
the changes in set A of the functional definition. These differences are manifested
in several places as discussed in the following sections.

3.6.1.1 Changing Premises

Although it is true that the outcome of the ethics value function remains the same,
the domain set itself has changed and will keep changing. The number of input
possibilities for every human action keeps on growing with new advances in computer technology. For example, take the act of forgery, which traditionally involves
taking somebody's document, making changes to it, and getting a benefit as a
result. Suppose the document is a check. Let us also assume, all other acts notwithstanding, that you have the document in your hand, in this case the check.
Traditionally, your inputs were limited to making changes to the signature and
probably changing the date, and cashing it meant literally walking to the financial
institution either to deposit it or asking the teller to cash it after producing identification. Although these acts are still possible and readily accepted, new and clev-
erer ways have emerged as computer technology has advanced. First, now the
inputs to set A of an act like this are numerous, no longer limited to the original
two. They range from scanning the check to electronically reproducing almost an
original check, to cashing it or depositing it without ever stepping in any financial
institution, even in the late hours of the night. All these offerings were of course
unheard of just a few years back, but they are giving thieves more ways to do their
job and making it very difficult for financial institutions and law enforcement
agents to do theirs.

3.6.1.2 Different Temptations

In traditional ethics there were few temptations prompting unethical actions. But
according to Richard Rubin [4], computer technology has generated many more
temptations for each input action. He outlines seven of these new temptations:

1. *Speed*: The speed of gathering information has greatly increased, causing unethical actions to be carried out in shorter times, thus decreasing the chances of

detection. When the chances of being caught are slim, many perpetuators think that they can get away with it.

2. *Privacy and anonymity*: The great availability of computers and computer-related technology in less visible places like people's homes; high, cheap and fast communication equipment; and software that can guarantee anonymity are creating a highly tempting environment for unethical acts.

3. *Nature of medium*: The ability to copy digital data without erasing or altering the original in any way causes little or no suspicion and hence encourages unethical activities.

4. *Aesthetic attraction*: Technology, especially when it is new, seems to offer challenges to those who try to use it. Thus, there is a sigh of relief and a sign of great achievement if one overcomes a technological obstacle. In the same way, if an intruder tries to break into a computer system, the sign of success and the euphoria thereafter overshadows the incivility of the act itself.

5. *Increased availability of potential victims*: With the widespread use of computers and the ever-widening reach of computer networks, an individual can now reach an unprecedented audience. This in itself creates an urge to attempt things that one would otherwise not have done.

6. *International scope*: The boundaryless nature of many computer networks, including the Internet, has created a temptation of its own. Now the entire world is well within reach by a touch of a button. This can tempt many intruders, many trying to circumvent their country's laws, and others thinking that an illegal act done in another country cannot be prosecuted in their own country. There are lots of temptations here.

7. *The power to destroy*: Computers seem to give this enormous invisible power to those who have them. This seemingly omniscient power may be a temptation to some. Although some of these temptations can still be found in the set of the old temptations, most of them are new.

3.6.1.3   Different Means of Delivery

What used to be the traditional means of carrying out an act like stealing has changed. With the expanded set of outcome possibilities come expanded delivery systems for the crime. For example, let us go back to the check. The traditional way of cashing a check was to go to the bank. With computers facilitating new ways of banking, you can get your check cashed without ever visiting the bank, even in the middle of the night.

3.6.1.4   Complacent Society

A majority of computer-related actions are either deliberately ignored by society for fear of publicity or they are hailed as novel science. This says that either members of society are still caught in the spell of the new wonder machine or that they have gotten so comfortable with the new wonder machine that they let their moral and ethical standards slide. Whatever it is, society is too complacent about computers, and until this attitude changes, computer ethics is likely to remain different from traditional ethics.

3.6.1.5   Ethical Muddles

With the possibility of numerous inputs from events, new difficulties of choice and justification cause ethical dilemmas, creating conflicting arguments and counterarguments on an input possibility of an event. This is because computers produce new situations that sometimes fall within our existing laws, rules, and moral principles, and sometimes fall outside these guidelines.

3.7   Technology and Values

Every now and then, a new technology is introduced in our midst, intended to make our lives easier. Some of these technologies do not last for more than a month; others take hold and become revolutionary in magnitude. Those which become successful most often influence society by creating new possibilities that may raise new moral and ethical concerns and consequently create vacuums and new dilemmas in that society's basic sets of moral values. Computer technology has been one of these successful technologies. In its very short duration, it has had such a strong impact and influence on society, and if it continues the present trend unchecked, it is likely to become one of the greatest revolutions in the history of humankind, far greater than the agricultural and industrial revolutions. Society as a whole seems to be engulfed in this revolution and no cultural and/or society norm will, in the end if there is an end, be left unaffected.

Successful technological revolutions tend to create tempting situations often resulting in a loosening of individual moral values, and the computer revolution tops that list. Worldwide cultural, political, and social underpinnings and values are undergoing a silent, but tremendous change as new computer products come on the market and the revolution gathers momentum. It is moving so fast that it is stripping us of our ability to cope. Although we are constantly in need of new moral principles and new ethical values to fit the changing landscape, we cannot formulate, debate, and put in place such principles and values fast enough before they are outdated. More important still, even if we were able to come up with new values and moral principles, we would still lack the conceptual models within which such values and principles can be applied.

There are many new situations resulting from the computer revolution that are outdating our basic sets of values. Take, for example, the processes of dealing in forgeries in monitory currencies. There are laws on the books in almost every country against forgeries of any kind let alone forgeries of currencies. These laws are further reinforced with individual moral values. One can, for example, reproduce and print millions of almost identical notes of a country's currency. Suppose even further that one produces a software program that reproduces the bank notes and enriches oneself. One's conscience of course tells the person that what one is doing is wrong, but the new technological advances are so tempting and making it so easy and so available that one can start rationalizing one's acts—I created or bought the program with my own money, did all the work by myself, and after all it is highly unlikely that I can be caught because people cannot even tell the difference. All one is doing is creating a vacuum in one's basic set of values, and society needs to find a way to fill that moral vacuum so as to prevent individuals from taking moral vacations! As computer and telecommunication revolutions pick up speed, creating new avenues of use and access like the Internet and the World Wide Web, thus giving users room and reasons to take moral vacations, there is an urgent need to do the following:

1. Formulate new laws to strengthen our basic sets of values, which are being rendered irrelevant by computer technology.
2. Construct a conceptual model in which the new laws can be applied successfully.
3. Launch a massive education campaign to make society aware of the changing environment and the impact such an environment is having on our basic values.

The first two objectives are beyond the scope of this book, which mainly focuses on the third objective, educating the public concerning ethical issues raised by the computer revolution.

Issues for Discussion: "Thou Shalt not kill" What does this mean? When can you kill and it is OK? What can you kill and it OK?

Exercises

1. How would you define ethics to the following audiences?

   • Seventh-graders
   • College students
   • Members of the clergy

2. Why are acts such as abortion legal in some societies and not in others?
3. Does technology bring relevant changes in ethics?
4. Use the traditional model of ethics to explain the effects of technology on ethics to seventh-graders.
5. What are the merits of computer ethics education?
6. Why should we study computer ethics?
7. There are two views on teaching computer ethics. State the views. What view do your agree with and why?
8. Why do we need ethical theories?
9. According to the human nature theory, you are supposed to develop your capabilities and your actions are based on those capabilities. If individuals have few developed capabilities (due to circumstances beyond their control for example), should they be responsible for their actions?
10. Discuss the existence of universal moral norms.
11. Discuss the effects of time on moral norms.
12. Using graphics, demonstrate the working of the functional definition of ethics.
13. Professional organizations usually use professional codes of ethics to enforce discipline in their members. Do codes always work?
14. Suggest an alternative to the professional codes of ethics and demonstrate that your alternative can work.
15. How does technology affect ethics? morality?

References

1. Solomon, R. Morality and the Good Life: An Introduction to Ethics Through Classical Sources, Second Edition. McGraw-Hill, New York, 1992.
2. Johnson, D.J. Computer Ethics, Second Edition. Prentice Hall, Englewood Cliffs, NJ, 1994.
3. Encyclopedia of Philosophy. http://www.utm.edu/research/lep/ni/
4. Rubin, Richard. "Moral Distancing and the Use of Information Technology: The Seven Temptations." In J. M. Kizza (ed.), Social and Ethical Effects of the Computer Revolution. McFarland, Jefferson, NC, 1996.
5. Fr. Austin Fagothey. Right and Reason, Second Edition. Tan Books and Publishers, Rockford, IL, 1959.
6. Manuel Velasquez, Dennis Moberg, Michael J. Meyer, Thomas Shanks, Margaret R. McLean, David DeCosse, Claire André, and Kirk O. Hanson. "A Framework for Thinking Ethically", Markkula Center for Applied Ethics at Santa Clara University. http://www.scu.edu/ethics/practicing/decision/framework.html

Further Reading

Edel, A., Elizabeth Flower, and Finarr W. O'Connor. Morality, Philosophy, and Practice: Historical and Contemporary Readings and Studies, Third Edition. Random House, New York, 1989.

Chapter 4
Ethics and the Professions

Learning Objectives

After reading this chapter, the reader should be able to:

1. Identify ethical issues that arise in professional decision making and determine how to address them.
2. Analyze global computing issues that influence professional decision making.
3. Describe the mechanisms that typically exist for day-to-day ethical decision making.
4. Identify progressive stages in a whistle-blowing incident.
5. Specify the strengths and weaknesses of relevant professional codes as expressions of professionalism and guides to decision making.

Real-Life Experiences
The Kansas City Pharmacist

In August 2001, Robert Courtney, a Kansas City pharmacist was indicted on 20 felony counts of product tampering, drug adulteration, and drug misbranding. Courtney illegally diluted Gemzar and other expensive chemotherapy drugs to make money.

What was more alarming was the fact that he had hundreds of cancer patients most of them relying on chemotherapy treatments for survival. According to the FBI, at least one patient who received the diluted drugs died.

Courtney was caught when a representative of Eli Lilly and Co., the pharmaceutical company that manufactures Gemzar, became suspicious from records that indicated that a Kansas City doctor was receiving much more Gemzar from Courtney's pharmacy than the actual amount of Gemzar the pharmacy was purchasing from the manufacturer.

After the doctor was notified and the drug was tested, US federal agents were then informed. It was found that Courtney was selling up to three times the amount of drugs he was purchasing from the drug manufacturer [13].

Discussion Questions

1. *What crime did Robert Courtney commit?*
2. *Was it proper to arrest Robert Courtney? Why or why not?*
3. *Do you think Robert Courtney was responsible for the assumed death?*

J.M. Kizza, *Ethical and Social Issues in the Information Age*, Texts in Computer Science, 55
DOI 10.1007/978-1-84996-038-0_4, © Springer-Verlag London Limited 2010

4.1   Introduction

What is a profession? It is a trade, a business, or an occupation of which one professes to have extensive knowledge acquired through long years of experience and formal education and the autonomy and responsibility to make independent decisions in carrying out the duties of the profession. To profess is to make a public declaration, a claim of something. In the case of a professional that something is knowledge in the knowledge domain of that which makes up that occupation or trade. Webster's dictionary similarly defines *profession* as "a : a calling requiring specialized knowledge and often long and intensive academic preparation b : a principal calling, vocation, or employment c : the whole body of persons engaged in a calling." [14]. Well-known professions are law, medicine, and engineering.

In our study of professions and the people who profess the deep knowledge of the profession, we focus on four themes: (1) evolution of professions, (2) the making of an ethical professional, (3) the professional decision-making process, and (4) professionalism and ethical responsibilities. These four themes cover all the activities of a professional life. First, we look at the beginnings of professions, describe the characteristics of professionals, and discuss how these characteristics are supported by commitment, integrity, responsibility, and accountability. We then describe the ways professionals are made: through both formal education and informal unstructured in-service. When professionals enter the work force, their duties involve decision making. We therefore look at the process of decision making, the problems involved, and the guilt felt about what are perceived as wrong decisions and how to avoid them. Professionals in their working environment encounter problems every day that require them to check in with their moral code. We focus on professionalism and ethical responsibilities as one of those areas that requires continual consultation with individual morality and discuss how these affect professions.

4.2   Evolution of Professions

4.2.1   Origins of Professions

The concept of a profession is actually not new, however, the word *profession* today carries a far different connotation than it did during the Middle Ages. According to Bolivar A. Senior [15], the word *profession* referred to a commitment formally *professed* by a person to become a member of a religious order, and a *professional* was the person who has *professed* the commitment. Senior writes, since early universities drew most of their faculty from religious orders, these teachers eventually were called *professors*. Richard Sizer [1] states that professions started in medieval times with the craftsmen's guild and in inns. These guilds were responsible for apprenticeship standards, competence, and performance of their members. Little distinction was made between manual labor and intellectual groups. But as small intellectual groups developed like those of clerics, the first requirements of achievements and maintenance of personal criteria started to emerge. This emphasis on intellectual capabilities for membership in a group became increasingly important as time passed. Sizer states that professions in eighteenth-century England were regarded as "occupations for the 'gentlemen,' offering a safe social niche but not large material rewards." The Industrial Revolution is credited with establishing professions in engineering, accounting, and banking [1]. Over the years, however, material rewards have increased and a set of requirements has evolved.

Over the years, the term profession and its requirements for membership evolved into two categories: the *learned* professions, which required individuals with a deep knowledge of the profession acquired through years of formal education; *common* professions, which required the individuals to be noblemen who in theory did not really need to work for a living: they were *liberated* from the need to work, but ought to learn the profession anyway. The first liberal profession was the military career [15]. When the life of nobility became less influential, especially after the French revolution, the *common* distinction of professions came to be known as *trades,* probably as we know them today. However, *trades*, as today, still required one to hold a higher ethical standard.

4.2.2 Requirements of a Professional

There are three basic professional requirements, and over the years as the professions evolved, these three elements have taken different forms. They are:

1. *A set of highly developed skills and deep knowledge of the domain.* Although professional skills are developed through long years of experience, such skills must be backed up by a very well-developed knowledge base acquired through long years of formal schooling. Acquiring a sophisticated level of knowledge is crucial because skills based on shallow knowledge of the domain could be damaging to the profession in cases involving decisions that require understanding, analysis, and adoption of concepts to suit the environment or the problem. This requirement alone is enough to differentiate between professionals and those who acquire considerable skills from long years of working in the same domain such as auto mechanics and landscape designers.
2. *Autonomy.* Because professionals provide either products or services, there is always a relationship between the provider of the service and the receiver of the service or the provider of the product and the receiver of the product. In this relationship we are concerned with the power balance. In the case of a professional, the power is in favor of the professional. Take the relationship between a lawyer and a client or a physician and a patient, for example. In either case, there is a power play in favor of the provider of the service. If we consider the example of an auto mechanic, however, there is also a power play in the equation, but this time the power is in favor of the customer, not the provider of the service. There are also marked differences in the way the service is provided by professionals and nonprofessionals. In the case of a professional, there is more room to vary the way a service or a product is provided without consulting the receiver of the

service or the product, meaning that professionals have autonomy to vary the way the service is provided without asking the receiver for confirmation or consent. However, in the case of nonprofessionals, the provider of the service cannot vary the way the service is to be delivered without checking with the customer. For example, when you take a car for repair, the mechanic cannot vary from what you agreed on without formally asking you.

3. *Observance of a code of conduct.* A working professional usually observes these four types of codes [2]:

- *The professional code*: a set of guidelines provided to the professional by the profession spelling out what a professional ought to do and not do. A professional code protects both the image of the profession and that of the individual members. Thus, it is a requirement for the profession that members adhere to the code.
- *A personal code*: a set of individual moral guidelines on which professionals operate. In many ways these guidelines are acquired by professionals from the cultural environment in which they grow up or live in and the religious beliefs they may practice. Whatever the case, a personal code supplements the professional code significantly.
- *The institutional code*: a code imposed by the institution for which the professional is working. This code is meant to build and maintain the public's confidence in the institution and its employees.
- *The community code*: a community standard code developed over a period of time based on either the religion or culture of the indigenous people in the area. It may be imposed by civil law or the culture of the community in which the professional works.

The interaction between the four codes can be explained as follows: Consider each code as a circle inside another circle with the community code at the center of these concentric circles. Outside the community code is the institutional code enclosed by the personal code, which is enclosed by the professional code (see Fig. 4.1).

Any action performed by a professional working at a local institution is contained in the outermost circle. Therefore, for such action to be ethical, moral, and legal, it must be in conformity with all the codes and intersect all codes.

Let us consider an example. Suppose a physician is working in a community hospital where the hospital and the community do not support euthanasia. If the doctor is asked by his or her patients to assist them in taking their own life, the doctor must examine all four codes before coming to a decision. First, the professional code may not support euthanasia whether his or her individual moral code does or not. So because the institutional, community, and the professional codes do not support euthanasia, the doctor may not find it in his or her best interest to grant the patients their wishes even if he or she agrees with the patient. As we discuss later, the requirement that any action taken by a professional must fall within the intersection of the four sets of codes may present moral dilemmas for the professional in the decision-making process and consequently tarnish the professionalism of the individual.

Fig. 4.1 Codes Governing Human Actions

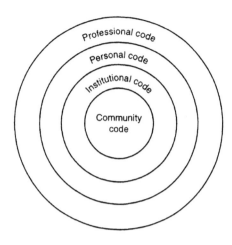

4.2.3 Pillars of Professionalism

Professionalism is supported by four pillars: commitment, integrity, responsibility, and accountability.

4.2.3.1 Commitment

Commitment, according to Humphreys, has these six characteristics [3]:

1. *The person making the commitment must do so willingly without duress.* The person executing the commitment must like what he or she is doing. If commitments are in the form of assignments with little autonomy, it is more likely the commitment may not be there.
2. *The person responsible must try to meet the commitment, even if help is needed.* Because commitments are not assignments, the person who has made the commitment is assumed to have the know-how, the autonomy to vary steps, and the skills to do the job. Professionals possess these characteristics, plus they have the ability to seek the necessary skills from others to circumvent obstacles that may arise, so more commitment is expected of them.
3. *There must be agreement on what is to be done, by whom, and when.* Professionals entering into a commitment must have advance knowledge of what is to be done and who is likely to do what part. Entering into a commitment without adequate advance knowledge is highly unprofessional. When the work is divided among other professionals, they themselves must make the same commitment for their respective parts and, in this case, commitment for those smaller parts is as important as the commitment for the whole job. If the smaller parts are assigned to nonprofessionals, they are considered assignments, and the commitment must

lie with the professional assigning the parts. Such commitment is carried out through supervision of the nonprofessional members of the team.

4. *The commitment must be openly and publicly stated.* Open commitments are transparent and easily correctable if there are problems. Professional commitments must fall within the allocated resources of time, material, and money. If a commitment is public, there are more chances that most of the sourcing, acquisition, distribution, and use of the resources will be transparent, and thus the job is likely to be done more smoothly.

5. *The commitment must not be made easily.* Before entering into a commitment, professionals should do research to make sure that what they are entering into is not a Trojan horse (something or someone intended to defeat or subvert from within).

6. *Prior to the committed date, if it is clear it cannot be met, advance notice must be given and a new commitment negotiated.* It is a sign of responsibility and commitment to have the courage to tell others of shortfalls in parts of the agreement so if there is anything to be done to meet the deadlines, it is done without acrimony.

4.2.3.2 Integrity

Integrity means a state of undivided loyalty to self-belief. It is honesty, uncompromising self-value, and incorruptible. The word "integrity" comes from the Latin word *integratas*, which means entire, undivided, or whole. To stay undivided in one's beliefs professionally requires three maxims of integrity: namely, vision, love of what one is doing, and commitment to what one has to do.

- *Vision.* Having vision is the capacity to anticipate and make a plan of action that will circumvent obstacles and maximize benefits. Vision is a sign of good leadership, and professionals who have the initiative, the autonomy, and the authority in the provider–client relationship exemplify leadership.
- *Love.* Numerous studies have shown that people who love what they do, do it better than those who do it because they have to. In school, children who have a love for a subject perform far better than those who do it because it is a requirement. When people choose professions, they should do so because they have a love for the work. The amount of love put in helps maintain morality in one's actions because what is being done is no longer chore but a creation, and we all know people love their own creations.
- *Commitment.* The vision and love applied to the work bonds the individual to whatever he or she is doing until it is done. This is commitment as we defined it earlier.

4.2.3.3 Responsibility

Responsibility deals with roles, tasks, and actions and their ensuing consequences. For example, as parents we have an obligation and a duty to bring up our offspring.

That is parental responsibility. But responsibility also depends on a person's value system, which is based on his or her environment and culture. There are various types of responsibilities, including personal, communal, parental, and professional, and these responsibilities vary depending on the age of the individual and his or her position in society. For example, the responsibilities of a 5-year old are far different from those of a 40-year old. Clearly the responsibilities of a country's chief executive are different from those of a janitor. When individuals choose a lifestyle implied in a career or a vocation, they choose and must accept the package of responsibilities that go with that lifestyle.

Responsibilities of a Professional as a Provider. A professional in either a provider–client or provider–customer relationship plays the role of provider of either a service or a product. This relationship, as we pointed out earlier, is a contract between the two parties. The relationship consists of three major types of responsibilities: service, product, and consequential.

Service Responsibilities. In order for a professional to provide a service to a client, there must be a contract binding the professional and the client. In this contract, as in any other contract, the professional has specific responsibilities regarding the time of delivery of the service, the quality of the service, and the consequences after the service has been rendered. For example, in the time-constraint responsibility, the service must be rendered within an agreed time frame; if not, a new time must be negotiated. In the quality of service responsibility, the service must meet its desired goal as far as the client is concerned, and it must have the expected value. The consequence responsibility involves the safety of the client from harm, both physical and financial, after receiving the service. The provider must take all these responsibilities seriously.

Product Responsibilities. If the contract between the provider and the client involves a product, the provider has the responsibility to deliver the product agreed upon on time, in good shape and of quality, and to provide documentation for safe use of the product. The provider of the product is responsible for all liabilities that might arise as a result of use of the product. In liability cases, the provider responsibility depends on the contract and the degree of harm. We say more about liabilities in Chapters 6 and 8.

Consequential Responsibilities. In a television medical drama episode I watched, an operating room scene showed a female doctor dancing to a reggae tune while operating on a patient and unknowingly sewing the patient up with a surgical metal clip still in the patient's chest. In the next scene the patient has died and the autopsy shows the metal clip is still in his chest. Before the results of the autopsy, the doctor remembers her error and naturally becomes remorseful, not knowing whether to tell the family right away or wait until the medical report is issued. She knows full well that whatever the case, the family is going to sue her and the hospital, and probably her job at that hospital and her medical career are over. There is remorse on the part of the doctor and anger on the part of the patient's family, all because one person did not fulfill her responsibilities.

Remorse and anger are aftereffects of an action gone wrong, in this case a professional service. Whether a professional has provided a service or a product, there are always aftereffects of that action. Oftentimes one is praised for a service well done and the best product ever provided, but there are also times when one is remorseful because a service did not produce what it was intended to or a product did not live up to expectations. In the worst-case scenario the service or product may cause physical or financial harm to the client. In such cases, one expects liabilities for the service or product, and the professional must accept those consequential responsibilities. In the case of the doctor, the service she provided fell short of what was expected, and she had to face the consequential responsibilities of her actions, which at times not only include the parties involved but may also involve innocent bystanders.

4.2.3.4 Accountability

One way we can define accountability is the obligation to answer for the execution of one's assigned responsibilities. This process involves the "cycle of setting measurable goals, planning what needs to be done to meet those goals, reporting progress towards goals, evaluating the reports, and using that feedback to make improvements" [4]. Accountability involves these three key elements [5]:

1. *A set of outcome measures that reliably and objectively evaluate performance*: In every profession there is a minimum set of measures that every individual in that profession must meet. This set must be carefully selected and those measures must be attainable. However, these measures vary according to the profession and the individual activity to be performed by the professional. For example, in the teaching profession, one of the measures might be the success rate of students when they take standardized examinations.
2. *A set of performance standards defined in terms of these outcome measures*: Like outcome measures, performance standards must be carefully chosen and attainable. These standards are also very dependent on the profession, but each profession must have a set of common performance standards for all its members for every type of service or product provided by that profession. For the teaching profession, the standard of output measures may be the passing of standardized examinations at a certain predetermined level. In the law profession, it might be the ability of a judgment to stand on subsequent appeals. Whatever standard measure is chosen, it must be plausible and measurable.
3. *A set of incentives for meeting the standards and/or penalties for failing to meet them*: The incentives chosen must be good enough so as not to create undesirable motives. For example, if the incentives are too good, they may force professionals to put the interest of their customers and clients below the interest of attaining the measures. If the incentives are monetary, they may force professionals to put the interest of making money ahead of the services they are supposed to offer. Similarly, the penalties prescribed must not be so harsh that they drive away those who intend to enter the profession. Harsh penalties also tend to make people in the wrong hide their actions and dig in deeper for fear of being discovered.

4.3 The Making of an Ethical Professional: Education and Licensing

In our discussion of the evolution of the professions, we have noticed the never-ending requirements of a an individual seeking membership in the chosen profession or trade to either have a deep knowledge of the profession acquired through formal education or to be intrinsically of a "gentleman's calling," willing to hold a higher ethical standard. In order to continue to uphold these essential requirements in both professions and trades, let us now discuss three items that encourage, maintain, and improve that higher ethical standard. These are: formal education, licensing, and professional codes of conduct. Professionals must follow a specific process to meet and maintain those professional requirements.

4.3.1 Formal Education

For formal education to be effective in teaching and enforcing the pillars of professionalism, it must be targeted and incremental. Let us walk through the making of an information technology professional as an example. In elementary school, as students are introduced to information technology, they should be told not to use machines to destroy other people's property or to hurt others. But these cautions should be explained in an age-appropriate way. For example, children should be taught responsible ways of using computers and the Internet.

They should be told not to visit certain web pages, to avoid getting involved in relationships online, not to give personal and family information online, and not to arrange for a rendezvous on or offline. In addition, they should be told to respect others' work and property, whether they are online or off. There are already reported cases of children as young as 14 years old breaking into computer systems and destroying records. In fact, many of the computer network attacks, and a good number of the headline-making incidents, have been perpetuated by young people, sometimes as young as 10-years old. For example, in a certain county in Tennessee, several ninth-graders broke into their school computer system and infected it with a virus that wiped out most of the school records. It is believed the students got the virus off the Internet [6]. The content of what is taught must be relevant and sensitive to different age groups and professionals.

As students go through high school, content should become progressively more sophisticated. The message on responsible use of computers should be stressed more. The teen years are years of curiosity and discovery and a lot of young people find themselves spending long hours on computers. Those long hours should be spent responsibly. While a good portion of the message should come from parents, schools should also be part of this partnership by offering courses in responsible use of computers. The teaching could focus on ethics; students should be given reasons why they cannot create and distribute viruses, download copyrighted materials off the Internet, and use the Internet to send bad messages to others. These are ethical reasons that go beyond "do it and you will be expelled from school" type of threats.

In college, of course, the message is more direct. There are several approaches to bring the message across:

(i) Students take formal courses in professional ethics in a number of professional programs in their respective colleges.
(ii) Without taking formal courses in their curriculum, students are taught a good amount of the information ethics sprinkled throughout their courses, either in general education or in their major.
(iii) Using a capstone course in the general education requirements and in that course add information ethics content. Many colleges now require computer literacy as a graduation requirement. Use that course to add ethics content.
(iv) Require an exit 1-h information ethics course which can be taken online.

Once they join the workplace environment, these professionals should be required to attend informal refresher sessions, seminars, and in-service workshops periodically.

4.3.2 Licensing Authorities

Licensing grants individuals formal or legal permission to practice their profession, which tips the balance of power in the giver–receiver equation in favor of the giver. Before a license is issued, certain formalities must be taken care of, for example, testing the competence of the aspirant for the specific knowledge and skills required. If such a test is not passed, the licensing authority may deny issuing the license. Beside testing for competence, the licensing authority also provides the licensee with a set of rules to follow to keep the license. If the rules are violated, the authority may have the prerogative of either sanctioning the licensee or recalling the license. Clearly a license is a privilege not a right, and if licensees want to maintain that right, they must follow the prescribed code. Licenses can be (and have been) used as both control and educating instruments to enforce rules, laws, and certain group or society norms.

Many professions license members and most of these professions require the potential licensee to take and pass examinations that sometimes test both knowledge and skills. Many professions, in order to keep members updated and compliant with their codes, limit the validity of their licenses to specific time periods so members have to renew their licenses. They then tie license renewal to passing of continuing examinations, which helps ensure that members stay knowledgeable in the profession. Professions also use periodic licensing examinations to check on members' compliance with codes. If members have in the past violated a code and been reported, such members may not have their licenses renewed even if they pass all examinations.

It is quite evident that in those professions with no licensing requirements, discipline has been and continues to be a problem, whereas in those maintaining vigorous licensing requirements, relatively few disciplinary problems have emerged. Because every profession strives for a good image, many legitimate professions require licensing for membership. Licensing enables professions to enforce their rules by law. For example, physicians can lose their license to practice if they do anything unlawful or unethical. Once such a license is withdrawn, a physician cannot practice medicine. Although there are many professions with licensing requirements but with no enforcement mechanism, an increasing number of professions are opting to require enforceable licensing to keep their image untainted.

4.3.3 Professional Codes of Conduct

The primary purpose of professional codes of conduct is to promote the public image of the profession by specifying and enforcing the ethical behavior expected from its members. Accordingly, and in most cases, professional codes consist of standards, canons, and rules of conduct that address the following areas [7]:

- Moral and legal standards
- Professional–client relationship
- Client advocacy
- Professional–public relationships
- Sanction mechanics
- Confidentiality
- Assessment
- Compliance
- Competence
- Certified professional credentials for those professions that use certification [6]

In order for professional codes of conduct to be effective, a profession must institute a system of enforcement, reporting, hearing procedures, sanctions, and appeals. Codes without such systems in place are completely ineffective.

4.3.3.1 Enforcement

Experience and studies have shown that professions with enforceable codes have fewer discipline problems among their members than those with no codes or those with codes but without enforcement mechanisms. Those professions with fewer disciplinary problems naturally have better images. Because the purpose of codes for any profession is to create and maintain a good image, those professions without codes should come up not only with codes, canons, and guidelines, but also with enforcement mechanisms, and those with codes but with no enforcement system should add them. It is common knowledge that laws, codes, canons, and/or guidelines are not obeyed until and unless some type of enforcement machinery is in place. There are various techniques of enforcement, most of them with no civil authority. The most widely used are professional ethics boards, standing committees, or review boards charged with:

- Drawing up the codes of ethics for the profession if none exist
- Revising codes if and when necessary
- Conducting education campaigns at the membership level
- Distributing copies of the codes to every member
- Developing disciplinary procedures
- Receiving complaints, conducting hearings, counseling members, and sanctioning members found guilty
- Promoting the image of the profession [8]

4.3.3.2 Reporting of Grievances

There are two main reporting procedures. The first is the typical organizational route in which a complaint is reported first to the local chapters if it exists. The complaint then makes its way to the top, usually to the national ethics committee. The second is the short-circuit procedure in which reporting can be done at any level and then from there a complaint is forwarded all the way to the top. Professions may vary these two types of reporting mainly in the area of who is supposed to report a professional in violation. In some professions, the reporting must be done by a member of the profession in good standing and nobody else. This means that concerned members of the public must report their complaint to a member of the profession, who then forwards the complaints to the committee. In other professions, any member of the public can initiate a complaint with the local professional board. Whichever way the reporting of a complaint is done, there should be a way to inform members of the profession and the public on the procedures of reporting and who can and cannot file a complaint, and there must be established channels of communication.

4.3.3.3 Hearing Procedures

Hearing proceedings are difficult to generalize about because of the many factors the hearing depends on: for example, the nature, the financial standing, and the structure of the profession; the kind of enforcement procedures being used; and the penalty to be imposed. If there is no enforcement procedure or if the penalty is not significant, the accused member may not even appear for the scheduled hearing. Professions should consider all these factors when drawing up the hearing procedures. For example, hearings should be held at the profession's nearest field office to save members from traveling long distances. If there is no field office, arrangements should be made to find a location convenient to both the accused and the hearing committee members, and the hearing process itself should be short if possible.

4.3.3.4 Sanctions

If a hearing committee decides that a member is guilty of the offenses charged, then the committee must come up with sanctions to fit the violations committed by the member. The committee may decide to recommend any one or a combination of the following: probation, revocation of certification, request for resignation, and suspension from the profession at the member's expense. If a probation option is taken, the committee must clearly specify the nature, duration, and conditions of the probation. Also there must be a person to whom the professional is to report for all requirements of the probation including supervision. After the sanctioned member fulfills the requirements of the penalty, a recommendation can be made to reinstate the member in good standing.

4.3.3.5 Appeals

A profession must have an appeals process on the books for the sanctioned professional who is not satisfied with either the ruling of the committee or the penalty imposed. Such guidelines should state clearly the procedure for appeals, how the appeal instrument is to be handled, who deals with the appeals, and the maximum amount of time an individual has between the time he or she receives a judgment and the filling of the appeal. The time allotted for a judgment on the appeal should also be stipulated. The profession must also state whether an appealing member should remain executing his or her duties or be prohibited from doing so until the appeal is complete. In certain professions, appealing members are either put on administrative leave, suspended, or allowed to carry on with their duties pending the decision of the appeal.

Here is an example of a professional code of conduct for:

The Institute of Electrical and Electronics Engineers, Inc.1

CODE OF ETHICS2

We, the members of the IEEE, in recognition of the importance of our technologies affecting the quality of life throughout the world, and in accepting a personal obligation to our profession, its members and the communities we serve, do hereby commit ourselves to the highest ethical and professional conduct and agree:

1. To accept responsibility in making engineering decisions consistent with the safety, health, and welfare of the public and to disclose promptly factors that might endanger the public or the environment
2. To avoid real or perceived conflicts of interest whenever possible and to disclose them to affected parties when they do exist
3. To be honest and realistic in stating claims or estimates based on available data
4. To reject bribery in all its forms
5. To improve the understanding of technology, its appropriate application, and potential consequences
6. To maintain and improve our technical competence and to undertake technological tasks for others only if qualified by training or experience, or after full disclosure of pertinent limitations

7. To seek, accept, and offer honest criticism of technical work, to acknowledge and correct errors, and to credit properly the contributions of others
8. To treat fairly all persons regardless of such factors as race, religion, gender, disability, age, or national origin
9. To avoid injuring others, their property, reputation, or employment by false or malicious action
10. To assist colleagues and coworkers in their professional development and to support them in following this code of ethics

4.4 Professional Decision Making and Ethics

Now we come to our third theme on professionalism and ethics: the process of professional decision making. Here we focus on professional dilemmas and guilt associated with decision making.

4.4.1 Professional Dilemma in Decision Making

Dilemmas in decision making are quite common in the everyday activities of a professional. The process of decision making resembles a mapping with input parameters and an output decision. The input parameters in the decision-making process are premises. To each premise is an attached value. The mapping uses these values along with the premises to create an output, which is the decision. For example, if I have to make the decision whether to walk to church or take the car, the set of premises might include, among others, time, parking, safety, and gas. The values attached to these premises are that if I go by car, I save time, I need a parking space, walking is good exercise, I need money to buy gas. If I decide to walk, my decision might be based on a set of premises including health and money to which I may attach the following values: walking to church 1 day a week is good exercise and it saves me money for gas. The mapping function takes these premises together with the values and outputs a "logical" decision. This mapping function is similar to the one we used in the ethics definition in Chapter 3. Dilemmas in decision making are caused by questioning the values attached to one's premises as inputs to the decision being made. One's input values may be clouded by conflicting codes of conduct, advances in technology, and/or incomplete or misleading information.

4.4.1.1 Conflicting Codes of Conduct

In Fig. 4.1 of Section 4.2.2, we showed that every decision made by a professional must take into account the interrelationships of professional, personal, institutional, and local codes. The decision must be made in such a way that all four codes agree.

Decisions outside the core intersection must be weighted carefully because they always result in controversy. Take the case of the famous Michigan pathologist Dr. Kevorkian, the so-called Doctor Death. Dr. Kevorkian became a hero to some who believed in assisted suicide and Doctor Death to others who did not. He managed to force a debate over assisted suicide on the entire nation by helping people to kill themselves using his "death machine" over and over for a total of at least 47 people. In the 7 years in which he accelerated his killing and before he was eventually charged and put in prison, Dr. Kevorkian actually scoffed at the law, scorned elected and religious leaders, and won over juries. Dr. Jack Kevorkian became more known for his stand on assisted suicide than on his long years of professional service. The controversy was generated by the conflict in the codes, namely, the medical professional code of conduct, which includes the Hippocratic oath, and the local code, that is, the code of the town, county, and the state of Michigan (the institutional code does not apply because he was retired).

4.4.1.2   Advances in Technology

Dilemmas in decision making may also be caused by advances in technology. Computer technology in particular has created more muddles in the decision-making process than any other technology. Advances in computer technology create a multitude of possibilities that never existed before. Such possibilities present professionals with myriad temptations (see Section 3.5.1.2).

4.4.1.3   Incomplete or Misleading Information

Not having all the information one needs before making a decision can be problematic. Consider the famous prisoners' dilemma. Two people are caught committing a crime, and they are taken to different interrogation rooms before they have a chance to coordinate their stories. During the interrogation each prisoner is told that the other prisoner has agreed to plead guilty on all charges. Authorities inform the prisoner that agreeing to plead guilty on the charges as the other prisoner has done will bring him or her a reduced sentence. But rejecting the plea will of course mean that the accused is not cooperating with the investigation, which may result in he or she receiving the maximum punishment allowable. Each prisoner has four recourses:

- Plead guilty without the friend pleading guilty, which would mean deserting a friend
- Refuse to plead guilty and the friend pleads guilty, which would mean betrayal and probably a maximum sentence
- Plead guilty and the friend pleads guilty, which means light sentences for both of them

- Both refusing to plead guilty and probably both receiving a light sentence or a maximum sentence

Whatever option the prisoners take is risky because they do not have enough information to enable them to make a wise decision. There are similar situations in professional life when a decision has to be made without enough information available and within time constraints. In such a situation the professional must take extra care to weigh all possibilities in the input set of premises and their corresponding values.

Taking all these into account and using the ethical framework we developed in the previous chapter can help the professional in making decisions that are just, fair, and plain ethical.

4.4.2   Guilt and Making Ethical Decisions

In an ethical decision-making process, decisions are made based on, and reflect, consequences, individual liberties, and justice. To achieve this, individuals can use any other ethical theories to frame or make ethical choices that reflect the selected criteria. However, whatever theory used, the outcome falls into one of the following three criteria:

- *Utilitarian criterion* – where decisions are made solely on the basis of their intended outcomes or consequences
- *Rights criterion* – where decisions are made based on the set of liberties the society enforces such as the Magna Carta and the Bill of Rights
- *Justice criterion* – which reflect justice. Decisions are made so that they are fair, impartial, and equitable to all

As we saw in Chapter 2 (Section 2.2.5), guilt is our natural internal judgment system, punishing ourselves based on our moral standards or the group's standards. So guilt, therefore, plays a crucial part in ethical decision making. In the decision-making process, guilt normally sets in right after the decision or a choice is made. And because guilt stays with the individual over a period of time, sometimes becoming cumulative, as we pointed out earlier, it may affect that individual's future decisions. Its effects on future decision-making processes center round new values being attached to the premises of the input set to the decision function. A guilty person reexamines his or her value set attached to all premises that come into play in the decision-making process. Sometimes guilt produces doubts about the present values attached to the premises without producing new and better values. Guilt causes decision makers to agonize over decisions. As we noted in Chapter 2, an excess of guilt could cause an individual to withdraw from society, which could be more dangerous because a withdrawn person may start to challenge the values attached to the premises as he or she tries to justify the guilt, resulting in bad decisions being made.

Although decisions are based on the outcome of an individual's deliberations, considering all input parameters and attaching values to these premises calls for a thorough examination of each premise by the individual. This process is aided by the individual reflecting on these basic steps [9]:

- Examining the ethically relevant issues, principles, standards, and practices
- Determining the different parties (and their special interests) who will be affected by the decision
- Deciding on an alternative course of action if and when the outcome of the decision is not what is expected
- Considering the probable consequences (short and long term) of each alternative on each of the different parties involved
- Thinking of consulting with a trusted colleague if the situation is complex, risky, or there is undue personal involvement
- Determining how personal values, biases, beliefs, or self-interests influenced the decision (either positively or negatively) and whether the consequences of the decision have been evaluated
- Being prepared to (1) assume responsibility for the consequences of the action, including correction of negative consequences, if any, (2) reengage in the decision-making process if the ethical issue is not resolved, and (3) evaluate the system(s) within which the issue arose, in order to identify and remove the circumstances that might facilitate and reward unethical practices

4.5 Professionalism and Ethical Responsibilities

This is the last of our four themes in professionalism and ethics. We focus here on professionalism and ethical responsibilities that include whistle-blowing, harassment, and discrimination.

4.5.1 Whistle-Blowing

The term whistle-blowing gives the impression of an act of seeking public attention. This is what we see in a sports event whenever a foul is committed. The referee blows a whistle to call public attention, including that of the athlete, to the unsportsman-like act committed. In some countries, law enforcement personnel use whistles to draw public attention to what they deem unlawful acts and to seek help.

The purpose of whistle-blowing in the workplace and the goal of a whistle-blower is the same as that in the sports arena – calling to public attention, including and especially to that of a higher authority such as a government, what is considered an illegal or mismanaged act. Whistle-blowing can be internal, in which case the attention is sought internally and remains within organizational channels, or it can be public, in which case it alerts everyone.

Everyday people, especially employees, witness wrongdoing on the job. What they witness usually can jeopardize not only their health, safety or lives but the well-being of others. Quite often many witness such illegal acts but choose to remain silent in the face of such misconduct because they think it is not their thing or they think it will not make a difference. Yet others fear to cause problems on the job. A few brave it out to save lives. However, quite often, instead of receiving praise for their brave actions and high integrity, they are often targeted for retaliatory acts such as investigations, ridicule, blacklisting (especially in their trade), harassment, intimidation, demotion, and sometimes outright dismissal.

So in light of these threats, the most important aspect of whistle-blowing is to remain anonymous. Revealing the identity of a whistle-blower could be dangerous. Besides the obvious risks of potential job loss and poor or inadequate legal protection, there is also a psychological and sometime emotional price to pay for whistle-blowing. Personal and family friends may turn against you. At work you may be labeled a troublemaker, leading people with whom you work to treat you as an outcast. So care must be taken before whistle-blowing to ensure anonymity. The most difficult decision may involve finding a good medium that will insure that confidentiality and anonymity. It is difficult and almost impossible to expect total anonymity, though, for a whistle-blower because there will be a need for sufficient information to support allegations which may result in giving away one's identifying details.

Different whistle-blowing methods have been used for years, ranging from traditional ones to more modern computer-aided ones.

4.5.1.1 Computer-Aided Methods

Most common methods are anonymous, including anonymous remailers that use a software program to take an original e-mail, strip its header and all other identifying data before forwarding it to its destination. Because the remailer does not include any return address on the e-mail, it attaches a pseudonymous address in case you need a reply. Before using anonymous remailers, however, exercise caution because the authorities can force the server administrator to reveal the owner of the pseudonymous name and address in cases of emergencies and other coercion.

4.5.1.2 Traditional Methods

There is a cross section of traditional methods used in whistle-blowing. Historically, whistle-blowing has used spy-like methods to pass on information to either the public or a higher authority. All methods that ensure anonymity can be used; the most common include face-to-face communication with a public person that will ensure your anonymity; talking with the news media, which can keep your identity a secret; hotlines that alert the caller identity; and writing letters.

Whistle-blowing has been praised by many as courageous actions taken by a few good people with a moral conscience who risk everything to call public attention to illegitimate business practices and illegal and immoral actions. Others have condemned whistle-blowing as acts of vendetta, revenge, and greed that should not be encouraged. In fact, most whistle-blowers are either fired employees or unhappy ones. The following situations can complicate whistle-blowing:

- *Fear of reprisals*: Many illegal and immoral acts go unreported because would-be whistle-blowers fear reprisals such as physical harm, job loss, reassignment to less desirable, sometimes demeaning jobs, suspension from work, and denial of promotions or training. In one survey, John Keenan and Charles Krueger report that this fear is real in potential whistle-blowers. Their survey indicated that not many organizations were willing to protect the whistle-blower. In fact, only one-half of the managers surveyed indicated a willingness to protect a whistle-blower [10].

- *Suspicion surrounding whistle-blowing*: Not every whistle-blower should be taken seriously because not all of them are sincere. Some whistle-blowers are driven by greed, vendettas, anger, or revenge. In fact, many known cases of whistle-blowing were provoked when management and the employee disagreed. In other cases, whistle-blowing is caused by booty promises, especially by governments, to reward anybody with a certain percentage of the proceeds coming out of whistle-blowing. In the United States, for example, private employees can sue any company on behalf of the government under the 1986 amendment to the False Claims Act (see Appendix B) commonly known as qui tam action, if that company has any dealings with the federal government. Under this law, a person who discovers fraud against the government can file a civil suit if the government does not take the case. As an incentive to whistle-blowing, any money recovered is shared between the government and the plaintiff, who can receive as much as 30% of the amount involved in the fraud.

- *Membership in organizational channels*: Sometimes a whistle-blower act may be ignored because the whistle-blower is a member of the company or business organizational channel. Vivian Weil [11] cites two whistle-blowers who are not considered as such because they called public attention to a serious ethical and moral problem but remained within the lines of command and, therefore, were not taken seriously. Both Roger Boisjoly and colleague Allan MacDonald of Morton Thiokol in Utah are known to have opposed the launch of the fated Challenger but were overwhelmed by management, and they then blew the whistle in the hearings of the Presidential Commission set by President Ronald Reagan.

Since whistle-blowing can save lives and reduce waste, the US government encourages people who witness illegal acts and government waste to whistle blow. Besides enacting laws such as the False Claims Act which seek to expose fraud in federal contracts, the government also suggests that the would-be whistle-blower observe the following steps [12]:

1. Before taking any irreversible steps, talk to family and close friends about your decision to blow the whistle.
2. Be alert and discreetly attempt to learn of any other witnesses who are upset about the wrongdoing.
3. Before formally breaking ranks consider whether there is any reasonable way to work within the system by going to the first level of authority. If this is not possible, think carefully about whether you want to "go public" with your concerns or remain an anonymous source. Each strategy has implications: the decision depends on the quantity and quality of your evidence, your ability to camouflage your knowledge of key facts, the risks you are willing to assume and your willingness to endure intense public scrutiny.
4. Develop a plan – such as the strategically timed release of information to government agencies – so that your employer is reacting to you, instead of vice versa.
5. Maintain good relations with administration and support staff.
6. Before and after you blow the whistle, keep a careful record of events as they unfold. Try to construct a straightforward, factual log of the relevant activities and events on the job, keeping in mind that your employer will have access to your diary if there is a lawsuit.
7. Identify and copy all necessary supporting records before drawing any suspicion.
8. Break the cycle of isolation, research, and identify and seek a support network of potential allies, such as elected officials, journalists, and activists. The solidarity of key constituencies can be more powerful than the bureaucracy you are challenging.
9. Invest the funds to obtain a legal opinion from a competent lawyer.
10. Always be on guard not to embellish your charges.
11. Engage in whistle-blowing initiatives without using employer resources.
12. Do not wear your cynicism on your sleeve when working with the authorities.

4.5.2   Harassment and Discrimination

Harassment is to verbally or physically create an environment that is hostile, intimidating, offensive, severe, pervasive, or abusive based on a number of parameters including one's race, religion, sex, sexual orientation, national origin, age, disability, political affiliation, marital status, citizenship, or physical appearance. Discrimination on the other hand is a process of making decisions that negatively affect an individual, such as denial of a service, based wholly, or partly, upon the real or perceived facts of one's race, religion, sex, sexual orientation, national origin, age, disability, political affiliation, marital status, or physical appearance. Harassment and discrimination are serious breaches of human rights. In fact, harassment is a form of discrimination. If not attended to, harassment does not only affect a few individuals, but it eventually grows to affect everyone in the organization. The following steps are needed in fight against harassment and discrimination:

(i) *Awareness*. There are no clear signs of harassment, but in most cases harassment is manifested in the following signs: unhappiness, anxiety, discomfort, stress, and lifestyle changes. If some or all of these signs start to appear in the environment where an individual is, then there is harassment. Discrimination is even harder to detect than harassment. However, there is discrimination if the decisions made are based upon the discriminatory factors above.

(ii) *Prevention*. The main tool for the prevention of harassment and discrimination is for an organization to have a clear and simple written policy framework setting out the procedures that must be taken if harassment and discrimination occurs. The procedures must include: awareness/education, complaint process, sanctions, and redress.

4.5.3 Ethical and Moral Implications

The act of whistle-blowing is meant to alert and call the public to be witnesses to illegal acts that may be hazardous to their health and well-being or to waste of public resources. Of course, as we pointed out earlier, there are many other reasons for whistle-blowing. Are whistle-blowers living saints who fight evil to bring serious problems to light, thus contributing to the protection of the public's welfare? Does this explain the small numbers of whistle-blowers, although it is known that there are organizations in which a high potential for catastrophe can develop and somehow remain unexposed despite many people being aware of the problems?

Even people with high moral standards can be prevented from doing what is morally right because of the privileges, rights, and freedoms they stand to lose within the organization if they become known. People who feel accused and those allied to them tend to hit back to deflect attention from the accused. Retaliation is very damaging. So a would-be whistle-blower either decides to stay in line and live with a moral dilemma, but survive, or resign and live with a clear conscience. For a professional, a decision like this presents a complex moral conundrum because if he or she stays within the organization, retaliation is almost predictable. Staying with the organization also presents other problems both to the whistle-blower and colleagues. For example, collegial relationships and networks are disrupted. However, whistle-blowing is morally justifiable when the activities involved pose serious danger and harm to human life. The moral concept of whistle-blowing is good; it helps those who dare not speak out and all others who are affected.

Harassment and discrimination are both evil acts that challenge not only the conscious of an individual doing the acts, but also they create a situation that brings discomfort and inferiority to the targeted individual. It is, however, unfortunate that most individuals perpetuating the acts of discrimination and harassment lack the moral conviction and conscience.

Exercises

1. Define professionalism and list three elements of professionalism.
2. Why are the following concepts important for professionalism? Justify your answers.

   - Commitment
   - Integrity
   - Responsibility
   - Accountability

3. Discuss the merits of licensing software professionals.
4. Give an example of a decision that involves the examination of all four categories of codes.
5. Why is whistle-blowing so controversial? What are its pros and cons?
6. Why is harassment and discrimination so difficult to detect?
7. Is computer technology negatively or positively affecting harassment and discrimination?
8. Discuss the effects of whistle-blowing on a whistle-blower.
9. Study and discuss the False Claims Act.
10. Has the False Claims Act been successful?
11. Why is ethical decision making like software engineering?
12. Are whistle-blowers saints or blackmailers?
13. Why is it so difficult to make an ethical decision in today's technologically driven society?
14. What role does guilt play in professional decision making? Why it is so important?
15. Does every valid ethical argument involve a set of layers of arguments?
16. Suggest a more fitting role for licensing authorities.

References

1. Sizer, Richard. "A Brief History of Professionalism and Its Relevance to IFIP." In Jacques Berleur and Klaus Brunnstein (eds.), Ethics of Computing: Codes, Spaces for Discussion and Law. Chapman and Hall, London, 1996.
2. Kizza, J.M. "Professionalism, Ethical Responsibility, and Accountability." In J.M. Kizza (ed.), Social and Ethical Effects of the Computer Revolution. McFarland, Jefferson, NC, 1996.
3. Humphreys, W.S. Managing for Innovation: Leading Technical People. Prentice Hall, Englewood Cliffs, NJ, 1987.
4. "The Minister Answers Questions on Accountability Framework." http://ednet.edc.gov.ab.ca/level1/news/in-focus/accountability.html
5. "References: California Community Colleges (6870)." http://www.lao.ca.gov/chf6870.html
6. McMahan, Myrna. "Hearing Set for School Computer Hackers." Chattanooga Free Press, March 22, 1997, sec. C1.
7. "References: For Codes of Ethics." http://rehab.educ.ucalgary.ca/lowser/edps581/references.html
8. Kizza, J.M. "The Role of Professional Organizations in Promoting Computer Ethics." In J.M. Kizza (ed.), Social and Ethical Effects of the Computer Revolution. McFarland, Jefferson, NC, 1996.
9. Tom Tomlinson, Nursing Ethics, Western Schools, 1993.
10. "The Canadian Code of Ethics for Psychologists (1991)." http://www.cycor.ca/Psych/pub.html; http://www.cycor.ca/Psych/ethics.html
11. Keenan, John, and Charles A. Kreuger. "Internal Whistle-Blower: How Your Organization Can Profit by Listening." Wingtips, May/June, 1995, pp. 28–30.
12. Weil, Vivian. "Whistle-Blowing: What Have We Learned Since the Challenger?" http://www.nspe.org/eh1.html

13. Government Accountability Project's handbook for whistleblowers, The Whistleblower's Survival Guide: Courage without Martyrdom http://www.whistleblower.org/www/Tips.htm
14. Carey Gillam. "Eli Lilly Sued in Missouri Cancer Drug Case," YahooNews. Reuters. http://dailynews.yahoo.com/h/nm/20010827/sc/crime_cancer_dc_2.html
15. Webster's Dictionary.
16. Bolivar A. Senior. "Profession: Brief History and Epistemology of a Challenging Word for Construction Management", *Proceedings of the 42nd Annual Conference*, Colorado State University Fort Collins, Colorado, April 20–22, 2006.

Further Readings

Johansson, Conny, and Lennart Ohlsson. "An Attempt to Teach Professionalism in Engineering Education." http://www.hk-r.se/bib/rapport/2–93.html

Thomas, J.W. "Integrity as Professionalism: Ethics and Leadership in Practice." http://www.fs.fed.us/intro/speech/jwt_saf.htm

Chapter 5
Anonymity, Security, Privacy, and Civil Liberties

Learning Objectives

After reading this chapter, the reader should be able to:

1. Summarize the legal bases for the right to privacy and freedom of expression in one's own nation and how those concepts vary from country to country.
2. Analyze stated security procedures for "weak points" that an attacker could exploit and explain how they could (or will) fail.
3. Propose appropriate security measures for different situations.
4. Describe current computer-based threats to privacy.
5. Explain how the Internet may change the historical balance in protecting freedom of expression.
6. Describe trends in privacy protection as exemplified in technology.

Scenario 3

Did You Say Privacy? What Privacy?1

Surveillance technology has progressed to the point that it is possible to identify individuals walking city streets from satellites in orbit. Telephone, fax, and email communications can routinely be monitored. Personal information files are maintained on citizens from cradle to grave. There is nowhere to run . . . nowhere to hide. Personal privacy is dead.

24/7 OF THE (UN)KNOWN CITIZEN

W. H. Auden (1907–1973) notes in his poem "The Unknown Citizen" that his unknown citizen was a "modern man" for "he was fully insured, and his Health-card shows he was once in hospital but he left cured. Both Producers Research and High-Grade Living declare he was fully sensible to the advantages of the installment plan, and he had everything necessary to the Modern Man, A phonograph, a radio, a car, and a frigidaire [1]. Our citizen is definitely a modern man, more so than the archaic Auden's, for he owns all modern life's amenities, plus a company car equipped with a cellular phone and a reserved parking spot. He is computer savvy, with a computer in his office and at home. The normal day of our citizen starts at 6 a.m. when he is awakened by soft music from a radio. The radio reports that futures are up, indicating higher stock price opening. He jumps out of bed and switches on his computer to put in a "buy" order for a stock he has been meaning to buy.

Snapshot #1: *Tempest*

Several yards outside his private home, someone with a Tempest (a criminal, government agent, private investigator) is recording all that our citizen is doing. The information our man has used on the computer has been recorded by the Tempest.

J.M. Kizza, *Ethical and Social Issues in the Information Age*, Texts in Computer Science, 79
DOI 10.1007/978-1-84996-038-0_5, © Springer-Verlag London Limited 2010

HEADLINER #1: "PRIVACY LOST: THE DEMISE OF PRIVACY IN AMERICA" [2]

As our citizen pulls out of the garage, he notices that he is low on gas, so he pulls up at the nearest Conoco gas station. Being a modern man he is, he decides to pay at the pump.

Snapshot #2: *The transaction record is entered into a Conoco database and, of course, Visa database.*

Without worry he pulls away, speeding to work.

HEADLINER #2: "SPYING ON EMPLOYEES: BIG BROTHER HAS HIS EYE ON YOU . . . SNOOPING SISTER IS SUPERVISING YOU" [3]

Snapshot #3: *"Wherenet Tracking Knows Where You Are at Every Moment"*

Just before 8 a.m., he arrives at his workplace, pulling into his reserved parking spot. He enters the lot with an electronic key. Snapshot #4: *Company network and surveillance cameras start their full day of recording his activities. At 8:02 a.m. he settles into his office. He starts the day's activities with several emails to read and a few calls to return.*

HEADLINER #3: "SNOOPING BILL TO BECOME LAW BY NOVEMBER" [4]

Snapshot #5: *Echelon*

At 12:01 p.m. he receives a call from the company representative in Greece to discuss the new company marketing strategy he proposed last month.

At 3:15 p.m. he heads to his doctor's appointment. He has been complaining of knee pains. His doctor orders for a few tests. They are done quickly, the labs taking as much details from him as possible and his doctor updating his medical record. His insurance will pay for part of the visit. So the insurance is billed and his other medical record is updated. He pays by check. His other financial record is updated.

Since he leaves his doctor's office at 4:30 p.m., he decides to call it a day and head home. He calls his office to inform his secretary that he is heading home!

Snapshot #6. *"Big Brother in the Flesh: New Technology Could Make Us All a Part of the Collective, Permanently Supervised from Above"* [5] *On the way home, he remembers that he needs a few groceries. So he heads to Kroger's. At the grocery store, he picks up a few things and he is* picked *up.*

Snapshot #7: *Kroger's Surveillance Cameras. At the checkout counter, he gives in a dollar coupon for the chicken soup and he also hands in a Kroger's card to save 75 cents off chili on the week's special for Kroger's most valuable customer.*

Snapshot #8: *Kroger's database records the day's transaction. To receive the card, the citizen provided Kroger with his home address, income, family size, and age.*

Snapshot #9: *Celeria*

At 5 p.m. he leaves Kroger's and heads home. But on the way home, he receives a call from his girlfriend on his private cellular phone inviting him for dinner at her place.

At 5:30 p.m. he turns into his private driveway only to notice spilt garbage. He wonders whether the city garbage collectors did it. He puts the car in the garage and comes back to clean the driveway. The neighbor informs him that he noticed two guys going through his garbage, and they later drove away.

HEADLINER #4: "FORGET THE FIREWALL: GUARD YOUR GARBAGE AGAINST 'DUMPSTER DIVING' HACKERS" [6]

After cleaning the driveway, he checks his snail mail. He notices that they are all bills!

HEADLINER #5: "WHO IS READING YOUR BILLS" [7]

At 6 p.m. before he leaves for his girlfriend's house, the citizen decides to check his email and complete some correspondence.

Snapshot #10: *Carnivore*

At 7 p.m. he leaves for his girlfriend's house. He might spend the night there! The girlfriend is also modern and lives in a "Digital Home."

HEADLINER #6: "LATEST SURVEILLANCE LEAVES NOTHING TO CHANCE: EXPLORING THE DARK SIDE OF THE DIGITAL HOME" [8]

Next morning, he will drive the company car to work! What else do we need to know? Is he happy?

That is absurd. As Auden would put it: Had he been unhappy, we would have known!
Discussion Questions
1. *Where do we go from here?*
   - *Legislation*
   - *Regulation*
   - *Self-help*
2. *Do they work?*
3. *Do you believe we still have individual privacy?*
4. *What do you think is the best way to safeguard privacy?*
5. *How much interference by government in your life can you tolerate in order to feel secure?*
6. *How much privacy are you willing to give up to feel secure?*

Scenario References
1. W. H. Auden. "The Unknown Citizen." Literature: An Introduction to Fiction, Poetry, and Drama. 6th Edition. X. J. Kennedy and Dana Gioia, eds. New York: Harper Collins, 1995, pp. 611–612.
2. "Privacy Lost: The Demise of Privacy in America." http://dorothyseeseonline.tripod.com/newsline/id3.html
3. *"Spying on Employees: Big Brother has His Eye on You . . . Snooping Sister Is Supervising You."* http://www.successunlimited.co.uk/related/snoop.htm
4. Ian Lynch. "Snooping Bill to Become Law by November" [27-07-2000]. http://www.vnunet.com
5. Katherine Mieszkowski. "Big Brother in the Flesh: New Technology Could Make Us All a Part of the Collective, Permanently Supervised from Above," September 21, 2000 Edition. http://www.lasvegasweekly.com
6. *Stuart McClure and Joel Scambray. "Forget the Firewall: Guard Your Garbage Against 'Dumpster Diving' Hackers". LISTSERV@SecurityFocus.com. Friday, 7 July, 2000.*
7. Daniel Eisenberg. "Who Is Reading Your Bills?" A court ruling on privacy riles the FCC. http://www.cnn.com/ALLPOLITICS/time/1999/08/30/privacy.html
8. *Trey Garrison. "Latest Surveillance Leaves Nothing to Chance: Exploring the Dark Side of the Digital Home." Realty Times. February 10, 1999. http://realtytimes.com/rtnews/rtipages/19990210_digitalhomes.htm*

5.1 Introduction

Social, economic, and technological advances have dramatically increased the amount of information any individual possesses. Increasing demand for information and easier access to it have also created challenges. We have come to learn that information is a treasure in itself: The more you have, the better. Having valuable intellectual, economic, and social information creates enormous opportunities and advantages for an individual because information has become a vital resource in this information age.

Even though information is a treasure, it can also be a liability; for example, we are constantly seeking ways to acquire, keep, and dispose of it. We want to make sure that what is seen and heard privately does not become public without our consent.

In our technologically advanced society, a number of factors have contributed to the high demand for information and the subsequent need for anonymity, security, privacy, and the safeguard of our civil liberties. Among the main contributing factors are the following:

- High digitalization of information and increasing bandwidth
- Declining costs of digital communication
- Increased miniaturization of portable computers and other communications equipment
- Greater public awareness by the news media of the potential abuse of digital communication, especially the Internet

5.2   Anonymity

The Greeks used the word ανωνυμία to describe the state of being nameless. Anonymity is being nameless, having no identity. Since it is extremely difficult for anybody to live a meaningful life while one is totally anonymous, there are types of anonymity that people usually use. Consider these several types:

- *Pseudo identity*: An individual is identified by a certain pseudonym, code, or number (compare with a writer's pen name). This is referred to as pseudo anonymity. It is used frequently in the "Witness Protection" program. This is the most common variant of anonymity.
- *Untraceable identity*: One is not known by any name including pseudo names.
- *Anonymity with a pseudo address to receive and send correspondence with others*: This technique is popular with people using anonymous remailers, user groups, and news groups [1].

5.2.1   Anonymity and the Internet

The nature of the Internet, with its lack of political, cultural, religious, and judicial boundaries, has created a fertile ground for all faceless people to come out in the open. In particular, the Internet provides two channels through which anonymous acts can be carried out:

1. *Anonymous servers*: With advances in software and hardware, anonymity on the Internet has grown through anonymous servers. There are two types of anonymity servers:
   (a) Full anonymity servers, where no identifying information is forwarded in packet headers.
   (b) Pseudonymous servers, which put pseudonym in forwarded packet headers,   keeping the real identity behind a pseudonym, but being able to receive and forward all packets sent to the pseudonym to the real server.

Anonymity servers are able to accomplish this through the use of encryption. We are not going to go further on the way this encryption is done.

2. *Anonymous users*: Another Internet channel to assure anonymity is for users to assume pseudonyms and use internet services such as bulletin boards and chat

rooms anonymously. Sensitive and sometimes highly personal or classified information has been posted to user groups, news groups, and chat rooms. Anonymity of postings is also assured through the use of data transmission protocols such as Simple Mail Transfer Protocol (SMTP) and Network News Transfer Protocol (NNTP), which accept messages to servers with arbitrary field information (1).

As we discuss anonymity on the Internet, we need to point out that both anonymity and pseudonymity are not 100% anonymous. As anybody with a rudimentary knowledge of computing networking would know, there is always a possibility to find those who misuse the Internet this way.

5.2.2   Advantages and Disadvantages of Anonymity

There are several advantages and disadvantages to anonymity and let us look at some of these here starting with advantages:

- Anonymity is good when a whistle-blower uses it to check unhealthy activities within the organization. Although whistle-blowers are controversial, they are good in a number of cases especially when there is abuse of office and resources. We discussed whistle-blowing in Chapter 4.
- Anonymity is good in case of national security. So underground spies can gather information that is good for national defense.
- Where there is intimidation and fear of reprisals, anonymity is good because useful information may be revealed.
- Anonymity is good for some relationships and the security of some people.

   There are also disadvantages to anonymity including:

- Criminals and embezzlers can use it to their advantage.
- Lots of disputes could be solved if information from individuals party to these disputes can reveal the necessary information.

5.2.3   Legal View of Anonymity

As we have pointed out in the last section, anonymity has its good and bad side. More important, society may not be safe, if a lot of criminals use anonymity to hide their criminal activities. Anonymity can also bring suffering in social relations in society. So in a number of cases, it is necessary either for a local authority or national legislatures to pass laws that regulate when and who can use anonymity legally. In the current environment of the Internet, there are serious debates on the freedoms of individuals on the Internet and how these freedoms can be protected in the onslaught of people on the Internet under the cover of anonymity.

Discussion Issues:

1. List and discuss roles in society that require one to be anonymous and it is beneficial to society.
2. Discuss the major disadvantages of anonymity especially in the age of the Internet.

5.3 Security

In general, security can be considered a means to prevent unauthorized access, use, alteration, and theft or physical damage to property. Security involves these three elements:

1. *Confidentiality*: to prevent unauthorized disclosure of information to third parties. This is important in a number of areas including the disclosure of personal information such as medical, financial, academic, and criminal records.
2. *Integrity*: to prevent unauthorized modification of files and maintain the status quo. It includes system, information, and personnel integrity. The alteration of information may be caused by a desire for personal gain or a need for revenge.
3. *Availability*: to prevent unauthorized withholding of information from those who need it when they need it. We discuss two types of security: physical security, which involves the prevention of access to physical facilitates like computer systems, and information security, which involves prevention of access to information by encryption, authentication, and other means.

5.3.1 Physical Security

A facility is physically secure if it is surrounded by a barrier such as a fence, has secure areas both inside and outside the facility, and can resist penetration by intruders. Physical security can be guaranteed if the following four mechanisms are in place: deterrence, prevention, detection, and response [2].

1. *Deterrence* should be the first line of defense against intruders who may try to gain access. It works by creating an atmosphere intended to scare intruders.
2. *Prevention* is the second line of defense. Prevention mechanisms work by trying to stop intruders from gaining access.
3. *Detection* should be the third line of defense. This mechanism assumes the intruder has succeeded or is in the process of gaining access to the system. So it tries to "see" that intruder who has gained or who is trying to gain access.
4. *Response* is an aftereffect mechanism that tries to respond to the failure of the first three mechanisms. It works by trying to stop and/or prevent damage or access to a facility.

5.3.2 Physical Access Controls

To ensure physical security, a regime of access controls must be put in place. In physical access control, we create both physical barriers and electronic protocols that will authenticate the user of the resource whose security we are safeguarding.

5.3.2.1 Physical Security Barriers

The physical barrier can be a fence made of barbed wire, brick walls, natural trees, mounted noise or vibration sensors, security lighting, close circuit television (CCTV), buried seismic sensors, or different photoelectric and microwave systems [2]. The area surrounding the facility can be secured using locks and keys, window breakage detectors, infrared and ultrasonic detectors, interior microwave systems, animal like dogs, and human barriers like security guards and others.

5.3.2.2 Electronic Access Controls

With advances in technology, we are moving away, though not totally, from the physical barriers to more invasive electronic controls that include card access control systems, firewalls, and the third and probably the most important area, the inside, may be secured using electronic barriers such as firewalls and passwords.

Passwords

A password is a string of usually six to eight characters, with restrictions on length and start character, to verify a user to an information system facility, usually a computer system. Password security greatly depends on the password owner observing all of these four "never" cardinal rules:

1. Never publicize a password.
2. Never write a password down anywhere.
3. Never choose a password that is easy to guess.
4. Never keep the same password for an extended period of time.

Password security is not only important to individuals whose files are stored on a system, it is also vital to the system as a whole because once an intruder gains access to one password, he or she has gained access to the whole system, making all its files vulnerable. So system security is the responsibility of every individual user of the system.

Firewalls

A firewall is hardware or software used to isolate the sensitive portions of an information system facility from the outside world and limit the potential damage that can be done by a malicious intruder. Although there is no standardization in the structure of firewalls because it depends on the system and the system manager's anticipated threat to the system. Most firewalls are variations of the following three models [3]:

- *Packet Filters:* These are packet-level filters. They contain gates that allow packets to pass through if they satisfy a minimum set of conditions, and choke or prevent those packets that do not meet the entry conditions. The minimum conditions may include packets to have permissible origin or destination addresses, as determined by the network administrator. The filter firewalls can also configure and block packets with specific TCP or UDP packet port numbers, or filter based on IP protocol types. As we will see later, packet filters have a weakness in that they cannot stop or filter a packet with malicious intent if the packet contains the permissible attributes.
- *Proxy servers:* Work on the protected portions of the network that usually provide information to outside users requesting access to those portions. That is, the firewall protects client computers from direct access to the Internet. Clients direct their requests for an Internet connection through the proxy server. If individual client requests conform to the preset conditions, then the firewall will act on the request; otherwise it is dropped. These firewalls require specialized client and server configuration depending on the application.
- *Stateful Inspection:* These firewalls combine both the filter and proxy functions. Because of this, it is considered complex and more advanced. The conditions for a stateful inspection are, like the filter, based on a set of rules. But unlike filters, these rules are not based on TCP or UDP but on applications like proxy servers. They filter packets by comparing their data with archived friendly packets.

5.3.3   Information Security Controls

Information security includes the integrity, confidentiality, and availability of information at the servers, including information in files and databases and in transition between servers, and between clients and servers. The security of information can be ensured in a number of ways. The most common are cryptography for information transmission and authentication and audit trails at the information source and information destination servers. Cryptography, the science of writing and reading coded messages, forms the basis for all secure transmission. This is done through three functions: symmetric and asymmetric encryption, and hash functions.

5.3.3.1   Encryption

Encryption is a method that protects the communications channel from sniffers—programs written for and installed on the communication channels to eavesdrop on network traffic, examining all traffic on selected network segments. Sniffers are easy to write and install, and difficult to detect. Cryptography uses an encryption

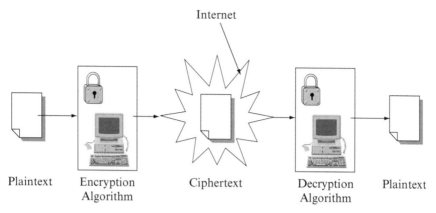

Fig. 5.1 Symmetric encryption

algorithm and key to transform data at the source, called plaintext, turn it into an encrypted form called ciphertext, usually an unintelligible form, and finally recover it at the sink. The encryption algorithm can either be symmetric or asymmetric.

Symmetric encryption, or secret key encryption as it is usually called, uses a common key and the same cryptographic algorithm to scramble and unscramble the message as shown in Fig. 5.1. The security of the transmitted data depends on the fact that eavesdroppers with no knowledge of the key are unable to read the message. One problem with symmetric encryption is the security of the keys which must be passed from the sender to the receiver.

Asymmetric encryption, commonly known as public key encryption, uses two different keys, a public key known by all and a private key known by only the sender and the receiver. Both the sender and the receiver each has a pair of these keys, one public and one private. To encrypt a message, from sender A to receiver B, as shown in Fig. 5.2, both A and B must create their own pairs of keys. Then A and B exchange their public keys—anybody can acquire them. When A is to send a message M to B, A uses B's public key to encrypt M. On receipt of M, B then uses his or her private key to decrypt the message M.

A *hash function* takes an input message M and creates a code from it. The code commonly referred to as a *hash* or a *message digest*, will be discussed more in the next section. A one-way hash function is used to create a digital signature of the message—just like a human fingerprint. The hash function is therefore used to provide the message's integrity and authenticity.

5.3.3.2 Authentication

Usually it is difficult for a system to verify the identity of a user, especially a remote user. Thus, authentication is a process whereby the system gathers and builds up information about the user to assure that the user is genuine. In data communication,

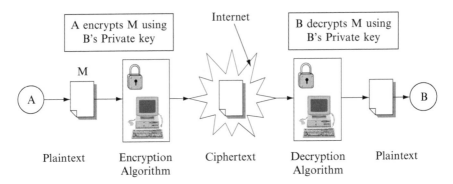

Fig. 5.2 Asymmetric encryption

authentication is also used to ensure the digital message recipient of the identity of the sender and the integrity of the message. In computer systems, authentication protocols based on cryptography use either secret-key or public-key schemes to create an encrypted message digest that is appended to a document as a digital signature.

The digital signature is similar to a handwritten signature in printed documents. Just like handwritten signatures, digital signatures ensure that the person whose signature the system is authenticating is indeed the true person, but digital signatures provide a greater degree of security than handwritten signatures. Also, digital signatures once submitted can never be disowned by the signer of a document claiming the signature was forged. This is called non-repudiation. A secure digital signature system consists of two parts: (1) a method of signing a document, and (2) authentication that the signature was actually generated by whoever it represents.

The process of signing the document, that is, creating a digital signature, involves a sender A passing the original message M into a hash function H to produce a message digest. Then A encrypts M together with the message digest using either symmetric or asymmetric encryption, and then sends the combo to B. Upon receipt of the package, B separates the digital signature from the encrypted message. The message M is put into a one-way hash to produce a message digest, and B compares the output of the hash function with the message digest A sent. If they match, then the integrity of the message M together with the signature of the sender are both valid (see Fig. 5.3).

Physical Authentication Methods. Authentication of users or user surrogates is usually based on checking one or more of the following user items [4]:

- *User name* (sometimes *screen name*).
- *Password.*
- *Retinal images*: The user looks into an electronic device that maps his or her retinal image; the system then compares this map with a similar map stored on the system.
- *Fingerprints*: The user presses on or sometimes inserts a particular finger into a device that makes a copy of the user fingerprint and then compares it with a similar image on the system user file.

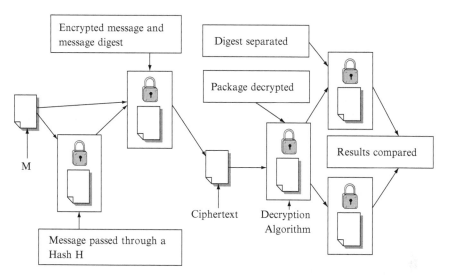

Fig. 5.3 Digital signature and authentication

- *Physical location*: The physical location of the system initiating an entry request is checked to ensure that a request is actually originating from a known and authorized client machine. To check the authenticity of such a client, the network or Internet Protocol (IP) address of the client machine is compared with the one on the system user file. This method is used mostly in addition to other security measures because it alone cannot guarantee security: If used alone, it provides access to the requested system to anybody who has access to the client machine.
- *Identity cards*: Increasingly, cards are being used as authenticating documents. Whoever is the carrier of the card gains access to the requested system. As is the case with physical location authentication, card authentication is usually used as a second-level authentication tool because whoever has access to the card automatically can gain access to the requested system.

5.3.4 *Operational Security*

Operation security involves policies and guidelines that organizations including all employees must do to safeguard the assets of the organization including its workers. These policy guidelines are spelt out in a document we call a security policy. It also includes guidelines for security recovery and response in case of a security incident.

5.4 Privacy

5.4.1 Definition

According to Jerry Durlak [5], privacy is a human value consisting of four elements he calls rights. We put these rights into two categories. The first category includes three rights that an individual can use to fence off personal information seekers; the second category contains those rights an individual can use to control the amount and value of personal information given out.

1. Control of external influences:

   - *Solitude*: The right to be alone without disturbances
   - *Anonymity*: The right to have no public personal identity
   - *Intimacy*: The right not to be monitored

2. Control of personal information:

   - *Reserve*: The right to control one's personal information including the methods of dissemination of that information

The notion of privacy is difficult to accurately define because the definition of privacy depends on things like culture, geographical location, political systems, religious beliefs and a lot more.

5.4.2 Types of Privacy

Although there are varied definitions of privacy, the several types of privacy we are going to discuss here are not influenced by the factors we have outlined in the previous section.

5.4.2.1 Personal Privacy

This type of privacy involves the privacy of personal attributes. The right to privacy of all personal attributes would mean the prevention of anyone or anything that would intrude or violate that personal space t where those attributes are. This would include all types of intrusions including physical searches, video recording, and surveillance of any type. In a number of countries, there are Statues and Acts similar to the US Fourth Amendment, which guarantees the right of the people to be secure in their persons, houses, papers, and effects, against unreasonable searches and seizures.

Discussion issue

Discuss a few of these statues and acts.

5.4.2.2 Informational Privacy

In the previous section, we discussed the privacy of an individual meaning that we want to ensure the privacy of an individual by preventing any intrusions through physical and electronic access to that individual's attributes. Informational privacy, unlike personal privacy, concerns the protection of unauthorized access to information itself. Of course there are different strands of information that we have to protect including:

- *Personal information*: Most personal information of value includes information on personal lifestyles like religion, sexual orientation, political affiliations, or personal activities.
- *Financial information*: Financial information is important not only to individuals but also to organizations. Financial information is a very valued asset because it gives the organization the autonomy it needs to compete in the market place.
- *Medical information*: Medical information is very personal and very important to all of us. For personal, employment, and insurance purposes, many people want their medical information to be private.
- *Internet*: In this new age, the Internet keeps track of all our activities online. With an increasing number of people spending an increasing number of time online in social networks and the digital convergence becoming a reality with every passing day, not only will our social life be online but soon all our lives also will. We want those activities and habits private.

5.4.2.3 Institutional Privacy

Institutions and organizations want their data private not only for business advantages but also for the life of the business. The research data, the sales and product data, the marketing strategies and the activities of the organization all need to be private.

5.4.3 Value of Privacy

Privacy has traditionally been perceived as valuable and has even gained more importance in the information age because it guards an individual's personal identity, preserves individual autonomy, and makes social relationships possible.

However, these days in the information age, the value of privacy has been eroded. We can no longer guarantee our privacy. It has left many wondering whether there is such a thing as privacy any more. As the scenario at the start of this chapter demonstrates, no one has guaranteed privacy any more unless such an individual is no longer part of the society. From the telephone calls you make that identify you through caller ID, to every transaction you pay for either by credit card or by check and to the multitude of forms you fill from getting your pet groomed to getting a prescription filled, you are identifiable and you have nowhere to hide. The most abused number, the Social Security number, is used as a personal ID by many companies including health insurance companies that use it as a customer ID in spite of the repeated warning from the federal government not to do so. In its effort to help stop the erosion of individual privacy, the U.S. Congress passed the Gramm–Leach–Bliley Financial Services Modernization Act of 1999, but put in reverse conditions—the so-called opt-out discussed in Section 5.4.3.1—that make the Act useless.

We consider three attributes of privacy: personal identity, autonomy, and social relationships.

5.4.3.1 Personal Identity

As information becomes more precious, it becomes more important for individuals to safeguard personal identity. Personal identity is valuable because it enshrines personal privacy. Unfortunately, with rapid advances in technology, especially computer technology, it has become increasingly difficult to protect personal identity, as discussed in Sections 6.2.5 and 11.3.5.

5.4.3.2 Autonomy

Humans need to feel that they are in control of their own destiny. They need their autonomy. The less personal information people have about an individual, the more autonomous that individual can be, especially in decision making. However, other people will challenge one's autonomy depending on the quantity, quality, and value of information they have about that individual. People usually tend to establish relationships and associations with individuals and groups that will respect their personal autonomy, especially in decision making.

5.4.3.3 Social Relationships

In some societies where marriages are arranged, parents on both sides try to collect as much information about each other as possible before they commit their offspring in marriage. In societies where there are no arranged marriages, the parties involved usually spend a period of time dating. The dating time is spent collecting as much information as possible about each other. The couple then uses this information to make a decision about marrying. However, each party may try to conceal some information because some seemingly valuable information may not be worthwhile and may even lead to breakup of the relationship.

5.4.4 Privacy Implications of Database Systems

5.4.4.1 Information Gathering

Have you paid enough attention to the number of junk mail, telephone calls during dinner, and junk emails you have been getting? If so, you may have thought about who has your name on a list and what they're doing with it. In recent years, telemarketers have been having a field day as technological advances have replaced the door-to-door salesman. Many companies you have done business with may have sold or shared your personal information to other companies, and tracing the source may be difficult. In many cases, we do not preserve our privacy as we defined privacy earlier. We have helped information seekers like companies in gathering and databasing information from us. We do this every time we apply for discount cards from grocery stores, gas stations, and merchandise stores, and every time we fill out information on little cards to enter contests, and every time we give out our Social Security number and telephone numbers to store clerks in department stores. The information they collect from us is put into databases and is later sold to the highest bidder, usually a marketer.

Information gathering is a very serious business that is increasingly involving a growing number of players that traditionally governments gathering mostly defensive information on weapon systems. However, with globalization and the Internet, the doors to the information gathering field have been cast open. Now individuals, companies and organization and of course governments are all competing, sometimes for the same information.

The tools of the trade have also improved tremendously, becoming more stealthy and a lot smaller and of course more accurate. With the modern tools of gathering information, no one is safe anymore. Because of our habits online, Internet crawlers are in action visiting our machines stealthy and gathering a wealth of information. There is no longer the need to get your information from cards you fill at shopping malls and grocery stores. There are better and faster ways now. There are tremendous legal and privacy issues that we have to deal with. First most of the information collected from us, the one we come to know of, which is a fraction of what they take, is collected without our consent.

Although the problem is skyrocketing, there is minimum effort to curtail the practice. This is a result of a number of reasons, the most important of which is that the rate at which technology is developing is continuously outstripping our legal systems and our ability to legislate late alone enforce the new laws. Several attempts have been made including the Gramm–Leach–Bliley Financial Services Modernization Act aimed to restrict financial institutions such as banks and brokerages from sharing customers' personal information with third parties.

Although the Financial Services Modernization Act has given financial institutions an information bonanza, the Act also tries in some way to protect the customer through three requirements that the institutions must disclose to us:

(i) *Privacy Policy*: Through which the institution is bound to tell us the types of information the institution collects and has about us and how it uses that information

(ii) *Right to Opt-Out*: Through which the institution is bound to explain our recourse to prevent the transfer of our data to third party beneficiaries
(iii) *Safeguards*: Through which the institution must put in place policies to prevent fraudulent access to confidential financial information

However, this same law, like many of its kind, has allowed these same US financial institutions to merge and form what have been called financial supermarkets. This one Act has opened a door for these companies to merge and consolidate customer data from several sources.

5.4.5 *Privacy Violations and Legal Implications*

Privacy, as we have defined it, is a basic human value that is at the core of human dignity and autonomy. Because of this recognition, many major and historical documents like the Fourth Amendment to the US Constitution, the UN Universal Declaration of Human Rights, the Council of Europe, and many national and multinational treaties contain enshrined clauses of the individual's right to privacy. It is believed that privacy forms the foundation of a free and democratic society.

However, this fundamental right is violated every day in many ways. While individual privacy rights have been violated for years, the advent of the Internet has accelerated the rate and scale of violations. There are numerous contributing factors or causes of violations. Let us look at some here:

(i) Consumers willingly give up information about themselves when they register at websites, shopping malls in order to win prizes, and in mailing solicitations.
(ii) Consumers lack the knowledge of how what they consider a little bit of information can turn into a big invasion of privacy.
(iii) Inadequate privacy policies.
(iv) Failure of companies and institutions to follow their own privacy policies.
(v) Internet temptation, as discussed in Section 3.5.1.2, that enable businesses to reach individuals in a very short time in the privacy of their homes and offices.

Because of the Internet's ability to reach many people with ease, major privacy violators have been Internet companies like DoubleClick, an Internet advertising company. DoubleClick used its dominant position on the Internet to reach as many people as possible. With this opportunity, DoubleClick quietly abandoned its original policy of providing only anonymous data collected from its Internet users to marketers and started combining its online user profiles with information from direct mailers and others. The combined information could easily be used to identify the Internet users since DoubleClick's tracking could now reveal names, addresses, and purchasing habits.

After massive user protests, the threat of lawsuits, and notices from the US Federal Trade Commission (FTC), DoubleClick gave up on their intended plan, putting the proposal on hold and claiming that they would seek user permission before launching the matching data plan [6]. Yahoo!, Inc, another Internet company, was sued by Universal Image, Inc., a company that makes educational videos. Universal sued Yahoo! for not living up to a contract to provide data, including customer email information that Universal had signed with Broadcast.com, Inc., before Yahoo acquired it [11].

Because of the anticipated growth of the Internet, there is widespread agreement that privacy rights are under serious attack and that something has to be done. The measures that are needed to protect both the user and consumer need to be varied to include legislation, like the US Consumer Protection Act, enforcement, and self-help.

Other privacy violations include intrusion, misuse of information, interception of information, and information matching.

5.4.5.1   Intrusion

Intrusion is an invasion of privacy by wrongful entry, seizing, or acquiring possession of the property of others. For example, hackers are intruders because they wrongfully break into computer systems whether they cause damage or not. With computer network globalization, intrusion is only second to viruses among computer crimes, and it is growing fast.

5.4.5.2   Misuse of Information

Human beings continually give out information in exchange for services. Businesses and governments collect this information from us honestly to provide services effectively. The information collected, as discussed in Section 5.4.3, is not just collected only to be stored. This information is digital gold to these companies. They mine the gold from us and sell it to the highest bidder. There is nothing wrong with collecting personal information when it is going to be used for a legitimate reason, for the purpose it was intended. However, the problem arises when this information is used for unauthorized purposes; collecting this information then becomes an invasion of privacy.

5.4.5.3   Interception of Information

Interception of information is unauthorized access to private information via eavesdropping, which occurs when a third party gains unauthorized access to a private communication between two or more parties. Information can be gathered by eavesdropping in the following areas:

- At the source and sink of information, where either client or server intrusion software can listen in, collect information, and send it back to the sender
- Between communication channels by tapping into the communication channels and then listening in

5.4.5.4   Information Matching

The threat of information matching can best be highlighted by an old story recounted by Richard O. Mason [7], who says it has been retold so many times that its accuracy is probably in doubt; however, its message remains the same.

Here is the story:

> A couple of programmers at the city of Chicago's computer center began matching tape files from many of the city's different data processing applications on name and I.D. They discovered, for example, that several high-paid city employers had unpaid parking fines. Bolstered by this revelation they pressed on. Soon they uncovered the names of several employees who were still listed on the register but who had not paid a variety of fees, a few of whom appeared in the files of the alcoholic and drug abuse program. When this finding was leaked to the public, the city employees, of course, were furious. They demanded to know who had authorized the investigation. The answer was that no one knew. Later, city officials established rules for the computer center to prevent this form of invasion of privacy from happening again [7].

The danger with information matching is that there is no limit to what one can do with the collected information, and no one knows what the profiles built from the matched information will be used for and by whom. Hundreds, maybe thousands, of databases with individual records are gathered from an individual over a lifetime. Can you recall how many forms you have filled in since you were a child? They may be in the thousands. Each one of these forms contains a set of questions asking for specific information about you. Each time an individual gives a certain answer to any one of these questions, the answer is used to establish a link with hundreds of other databases [7]. Hundreds, perhaps thousands, of databases have personal Social Security numbers. Such databases include driver's records, vital statistics, Social Security administration, medical records, schools, work, and public local, county, state, and federal databases. With the Social Security number as the search key, all these databases can very easily be linked together. In addition to these two links, many other keys can be used as links between databases.

The threat to information matching does not only originate from linking individual records in different databases. It also can come from erroneous or outdated (stale) information. Errors can enter information in basically three areas: (i) at the source, where it occurs mainly through incorrect input such as typing the letter "l" of the alphabet instead of a "1" (one), (ii) during transmission because of transmission interference, and (iii) at the sink, mainly as a result of poor reception. Information becomes stale when it gets outdated. Unfortunately, erroneous and stale information is frequently used. For example, in the USA alone, according to Mason, more than 60,000 local and state agencies by 1986 had routinely provided data to the National Crime Information Center where on a daily basis close to 400,000 requests were made to the center from law enforcement agents across the country. However, studies showed that the data was in error 4–6% of the time [7]. This means that an equal number of requests from law enforcement agents were filled with false information, probably placing many innocent individuals in awkward situations. Another example, which may not involve crime information, would be erroneous information collected by a credit reporting agency and used in approving services like loans, mortgages, and credit cards. If stale information is used, there is a danger that an individual could be denied credit unfairly and it is widely known how difficult it is to remove that stale information off an individual's credit record.

5.4.6 Privacy Protection and Civil Liberties

Perhaps there is no one agreed upon set of civil liberties. Many rights scholars have different sets of rights that they put under the umbrella of civil liberties. But the most accepted set of civil liberties are grouped into the following four categories: (i) criminal justice that includes police powers, personal liberty, and the right to a fair trial; (ii) basic freedoms of speech, assembly, association, movement, and no discrimination; (iii) freedom of information; and (iv) communications and privacy.

Rapid advances in computer technology, and in particular the advent of the Internet, have all created an environment where detailed information on individuals and products can very easily and cheaply be moved, merged, compared, and shared. With the help of sophisticated network scanning and spying software such as STARR, FreeWhacker, Stealth Keyboard Logger, Snapshotspy, Surf Spy, Net Spy, PC Activity Monitor, and others, no personal information on any computer on any network is safe.

Although this is good for law enforcement agencies like the local police and FBI to track down criminals, and to banks to prevent fraud, and to businesses to move data and process customer order quickly and efficiently, the accessing and sharing of personal data by companies, associations, government agencies, and consumers without an individual's knowledge is a serious threat to the security and well-being of the individual. So there must be ways to take precautions to protect against the misuse of personal information without consent. We have already indicated that personal privacy is a basic civil liberty that must be protected like any other civil liberty such as the right to free speech. In many countries, there are guidelines and structures that safeguard and protected privacy rights. These structures and guidelines, on the average, fall under the following categories:

1. *Technical*: Through the use of software and other technically based safeguards, and also by education of users and consumers to carry out self-regulation. For example, the Electronic Frontier Foundation has the following guidelines for online safeguards [7]:

   (a) Do not reveal personal information inadvertently.
   (b) Turn on cookie notices in your Web browser, and/or use cookie management software or informdiaries.
   (c) Keep a "clean" email address.
   (d) Don't reveal personal details to strangers or just-met "friends."
   (e) Realize you may be monitored at work. Avoid sending highly personal emails to mailing lists, and keep sensitive files on your home computer.
   (f) Beware of sites that offer some sort of reward or prize in exchange for your contact or other information.
   (g) Do not reply to spammers, for any reason.

(h) Be conscious of Web security.
(i) Be conscious of home computer security.
(j) Examine privacy policies and seals.
(k) Remember that you alone decide what information about yourself to reveal—when, why, and to whom.
(l) Use encryption!

2. *Contractual*: through determination of which information such as electronic publication, and how such information is disseminated, are given contractual and technological protection against unauthorized reproduction or distribution. Contractual protection of information, mostly special information like publications, is good only if actions are taken to assure contract enforceability

3. *Legal*: through the enactment of laws by national legislatures and enforcement of such laws by the law enforcement agencies. For example, in the United States the following acts are such legal protection instruments [9, 10]:

(a) Children's Online Privacy Protection Act.
(b) Consumer Protection Act.
(c) Freedom of Information Act (1968) as amended (5 USC 552).
(d) Fair Credit Reporting Act (1970).
(e) Privacy Act (1974): regulates federal government agency record keeping and disclosure practices. The act allows most individuals to seek access to federal agency records about themselves and also requires that personal information in agency files be accurate, complete, relevant, and timely.
(f) Family Educational Right and Privacy Act (1974): requires schools and colleges to grant students or their parents access to student records and limits disclosure to third parties.
(g) Tax Reform Act (1976): restricts disclosure of tax information for nontax purposes.
(h) Right to Financial Privacy Act (1978): provides bank customers the privacy of financial records held by banks and other financial institutions.
(i) Electronic Funds Transfer Act (1978): requires institutions providing EFT to notify its customers about third-party access to customer accounts.
(j) Privacy Protection Act (1980): prevents unannounced searches by authority of press offices and files if no one in the office is suspected of committing a crime.
(k) Federal Managers Financial Integrity Act (1982).
(l) Cable Communications Policy Act (1984).
(m) Electronic Communication Act (1986): broadens the protection of the 1968 Omnibus Crime Control and Safe Streets Act to include all types of electronic communications.
(n) Computer Matching and Privacy Protection Act (1986): sets standards for the U.S. government computer matching programs, excluding matches done for statistical, law enforcement, tax, and certain other causes.
(o) Computer Security Act (1987).
(p) Video Privacy Protection Act (1988): prohibits video rental stores from disclosing which films a customer rents or buys.

(q) Driver's Privacy Protection Act (1994): prohibits the release and use of certain personal information from state motor vehicle records.

(r) Telecommunication Act (1996): deregulates the cable and telephone companies to enable each company to become involved in the business of the other.

(s) Medical Records Privacy Protection Act (1996):

    (i) Recognizes that individuals possess a right of privacy with respect to personally identifiable health information

    (ii) Provides that this right of privacy may not be waived in the absence of meaningful and informed consent and

    (iii) Provides that, in the absence of an express waiver, the right to privacy may not be eliminated or limited except as expressly provided in this act

(t) Digital Millennium Copyright Act (2000).

(u) The Gramm–Leach–Bliley Financial Services Modernization Act (2000).

5.5 Ethical and Legal Framework for Information

5.5.1 Ethics and Privacy

The issues involving ethics and privacy are many and cover wide areas including morality and law. The rapid advances in computer technology, especially the Internet, have resulted in rapid changes in these issues and the creation of others. For example, before the Internet, the best way to correspond with a colleague was to either write or type a note, mail it, and, of course, trust a postal carrier. Your worry was not that the carrier would snoop and read its contents, but whether the carrier would deliver it in a timely fashion. Many people never worried because they knew that tampering with mail was a federal offense.

Now, however, with the advent of the Internet and electronic messages, confidentiality is a great concern. Computer technology has raised more privacy questions than it has found answers to. Is there any confidentiality in electronic communication? Is anything that goes in the clear over public communication channels secure anymore? Are current encryption protocols secure enough? What laws need to be in place to secure anyone of us online? Who should legislate them? Who will enforce them? We need a first an ethical framework like the one we developed in Chapter 3. But in addition to this, we also need a legal framework. Both these frameworks would probably help. The question is who will develop these frameworks? Who will enforce them?

5.5.1.1 Discussion Issues

Attempt to draft an ethical framework discussed here. What do you need to include?

What should be in the legal framework? Who should enact the laws in the framework?

5.5.2 *Ethical and Legal Basis for Privacy Protection*

The explosion of interest in the Internet, with growing numbers of people obtaining access to it, has also increased the potential for Internet-related crime. The arrest of Kevin D. Mitnick, one of the Federal Bureau of Investigation's (FBI) most wanted computer criminals in 1995, ignited anew the debate on the issue of ethics and security. Mitnick was arrested by the FBI after several years on the agency's most wanted computer criminals list. His arrest was a result of months of work by Tsutomu Shimomura, a renowned cybersleuth.

Mitnick's acts and many after him, are highlighting how vulnerable the Internet is and how vulnerable we are whenever we use it. Security and ethical issues do not and should not only come into play when there is a crime committed. These issues are also raised when individuals and companies act in ways that are considered harmful or have the potential of being harmful to a sector of society. Consider Internet postings, for example. As the Internet grows, companies and individuals are flocking to the Internet to post and advertise their wares. Until recently, the focus of Internet security and ethics was on pornographic images accessible to children. But of late a multitude of concerns have sprung up as new internet technologies and services have sprung up like social networking and twitter.

What is the way forward? How can we ethically and legally encounter the new internet technologies and services without interfering into people's love and business as they use these new services?

Exercises

1. Define security and privacy. Why are both important in the information age?
2. What is anonymity? Discuss two forms of anonymity.
3. Discuss the importance of anonymity on the Internet.
4. Is total anonymity possible? Is it useful?
5. Develop two scenarios—one dealing with ethical issues involving security, and the other dealing with ethical issues involving privacy.
6. Is personal privacy dead? Discuss.
7. List and discuss the major threats to individual privacy.
8. Identity theft is the fastest growing crime. Why?
9. Why is it so easy to steal a person's identity?
10. Suggest steps necessary to protect personal identity.
11. Governments are partners in the demise of personal privacy. Discuss.
12. Anonymity is a doubly edged sword. Discuss.
13. Are the steps given in Section 5.4.5 enough to prevent identity theft? Can you add more?
14. What role do special relationships play in identity theft?
15. Modern day information mining is as good as gold! Why or why not?
16. How do consumers unknowingly contribute to their own privacy violations?
17. How has the Financial Services Modernization Act helped companies in gathering personal information?

References

1. Detweiler, L. "Identity, Privacy, and Anonymity on the Internet." http://www.fwn.rug.nl/fennema/marko/archive/privacy.txt
2. Seven, Gary. "Lex Luthor and the Legion of Doom/Hackers Presents: Identifying, Attacking, Defeating, and Bypassing Physical Security and Intrusion Detection Systems." *The Lod/H Technical Journal.* http://underground.org/publications/lod/lod-1.3.html
3. Lowe, D. V. "Security Overview: Introduction." http://www.compclass.com/~vincent/fin4/fin4.html
4. Scherphier, A. "CS596 Client–Server Programming Security." http://www.sdsu.edu/~turtle/cs596/security.html
5. Durlak, Jerry. "Privacy and Security." *Communications for Tomorrow.* http://renda.colunato.yorku.ca/com4tom/1296.html
6. Will Rodger. "Sites targeted for privacy violations." *USA Today,* June 13, 2000.
7. Mason, Richard. "Four Ethical Issues of the Information Age." In R. Dejoie, G. Fowler, and D. Paradice (eds.), *Ethical Issues in Information Systems.* Boston, MA: Boyd & Fraser, 1991.
8. Johnson, Deborah. *Computer Ethics,* 2nd ed. Englewood Cliffs, NJ: Prentice Hall, 1995.
9. Landon, Kenneth. "Markets and Piracy," *Communications of the ACM,* 39(9), 1996, pp. 92–95.
10. "Second Amended Verified Original Petition and Application for TRO and Temporary Injunction," *Universal Image, Inc.* v. *Yahoo, Inc.* http://www.tomwbell.com/netlaw/universal/yahoo.html

Further Readings

Rachels, James. "Why Privacy Is Important." In R. Dejoice, G. Flower, and P.A. Radice (eds.), *Ethical Issues in Information Systems.* Boston, MA: Boyd & Fraser, 1991.
Schiesel, Seth. "On the Web, New Threats to Young Are Seen." *New York Times,* March 7, 1997.
"Tactics of a High-Tech Detective." *New York Times.* http://www.takedown.com/coverage/tactics.html

Chapter 6
Intellectual Property Rights and Computer Technology

Learning Objectives

After reading this chapter, the reader should be able to:

1. Distinguish among patent, copyright, and trade secret protection.
2. Discuss the legal background of copyright in national and international law.
3. Explain how patent and copyright laws may vary internationally.
4. Outline the historical development of software patents.
5. Discuss the consequences of software piracy on software developers and the role of relevant enforcement organizations.

Scenario 4
Cybersquatting: Is It Entrepreneurship or Intellectual Theft?

Just before the 2000 New York senatorial campaign, Chris Hayden paid $70 each for the exclusive 2-year rights to the following Internet addresses: www.hillary2000.com, www. hillaryclinton 2000.com, and www.clinton2000.com. A few weeks later, Mrs. Hillary Clinton, the then US first lady, declared her candidacy for the state of New York senatorial race. The Clinton campaign team wanted her presence on the web, but they could not use any of the three names, though they rightly belonged to Mrs. Clinton. Deciding not to challenge Mr. Hayden in the middle of an election campaign, the team opted to buy the rights for www. hillary2000.com from Mr. Hayden. However, Mr. Hayden decided to engage a broker to demand $15,000 for the use of the name [10].

Cybersquatting, as the practice of grabbing somebody's name and registering it with an Internet registration company in anticipation of reaping huge rewards, is becoming widespread.

Discussion Questions

1. *Is Mr. Hayden violating Mrs. Clinton's intellectual rights?*
2. *Can Mr. Hayden claim free speech protection for the use of the names?*
3. *Should there be laws to make the practice illegal?*

6.1 Definitions

Intellectual Property (IP) broadly describes tangible things such as ideas, inventions, technologies, artworks, music and literature, and others that one can claim ownership to. Ownership to IP to any of these things may result in economic gain as rewards to personal initial investments before they acquire value. It is a set of legal

J.M. Kizza, *Ethical and Social Issues in the Information Age*, Texts in Computer Science,
DOI 10.1007/978-1-84996-038-0_6, © Springer-Verlag London Limited 2010

rights which result from intellectual activity in the industrial, scientific, literary, and artistic fields [11]. Intellectual property rights (IPR) are legal rights bestowed to an individual or a group that created, designed, or invented the activities that led to the intellectual property in domains such as science and technology, business, industry, and the arts. These legal rights, most commonly in the form of patents, trademarks, and copyright protect the moral and economic rights of the creators, in addition to the creativity and dissemination of their work [11].

6.2 Computer Products and Services

Computer products consist of those parts of the computer you can see and touch (e.g., the keyboard, CPU, printer, and monitor). They are considered products because they have tangible form and intrinsic value. A service is an act carried out on behalf of someone, usually a customer. If the service is going to be paid for, the provider must strive to please the customer; it is crucial. If the service is not to be paid for, the act must then be performed to the liking of the provider.

Services have intrinsic value to the customer or recipient, but have no tangible form. For example, a patient going to a doctor for treatment receives a service that has an intrinsic value, especially if the patient gets better, but it has no tangible form. A computer service can take the form of repairing a computer product and/or configuring and installing a computer network, neither of which has a tangible form but do offer considerable intrinsic value to the owner. Computer products can be defined easily because they have tangible form and intrinsic value. Services can also be defined easily because they have intrinsic value to the customer or the recipient, and in most cases to the provider, although they have no tangible form. Computer software, however, cannot be so easily classified as either a product or a service. Since it entered the marketplace, therefore, legal protection of computer software has been very problematic.

Computer software is a set of logical instructions to perform a desired task. This logical sequence follows an algorithm. The development of this sequence of instructions goes through the following phases:

1. *Logic map*: the plan of the idea or an algorithm to accomplish the task. A plan is a flowchart of logic control with four major stations, namely, the input, output, processing, and decision box connected by arrows indicating the direction of flow of logic. See the flowchart in Fig. 6.1. Within the flowchart itself, there may be loops that express repetition of certain parts of the logic of that flowchart. Effective implementation of the flowchart achieves the desired effects of the program for the designated task.
2. *The source code*: a result of the implementation of the flowchart, turning the flowchart into a set of instructions using a programming language of choice.
3. *The object code*: the second stage of the implementation of a flowchart in which the source code, with the help of either a compiler or an assembler, is turned into strings of zeros and ones. In this form, the program is referred to as an object

Fig. 6.1 Flowchart

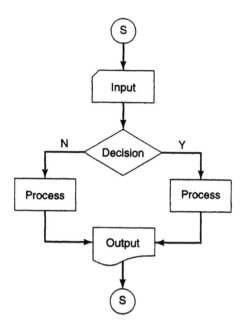

code. This is not yet fully an operational form of the program because at this stage the program lacks variable addresses that have yet to be reconciled. It is also missing library routines that are added in the next stage.

4. *Memory-based executable code*: After the object code is done, it is passed to the linker, another one of the system programs, whose job is to look for all missing variable addresses and library and personal routines and include them in the object code to produce a load module. The load module is now ready to be loaded if execution is needed. The job of loading the module is done by another system program called a loader. Most programs bought from vendors and software producers are in this executable form. The program at this stage has intrinsic value to the software producer and probably to the buyer, but it has no tangible form if you do not consider the medium it is on.

5. *Microcode*: another form of executable code, but unlike the type of code we have just described, this code is not loaded in physical memory. It is coded and loaded on ROM (the read-only memory of the computer, which cannot be written on by the user) or burned into the computer hardware at the time of manufacture. If this code is loaded in ROM it can only be erased electronically or by using ultraviolet light. If, however, it is incorporated into the hardware, it is not easily changed and it cannot be erased. In this form the program is referred to as microcode. For a program in hardware, execution is normally achieved through the logical flow in the assemblies of hardware components.

In support of either hardware-based or memory-based programs, programmers, usually the creators of these programs, write documentation and technical manuals to accompany the program and help the user of the software. Our references to computer programs here, therefore, include memory-based and hardware-based programs together with the technical manuals and all related documentation.

In our definition of computer software, whether hardware-based or memory-based, including technical writings, note that computer software, if it is considered at the execution stage without the technical documentation, has an intrinsic value both to the developer and the buyer, but it may not have a tangible form unless you consider the medium it is on (e.g., the disk). For example, during tax filing season when you buy a tax program to help you with taxes, you normally get a couple of disks with the program on them and a number of manuals and flyers. You can ignore the flyers in your package because they are usually for commercial purposes, but the purpose of the manuals is to help you learn how to use the program. You can touch the manuals, the disks, and so on, but you cannot touch the program itself. That is, the manuals and disks all have a tangible form and probably some intrinsic value, but the program itself does not have a tangible form, although it has the most intrinsic value. In this case we can classify such software as a service.

But not having a tangible form does not by itself rule out software as a product. According to Deborah Johnson [1], the courts do not equate products with what is tangible. Courts have defined things such as energy and leases as products, although none has a tangible form. So there are cases when we can consider software as a product.

In his article "Negligence for Defective Software," Jim Prince [2] puts software into three categories. The first category is made up of off-the-shelf software such as Windows, Lotus, and others that one can buy ready-to-use with no alterations allowed by the producer. This category he calls the "canned" software. The customer gets it as is. The second category is the software specifically ordered by the customer from the software house or producer to fit the customer's very specific needs, similar to going to your physician for a specific illness. The third category is software the customer buys off the shelf, but with changes allowed, or the customer adds certain parts to the software to meet some specific needs. According to Prince, category 1 software is considered to be a product, whether it has a tangible form or not; category 2 software is considered to be a service; and category 3 software is a new class he calls "mixed case."

6.3 Foundations of Intellectual Property

Gaining the skills to provide computer technology products, services, and software requires a considerable investment both in time and money. So the individuals who do this work should reap financial rewards for their efforts. Such rewards create an atmosphere of creativity and competitiveness, which in turn creates jobs that drive the economy. This creativity must therefore be protected, for if it falters because of lack of protection, then the economy of the country falters along with it.

Computer technology in particular was born out of this individual creativity and the adventurism of young entrepreneurs. In order to encourage these innovators, society must protect their efforts and resources. To do this, a specific set of rights, collectively known as intellectual property rights, has been recognized, and laws have been enacted by different countries and groups of countries to protect those rights.

Intellectual property rights form a wide scope of mechanisms that include copyrights, patents, trademarks, protection of trade secrets, and, increasingly, personal identity rights. Each of these instruments of protection is regulated by a body of laws and statutes we discuss throughout this chapter. Unfortunately, some of these laws are not universal; they only apply in one country. And even within the United States, the same laws may not apply in all states. In particular, we look at intellectual property rights as they apply to computer products, services, and software.

6.3.1 Copyrights

Internationally, copyright is a right, enforceable by law, accorded to an inventor or creator of an expression. Such expressions may include creative works (literary, dramatic, musical, pictorial, graphic, and artistic) together with audiovisual and architectural works and sound recordings. In general, every original work that has a tangible form and is fixed in a medium is protectable under the copyright law. The history of copyright laws can be traced back to eighteenth-century England with the so-called statute of Queen Anne around 1710 setting a pattern for formal copyright statutes. England was followed by the United States in 1790 when the first US copyright law was enacted by Congress, and by France in 1793 [3].

Since then, copyright laws have spread worldwide. Examples of international copyright bodies include the Berne Convention in 1886, of which the United States was not a signatory until 1989, the 1952 Universal Copyright Convention (UCC), and the Berne and Paris conventions in 1971. To make sure that conventions stay current and signatory countries observe them, a number of world bodies have been created mainly to administer the conventions. The World Intellectual Property Organization (WIPO) created in 1967 was the first to be charged with such a task. Later, the UN Educational Scientific and Cultural Organization (UNESCO) together with WIPO were assigned to administer the UCC, and finally the World Trade Organization (WTO) is now charged with administrating the Trade-Related Aspects of Intellectual Property Rights (TRIPPS) agreement concluded under the Uruguay round of the General Agreement on Tariffs and Trade (GATT). Besides these large and more comprehensive organizations, there are also numerous small regional organizations like the North American Free Trade Agreement (NAFTA) [3].

These organizations, together with national legislatures, keep these conventions and national copyright acts current through amendments. For example, in the United States the 1790 copyright law was amended in 1831 and then in

1870. In 1909, Congress enacted the Copyright Act, which underwent two amendments, and in 1976 Congress enacted the current Copyright Act, which came into effect in 1978. This act has already undergone several amendments mainly because of advances in computer technology.

Each country has its own requirements for the issuance of a copyright. In the United States, for example, there are three requirements for copyright protection of a work under the 1978 US Copyright Act: originality, fixation, and expression; in Canada, it is originality and fixation. The US copyright laws cover all original works fixed in tangible forms regardless of medium, and such works must be expressions, not ideas [4]. The scope of works or creations meeting these criteria is wide. It includes artistic, pictorial, graphic, and sculptural works; musical and sound recordings; audiovisual works including television and motion pictures; and literary works and other printed materials such as books, greeting cards, journals, flyers, and leaflets, and the list goes on.

But a number of creative fixable works are excluded from this extensive list because they are considered either trivial or utilitarian. The list for these is also a long one. It includes calendars, schedules of events, scorecards, ideas, facts, names, common language phrases, titles, blank forms, and many others. Although some of these may not be protected by the copyright laws, they may be protected somewhere else – for example, by trademark or patent laws.

6.3.1.1 Works in the Public Domain

When the copyright on a work expires, that work goes into the public domain. Other works in public domain include those owned by governments, non-copyrightable items we listed earlier such as ideas, facts, and others, works intentionally put in the public domain by the owner of the copyright, and works that lost copyrights for various reasons before the copyrights expired.

Works in public domain are not protected by the copyright law and can be used by any member of the public without prior permission from the owner of the work. Examples of such works in the United States include works published before 1978 whose copyright has not been renewed and, therefore, have no valid copyright notice. A copyright notice consists of a copyright symbol denoted by: ©, the word "copyright," the year the copyright was granted, and the name of the copyright owner. For example: Copyright © 1995 John Mukasa.

6.3.1.2 Application for a Copyright

For authors and/or creators of works who need this kind of protection, the process begins with an application to the copyright office. Each country's copyright office has different requirements. The US Copyright Office requires an applicant to include with the application a copy of the work for which a copyright is sought and to file for copyright within 3 months of the first distribution of the work.

Upon receipt of the application by the Copyright Office, it is reviewed to make sure it meets the three criteria of originality, fixation, and expression for the issuing of a copyright.

Fixation, a remnant of the Gutenberg era, and now the most controversial element in the current debate about intellectual property rights in the digital age, refers to the tangible form in which the creation is perceived by others. For example, computer programs are fixed in binary code. For performing arts like drama, the script is the fixation. In the fine arts the painting or the sculpture is the fixation. It is important in creative work to have fixation because it clearly demonstrates and defines the tangible form of the creation and the domain and parameters of such a creation.

Like fixation, the protection of a creation requires proof of originality. The originality requirements differentiate among facts, ideas, and expressions as creations. Facts are considered common property for all humanity; no one has a right to an unknown or known fact because it is not considered an invention; the same principle applies to theories – mathematical, scientific, and others. Ideas, like facts, are also considered common property and therefore are not copyrightable. Thus, originality is only possible through expressions. Such expressions may include ideas, theories, and other inventions. The packaging must be original if protection is sought. Packaging includes remakes of protected works. This type of packaging is what scholars of copyrights call derived works. For an interesting discussion of this, refer to The Copyright Book by William E. Strong [4]. The review process is very extensive and thorough and takes some time before it is complete. Upon approval, the recipient must place a notice of copyright ownership in all parts and copies of the work.

6.3.1.3   Duration of a Copyright

In the United States the duration of copyright protection falls into two periods: those copyrights granted before the 1978 Copyright Act and those granted after that date. If a copyright was received for a published work before 1978, that copyright lasts for 75 years after the date of issuance. For unpublished works the copyrights will expire on December 31, 2002 regardless of when they were issued. If the copyright was received after 1978, the work remains protected by copyright laws for the lifetime of the author plus 50 years. In the case of more than one author of the works, the protection lasts for the lifetime of the longest living author plus 50 years. For all works made for hire, that is, works made as part of contracted employment, the coverage lasts 75 years from the date of the first publication or 100 years from the date of creation (5).

6.3.2   Patents

Unlike the copyright that protects expressions, patents protect inventions or discoveries. In the United States, patent rights are protected just like copyright rights.

In many countries, patent protection rights like those of copyrights are provided for by the constitution. The US Constitution, for example, states it this way: "to promote the progress of science and useful arts, by securing for limited times to authors and inventors the exclusive right to their respective writing and discoveries." In accordance with this, the Congress has enacted and continually revised patent laws to suit the times. These laws give inventors or discoverers living within US borders and territories the exclusive rights to make, use, or sell their invention or discovery for a specific period of time as long as there was full disclosure of the invention or discovery at the time the patent application was filed.

Because of the disclosure requirement that every patent applicant must meet, the patent is more of a contract between the inventor or discoverer and the government. For this contract to be binding, each party to the contract must keep its part: the government's part to protect the exclusive rights of the inventor or discoverer while such a person recovers his or her investments for a period of time, that of the inventor or discoverer to make a full disclosure to the government of the invention or discovery. With this disclosure the government makes sure the public benefits from the discovery or the invention while it is still under patent protection.

6.3.2.1 What Is Patentable?

In the United States, an invention or discovery is patentable if it meets two basic requirements. The first requirement is that the invention or discovery for which the patent is sought is new and useful, or is a new and useful improvement of any of the following: process, manufacture (covering all products that are not machines), and machine (covering all mechanisms and mechanical products and composition of matter, which includes all factory-manufactured life-forms).

The second requirement is that the invention or discovery must satisfy the following four conditions and all must apply:

1. *Utility*: An invention or discovery serves a basic and minimum useful purpose to the general public or to a large percentage of the public without being a danger to the public, illegal, or immoral.
2. *Novelty*: The invention or discovery for which a patent is sought must be new, not used, known, or published somewhere before.
3. *Nonobviousness*: The invention or discovery for which patent protection is sought must not have been obvious to anyone with ordinary skills to produce or invent in its disclosed form.
4. *Disclosure*: There must be adequate disclosure of the product for which a patent is sought. Such a disclosure is often used by the Patent Office in its review to seek and prove or disprove the claims on the application form and also to enable the public under the contract with the government to use the invention or discovery safely and gainfully.

6.3.2.2   Application for a Patent

In many countries, the process of obtaining a patent begins with the filing of an application with the patent office. As we already discussed, the application must give a clear and detailed disclosure of the invention or discovery including its workings, experiments made, data used, results obtained, safety record, and effectiveness if used properly. Its weaknesses, if observed, and all pertinent information that may be required if the Patent Office is to carry out a similar experiment must also be submitted.

6.3.2.3   Duration of a Patent

After the review process is completed – and this may take some time depending on the disclosure provided and the type of invention or discovery – the patent is then issued to the applicant for the invention, and only for that invention, not including its variations and derivatives. The protection must last for a number of years – 17 years in the United States. During this time period, the patent law protects the inventor or discoverer from competition from others in the manufacture, use, and sale of the invention or discovery.

6.3.2.4   Public Domain

The patent law does not protect ideas, but only the process of carrying out an idea. Competitors may take the same idea and use a different process to arrive at their own inventions or discoveries, which can then be patented as novel. When the patent protection expires, the patent together with all disclosures go into the public domain for anyone to use.

6.3.3   Trade Secrets

A trade secret is information that gives a company or business a competitive advantage over others in the field. It may be a formula, a design process, a device, or trade figures. Thus, there is no one acceptable description or definition of trade secrets. The generic definition is that it is a collection of information in a given static format with strategic importance. The format may be a design expressing the information, a formula representing the collection of information, a pattern, a symbol, or an insignia representing the information. Whatever the format the collected information takes, it must have given or offered an advantage to the owner which places that owner a degree above the competition.

In the United States, unlike the other intellectual properties we have described so far, trade secrets have no federal protection. All trade secret laws are state laws.

But trade secret owners are further protected by express or implied contract laws and laws of unfair competition which are backed by federal statutes.

6.3.3.1 Characteristics of Trade Secrets

Because it is difficult to define a trade secret, it is important that we characterize what makes a trade secret. According to Neitzke [6], a trade secret is characterized by the following:

1. The extent to which the information is known outside the business. If a lot of people outside the company or business know or have access to the collection of information that constitutes the trade secret, then it is no longer a trade secret.
2. The extent of measures taken by individuals possessing the trade secret to guard the secrecy of the information. If the information is to remain known by as few people as possible, there must be a detailed plan to safeguard that information and prevent it from leaking.
3. The value of the information to the owner and to the competitor. If the collection of information forming the trade secret has little or no value to the competitor, then it can no longer be a trade secret because it offers no definite advantage to the owner over the competitor. It does not matter whether the owner values the information; as long as it is not valued in the same way by the competitor, it is not regarded as a trade secret.
4. The amount of effort or money spent by the owner to develop or gather the information. The logic here is usually the more money the developer puts in a project, the more value is placed on the outcome. Because there are some information or project outcomes that do not require substantial initial investments, the effort here is what counts.
5. The ease or difficulty with which the information could be properly acquired or duplicated by others. If it will take a lot of effort and money to duplicate the product or the information, then its value and therefore advantage to the competitor diminishes.

The conditions that characterize a trade secret are in direct conflict with the requirements of a patent. Remember the main requirement for obtaining a patent is the full disclosure of all the information surrounding the product and its workings. This directly conflicts with the need for secrecy in trade secrets. So the patent applicant cannot claim a patent and at the same time claim protection using the trade secret laws.

6.3.3.2 Duration of Trade Secrets

Trade secrets have an indefinite life of protection as long as the secrets are not revealed.

6.3.4   Trademarks

A trademark is a product or service-identifying label. It is a mark that attempts to distinguish a service or a product in the minds of the consumers. The label may be any word, name, picture, or symbol. It is very well-known that consumers tend to choose between products through association with the product's brand name. For example, the Golden Arch is a trademark for McDonald's restaurants. There are many other fast-food restaurants (e.g., Burger King), but none of them can use the Golden Arch as their trademark. The Golden Arch differentiates McDonald's from all other fast-food restaurants and may give it an advantage over its competitors in the industry. Because trademarks are used by consumers to choose among competing products, they are vigorously protected by their owners.

Unlike patents and copyrights, however, trademarks are not so protected and enshrined in constitutions. For example, in the United States, trademark laws, like trade secrets, are based on state statutes. At the federal government level the trademark laws can be found in the Lenham Act and the new Trademark Cyber-piracy Prevention Act 1999 [7].

Whereas the patent gives owners the exclusive right to use, sell, and make use of the invention or discovery, and the copyright law gives owners the exclusive rights to copying their works, the trademark gives its owner the right to prevent others, mostly competitors, from using the same or similar symbol to market their products.

6.3.4.1   Categories of Trademarks

Trademark is a general term that includes a service mark, a certification mark, and a collective mark. A service mark is usually used in the sale or advertising of a service. It is supposed to uniquely identify that service. A circle with checked lines distinguishes AT&T telecommunication services from those of BTT, MCI, and many others. A certification mark is used as a verifier or to authenticate the characteristics of a product, a service, or group of people who offer a certain service. For example, colleges attach seals to diplomas as marks to certify the educational attainment of the holders. A collective mark is mainly used by a group of people to indicate membership in an organization or association. For example, people who take and pass certain specialty examinations can use a mark like CPA, PhD, or MD to indicate their belonging to those groups.

6.3.4.2   Characteristics of Trademarks

It is said that a picture is worth a 1,000 words. So, it is assumed by trademark owners that a symbol is worth a 1,000 words and, therefore, their marks are always saying something to the customers, at least in theory. A variety of marks are used by product and service companies to enhance the commercial value of their products or services in the eyes of the public by association. General wisdom is that the more recognizable the mark is, the more valuable will be the product or service.

In addition to categorizing trademarks by what they cover, as we did in the last section, let us also group them according to what they say. Trademarks as symbols of sales to the consumer are generally supposed to tell the consumer about the services or the products they are intended to boost. The impression the mark gives to a consumer, the likelihood of the existence of such a mark, and the ease of obtaining registry put it in one of the following characteristic groups:

- *Arbitrary marks*: trademark symbols that say nothing about the product or service. They are usually used arbitrarily with a product or service, but over time they begin to get associated with that product or service. The majority of arbitrary marks are usually one or more words or a collection of letters already in linguistic use but with no associated meaning at all. Many established trademarks start as arbitrary marks and consumers eventually come to associate them with the product or service. For example, McDonald's Golden Arch may have had no meaning at the beginning and still may have no meaning to "aliens" unless they know of the association.
- *Suggestive marks*: symbols or writings that are usually in the public domain, but people twist them to say something about their products or services. They may suggest to the customer the features, qualities, and other characteristics of the product or service. A good example here would be a mark like "GolfRight" as a trademark for a company manufacturing a new brand of golf balls. It took out of the public domain the two words "golf" and "right" and combined them to describe the product with the creation of a new word "GolfRight."
- *Descriptive marks*: usually contain a description of the intended purpose of the mark but say nothing about the product or service. For example, if you create a program that you think simplifies the tax-preparing process you may use a trademark called "Easy-Tax."
- *General marks*: new marks, unrelated and with no suggestive features, qualities, and characteristics of the products or services they are said to represent. Unlike the arbitrary marks, general marks are not linguistically bound. A general mark could be any symbol. General marks are desirable because they are easy to register, since the likelihood of the existence of a similar mark is minimal. Example of such a mark is the use of a graphic symbol like an arrow for a product or service.

6.3.4.3 Registration of a Trademark

An application for a trademark must contain and present all relevant information. It must also describe the product or service for which the trademark is being sought, the class of goods and services, and the date of first issue of the mark. Marks are registered only if they meet certain criteria. The core requirement is that the mark must not cause confusion with similar marks used by others. In the United States a mark is registered as a trademark only if it meets the following criteria:

1. It must be in good "taste" for the public – not immoral, deceptive, or illegal.
2. It must not have suggestive connotations to its origin.
3. It must not be a symbol of any recognized country.
4. It must not use people's likenesses either in death or living without prior consent.

6.3.4.4 Duration of a Trademark

In the United States, a valid trademark is protected for 10 years. If an extension is needed it can be granted for another 10 years.

6.3.5   Personal Identity

Identity theft is a crime committed when one misrepresents oneself, with or without success, as another person in order to get the victim's information so that the perpetrator can receive goods and services in the fraud victim's name. Identity theft is now one of the fastest growing crimes in the United States and in a number of other countries as well. Although it is still not considered to be a crime in some countries, national legislatures are in full gear enacting laws to criminalize it. When it happens, it takes probably an instant, but it can take a long period of time before it is discovered. By then, the information misuse, financial loss, and psychological damage can be devastating. But this is nothing compared to the agony one goes through trying to control, manage, and recover from the damage caused. Doing this can sometimes take years and be very costly.

Techniques to steal personal identity include the following [8]:

(i) Advertising in newspapers and mostly on the Internet. The most common technique now, pretext calling, is where people misrepresent themselves as law enforcement agents, social workers, and potential employers to obtain the private data of others from banks and other financial institutions.
(ii) From readily available how-to books and discussion groups perpetrators get foolproof methods of wangling financial information out of bank employees.
(iii) Use of telemarketing scams to trick consumers into revealing personal data.
(iv) Abundant authentic-looking fake IDs, including Social Security cards, birth certificates, and driver's licenses, are on sale online.
(v) Going through one's trash for personal information.
(vi) Using the post office to redirect one's mail to a perpetrator's box number.
(vii) Criminals are increasingly using radio scanners to eavesdrop on personal calls.

6.3.5.1 Prevention

After being the victim of identity theft, it is extremely difficult to straighten out one's record, let alone recover the stolen personal attributes. The best course of action is for individual defense. The following steps are considered minimal but effective:

(i) Shred all credit-card receipts, cancelled checks, and other financial documents.
(ii) Seek employer personal information protection plans.
(iii) We are leaking vessels of personal information. At every stop we make, we involuntarily give out crucial personal information such as sensitive financial data, telephone numbers, Social Security numbers, and other vital personal data.
(iv) Where possible get all your payments deposited electronically in your bank account.
(v) Periodically check your credit report. It is better still if you review credit reports from all three credit bureaus for erroneous data on your personal credit report. Once you get your credit report, look for things such as who is using your information. Check and make sure you know who requests for your information from these companies.
(vi) Shred all your credit card solicitations and all other mail that bears personal identification.
(vii) If you become a victim, report the incident to law enforcement personnel.
(viii) Although not as effective so far, legislation is also important. The US Congress recently passed a law that makes it a federal crime, punishable by up to 5 years in prison, for anyone to misrepresent himself/herself to obtain someone's private financial data.

6.4   Ownership

As we discuss ownership in this section and indeed the whole book, we confine ourselves to intellectual property ownership. Ownership of everything else other than intellectual property is outside our scope here. An idea is novel if it is original, authentic, and new. Inventiveness, creativity, and discoveries are born out of individual ideas. Good ideas are the source of substantial benefits to individuals and the public. Before an idea can be useful, however, it must be put into utilizable form, either as a process or as an application. It is this idea in a utilizable form that is the core of intellectual property rights. In many countries the owner of such an idea has a set of legal rights to its expression as a creation, work, invention, discovery, information, or any other form.

Via the copyright law, the patent law, the trademark law, and trade secret statutes, governments have indicated that they can protect owners' rights under certain conditions, and, therefore, legal ownership to creations, discoveries, information, inventions, and the like, is protectable. As we have already seen, the domain of all these rights constitutes intellectual property. Within this domain, these rights are grouped into subsets defining specific areas of interests such as the right to make, use, or sell one's works of discovery or creation. Each such subset is protected by the four well-known instruments we discussed in Section 6.3.

6.4.1 The Politics of Ownership

Recently a lot has been written about the concept of intellectual property rights, and the issue has been in the news, such as when the US government negotiated with China, the country many in the West believe has the highest rate of abuse of the intellectual property laws. There have been many statements made about the effects of cultural differences between Western countries and other cultures of the world regarding the issue of intellectual property rights.

In fact, this issue alone has become a defining factor between Western and other cultures. Western culture emphasizes individuals, rewards individual achievements, and hence upholds intellectual property issues as a golden egg. Non-Western cultures, in contrast, which emphasize community responsibility, do not understand the West's focus on intellectual property rights. To many non-Westerners, a good manifestation of an idea that benefits a community should be enjoyed by the whole community, not just by one or a few members, because individuals make up the community.

As global economies become more and more intertwined, and as the West continues to keep the lead in technological development, many of the non-Western cultural underpinnings are likely to change as these cultures devour the new imported Western technology. Already a number of countries in Southeast Asia have been forced to abide by the intellectual property laws as dictated by the West.

In addition to the cultural politics of intellectual property issues, there is also a perception controversy. Many people believe the protection of the manifestation of one's ideas by copyrights, patents, trademarks, and trade secrets laws automatically constitutes a monopoly of the benefits that come with the ideas. Because of this misconception, the US Congress and indeed other governments have passed anti-trust laws to calm the public. The antitrust laws in themselves prevent or restrict patent, copyright, or trademark holders from collecting large loyalties beyond the term of the license by opening up the competition.

6.4.2 The Psychology of Ownership

Whether we grew up in a culture that rewards individual achievements or in those cultures that pride themselves on community achievements, we are aware of the distinct psychology about individual ownership. We tend to classify those items that we individually own, whether they are few or abundant, according to their intrinsic value to us. We may believe our self-worth and status in the community depend on the intrinsic value of the items we own. So the intrinsic value we attach to these items is one of the most important aspects of ownership. Another aspect of ownership is the tangibility of what we own. When what we own has a tangible form with glamour and value to others – whether it has any intrinsic value to us or not – it tends to raise our status in the community. We therefore gain the respect of others, which in turn affects our self-esteem and our egos.

6.5   Intellectual Property Crimes

An intellectual property crime (IPC) is the act of infringe on the rights of the owners of the intellectual property. IPC refers to all activities that involve infringement, counterfeiting, piracy of products and services for profit without. It also includes misappropriation, misrepresentation, cybercrimes, corruption and bribery, and espionage. The cost of intellectual property crimes to industry and nations is huge.

Technological advances have made these crimes grow like a wild fire in the past decade by making committing these crimes a lot easier and making the field of crimes global, in the process making the threat of apprehension less. Technology has also increased these crimes by making the costs of making duplicated products low and easy to make.

6.5.1   Infringement

In Section 6.3 we discussed the legal protection over a domain of rights for an individual's manifested idea. This legal protection is offered in subsets of laws that define the boundaries within which such laws can be enforced. Anybody else with no rights within this domain is considered an infringer, defined as one moving within the protected domain to claim rights for the use of someone else's manifestation of an idea without permission from the holder of the rights.

This is an abstract concept and the difficulty in understanding it illustrates the elusiveness of the boundaries of these rights. There are three types of infringements:

1. *Direct infringement*: The infringer knowingly or otherwise makes, uses, sells, or copies a protected item without any alteration.
2. *Inducement infringement*: The infringer intentionally supports infringement activities on a protected item without individually taking part in the infringement activities.
3. *Contributory infringement*: The infringer takes part in the infringement of a protected item. Let us now look at infringement under each one of the subdomains of the intellectual property domain.

6.5.1.1   Copyright Infringement

Copyright infringement is very difficult to prove. However US courts have provided guidelines that many courts normally follow [4]. Here are some of the items that courts look for in an infringement suit:

- Whether the infringer has knowledge or visual contact with the work
- Whether the individual claiming to be the owner has a valid copyright
- Whether the work under dispute is a major revision with substantially new contents of the original or just a variation

6.5.1.2   Patent Infringement

Like copyright infringement, patent infringement is also difficult to detect. Highly sophisticated methods of policing and investigative work need to be laid down and followed. No public law enforcement can be used in these cases. It is purely the efforts of the owner of the patents, and he or she must meet all expenses incurred during the investigation and prosecuting of the infringer if caught. Once the infringer is caught and determined guilty by the court, a hefty settlement is collected from the perpetrator. There may also be punitive damages.

Because the policing and investigation can be difficult, lengthy, and expensive, patent owners tend to use a device that uses the public to do the policing for them. They achieve this by using patent markings on their products, for example "Pat." followed by the number of the patent. With this mark on the product, patent owners hope the public will police the marketplace and inform them if they suspect any patent infringement. If the patent owner confirms that an infringement on his or her patent has taken place, the first course of action is usually litigation to collect the damages and most importantly to send a message to the public and mostly to those who had intentions of infringing on the patent to keep off. Another channel of action open to the patent owner is through an independent arbitrator to obtain some compensation from the infringer.

6.5.1.3   Trademark Infringement

To prove infringement of a trademark, one must prove beyond doubt that the infringer's action was likely to confuse the public. Because of this, it is very difficult to prove trademark infringement. If the owner of the trademark can successfully prove and convince the courts that the infringer's mark has or is likely to cause confusion, then the infringer may be asked to pay any or a combination of the following: monetary awards based on the profits he or she made on the product displaying the mark, losses the owner supposedly incurred due to the infringement, and/or punitive damages and legal fees.

6.5.2   The First Sale Doctrine

A copyright owner under the first sale doctrine has the right to distribute copies of copyrighted materials by means of sale, transfer of ownership, rental, release, or by any other means. In the United States, under the first sale doctrine section 109(a) of the Copyright Act, artists, authors, inventors or discoverers can control subsequent use of their works through a lease or license. Anybody else who uses that work without either a lease or license is an infringer.

6.5.3   The Fair Use Doctrine

The fair use doctrine establishes a bridge between the protection of rights of artists, authors, inventors, or discoverers to benefit from their works and the basic rights of the community to gain from each member's contributions for the betterment of all and the upholding of the principle of economic competition. The use of copyrighted material is considered fair if it does not exploit the commercial value of the work.

There are four ways to judge whether the use of an invention, discovery, or work is fair or not. We list them here and discuss them in depth in Chapter 11:

1. The purpose of use, commercial or educational
2. Nature of use
3. Percentage of use
4. The effect of use on the commercial value of the invention, discovery, or works

The fair use doctrine has also given rise to conflicts between the separation of free speech and copyrights. According to Strong [4], a "citizen may be free to speak, but he is not entitled to speak his mind in the same words as his neighbor. He is free to speak the idea if you will, but not the expression." There are so many exceptions and inclusions under the fair use doctrine that it is difficult to be sure what is fair use unless one talks to a copyright lawyer or other experts knowledgeable in copyright law. The rule of thumb advocated by many copyright lawyers is that any time you have to copy any part of a copyrighted work outside personal educational use, even in the case of just one copy, talk to somebody who knows the law.

6.6   Protection of Ownership Rights

In Sections 6.3 and 6.5 we discussed the intellectual property rights' instruments of protection and how they can be infringed upon. In this section we look at how an owner of these property rights can use these instruments. We approach this by discussing the domain, source and types, duration, and the strategies of protection.

6.6.1   Domain of Protection

During our discussion of intellectual property rights, we defined the domain as the set of all different rights enjoyed by the owner of a manifested idea. Within this domain, there are subsets of rights enjoyed by the owner, depending on the manifestation of the idea. These subsets are protected by the body of laws discussed in Section 6.3, namely, copyright, patent, trademarks, and trade secret laws. Under each of these subsets, different rights are protectable as shown here:

1. *Copyrights*: Copyright laws protect all rights embodied within the copyrighted work by the copyright act of the particular country, including the right to use, transform, sale, copy, and modify.
2. *Patents*: Patent laws protect all rights embodied in the particular country's patent law.
3. *Trademarks*: Trademark laws protect all rights in the different trademark statutes depending on the state and country.
4. *Trade secrets*: Trade secret statues and laws protect all rights within the different states, local authority, and country's statutes.

Anything else outside of these sets, except the various laws that protect personal identity, should be in the public domain and, therefore, is unprotectable.

6.6.2 Source and Types of Protection

Because intellectual crimes have become global with the growing technological advances, there has been a realization in countries that there must be protection of national interests. Thus, a number of national and global organizations have been put in place and national Acts and international treaties signed to fight these crimes. In the United States, intellectual property rights are protected by the copyright and patent laws are protected by the federal courts because they are protected by the Constitution. Other intellectual property laws in United States include:

- The Antipiracy Act of 1976
- The Communication Act of 1984 The No Electronic Theft Act (NET Act)
- The Digital Millennium Copyright Act (DMCA)
- The Economic Espionage Act of 1996
- Money Laundering Act of 1956

These and a number of state statutes or local ordinances protect the IPR. But because neither federal nor state protection is extended outside US borders, different organizations have over the years been set up to fight these crimes. Among these are:

- The World Trade Organization (WTO)
- Interpol
- The Universal Copyright Convention (UCC)
- Berne Convention
- The Trade-Related Aspects of Intellectual Property Rights (TRIPPS)
- The World Intellectual Property Organization (WIPO)

Remember that although intellectual property rights are protected by a body of laws, the burden of policing, detection, and prosecution in any country is squarely on the shoulders of the owner of the specific intellectual property rights protected.

6.6.3 Duration of Protection

As we saw in Section 6.3, the period during which intellectual property is protected depends on a number of factors, including the body of laws protecting your rights and your geographical region.

6.6.4 Strategies of Protection

The burden of safeguarding the intellectual property rights of an individual is with that very person owning the work. It is the duty of individual owners of copyrights, patents, trade secrets, and trademarks to devise strategies to safeguard these rights.

Various methods have been used by individuals and companies who hold these rights to defend themselves. Large companies and individuals have been known to use methods ranging from spying on competitors and suspected infringers using private undercover operatives to collaborating with government officials to check on imports and exports. Some companies call in their respective governments when they suspect foreign infringements. When governments step in, they negotiate joint policing within the respective countries and sign treaties to protect these rights. For example, the US government has negotiated with and sometimes pressured foreign governments on behalf of US-based companies to observe the intellectual property rights of US technology companies after these companies suspected infringement by individuals and companies in these countries.

Within the United States, some corporations, especially software companies and computer chip manufacturers, have started using local law enforcement agencies to raid suspected infringers both in the United States and in other countries. Another approach used by private companies is a blitz of publicity about suspected countries and counterfeit products. Education campaigns via the mass media are also being used as a viable and effective protection strategy.

6.7 Protecting Computer Software Under the IP

We know that algorithms and ideas are not classified as intellectual property and, therefore, are not in any way protected. Ideas and algorithms belong to everybody, and no one can put a claim on them. Software, although it comes out of and strictly follows an algorithm, is not considered an algorithm but rather a manifestation, an expression of that algorithm. Many people may have many different ways of expressing, and, therefore, representing the same algorithm and hence have different programs that are considered clear intellectual property and are, therefore, protectable. But for computer software, there are no guidelines one can use to claim that because software is considered a derivation of an algorithm, it is, therefore, protectable. Computer products, in particular computer software, are more elusive and thus have been presenting many problems for those seeking protection under intellectual property rights law. The difficulty with software protection comes from the difficulty in categorizing it. As we said earlier, software can be a product, a service, or a mixture of both.

6.7.1 Software Piracy

Discussing the intellectual property rights (IPR) one cannot fail to think about the modern wonder of technology, the computer software, and its relationship with IPR. The biggest problem concerning computer software and IPR is software piracy. Generally speaking, we can define software piracy as the act of copying, distributing, or using proprietary software belonging to somebody else who bought it. This act is and has been illegal ever since software started being protected by law after software manufacturers started filing for patents and copyrights for their products and creations. However, this has not always been the case. In the early days computers, mainly mainframe, came with software preloaded. There were few computers and few users, nobody cared about the software the least understood let alone knowing how to use it and when to use it. With the miniaturization and widespread use of computers together with the high costs of production and purchase costs of software, this changed. A demand for software was created that lead to the piracy problems. We will come around to this issue when we discuss the transnational software issues in the next section.

The issue of software piracy is a complex one. There are several other issues that complicate software piracy. Some people use illegal software without knowing that the copies they have are illegal. Others use it with the full knowledge that the copies they are using are illegal but they go ahead anyway. Others are confused by the software terminology that includes freeware, shareware, and commercial software. Yet others, especially those in educational institutions are confused by the IPR principle of fair use. They cannot tell how much is fair. There is also a large percentage of illegal software users who do it purposely to get even with software manufacturers who frequently upgrade software versions making older versions of the product obsolete. We will discuss these and other issues in the coming section.

Is there a solution to this problem? Yes and no. Yes in that software companies and governments are working together in efforts to eliminate or downgrade the problem.

6.7.2 Protection of Software Under Copyright Laws

Computer software, along with its documentation can be protected under the copyright laws. According to Section 101 of the 1980 US Copyright Amendment, a computer program is defined as "a set of statements or instructions to be used directly or indirectly in a computer in order to bring about a certain result" [9]. This automatically implies that such a set of instructions or statements is a written creative work by someone, hence a literary work. Therefore, copyright laws that protect creative works also protect computer programs including technical manuals and documentation. The developer of a program thus has protective rights to authorize others of his or her choice to reproduce the format of the program en masse any time, to update and upgrade the program and distribute it for free, or to sell or transfer ownership. The copyright laws in this case protect the source code, the object code, and the executable codes – including the manuals and documentation – from illegal copying and piracy.

Although the developer has such rights, there are limitations or exceptions in some instances. For example, a buyer of such a program has some protected rights also. The buyer has the right to make another copy as a backup, provided that a copy is not used on another machine. Software registration for copyright, however, does not stop a software developer's worries because by registering software, the developer is opening up the secrets of the whole project as part of the requirements of the copyright issuance. According to Neitzke, there are two roadblocks in copyright registration in some countries:

1. Some courts have taken the position that copyright registration precludes maintaining software as a trade secret.
2. In some countries registration requires submitting at least the first and last 25 pages of the program for public inspection.

So before a developer goes ahead with a copyright application he or she should weigh the pros and cons of copyright protection.

6.7.3   Protection of Software Under Patent Laws

In Section 6.3.2 we defined a patent as the protection of the manifestation of an idea on condition that the patent owner discloses the methodology for the manifestation and workings of the product from the idea. Unlike the copyright laws, however, patents protect the processing of the idea; they also protect the implementation of the idea as a machine, a manufacturing process, or a composition of matter or materials. Under these conditions, computer hardware components, by their very nature, are protected under the patent laws. Software also may be protected under the patent laws under certain circumstances. Under these conditions, how can software be protected?

This is a difficult question, and we must answer it first by explaining that patent issues for computer programs are not yet settled. There are various reasons for the debate, among which are the following:

1. The requirement of the patent system for total disclosure of all information pertaining to the application of the patent is still a big issue. Given that the patent

protection lasts for 17 years and 2-year-old software is as old as software can get and still be really viable, requiring developers to disclose the secrets of their software before the 17-year deadline opens them up to stiff competition and better variations of the applicant's software format.
2. Most of the computer programs on the market are simple one-person ventures. Such persons, many of them independent-minded individuals, may not support yet let alone be able to afford the expense of the patent process application.
3. It has been and it is still very difficult, as we saw earlier in this section, to prove to courts and patent offices that algorithms are processes and therefore a form of manifestation of an idea and not mere mental gymnastics that any human being can do and, therefore, not patentable because mental steps and mathematical formulas are not patentable items.

Although computer programs are not suited for patent protection, there have been successful applications that have received patents. For specific examples of some of these cases, see Gervaise Davis's book Software Protection [5].

6.7.4 Protection of Software Under Trademarks

In Section 6.3.4 we defined a trademark as a symbol or mark with financial value that helps customers connect to the product. The main purpose of a trademark is to make the product stand out against the competitors. All hardware companies and a few software ones like Microsoft have their trademark protected under the trademark laws and statutes. But how is a mark or symbol be used to protect computer programs?

The protection of computer programs by trademarks is achieved through self-realization by the infringer that it is not easy to copy, change, or redistribute copies of well-known software works. For example, it is not easy to make copies of Windows 9X, NT or any other Windows product, and resell them, although there have been instances of this. So for big-name software developers, this realization by would-be infringers works far better than law enforcement. But the trick does not work all the time, especially in countries where this sort of realization does not have as much appeal because of lack of publicity of the products. Apart from these measures software developers do include their symbols and marks within the product so that during use, the symbols and marks are displayed automatically. However, there are no effective global trademark laws to protect computer programs.

6.7.5 Protection of Software Under Trade Secrets

So far we have defined a trade secret as information one has about a manifestation of an idea and that no one should disclose or use for the benefit of themselves or a competitor. As pointed out in Section 6.3.3, there are basic laws to protect trade secrets. How do these laws help protect computer products, especially software?

The manifestation of an idea into a computer program usually starts with the blueprint and flowchart, as we saw earlier. This then goes through the remaining stages of object code and executable code. One's knowledge of the process anywhere during these stages forms a trade secret and should not be revealed for personal gain or to a competitor.

It is generally known to computer programmers and software developers, as it is known to all hardware engineers, that once the blueprint and flowchart of a computer program is known, it is easy to develop a program. It is, therefore, of the utmost importance that at the early software development stages, the blueprint and flowchart not be known outside design circles. Typically the trade secret laws require an infringer, if caught, to stop, return the material under dispute to the rightful owner, and pay damages. But there are difficult cases, such as when former employees leave their employers without written material but with years of acquired know-how of product development. Here the law is difficult to apply. Some companies make the employees sign nondisclosure contracts for a specific number of years after leaving the company. This works to some extent, but it is very difficult to enforce except in high-profile and rich companies.

6.8 Transnational Issues and Intellectual Property

A number of studies concerning the international IP system show that there is an extensive and growing number of losses being incurred by businesses in the developed world as a result of nonenforcement of IP laws in the developing world. The developed world is charging that the lack of IP legislation in some development countries and the absence of enforcement in others are amounting to sanctioning pirates and leading to losses amounting to tens of billions of dollars worth of goods of multinational corporations every year. Developing countries, however, are not amused with the charges lobbed on them. They argue that:

- The IP system, if instated in full in their countries, results in significant social costs on that country; this may include developing the cost of acquiring and maintaining the IP rights and defending those rights whenever there are international legal disputes.
- Country memberships in the present IP system are costly and exacerbate the costs of enforcement.
- Loosely enforcing the IP laws will speed their industrialization and development by enabling them to copy state-of-the-art technologies.
- The IP protection is not as profitable as was toted by developed countries. There is evidence that the innovation for developing countries is not visible. For example the introduction or strengthening of patent protection for pharmaceutical products has not increased national or foreign direct investment, production or R&D in developing countries. On the other hand, the Indian pharmaceutical

industry became a global producer of active ingredients and medicines in the absence of patents on such products, which was only introduced in January 2005, at the expiry of the transitional period allowed by the TRIPS Agreement [10].

• The industrialized world, when in the process of development, did not depend on the patent system but rather the lack of the IP system which promoted innovation.

So the developing world is reluctant to accept the IP system wholesale without concessions unless the industrialized countries guarantee them greater access to their markets for their goods and agricultural products. There other issues pertinent to the IP system but we will not go into those here.

Discussion Issues:

1. Do you think the developing world has relevant issues to their development?
2. Is the developing world being misled by a few powerful countries within their ranks?
3. What kind of concessions should the developed world make?
4. Does this represent the worst of in world politics?

Exercises

1. Discuss the problems faced by software developers trying to apply for protection under trade secret statutes.
2. Why is it difficult to apply patent laws to software?
3. Why is it possible to apply patent law to software?
4. Is it possible to trademark software?
5. Discuss the ethical and legal issues surrounding software ownership.
6. There is a move to do away with the current copyright law. Why?
7. Why is the copyright law, in its present form, considered to be unenforceable?
8. What changes would you suggest in the current copyright laws to make it enforceable in cyberspace?
9. Has the Internet made software protection easier or more difficult? Why or why not?
10. There is a movement (that includes hackers) that is advocating for free software! Discuss the merits of this idea, if any.
11. Because of income disparities between north and south, and haves and have-nots, fair pricing of computer products is impossible. Discuss.
12. Most copyright violations are found in developing, usually, poor countries. Why?
13. Does the high price of software marketing in developing countries justify the high rate of software piracy in those countries? Why?
14. What do you think is the cause of the rising cost of software?
15. Is globalization a means through which the developed, usually northern countries, will enforce the copyright laws?

References

1. Johnson, Deborah G. Computer Ethics (2nd ed.). Englewood Cliffs, NJ: Prentice Hall, 1994.
2. Prince, Jim. "Negligence: Liability for Defective Software." Oklahoma Law Review 33, 1980, pp. 848–855.
3. Gow, Gordon A. "Copyright Reform in Canada: Domestic Cultural Policy Objectives and the Challenge of Technological Convergence" http://www.ucalgary.ca/~gagow/cpyrght.html

4. Strong, William E. The Copyright Book: A Practical Guide (2nd ed.). Boston: MIT Press, 1984.
5. Davis, Gervaise G. Software Protection. New York: Van Nostrand Reinhold, 1985.
6. Neitzke, Frederick, W. A Software Primer. New York: Van Nostrand Reinhold, 1984.
7. "Personal identity theft on the rise" USA Today, Tech Report. 09/14/00.
8. Burge, David A. Patent and Trademarks: Tactics and Practice (2nd ed.). New York: Wiley, 1984.
9. Scott, Micheal D. Computer Law. New York: Wiley, 1984.
10. Andrew Glass. "Cybersquatters frustrate political candidate", Cox News Service, Sept. 7, 1999.
11. Hedi Nasheri. "Addressing Global Scope of Intellectual Property Law". http://www.ncjrs.gov/pdffiles1/nij/grants/208384.pdf

Further Readings

Davis, Randall. "A New View of Intellectual Property and Software." Communication of the ACM 39(3), 1992, pp. 21–30.
Oz, Effy. "Protecting Software as Intellectual Property." In Ethics for the Information Age. Barr Ridge, IL: Business and Education Technologies, 1994, pp. 273–285.
Samuelson, Pamela. "Information and Property." Catholic Review 38, 1989, pp. 365–410.
——"Is Information Property?" Communication of the ACM 34(10), 1991, pp. 15–18.
——"Copyright Law and Electronic Compilations of Data." Communication of the ACM 35(2), 1992, pp. 27–32.
——"Regulation of Technologies to Protect Copyrighted Works." Communication of the ACM 39(7), 1992, pp. 17–22.
Suapper, John. "Intellectual Property Protection for Computer Software." In Deborah Johnson and Helen Nissenbaum (eds.), Computer Ethics and Social Values. Englewood Cliffs, NJ: Prentice Hall, 1995, pp. 181–190.

Chapter 7
Social Context of Computing

Learning Objectives

After reading this chapter, the reader should be able to:

1. Interpret the social context of a particular software/hardware implementation.
2. Identify assumptions and values embedded in a particular computer product design including those of a cultural nature.
3. Evaluate a particular computing tool implementation through the use of empirical data.
4. Describe positive and negative ways in which computing alters the modes of interaction between people.
5. Explain why computing/network access is restricted in some countries.
6. Learn the impact of the digital divide.
7. Understand how income, geography, race, and culture influence access to information technology and technology in general.
8. Analyze the role and risks of computing in the implementation of public policy and government.
9. Articulate the impact of the input deficit from diverse populations in the computing profession.

Scenario 5
Electronic Surveillance and the Bodyguard

> *Jon Kiggwe is a young aggressive entrepreneur, with a bright future. With several businesses doing well and a few start-ups with promising financial status, Jon is on his way to making a million dollars before his 25th birthday. Jon's business meetings take him into tough neighborhoods. So, for him to feel secure, Jon uses a team of professional security bodyguards to shadow him almost 24 h a day.*
>
> *In his big 10 million dollar home, Jon receives a stream of guests, including both business associates and friends. His bodyguards, besides keeping an eye on him, also see to the orderly arrival and departure of the guests. Because of this, the bodyguards keep a permanent office and sleeping quarters at Jon's mansion.*
>
> *Without informing them, Jon installed video recording and listening gadgets in the guards' office and sleeping quarters to record their every conversation and movement. He feels safe that way!*

Discussion Questions

1. *Is Jon violating any law?*
2. *Do the bodyguards have any right to privacy on Jon's premises?*
3. *Does Jon have a right to know what the bodyguards are doing in his house?*

7.1   Introduction

In the last 20 years or so, we have witnessed an invasion of computers and computer-related equipment in workplaces, homes, and schools. The advent of the Internet, wireless communication, and miniature computer technology has considerably expanded this invasion into planes, trains, and automobiles. The widespread use of computers and computer technology in its present form has also resulted in a shift in computer usage. The computer started as a utilitarian tool, but has now also been embraced as a social tool. Probably due to the popularity of the Internet, both young and old have found solace in the computer at home. Playing this double role as a utility and an entertainment tool, the computer has become an integral part of our social fabric.

However, in the meantime, two worlds have been created for humanity: the unreal world of entertainment and a real computer technology-driven world, which augments our familiar environment and makes our daily activities easier and more enjoyable. This in turn has led to an influx of computer technology into the workplace, the schools, and the home. Indeed, the home has turned into a hub of technology. No one knows, as yet, the social, psychological, and intellectual implications that may result from this. Predictions abound that this will enhance our intelligence and improve our performance at whatever we do. This belief alone has been a driving force for the computerization of schools and homes, with parents hoping to produce young geniuses.

These beliefs about the value of technology, whether supported by scientific research or not, are not new. Ever since the beginning of the industrial age when technology started entering the workplace and homes, the aim has been to utilize it and help make us wiser and more productive. It is, therefore, no wonder that as technology has developed, progress and fundamental changes have been taking place almost daily. Our focus in this chapter is on both the social and ethical effects of computer technology on people, whether we are at home, school, or work. We will focus on the "digital divide," the workplace, the monitoring of employees, and the well-being of employees.

7.2   The Digital Divide

The technological inequalities among peoples in one country and between countries, commonly known as the digital divide, arose from the landmark 1994 US Commerce Department's National Telecommunications and Information Administration (NTIA) report, "Falling Through the Net", commonly referred to as NTIA I. The NTIA I report used the Information and Communication Technologies (ICT) *access* indicator, one of the many digital divide indicators, to highlight sectors of the US population that were technologically deprived. Since then, the digital divide debate has been raging, centered on a number of key critical issues including:

- Whether there is such a thing as a digital divide
- Indicators that should be used to measure such a divide if it exists and
- The best ways to close such a divide

Much of the debate is the result of a lack of understanding about the digital divide—its origins, inputs, and responses to inputs. In general, the study of the digital divide involves the study of the impact of communication technologies such as radio, television, the press, post offices, fixed and cellular telephones, fax machines, airports, computers, and connectivity to the Internet on society's social, economic, political, and cultural institutions.

While all these are means of modern communication, some are not actually digital; we will focus on a few more modern communication technologies such as telephones, personal computers, and connectivity to the Internet. Indeed, NTIA I itself focused on these three media. Let us focus on five indicators of the digital divide, namely, access, technology, humanware (human capacity), infrastructure, and enabling environment.

7.2.1 Access

Access is a crucial component in the digital divide. It involves obstacles that exist even if all the other remaining indicators are in place. Such obstacles may include, but are not limited to, costs involved in acquiring the technologies, availability of free or low-cost facilities in the neighborhood, the ability to travel to places where there are low-cost access points such as libraries and community centers, and having the capacity needed to utilize the technologies. These obstacles can broadly be grouped into five categories: geography, income, ethnicity, age, and education.

7.2.1.1 Geography

According to the UN Human Development Report 2000, there is a big digital divide between the rich industrialized countries of the northern hemisphere and the poor, less industrialized countries in the southern hemisphere. The poor, developing countries, geographically in the southern hemisphere and mostly in the southern axis of development, are deprived of the access to information in all the eight information access categories surveyed in the UN Development reports from the 1994 to 1998 as shown in Tables 7.1 and 7.2 below [2]. Data from both tables show that people in the developed world enjoyed increased percentages of every category of information access, including computer ownership, Internet connections, and fixed telephone lines, between 1994 and 1998. However, the corresponding ratios are very low for all developing countries and almost nonexistent in some categories in the least developed countries.

For more modern communication technologies such as computers and Internet access, the ratios and, therefore, the gaps, are even more daunting. For example,

Table 7.1 UN Human Development Report on distribution of communication technologies (1994)

HDI Rank	Television (per 1,000 people) 1995	Main telephone lines (per 1,000 people) 1995	Public pay phones (per 1,000 people) 1995	International phone calls (minutes per person) 1995	Fax machines (per 1,000 people) 1995	Cellular phone subscribers (per 1,000 people) 1995	Internet users (per 1,000 people) 1995	Personal computers (per 1,000 people) 1995
Industrial countries	523.6	413.5	3.7	41.6	23.2	61.1	17.9	156.3
All developing countries	145.3	38.7	0.7	2.8	–	3.6	0.5	6.5
Least developed countries	32.4	3.2	(•)	0.5	0.1	–	–	–

Table 7.2 UN Human Development Report on distribution of communication technologies (1998)

HDI Rank	Television (per 1,000 people) 1995	Main telephone lines (per 1,000 people) 1995	Public pay phones (per 1,000 people) 1995	International phone calls (minutes per person) 1995	Fax machines (per 1,000 people) 1995	Cellular phone subscribers (per 1,000 people) 1995	Internet users (per 1,000 people) 1995	Personal computers (per 1,000 people) 1995
OECD countries	594	490	4.9	–	–	223	37.86	255
All developing countries	162	58	1.3	–	–	18	0.26	–
Least developed countries	29	4	(•)	0.5	0.1	–	–	–

88% of the world's 143 million Internet users are in about one or two dozen wealthy countries [3]. Currently the developing world has just about 4% of the connections while the developed world is 40% cyber connected [4]. Yet almost 90% of the world's population still lives in the developing world. Geographical disparities are not only between countries but also within countries. In the United States, one of the countries enjoying high access percentages, people in rural areas and inner cities are far less likely to have computers and even far less likely to have Internet connections. The statistics in the tables and figures below tell the story. According to the NTIA Technical Report 2000 (NTIA 2000) survey of US households with a computer and online access in Table 7.3, if one lived in a suburb, one was more likely to own a computer and have an online access to information than somebody in a rural area or in an inner city [5].

7.2.1.2 Income

The NTIA 2000 data in Table 7.4 and the UCLA Internet Report [6], Table 7.5, indicate that income greatly affects one's ability to have access to ICT As Table 7.4 shows, those with incomes of $75,000 and above were four times more likely to have online and computer access at 86.3% computer access and 77.7% online access as compared to 19.2% computer access and 12.7% online access for those earning $15,000 or less. In a similar manner, the UCLA Internet Report in Table 7.5 shows that those earning $50,000 or more were twice as likely to have an Internet connection than those earning $15,000 or less.

Table 7.3 Percentage of US computer households with a computer and online access by region

	Rural (%)	Suburb (%)	Central city (%)
Online access	38.9	42.3	37.7
Computer access	50.4	51.5	43.7

Table 7.4 US households with a computer and online access by income

Groups	Computer access	Online access
Under $15,000	19.2	12.7
15,000–24,999	30.1	21.3
25,000–34,999	44.6	34.0
35,000–49,999	58.6	46.1
50,000–74,999	73.2	60.9
75,000+	86.3	77.7

Table 7.5 Internet users based on income (UCLA Report)

Income	$0–$14,999	$15,000–$49,999	$50,000–$99,999	$100,000–$149,999	$150,000+
Percentages	41.0%	61.5%	81.6%	88.6%	87.3%

Table 7.6 Global ICT (Information Communications Technologies) access based on income

	Fixed main telephone hosts	Cellular telephone	Television	Personal computers	Internet
High income	470	569	674	315	48.18
Low income	6	36	145		0.02

Table 7.7 US households with computer and online access by race/origin

Category	Computer access	Online access
White non-Hispanics	55.7	46.1
Black non-Hispanic	32.6	23.5
Asian American and Pacific Islanders	65.6	56.8
Hispanic	33.7	23.6

Figures from the Media Metrix June 2000 survey also show similar US household income patterns. The report shows that of those households earning less that $25,000, while they form 32.1% of the US population, only 9.7% are online. The largest income group active online according to the report earns between $40 K and $60 K per year, with a 27.3% online share, while those earning, $100k+, the highest earning bracket, have 18% online share [7].

Income data from the latest UN Development Report shown in Table 7.6 above confirm the US data in Table 7.4. Globally, irrespective of the geographical locale, people with high incomes have a higher percentage of ICT access than those with low incomes. For example, Table 7.6, comparing people with high income to those of low income, shows an access ratio of 569 to 36 fixed telephones, 265 to 8 cellular phones, 674 to 145 televisions, 315 to almost negligible personal computers, and 48.18 to 0.02 Internet connections per 1,000 people in 1998.

7.2.1.3 Ethnicity

According to NTIA 2000, one's ethnicity has a great influence on ICT access. For example, in the United States, blacks and Hispanics, the two main US minority groups, are twice as likely as their white counterparts not to have a computer and access to the Internet (see Table 7.7).

Although there has been no comprehensive study of global ICT access based on ethnicity and race, one can make a generalization based on the US NTIA studies that there are significant gaps in ICT access among ethnic groups both within and among countries.

7.2.1.4 Age

There is a myth that young people use computers and the Internet far more than any other age group. There is also conventional wisdom that young people under age 18 do more surfing of the Internet than any other age group. However, contrary to this

Table 7.8 US households with computer and online access by age

Category	%
Under 8	15.3
9–17 years	53.4
18–24 years	56.5
25–49 years	55.4
50+ years	29.8

Table 7.9 Age and internet usage (UCLA report)

Age group	12–15	16–18	19–24	25–35	36–45	46–55	56–65	65+
Average hours per week	5.6	7.6	9.7	11.3	9.4	10.3	8.5	6.8

wisdom, there is consistent data from NTIA 2000 and the UCLA Internet Report showing that the highest usage of computers and the Internet is among people between the ages of 18 and 49. NTIA 2000 (in Table 7.8) and correspondingly the UCLA Internet Report (Table 7.9) both show that older people and those under ten use computers and online access far less than any other age group. Also, the latest figures from Media Metrix show similar global patterns with a bell-curve-shaped pattern of usage peaking between 18 and 54 years [7].

7.2.1.5 Education

Ever since the NTIA I report showed that the higher the education level one achieves, the more likely one is to use a computer and, therefore, the Internet, study after study has shown the same thing. Data from NTIA 2000 and the UCLA Internet Report, in Tables 7.10 and 7.11, show the same trend. For example, the very highly educated with advanced degrees in both NTIA 2000 and the latest UCLA Internet Report, have 69.9% and 86% Internet usage, respectively, compared to 11.7% and 31% usage, respectively, for those with less than a high school diploma.

Although these figures are based on the US population only, there are strikingly similar patterns in other developed and developing countries.

7.2.2 Technology

The computer-driven technological revolution has brought the countries of the world closer together. In their study of the digital divide, Rodriquez and Wilson observed that all developing countries, including the poorest, are improving their access to the use of ICT [1]. But as Tables 7.1 and 7.2 from the U.N. Development Reports (1994 and 1998) show, industrialized countries grew between 1994 and

Table 7.10 US households with computer
and online access by education

Category	Computer%	Online%
Elementary	18.2	11.7
High school diploma	39.6	29.9
Some college	60.3	49.0
College diploma	74.0	64.0
Postgraduate	79.0	69.9

Table 7.11 Internet use and education (UCLA Report)

Education level attained	Less than high school	High school graduate	Some college	College graduate	Advanced degree
Percent using Internet	31.2%	53.1%	70.2%	86.3%	86.3%

1998 from 523 to 594 per 1,000 people, and correspondingly the least developed countries grew from 32 to 29 television sets; 413 to 498, against 3.2 to 4 fixed telephones; 61 to 223, against less than zero to one cellular phones; 156 to 255, against less than zero to still less than zero computers; and from 17.9 to 37.8, against less than zero to still less than zero Internet connections per 1,000 people.

The gap is even larger for the newer technologies. Technologies such as faxes, cellular phones, computers, and Internet connections registered almost zero growth per 1,000 people in developing countries compared to their counterparts in the developed countries during the same period.

This state of affairs is the result of a lack of broad-based technological skills and know-how. The acquisition of technological skills and, therefore, the development of a good technological base, depends a great deal on relevant inputs that include investment capital, infrastructure, and humanware (human capacity). However, the situation with the technology inputs and outputs is no better either. New technological innovations require huge amounts of money to be invested in research and development. Unfortunately not enough capital investment is done in developing countries. According to the UN Human Development Report 1999, while developed countries have 21% of the $(US) 21,000 billion GDP in 1999 invested, the least developed countries had 20% of the $(US) 143 billion GDP invested [8]. Because capital investment in technology is usually in form of hardware and software, let us focus on those here.

7.2.2.1 Hardware

Although there has been a steady increase in the number of computers, telephones, and other modern communication technologies in almost all countries of the world in the last couple of years, as noted by Rodriguez and Wilson, the quantity, quality, and maintenance of these technologies is still a big problem challenging the narrowing of the ICT digital divide. There is a serious regression in hardware acquisition and maintenance. Computer components for example, are being acquired, but they are being disposed of at probably the same rate as they are acquired. Uncertain and unreliable power supplies contribute to the shorter life spans of ICT products in developing countries; many of the unusable ICT products are so because they were probably hit by a power surge.

Replacement of the bad parts is hampered by the price of new ones. ICT parts are very expensive in a number of developing countries because either governments levy high tariffs on imports to raise local revenue, or they impose luxury taxes because they are classified as luxury items.

ICT products are also expensive because most outlet owners are not indigenous people; they are foreign investors who usually raise prices to cover their local and infrastructure expenses plus profits. In addition to that, like all equipment and software produced in developed countries and imported into developing countries, by the time such items arrive in the developing world, their prices have been inflated three to four times their original values.

7.2.2.2 Software

Along with the problems presented by hardware are the problems of software. For ICT equipment to be helpful, it must have good and relevant software. Countries that have seen benefits from ICT, like those in OECD, either produce their own software or they have enough financial capacity to source software with few problems. This is not the case in many developing countries. There is very limited humanware to have software locally produced. In addition, they do not have enough money to source the software from their northern counterparts where it is produced. Even if they have some money to buy software from developed countries, as we pointed out earlier, by the time software arrives in developing countries its list price is much higher. The end result, at least for the time being, is that most ICT software in developing countries comes with the bulk of the donated ICT equipment. But more often than not, the software shipped on donated company computers rarely meets the needs of the recipients. Consequently, they end up using a product that in most instances produces outputs that have very little value to them, irrespective of the inputs. In such a situation, that equipment ends up not benefiting the locals.

7.2.3 Humanware (Human Capacity)

In this section we want to look at the complex issues related to human capacity development. The availability and easy access to ICT does not always solve the digital divide problem. As Rodriguez and Wilson pointed out, it is only a partial solution to a complex problem. Even if we were to provide everyone on the globe with first class ICT equipment, the reality would remain that only a few would be able to maintain and gainfully use the provided technologies. This is likely to remain the case until there is a corresponding degree of technical capacity and knowledge acquired by the people intended to use the technologies so that they can maintain the equipment and derive value-laden outputs. The first problem is lack of human-ware in developing counties to maintain the equipment. There is a shortage of teachers, technicians, and institutes to train them. The next challenge is to ensure that people can gainfully use ICT to add value to local inputs. People will take ICT seriously when it meets and serves their own local needs. Human capacity develop-ment is a complex multifaceted endeavor consisting of many parts including [24]:

- Creating awareness of the potential for ICT to meet one's needs
- Creating, developing, and strengthening capacity to use information and ICT effectively, using local inputs
- Building capacity to produce and package information so that it adds value to local inputs
- Ensuring ongoing technical capacity development, and developing a format for knowledge and information sharing
- Preventing the local capacity from being drained to other, usually developed countries

The challenge, therefore, in tackling human capacity development is to deal with each of these issues so that the locals using ICT may find meaningful answers to their local problems. ICT capacity development should take into account equity, fairness, and cultural and other contextual factors at the local levels.

7.2.4   Infrastructure

As noted by many, the digital divide infrastructure is related to access in many ways. They both present obstacles to gaining access to ICT. For us, infrastructure will mean fixed communication structures. In those countries with good fixed com-munication structures like electricity, telephones, good roads, and airports, ICT development is a lot faster. Lack of such resources hinders the development of ICT. In his communication to the Digital Opportunity (DIGOPP) discussion list, Robert Krech, drawing from his experience in Nepal, noted the enormous difficulties in "the logistics of reaching people located in remote rural areas with limited or no access to formal educational systems, healthcare, portable water, electricity or jobs related to the new information economy" [9]. Krech was expressing the necessity or lack of good fixed communication structures that are crucial to the development of ICT.

The availability of these resources helps to speed up the development of ICT structures like telecenters. ICT access enablers such as personal computers, per-sonal assistants, Internet-enabled cellular phones, and other miniature Internet-enabled gizmos in developed countries and the urban areas of developing countries, together with civic centers in developed countries and telecenters in developing countries, have all been hailed in advancing global communication. But in order for them to work, there must be a basic communication infrastructure in place. So if digital communication is to be developed in the developing world, ICT-accessible points such as telecenters, civic centers and Internet or cyber cafes must be opened up where there are none and expanded where there are a few.

7.2.5 Enabling Environments

As Rodriguez and Wilson [1] noted, there are many countries with similar levels of per capita incomes and economic structures exhibiting widely varying ICT performances. There are no good explanations for this except for the existence, or lack thereof, of enabling environments. An ICT-enabling environment is an environment in which ICT can thrive. There are several things that can bring about such an environment, including politics, public policy, and management styles.

7.2.5.1 Politics

According to Rodriquez and Wilson, ICT thrives in a good political environment that ensures:

  (i) A climate of democratic rights and civil liberties conducive to ICT adaptation
 (ii) Respect for the rule of law and security of property rights
(iii) Investment in human capacity
 (iv) Low levels of government distortions

One sure way of creating such environments in the different political systems that make up the landscape of the developing world is for the two leading nongovernmental organizations, the G8 Dot Force and the Commonwealth Expert Group on Information Technology, and other development organizations working toward the elimination of the digital divide, to develop a policy that charges governments in individual countries with the task of creating the enabling environments for ICT to shrive. One approach is to develop a Leadership Mobilization Strategy (LMS) to target and educate first the top political leadership at all levels within and outside government about the benefits of ICT to the country's development. These officials must be made to understand the need for ICT and then articulate it to others. This is crucial to get leaders to mobilize people and bring ICT awareness to the general population. While politics is conducive to a good ICT environment, a great deal of ICT development also depends on good public policy and management styles.

7.2.5.2 Public Policy and Management Styles

Governments must put in place streamlined regulatory policies for the importation and licensing of ICT technologies. Laws must be enacted and enforced uniformly so that nongovernmental organizations (NGOs) and other organizations interested in investing in ICT economic activities do so with ease.

In many developing countries, there are currently ICT-related laws and policies on the books which are not enforced. Such policies must be updated where necessary and enforced strictly and fairly. New competitive policies such as the liberalization of the telecommunication and energy sectors must be developed and the sectors must be staffed with competent managers with appropriate expertise. These ICT regulatory policies need to be efficient, predictable, and easy to understand. Licensing bodies need to be efficient and staffed with professionals. In addition, there must be government support for taxing policies that grant favors like tax holidays to ICT equipment and investment firms. Finally, there must be transparency in government to create a moral bar for the rest of the country.

7.3   ICT in the Workplace

The automation of the workplace has been the most vigorously pursued concept since the industrial age. Despite the original fear that workplace automation would mean the end to human work, except in a few areas workplace automation has proceeded hand-in-hand with increases in employment numbers [10]. This is, of course, not to deny that automation has caused some human displacements in the workplace. But overall numbers are steady, and according to the International Labor Office report, the introduction of computers into offices did not bring about any significant dismissal of personnel, nor did it result in a decline in the general level of employers [10]. Among all the different technologies that have thus far entered the workplace, computer technology has entered at an astonishingly high rate of speed.

7.3.1   The Electronic Office

We can define an electronic office as a technology-augmented office with knowledgeable employees. The technology in the environment may include computers and computer-driven devices that help in interpersonal oral and electronic communication, distribution, and receipt of correspondence, telecommunication devices with text-processing and storage capabilities to enable the office staff to design, develop, edit, and store material electronically; and other office support equipment to streamline decision-making tasks. The evolution of the electronic office began with industrialization but took giant steps beginning in the 1950s with rapid advances in computer technology and telecommunications. Since then the workplace has been undergoing a rapid transformation of its own. Gone are notepads, typewriters, large cabinets filled with manila folders, the rotary telephone, and rotary fans. Computers have replaced most of the filing cabinets, the files, and typewriters. Electronic notepads, automatic answering systems, office intercoms, copiers, and fax machines have moved in. Living plants and air-conditioning have become standard. Increasingly, office job descriptions at all levels and in all professions are being transformed to incorporate computer and telecommunication skills.

Two factors have been and are still fueling the growth of the electronic office. The first is the increasing productivity of office employees, both clerical and professionals, to counter the rising costs of office operations, which according to Olson and Lucas [11] have been increasing faster than office employees' productivity. The second is the acquiring of technology necessary to handle the ever-increasing complexity and modernization of office communication and decision-making processes.

7.3.2   Office on Wheels and Wings

As electronic gadgetry has been invading the office and the overall workplace, workers have been leaving the office in droves, a few of them replaced by the new technology, others transplanted by it, but many for the experience of working outside their original office confines.

The advent of laptop computers, cellular phones, and personal digital assistants (PDAs) have accelerated the mobility of the office. Busy executives, white-collar workers, and, this time around, blue-collar workers, especially those in the service industry, can be seen in airports, hotel lobbies, restaurants, and aboard airplanes and in trains, keying in data and putting in a day's work as they would have done previously in their offices.

Mail and package service company drivers are also keying in their locales and speed, transmitting the data to the company computers so a package can be continuously traced from the time of departure to within minutes of the estimated time of arrival. Many companies are embracing this new office on the go. Among the industries that have found the edge in this phenomenon is the home service industry, which is utilizing the new office technology to improve services and of course increase business. Others include delivery services, home repair, and heating and air-conditioning services to keep workers on location and in the office in constant contact.

7.3.3   The Virtual Workplace

With the latest developments in telecommunication and computer technology the virtual workplace is home to an increasing type of employees who work very briefly in their corporate workplaces, are mostly on the road, and often telecommute using personal or company-provided equipment. This breed of worker is rarely in a fixed workplace, but nevertheless he or she performs a full day's work even if at the beach.

According to Snizek [12] the most important element of the virtual workplace is the use of computers and other telecommunication devices to link up employees and the massive worldwide databases of vital information and other human resources. As computer and telecommunication technologies improve and the bandwidth and computer miniaturization increase, this will not only lead to more workers opting for the virtual workplace but will also increase vital information flow into the company and corporate offices, which may lead to companies gaining a higher level of vital data, employee expertise, and experience from colleagues around the globe. The virtual workplace's increasing popularity is mainly due to recent changes in computer and telecommunication technology and organizational changes as a result of corporate downsizing and outsourcing. For example, during the dot.com boom, in order for corporations to keep the same level of overall effectiveness and efficiency and even to surpass it sometimes with fewer employees, companies encouraged virtual offices, and the trend is likely to continue [12].

There are other benefits of the virtual office in overhead savings and other costs. With virtual employees rarely in their offices, a number of other employees can share their office space and other office resources, thus saving millions of dollars in facilities, and equipment costs. The company may no longer need to have a large work force on a permanent full-time basis. Companies can now use a limited staff and seek out contract expertise on a case-by-case basis as the situation arises.

In addition to the transformation of traditional workers, the virtual office is also opening doors to a new group of workers such as the disabled, the home-bound, and the elderly who have traditionally been left out of the work force.

It is probably too early to talk about the long-term effects of the virtual office on both the employees and employer, but there are some difficulties already visible both in the employee and employer communities. Because most employee time is spent outside the physical office, employees rarely meet face to face, so there is a lack of collegiality and of community spirit. Also, since most employees, especially experts, are not full-time employees of the corporation, there is a lack of belonging that affects employees and eventually undercuts their loyalty and hence their effectiveness. A company built on a transient work force lacks the moral force and legitimacy in the community in which its operations are based.

7.3.4 The Home Worker: A Growing Concept of Telecommuters

As workers have changed their work habits from working 40 h a week in the workplace environment to sharing those 40 h between being at the workplace and commuting to the workplace, the 9-to-5 time schedule for the majority of workers has started to crumble, with many moving their work locales outside of the normal confines of time and space. Studies show that the largest number of workers doing their work outside their primary place of work do it in their homes. According to figures reported by Kraut [13], the percentage of home office workers or telecommuters in the total US work force by 1960 was 3%, but numbers have been on the rise ever since. Snizek [12], quoting a US Bureau of Statistics report, puts the percentage of the US total work force working at least 6–8 h per week telecommuting at 30% as of 1995. This is a significant rise and can be attributed to advances in office technology and the plummeting of prices for computers and telecommunication devices, the diminishing sizes of communication devices, and the increase in speed and bandwidth of communication devices. The US National Association of Home Businesses reported that the number of home-based workers increased more than seven times between 1984 and 1994. The association report said that there were 45 million telecommuters in 1994 compared to six million in 1984, a 750% increase [12].

As office technology improves, a large number of workers outside the self-employed professions of artists, writers, and craftspeople are potentially able to work at home. The advances in technology are making many types of jobs that used to require a worker to stay in an office environment more mobile. This is being helped further by the shift in global economies from manufacturing-based to information-based. For example, Porat [14] reports that by 1975 the US economy had about 50% of the work force engaged in information-related work, and since then this has changed a great deal.

7.3.4.1 Categories of Telecommuters

There are three categories of telecommuters. The first category of telecommuters consists of workers who use their homes as an adjunct to their conventional office jobs. These workers are usually in white-collar jobs in areas such as management, research, market studies, and education. They are highly motivated. For them, occasional work-at-home is a flexible alternative used most in cases of critical work that can best be done at home to avoid the office environment. Kraut [13], reporting on a study he did in 1983 and 1984 at AT&T Bell Laboratories, states that these workers put in a full day's work at the conventional office in addition to taking some of their office work home. They additionally work at home on weekends and in the evenings.

The second category of telecommuters consists of workers who use their homes as the base for their businesses. The majority of these are in telemarketing, small start-up companies, and human services such as child care and elderly care. Unlike the first category, these individuals are less educated and less likely to use a fully equipped electronic home office. Others in this category are the dispatchers in the home service industry. They are more likely to use a telephone and a computer without much data transmission.

The third category of telecommuters consists of those who have full-time jobs with large companies, but prefer through their own initiative to work from home. This category includes computer programmers, sales specialists, editors, writers, and those whose work depends on a high degree of creativity such as artists, musicians, and composers. This third category is a mixed bag of highly educated, independent, and specialized workers, and those who are not so highly educated but very talented and skilled.

As computers and telecommunication technology become cheaper and people get more access to smaller more portable computers and other communication devices become more readily available, the home is becoming more and more a place of refuge for conventional office workers. Although it is not possible to predict the future direction of the home office, it is likely that if the technology that has caused the increase in the home office keeps on track, the number of telecommuters is likely to continue growing, with the majority of workers remaining in home offices for economic benefits and convenience.

7.3.4.2 Company Role in Telecommuting

To many, the home office is a revisit to the cottage industry of the fifteenth through eighteenth centuries in Europe: Raw materials were dropped off at the workers' cottages and finished products later picked up for market. Ever since industrialization, factories and later companies have been using home workers. Thus, company experimentation with their employees telecommuting is not a new idea.

The home office has always been prompted by new advances in technology and by the need of businesses to become more productive with minimum expenditures. As the Internet and globalization open up new international competition and as new technologies make telecommuting more acceptable to employees, company-sponsored telecommuters will increase.

By the 1960s, according to Kraut [13], telecommuters accounted for 3.6% of the US work force, and a small portion of this was company sponsored. But by the late 1970s and early 1980s, big companies such as IBM and AT&T were deeply involved with telecommuting experiments. Kraut estimates that by 1983, IBM had over 8,000 employees telecommuting. These big companies and other smaller ones spent money in this experiment expecting a benefit in return. The experiments were also meant to provide information on the classification of work suitable for the home, to identify individual workers who could work at home, and to throw light on how workers were to be monitored as they worked from their homes.

Although no study has yet reported big monetary benefits for companies from these experiments, some studies on other related issues have provided some results. For example, on the issue of remote supervision, classification of jobs fit for telecommuting, and identifying individuals better suited for telecommuting, a study by Olson and Lucas [11] provided some partial answers. On the issue of classification of work, the study found that work with possible measurable milestones is most suited for telecommuting. On the issue of identifying individuals most suited to telecommute, the study found that people who usually need less supervision at the office and those who do volunteer work are the most suited to telecommute. As we see in Section 7.3.4.3, these conclusions are also influenced by the nature of the work, gender, age, and labor supply. The study also highlighted difficult issues such as the effect of telecommuting on the promotability of employees because visibility is key to promotion. There was also some light shed on the issue of pay. Telecommuters tend to be paid less because their pay is based on output, which makes output the real mechanism of monitoring telecommuters [11].

7.3.4.3 Effects and Benefits of Telecommuting

Whenever there is a change in the environment of workers, there is always bound to be some social, psychological, and financial effects on both employee and employer. If the effects are financial, they become benefits. However, if they are psychological, they become health issues; if they are social, they become organizational issues. In this section we concentrate on social and financial issues. We discuss psychological issues in Sections 7.5 and 7.6.

An employer–employee arranged home office is supposed to reap benefits for both parties. Let us start by qualifying our discussion to include only those telecommuters who are company employed, have traditional offices at companies' premises, and through mutual arrangements with their companies have decided to work from their homes. This group truly exemplifies the benefits, if there are any, for both the employer and the employee. Because these workers have a choice of either staying at the office or working from home, they can work only from their homes if they experience a benefit and the companies can only let them work from their homes if the companies expect a benefit from the arrangement. For those working at home with no choice but to work at home, like those in the majority in category 2, the benefits are already clear. Defining benefits for telecommuters is not easy because each participant in the arrangement perceives the benefits the way they would like them to be. For example, the company may see the benefit as savings on office space so that other workers can use the space, or as savings in office supplies, or a reduction in the likelihood of employee risks while on company premises. The employee may see benefits as spending more quality time with their loved ones at home, or spending less time in traffic commuting to and from work, or the flexibility and independence in decision making concerning the work the employee has to do. The value of benefits from this arrangement depends on individual circumstances as discussed by Kraut [13] and reported as follows:

1. *Gender*: Women have traditionally given care to children and the elderly, the two groups most homebound; women would therefore draw maximum benefits from telecommuting arrangements with their employees, if their primary objective for telecommuting is to take care of their families.
2. *Nature of work: managerial, clerical, sales, or service*: The nature and type of work one does also influences the kind of benefits one gets. For example, clerical work tends to be more supervision intensive than managerial and professional work. In these types of work where supervision is not as intensive, there is a high degree of latitude for one to make decisions. However, jobs that are supervision intensive are less likely to be moved into home environments. If such jobs are to be moved to a home environment, chances are that the company may not garner any benefits, but employees may benefit by getting more freedom and flexibility in the work routine and in decision making.
3. *Labor supply*: When there is a limited supply of one type of workers, companies try to find innovative ways of attracting and keeping workers in those limited-supply areas. For example, in 1981, IBM, anticipating a demand in programmers

and engineers, started a telecommuting program to attract young talented programmers and engineers. Members of such groups usually garner great benefits with such an arrangement.

4. *Age*: Age may be a factor in home office productivity. For example, in sales, young people are more productive outside of offices than older workers. In management, older people are more productive in offices than outside offices. Women in their childbearing years are more productive when they telecommute than when they work in company offices. So using the age factor, both employer and employee can benefit from home offices.

The US Department of Transportation summarizes the benefits of telecommuting for both employees and employers as [25, 26]:

- An individual benefits from telecommuting because he or she immediately eliminates the time, trouble, and expense of physically commuting to work. This gives the average person an extra hour per day, right off the top, to use for the thinking, writing, telephoning, planning, and reporting work that keeps the business organization moving forward.
- The benefits of telecommuting also translate directly and immediately into more discretionary time, less stress, and general health improvements.
- More autonomy in work decisions and having more control over time and more flexibility in job variations.
- Less commuting expenses on an individual.
- More quality time with family with less to no frustration at home.
- Employers benefit from the extra productivity that has been reported to be consistently at 10–15% in many studies in the last 2 decades.
- Employers also save on expenses through having fewer employees on company premises. Such savings come from the daily need for offices, desks and chairs, bathrooms, copy machines, parking spaces, heating and lighting, and all the rest.
- In addition, telecommuting helps the best and satisfied employees stay longer, thus saving on recruiting and training costs.
- Society benefits from telecommuting through benefits to the environment.

But the overall benefit to employers of home office workers is evaluated through measures like the productivity of the employee. According to the report of the National Academy of Sciences and Electronic Services Unlimited [13] conducted in 1984, productivity among both clerical and managerial telecommuters of the 24 projects evaluated in the report increased about 15–25%. Reductions come from office space, equipment purchases and wear, and office supplies. Businesses also reduce costs by hiring contract workers as the need arises, hence reducing the overall worker benefit expenses. Beside the reductions in overhead costs, by employing contract home workers, companies tap into the scarce resources of the professional expertise they would not otherwise find.

Telecommuting is not all positive, however. Among the issues that negatively affect the company image are employee morale and alienation. Because of the lack of professional contacts, employees' morale may suffer and they may feel abandoned by the company. If this happens, productivity falls. Another negative impact is the public's perception of the company when they see an employee mowing the lawn at 3 p.m. on a workday.

7.3.5 Employee Social and Ethical Issues

Mention of the phrase *office automation* used to conjure up nightmarish images of less control, helplessness, joblessness, and the stagnation of humanity. Within the context of office automation, the concept implies the idea of massive layoffs because offices with intelligent machines may require fewer people. Besides the fear of layoffs, workplace automation has also been plagued with the issue of *diskilling*, meaning stripping an employee of job skills as a result of changes either in job content or procedures. Diskilling, according to Attewell et al. [15], can either be intraoccupational, in which case the skill content of the job decreases over time, or entraoccupational, in which very few people gain the skills needed for the job, causing either low-paying jobs or layoffs. James Driscoll [16] expressed the fear of diskilling in a more sarcastic way by saying that the office of the future would "leave people in only two roles: bosses and garbage collectors." But so far these horrific fears of diskilling have not been realized, even with the heavy office automation of the last 10 years.

There have been some layoffs and diskilling of employees, but the numbers have been very small. Several factors have prevented this from happening; among them are the following:

1. The willingness of employees to retrain and use the newly acquired technology. This, of course, has lead to the upgrading of skills in the workplace. In fact, according to Attewell et al., computerization has led to reskilling of employees rather than diskilling.
2. The historical patterns show that more efficient production techniques lead to expanded operations and added growth, which leads to more hiring rather than firing of existing employees.
3. In anticipation of automation more employees are usually hired to cope with the new technology and to handle the expanded work capacity.

7.4 Employee Monitoring

In the last decade most of the large industrialized economies have been shifting from a heavy manufacturing base to an information management base. Along with this shift has been stiff competition resulting from globalization. Competition coming from not only large economies but also from upcoming developing countries. These developing economies with their cheap labor costs are making this competition more costly for a number of older, more established and mature economies.

This shift in the economies and the stiff competition have resulted in a shift in management styles to bring more efficiency and quality in the established economies. This is not the first time such management styles have shifted. Styles in management have been changing with shifts in economies since the dawn of the Industrial Revolution. In those early days, management followed a style now commonly known as Theory X, after Douglas McGregor. Theory X management, with all the trappings of the industrial era, was characterized by a top-down autocratic style of management in which the manager—literally from the top floor—commanded the activities of the factory workers on the factory floor with almost omniscient and demeaning power.

As economies grew bigger and employees became more elite, a new management style started to evolve that became known as Theory Y. Theory Y put more faith and empowerment in the hands of the employees. The style was hierarchical with the employee ranks broken down into small semi-independent units. Each unit was headed by a supervisor. The supervisors themselves formed another top-down hierarchy ending with the top management. Theory Y, or scientific management, as this management style is commonly known because of its hierarchical structure, gave more flexibility and partial decision-making powers to employees at different levels of the management hierarchy. The workers themselves were more removed from the top management, but at the same time they were closer to management decisions and control from the smaller units. Scientific management has been in effect for years.

But with the recent shifts and globalization of world economies, scientific management has been slowly giving way to a new style in which management is trying to wrest back control of the work process away from the workers and slowly bring back the techniques of Theory X. Given the technological advances of recent years and the abundance of educated and highly skilled workers, though, it would be unwise for today's management to bring back these techniques. So a new technique in the works is called "fear management." It is aimed at keeping workers in line, just like all other management styles, but with "voluntary" compliance by workers to company management policies and practices they would normally have questioned or challenged.

Unlike theories X and Y, which achieved worker control through autocratic and supervisory unit means, fear management uses both worker surveillance and control as enforcement means. Fear is transmitted to workers through policies like "downsizing," "contingent work force," and "outsourcing." To workers these policies spell disaster and fear of losing job security and being replaced by part-time, temporary, and contract workers. According to Karen Nussbaum [17], temporary workers now make up one-third of the U.S. work force less than one-half are covered by any pension, and many have no health insurance.

Management is using a wide array of surveillance gadgets and techniques. These include, among others, employees taking polygraph tests if they are suspected of a breach of any kind. Although in the United States compulsory use of the lie detector is banned, it is still used on a voluntary basis. Drug testing is widely used by many companies and required by all U.S. government employees in some categories. Handwriting analysis, the honesty test, electronic monitoring, mind control, and many other techniques are also being used.

7.4.1 Workplace Privacy and Surveillance

The electronic office or workplace has provided management with a bonanza of new possibilities for monitoring employees in their drive to reduce ever-increasing workplace costs. The issue of employee monitoring is not new because of advances in computer technology. Ever since the Industrial Revolution workers have been monitored for performance evaluation because performance has been used as the basis for pay and for decisions about employee advancement. Monitoring has also been employed to control employees and impose overall discipline in the workplace. But before the advent of surveillance gadgets, workplace monitoring was done through human eyes—the supervisor's.

As workplace modernization picked up speed with advances in technology, the techniques and debate surrounding employee surveillance intensified. The battles were fought on two fronts: those who see monitoring as good management control tools with plausible reasons such as increased production, more accurate assessment of employee performance, greater organizational control over employees, immediate feedback on individual employees (which can lead to high motivation), and more flexibility in work location, and those who see surveillance as an outright transgression of employee privacy, causing problems such as stress, decreased job satisfaction, and an affront to human dignity. The replacement of the human eye with an electronic one, on guard 24 h a day, 7 days a week, without taking a break, and easily concealed, really started the actual erosion of employee privacy.

Employers collect information from employees through two channels. The first is the voluntary channel in which employees surrender the information through forms, interviews, worker sessions, and worker get-togethers. The first work-related information collected from the employee by the prospective employer is collected from the job application, followed by more information surrendered by the prospective employee during the interviewing process. Most of the time this information is given voluntarily because the person wants to get a job and of course employers need employees they can trust. After being hired, especially during the first few days at the job, the new employee usually fills out myriad forms for an employee folder so the employer can pay for the new employee's benefits, taxes (part of them anyway), and salary.

The second channel is the private information the employer gathers through surveillance. The degree, rate, and method of surveillance depend on the employer and how much information is needed from the employee and the value of that information to the employer. The information collected is supposedly used solely for managerial decision making regarding employee work assignments, individual feedback, pay increases, bonuses, promotions, and other benefits, and, of course, termination. If most of this information, legitimately collected or otherwise, was used solely for employee benefits, very few would complain. But sometimes it is not, which is when employee privacy issues arise. For example, how much personal information is needed by the employer for employee benefits before it becomes an invasion of the employee's personal privacy? Are there restrictions on the use of that information? Does the employee have the right to view any information collected on him or her? Is employee surveillance legal, and if so, what legal avenues does an employee have?

According to Adler et al. [18], there are no general explicit constitutional rights to privacy in the United States except in a few states. The US Privacy Act of 1974 has limited applicability mostly to federal employees. Private employees are not adequately covered by this act; they are only covered by a threat to sue for libel, discrimination, and ethical consideration. In light of the limitation of both the US Federal Privacy Act and state statutes, courts started to recognize independent torts, according to Adler et al. (1994). This may be true in many other countries.

Is employee surveillance an invasion of employee privacy? That depends. Notice that invasion of privacy does not mean collection of information on an individual without the individual's knowledge but rather the disclosure of collected information on an employee without legitimate reason or interest. An employer can gather information from the employees with whatever means as long as that information is not used maliciously. For example, an employer can collect information from an individual employee through covert actions like electronic monitoring and use that information solely to further business interests without disclosure to the employee. According to Adler et al. (1994), this procedure is legal and most courts have recognized it as a legitimate business interest and have sided with employers.

Adler et al. cite a case that further clouds the employee privacy issue. An employer was requested by a court to provide an employee's records. In such a case the employee may not have any legal rights regarding the information the employer has. If the employer refuses the request, the employer can be cited for contempt of court. But if the employer obliges, he or she may be charged with violating the employee's privacy rights.

Why are the employee privacy issues becoming so important? As the US and many other economies shift toward information-based economies, the value of owning information for economic advantages becomes even greater. Many companies are trying to obtain information on individuals to market their products, to approve loans, to offer audits, and many other revenue sources. Because companies like insurance, banks, loan assurance, and legal investigations want the information on their clients to be as accurate as possible (their businesses depend on it), information-gathering companies see the employer as their best source of such accurate and reliable information.

Individual information has become valuable not only to banks and insurance companies that want security for their money but also to a cross section of manufacturing and service companies. These companies want to find new markets for their products. In order to do that, they need a source from which to launch their marketing and get a foothold in specialized markets. This kind of information can best be gotten from employers. Once a company has gathered that information about individuals, it can model its market strategies around the characteristics exhibited by these individuals. Such information may include income levels, leisure activities, foods, favorite wines and beers, whether one eats chili, and so on.

In this rush for personal information, the employer takes center stage as the best source of such intriguing tidbits. Statistics show that the workplace is only second to the home as a place we spend most of our time. It is common sense, therefore, that the workplace should be the next best place to look for information on an individual.

7.4.2   Electronic Monitoring

Electronic monitoring is generally the monitoring of employees using electronic devices like video cameras, computer equipment, audio devices, and many other concealed gadgets. In most cases it measures the quality and usually the quantity of work and the ability and effectiveness of the worker. In other cases it also measures the worker's habits on and off the work premises because some employers believe these habits have a great bearing on employee performance. For example, if the employee is a drug user, the effects of drugs will eventually affect the quality of that employee's work.

Electronic monitoring of employees is characterized by workers' ignorance that they are being monitored, fear of the ever-watching eyes of the supervisor, and fear of how much that supervisor knows about them. Let us illustrate these fears by two short examples from Nussbaum [17]. She first cites the case of *Mary Williams* v. *United Airways* in which Mary Williams was first disciplined for her remarks to a coworker, sent to a psychiatrist, and subsequently fired from her work at United Airlines because she confided to a coworker about an obnoxious customer while management was listening in. In another example in the same paper, Nussbaum cites a New York data processor whose boss kept flashing the message "you are not working as fast as the person next to you" on her computer screen.

There are thousands of cases like these two arising from employee monitoring. Although there are no comprehensive studies on the spread of electronic monitoring in the workplace, it is generally believed that electronic monitoring of employees is on the rise and is already enshrined in the banking, insurance, and airline industries, to name but a few.

As technology becomes cheaper, therefore more affordable, smaller, and easier to conceal, the trend is likely to pick up momentum as the pressure for quality, quantity, and standards increases because of global competition. This is likely to force more companies to resort to electronic monitoring as a way to control employees to extract more performance, compliance, and probably more money. In fact, in some sectors of employment the percentages are already high. For example, according to Grant et al. [19], in the United States 25–35% of all clerical workers are electronically monitored for work performance.

7.4.2.1   Effects of Electronic Monitoring on Employees

Recently, I watched a British television comedy in which the theme was employee monitoring. The setting was a department store. The managers of the store found out they were losing merchandise and decided the employees were the most likely culprits, so they hired a security guard to check all employees' bags and pockets at the end of each day as the employees left the premises. They also installed video cameras throughout the store including the rest rooms. With the cameras in place, all human movements could be monitored in the comfort of the manager's office. Employee morale and performance declined considerably because employees, already aware of cameras watching their every move and carefully recording their every word to customers, were more concerned about being seen sweet-talking their customers and looking smart than actually working. Employees neglected those parts of the store where they could not be seen "working" by management. Also there were fights between employees to take those strategic places. Funny as the television episode was and indeed as it was intended to be, it illustrates a number of issues research has shown to exist among electronically monitored employees.

In research conducted by a North American insurance company reported by Grant et al. [19], results like those portrayed in the television comedy were observed. The research studied a monitored group of the group-claims processing division of the insurance company and a nonmonitored group of the same division. In these two groups, the researchers included some supervisors and department managers. The monitored group was responsible for entering and paying claims using an automated claim-processing system and dealing directly with subscribers answering their questions and settling their disputes as far as payments were concerned. Their work included printing checks and talking to customers on phones.

The computer "monitor" counted the number of checks produced by an individual on a daily basis. According to the findings of the research, the group that was monitored considered the number of checks printed as the most important part of their work. In fact, they thought that talking to subscribers was an impediment to their job of printing checks. These employees, just like those in the British comedy, focused on those parts of their jobs they thought were being monitored and neglected all other essential parts. Although the monitored group did their work this way, the researchers found that the employees in the nonmonitored group had a different perception of their work. This group thought that dealing with customers was the most important part of their work.

Another research project conducted by Irving et al. [20] compared two groups of employees working in insurance companies, financial institutions, and government. One group was electronically monitored and the other was not. The researchers looked at the effects of monitoring on issues such as job satisfaction, what employees consider as a measure of performance, amount and usefulness of feedback, and relationships among employees and between employees and supervisors. The results of the study were very similar to those of Grant's study and the British television comedy. Employees put much more emphasis on quantity as a measure of performance; there was no significant usefulness in the timely individual feedback; rewards were based on electronic performance evaluations in the monitored group, and those in the monitored group felt, and rightly so, that they were more supervised than any other group in the company. From these studies two important issues emerge:

1. Very often an intended goal of a monitoring program may be clouded by a different goal perceived by the monitored group. Therefore, without a well-thought-out electronic monitoring program, the intended goal of the company may be lost in the resulting perceptions of the employees.
2. The psychological effects on the monitored employees may be more severe than previously thought and anticipated. The philosophy that "if it isn't counted, it does not count" should not be allowed to flourish among employees. Besides what has been observed in Grant's study and the British comedy, there are social, ethical, and mental effects on the monitored employees.

7.4.2.2 Consequences of Electronic Monitoring

The most devastating effect of electronic monitoring on employees is fear of losing their jobs. For many of us a job is the only source of a livelihood and any sign of losing it triggers fear. In addition to fear of job loss, electronic monitoring also causes the following problems:

- *Reduced task variety*: The type of work monitored most is of a low-skilled, repetitive nature. In these jobs employees take the quota to be the measure of work and usually cannot afford to take a break, let alone slow down, thus increasing the monotony of their activities.
- *Lack of individual initiatives*: Most monitored jobs do not require personal creativity because they are of a low-skilled, repetitive nature. The employee usually is not allowed to vary the procedures but follows them to the letter.
- *Reduced or no peer social support*: Monitored groups are always given separate stations where gadgets can monitor them in full view. So an employee must remain where he or she can be "seen."
- *Lack of self-esteem*: The isolation, the monotony of work, the lack of creativity, and the lack of freedom to vary job steps lower employee morale and consequently self-esteem.
- *Lack of interest in the job*: With low self-esteem, many people definitely lose interest in their jobs.
- *Lack of trust among workers, between workers and supervisors, and between supervisors and management*: This lack of trust can result in low company morale, and later production levels may begin to fall. As employee morale plummets and dislike of the employer rises, workers turn to litigation, filing privacy suits against their employers. Nussbaum reports that in the United States there were twice as many lawsuits of workplace privacy filed between 1984 and 1987 as between 1978 and 1980. In the courts, although workers' privacy rights have not been successful in the number of lawsuits filed, there is a growing recognition of workplace privacy rights. A number of states in the United States and indeed in other countries have been working on legislation to protect workers. The trade union movement has also been actively negotiating languages in worker contracts to help curb unnecessary workplace monitoring.

- *Alienation*: Sociologists define the concept of worker alienation as lack of worker freedom and control, purpose and function, and self-involvement in their work. Alienation, according to Shepard [21], is lower among workers in industries with automated technologies.

7.5 Workplace Employee Health and Productivity

Productivity of workers depends on the quality of their physical and mental state. Employers have always strived to make their workers happy, healthy, and productive. Although some have partially succeeded in this mission, many by changing working rules and the environment and adding facilities such as employee gyms, cafeteria, daycare centers, and worker facilities for their employees, overall the majority of employers have never fully succeeded in this endeavor. There has always been a feeling of powerlessness among employees to control the state of working conditions because they lack freedom and control. According to Shepard [21], a worker has freedom and control at work if he or she can vary steps involved in doing the job, determine work methods and workload, and increase or decrease speed at which the work is done. With the changing work environment due to advances in computer technology, employers are finding themselves achieving what has eluded them for years, offering their employees happiness, healthier environments, and high productivity through empowerment.

Human beings always want to feel they are in control of their work and other aspects of their lives. The changing work environment gives the workers exactly that. It gives them a choice either to work in a traditional office or from home. Choice brings commitment and obligation. When people make a choice of their own, they tend to commit to the requirements of their choice. The commitment to work always translates into higher productivity quotas. Although computer technology has given workers more control in decision making, it has also given them new dangers in the workplace. These dangers are collectively discussed next as ergonomics.

7.5.1 Ergonomics

Ergonomics is an applied science concerned with designing human–machine interactions that offer and maintain a safe, comfortable, healthy, and habitable work environment. With the increasing automation of the workplace, our dependence on machines is on the rise, and the field of ergonomics is correspondingly expanding. It now covers a wide array of work environments and factors that influence the employee's health and wellness through prevention of occupational diseases. In particular, ergonomics studies the design of human work and production because when the demands for human performance of a task exceed human capacity then ergonomic injuries start to occur and human wellness declines.

An ergonomic injury results when the demand on a person to perform a task exceeds that person's working capacity. Examples of ergonomic injuries include work accidents that occur due to the overwhelming demand for performance and all work-related musculoskeletal disorders such as back pain, neck and shoulder pains, and repetitive strain injuries (RSI), with most studies now focusing on RSI.

7.5.1.1 Repetitive Strain Injuries

RSI is a set of work-related musculoskeletal disorders caused by repeated and prolonged body movement resulting in damage to the fibrous and soft body tissues like tendons, nerves, and muscles. Some RSI conditions are well known in medical communities, but a number of others are still very obscure and difficult to diagnose because they present with different and very often unpredictable patterns. RSI as a disease is not new; it has been affecting people performing repetitive motions like cashiers, musicians, assembly and data entry workers for years; it has just recently gained prominence because of the rise in computer availability and widespread computer use. Recent studies have isolated some of the main causes of RSI as repetitive motion, forced gripping, performance stress, alienation, static loading, fixed posture, deviated wrists, and boredom. Computer users of keyboards, mouse, tracking balls, touchscreens, and footmouse are among the groups most prone to RSI. RSI attacks those body parts such as tendons, wrists, shoulders, nerves, and arms and sometimes the neck that receive tremendous stress exerted by body movements. This condition, which has come to be known by a string of names like occupational overuse syndrome (OOS), cumulative trauma disorder (CTD), carpal tunnel syndrome (CTS), and upper limb disorder (ULD) causes serious pain and if not treated early may cause even permanent disability. As a result of the damage to the nerves, wrists, arms, tendons, and muscles, the disease also causes eyestrain, fatigue, headaches, usually back pain, tingling, coldness, hand numbness, and stiffness and discomfort in body movement especially fingers, arms, and the head. When RSI is caught in time, it can be cured with proper care and prescriptions that emphasize changes in individual work styles and techniques. Among the suggested changes in work styles and techniques are the following:

1. *Use ergonomically correct work equipment.* These may include chairs, tables, computer equipment like new keyboards, monitors, new software, and new lightning in the workplace.
2. *Use a light touch on the keyboard to place less stress on body parts.* Also keep the wrists straight in line with your arms.
3. *Take frequent breaks from your work.* Do not work for long hours without a break. Once you get a break, walk around and do some stretching exercises.
4. *Educate yourself about RSI.*
5. *If necessary reduce the time you spend at the computer terminal.*

Improvements in the design of human work and occupational environments can result in benefits to the employee and the employer. Among such benefits are the following:

- Reduced medical bills
- A higher level of self-esteem
- Increased productivity because of fewer employee errors. High attendance rate and retention skills increase per capita output

Studies have shown dramatic increases in the range of 20–50% in increased productivity after effective ergonomics remedies were implemented for people working with visual display units (VDU) [22].

7.5.1.2   Stress

Besides RSI, stress has also recently drawn public attention as a work hazard. Like its counterpart RSI, stress has been targeted to explain a lot of worker discomfort and frustration that may lead to poor job performance, strained interpersonal relations, and erratic employee behavior. Stress is believed to have its origins in environmental inputs and it appears through symptoms such as fear, anxiety, and anger. Anything that increases the stress level of an individual ultimately endangers that individual's health.

In the work environment stress is mainly caused by a variety of factors including impending deadlines, long hours at work, uncooperative colleagues, lack of management support and understanding, constantly changing requirements, and lack of job capacity either because of changing work procedures or the workplace environment. Stress onset affects individuals differently depending on the environment they are in, and different individuals react differently to stress. For example, Ivancevich et al. [23] report that under stress women consume less coffee than men, shout less but consume more aspirin, and visit doctors more frequently than men.

Employers can significantly reduce employees stress by enhancing the overall work environment, keeping consistent work schedules, giving fewer deadlines, and making fewer management demands. Health awareness and knowledge of the causes of stress are always the first step in controlling it.

Exercises

1. Discuss the effects of telecommuting on family life.
2. If there are benefits to the employer for telecommuting, why is it that not many companies have embraced telework?
3. Ergonomics is turning into a multimillion dollar business. Discuss.
4. Electronic monitoring has more negative effects on both employers and employees. Discuss.
5. Work productivity is directly related to the well-being of the employee. Discuss.
6. Has automation caused any massive worker layoffs?
7. Has technology in the workplace created jobs or trimmed job rolls?
8. There has been a debate on the existence of the digital divide. What is your opinion? Is there one or not?

9. Is there anything like equal access to computing technology? In otherwise is it achievable in any society?
10. The concept of telecommuting has not realized its earlier potential, and therefore, has not been successful. Is this a true statement? Why or why not?
11. Has the Internet, together with new developments in telecommunications, increased the value of telecommuting?
12. Has the Internet and related technologies helped to lessen the problems experienced by the telecommuter?
13. Discuss the social implications of telecommuting.
14. What, if any, are the ethical implications of telecommuting?
15. What are the benefits, if any, of employee monitoring?
16. What are the social and ethical problems resulting from employee mandated drug and polygraph testing?
17. Why do you think employee monitoring is such a hot issue?
18. There are benefits to employee monitoring! Discuss
19. Should employees sacrifice their privacy because of fear of losing a job?

References

1. Francisco Rodriguez and Ernest J. Wilson, *Are Poor Countries Losing the Information Revolution?* InfoDEV, The World Bank.
2. *United Nations Human Development Report 2000.* United Nations Development Program. http://www.undp.org/hdro/
3. "(fwd:) Information Age Have and Have-nots." http://www.library.wustl.edu/~listmgr/devel-l/august1998/00058.html
4. "Vital Signs". CNN Headlines News. Saturday, May 28, 2000.
5. National Telecommunications and Information Administration, Technical Report 2000 (NTIA 2000). "Falling Through the Net: Toward Digital Inclusion." http://www.ntia.doc.gov.ntia-home/ftfn00/front00.htm
6. Harlan Lebo, *The UCLA Internet Report: Surveying the Digital Future.* http://www.ccp.ucla.edu
7. Anne Rickert "The Dollar Divide: Web Usage Patterns by Household Income." Media Metrix, Inc., August 2000. http://www.mediametrix.com/data/MMXI-USHHI-0600.pdf
8. *United Nations Human Development Report 1999.* United Nations Development Program. http://www.undp.org/hdro/; http://www.ntia.doc.gov.ntiahome/net2/falling.html
9. Robert Krech, email communication to DIGOPP, March 8, 2001. http://www.edc.org/GLG/Markle/dotforce/digopp/
10. Gottieb, C.C., and A. Borodin. Social Issues in Computing. New York: Academic Press, 1973.
11. Olson, Margrethe, and Henry Lucas. "The Impact of Office Automation on the Organization: Some Implications for Research and Practice." *Communications of the ACM,* 25(11), 1982, pp. 838–847.
12. Snizek, William. "Virtual Office: Some Neglected Considerations." *Communications of the ACM,* 38(9), 1995, pp. 15–17.
13. Kraut, Robert. "Predicting the Use of Technology: The Case of Telework." In Chuck Huff and Thomas Finholt (eds.), *Social Issues in Computing: Putting Computing in Its Place.* New York: McGraw-Hill, 1994, pp. 312–334.
14. Porat, M. "The Information Economy: Definitions and Managements." U.S. Department of Commerce, Office of Technology Report, U.S. Government Printing Office. Stock number 003–000–00512–7, Washington, DC.
15. Attewell, Paul, and James Rule. "Computing and Organization: What We Know and What We Don't Know." *Communications of the ACM,* 27(12), 1984, pp. 1184–1193.

16. Driscoll, J. "Office Automation: The Dynamics of a Technological Boondoggle." In Robert M. Landau, James H. Bair, and Jean H. Siegman (eds.), *Emerging Office Systems*. Norwood, NJ: Ablex, 1982.
17. Nussbaum, Karen. "Computer Monitoring: A Threat to the Right to Privacy." In Ray Dejoie, Geroge Fowler, and David Paradice (eds.), *Ethical Issues in Information Systems*. Boston, MA: Boyd & Fraser, 1991.
18. Adler P.A., L.K. Parsons, and S.B. Zolke. "Employee Privacy: Legal and Research Developments and Implications for Personal Administration." In Chuck Huff and Thomas Finholt (eds.), *Social Issues in Computing: Putting Computing in Its Place*. New York: McGraw-Hill, 1994, pp. 312–334.
19. Grant, Rebecca, Christopher Higgins, and Richard Irving. "Computerized Performance Monitors: Are They Costing You Customers?" In Chuck Huff and Thomas Finholt (eds.), *Social Issues in Computing: Putting Computing in Its Place*. New York: McGraw-Hill, 1994, pp. 312–334.
20. Irving, R.H., C.A. Higgins, and F.R. Safayeni. "Computerized Performance Monitoring Systems: Use and Abuse." Communications of the ACM, 29(8), 1986, pp. 794–801.
21. Shepard, John. *Automation and Alienation*. Cambridge, MA: MIT Press, 1971.
22. Grandjean, Etienne. *Ergonomics in Computerized Offices*. London: Taylor & Francis, 1987.
23. Ivancevich, John, Albert Napier, and James Wetherbe. "Occupation Stress, Attitudes, and Health: Problems in the Information Systems Professions." *Communications of the ACM*, 26(10), 1983, pp. 800–806.
24. DIGOPP Working Group of the Education Development Center. http://www.edc.org/GLG/Markle/dotforce/digopp/
25. "Benefits of Telecommuting" U.S. Department of Transportation's Departmental Office of Human Resource Management. http://dothr.ost.dot.gov/Telecommuting/benefits_of_telecommuting.htm
26. Paul Boyd. "Six Organizational Benefits of Telecommuting." http://pw2.netcom.com/~pboyd/orgbens.html

Further Readings

Bailyn, Lotte. "Towards a Perfect Workplace." *Communications of the ACM,* 32(4), 1989, pp. 460–471.
Flynn, L. "They Are Watching You: Electronic Surveillence of Workers Raises Privacy Concerns." *San Jose Mercury News,* June 13, 1993, p. 1 F.
Payser, Marc. "When E-mail Is Oops-Mail: Think Your Private Messages Are Private? Think Again." *Newsweek,* October 16, 1995, p. 82.
Sauter, Steven, Mark Gottlieb, Karen Jones, Vernon Dodson, and Kathryn Rohner. "Job and Health Implications of VDT Use: Initial Results of the Wisconsin NIOSH Study." *Communications of the ACM,* 26(4), 1983, pp. 284–294.

Chapter 8
Software Issues: Risks and Liabilities

Learning Objectives

After reading this chapter, the reader should be able to:

1. Explain the limitations of software testing as a means to ensure correctness.
2. Describe the differences between correctness, reliability, and safety.
3. Discuss the potential for hidden problems in reuse of existing software components.
4. Describe current approaches to manage risk and characterize the strengths and shortcomings of each.
5. Outline the role of risk management in software systems design and construction.

Scenario 6
Who Will Pay the Price for Flawed Software?

Peter Efon works as a programmer for a major software company. The company, Cybersoft, is launching itself to be a major Internet-based platform developer and it is soon to launch a web initiative. Peter is involved in the development of a crucial component of the initiative. The company has trust in Peter for he has worked for it since he left college 15 years ago. Since his arrival at the company, Peter has pioneered a number of major software development projects. Peter has followed, and is very much aware of, the losses suffered by other businesses due to defective software. He even knows that in 2000, US companies suffered a whopping $100 billion loss due to bad software. He and his company, Cybersoft, are determined to target quality as the major focus of their new web initiative. Peter dreams of the success of the web initiative and the recognition it might bring both to his company and him. However, a few days before the launch of the much-awaited initiative, as Peter makes his final quality checks, he discovers a flaw in the core component of the initiative whose magnitude he could not determine. To do so would mean a few weeks delay at best, a major blow to the company's efforts. The company had mounted an advertising blitz on all major media outlets. Even a few weeks delay would cause major financial losses and the public's loss of confidence in the right company. This must never happen. Peter decides to see to it.

Discussion Questions

1. Is Peter Eflon wrong?
2. What damage would Cybersoft have suffered had there been a delay?
3. What do you think would have been the right course of action for Peter and Cybersoft?
4. Can you estimate the damage?

J.M. Kizza, *Ethical and Social Issues in the Information Age*, Texts in Computer Science, DOI 10.1007/978-1-84996-038-0_8, © Springer-Verlag London Limited 2010

8.1   Definitions

Software is a set of computer programs made up of a sequence of short commands called instructions that tell the computer what to do. Normally software is in two forms, either built into the computer's more permanent memory, called ROM (read-only memory) or loaded on demand in less permanent but more volatile memory called RAM (random access memory). A *software producer*, or *developer*, creates or develops a set of programs to meet the specifications of a user, if there is a contract, or of a specific problem if it is a general software. Developers are either individuals working alone or companies such as Microsoft, which employs hundreds of software engineers including analysts and programmers. *Software buyers*, or *customers*, obtain the finished software from the developer to satisfy a need, basing their decision on developer claims. The buyer may be an individual or a company.

In this chapter, we focus on the issues that arise out of the relationship between the developer and the buyer, including claims, user expectations, and the legal ramifications that may follow an unhealthy relationship. The discussion touches on standards, reliability, security, safety, quality of software, quality of service of software products, causes of software failures, developer and buyer protection, and techniques for improving software quality. Let us begin by defining these terms.

8.1.1   Standards

Software developers must convey to buyers' satisfaction that their products are of high quality. The buyer, however, has little leverage in disputing the claims of the developer in these areas because there is no single universally acceptable and agreed upon measure of software standards. But there are universal basic standards that a software product must meet. Such standards include the mutually agreed upon criteria and expectations of the buyer. In this case, the law imposes such standards, and if the product does not live up to them, the buyer has the right to pursue legal action. There is no one criterion that can be used to measure software standards but rather a collection of criteria such as development testing, verification and validation of software, and the programmer's professional and ethical standards.

8.1.1.1   Development Testing

According to Richard Hamlet [1], "programs are complex, hard to understand, hard to prove, and consequently often riddled with errors." But might not a small set of tests on a program pinpoint problems? Answering yes to this question has been the driving force behind testing, which helps reveal the discrepancies between the model being used and the real situation. Testing tries to assure that the program satisfies its specifications and it detects and prevents design and implementation faults. But testing is limited by an exponential number of states, which makes exhaustive testing very expensive and unworkable for large projects. Thus, a number of other selective testing techniques are being used. One such technique is *development testing*, which consists of a series of random tests on the software during the development stage. However, the use of mathematical techniques in developmental testing, which seems to offer good assurances and is widely used, does not ensure error-free code. Neither does refocusing verification of code to the underlying algorithm and basic computation, because not all errors may be in these areas. So testing alone does not eliminate all the bugs.

8.1.1.2 Verification and Validation

The process of V&V involves static formal mathematical techniques such as proof-of-correctness and dynamic techniques such as testing to show consistency between the code and the basic initial specifications. It works from the specifications of the software and develops tests that can show that software under review is faulty. Tests are randomly chosen. But as any programmer will tell you, as the level of programming gets lower and lower toward machine code, software bugs get harder and harder to detect, and no amount of V&V is able to prevent those bugs from falling through the cracks.

8.1.2 Reliability

Unlike hardware products whose reliability is measurable from age and production quantities, software reliability cannot be measured by wear and tear, nor can it be measured by copies produced at manufacture time, although experience has shown that it exhibits some degree of stochastic properties on unpredictable input sequences. A software product can fail to deliver expected results because of an unexpected input sequence. Reliability of software can, therefore, be defined in relation to these input sequences. According to Parnas et al. [2], reliability of software is the probability that such a software does not encounter an input sequence that leads to failure. A software product, therefore, is reliable if it can continue to function on numerous unpredictable input sequences. Other measures of reliability include the number of errors in the code. But this also is difficult to take as a good measure because a program with fewer errors is not necessarily more reliable than one with many. Because no system can be certified as error free, including software systems, there have been numerous cases and will continue to be, in which systems have and will fail the reliability standards.

Consider the example of the Denver International Airport baggage system [3]. When the city of Denver, Colorado, wanted to replace Stapleton International Airport, they contracted an automated baggage company, BAE Automated Systems of Dallas, to design and build a baggage delivery system. When BAE delivered the system, it failed all initial tests. Bags flew out of carts, and jams were frequent. After a number of failed test runs, and knowing they were running out of time, city officials hired another firm, which recommended a smaller, less expensive, but working manual system to run as a stand-alone alongside the automated system. When it opened, the airport was $2 billion over budget due to the delay caused mostly by this system.

In his book *Computer Related Risks*, Peter Neumann gives numerous examples of system failures due to unreliable products [4]. Like standards, reliability is another very difficult concept for a buyer or customer to understand because there are no universally accepted criteria for ascertaining the reliability of a product.

8.1.3   Security

In Section 5.3 we discussed the general concepts of system security including information security. In this section we focus on software security. As computer technology makes giant advances, our dependence on it increases and so do our security concerns as more and more of the vital information that used to be secured under lock and key is now on giant computer disks scattered on numerous computer systems.

Software is an integral part of a computer system, and the security of such a system depends on its hardware but even more so on the software component. There are more security attacks on systems through software "holes" than hardware, mainly through piracy, deletion, and alteration of programs and data. A computer system software is secure if it protects its programs and data—in other words, if it does not contain trapdoors through which unauthorized intruders can access the system.

According to Neumann [5], improper encapsulation, inheritance of unnecessary privileges, and inadequate enforcement of polymorphism are the most common sources of software security flaws. Polymorphism is a state or a condition of passing through many forms or stages. Software development passes through many different forms. In addition to these as common causes of system insecurity is the human element. A computer system software can be protected from undetected modification through strong and sound design principles, enforcement of proper encapsulation, separation of all privileges, and ethical education of system developers and users about security issues.

The human and probably ethical side to system security, according to Ahl David [6], is that most computer crimes are not committed by hackers but by trusted employees, programmers, managers, clerks, and consultants in the company who know and can manipulate the working of the software. If David's observation is true, then computer security and hence system software security greatly depends on the education of system developers and knowledgeable users.

8.1.4   Safety

Recent advances in computer technology have resulted in wider computer applications in previously unthinkable areas such as space exploration, missile and aircraft guidance systems, and life-sustaining systems. In these areas the safety of software has become one of the most prominent components of the whole security system. Such a system cannot afford an accident or an error because of software failure without dire consequences to human life, property, and the environment.

A software system is unsafe if a condition is created whereby there is a likelihood of an accident, a hazard, or a risk. The function of software safety in system safety is that software executes within a prescribed context so as not to contribute to hazards or risk either by outputting faulty values and timing or by failing to detect and respond to hardware failures that may cause a system to go into a hazardous state.

According to Nancy Leveson [7], software safety depends on the design and environment in which such software is used. So software that is considered safe in one environment may be unsafe in another. Because software is designed and produced by different people in different environments and used in different applications in a variety of environments, no one software product can conform to all requirements in all environments; in other words, one cannot assume that because a software product is hazard free in one environment, it is hazard free in all environments. For example, according to Strigini and Littlewood [8], whereas the requirement for rate of occurrence of failures as a dependability measure is appropriate in systems that actively control potentially dangerous processes, the same measure is not as appropriate for life-critical processes in which the emphasis is on failure-free survival.

In the final analysis, good and safe software depends on good programming practice, which includes control techniques, application of various types of safety analysis during the development cycle, and evaluation of the effectiveness of these techniques. Whether these techniques are enough depends on the chosen and acceptable risk level, which tends to vary with the application environments [9]. For other dependability measures, consult Littlewood's article.

8.1.5 Quality

The emergence of a global software market, the establishment of powerful software development warehouses in different countries, and the improving standards of global software have all brought software quality to the forefront of software issues. A software product has quality if it maintains a high degree of excellence in standards, security, safety, and dependability. Many software vendors are starting to develop and apply quality improvements techniques such as total quality management (TQM).

A TQM technique that tries to improve software quality through a software development process known as the software quality function development (SQFD) represents a movement from the traditional techniques of TQM to the software development environment by focusing on improving the development process through upgrades in the requirement solicitation phase [10]. This technique focuses on this phase because software problems occur when user requirements are misunderstood, which causes overruns of development costs. Introducing design techniques that focus on user specification in this early phase leads to fewer design changes and reduces transfer errors across design phases.

8.1.6   Quality of Service

For a product, and in particular, a software product, quality of service (QoS) means providing consistent, predictable service delivery that will satisfy customer application requirements. The product must have some level of assurance that the customer's service requirements can be satisfied. For example in the case of the Internet, QoS would mean that the network elements like routers and hosts expect a high level of assurance that its traffic and service requirements can be satisfied. This requirement and expectations are important because the working and the architecture of the Internet are based on "dumb" network concept, which at its simplest involves two smart end routers, one transmitting and one receiving and no intelligence in between. Then datagrams with source and destination addresses traverse a network of routers independently as they move from the sender to the receiver. IP provides only an addressing mechanism and nothing else. It provides no guarantees of the delivery of any independent datagram in the network. So QoS is needed in network protocols.

8.2   Causes of Software Failures

Failure or poor performance of a software product can be attributed to a variety of causes, most notably human error, the nature of software itself, and the environment in which software is produced and used.

8.2.1   Human Factors

In the human factor category, poor software performance can be a result of:

1. *Memory lapses and attentional failures*: For example, someone was supposed to have removed or added a line of code, tested, or verified, but did not because of simple forgetfulness.
2. *Rush to finish*: The result of pressure, most often from management, to get the product on the market either to cut development costs or to meet a client deadline, rushing can cause problems.
3. *Overconfidence and use of nonstandard or untested algorithms*: Before algorithms are fully tested by peers, they are put into the product line because they seem to have worked on a few test runs.
4. *Malice*: Software developers, like any other professionals, have malicious people in their ranks. Bugs, viruses, and worms have been known to be embedded and downloaded in software as is the case with Trojan horse software, which boots itself at a timed location. As we will see in Section 8.4, malice has traditionally been used for vendetta, personal gain (especially monetary), and just irresponsible

amusement. Although it is possible to safeguard against other types of human errors, it is very difficult to prevent malice.

5. *Complacency*: When either an individual or a software producer has significant experience in software development, it is easy to overlook certain testing and other error control measures in those parts of software that were tested previously in a similar or related product, forgetting that no one software product can conform to all requirements in all environments.

8.2.2 Nature of Software: Complexity

Both software professionals and nonprofessionals who use software know the differences between software programming and hardware engineering. It is in these differences that many of the causes of software failure and poor performance lie. Consider the following:

1. *Complexity*: Unlike hardwired programming in which it is easy to exhaust the possible outcomes of a given set of input sequences, in software programming a similar program may present billions of possible outcomes on the same input sequence. Therefore, in software programming one can never be sure of all the possibilities on any given input sequence.
2. *Difficult testing*: There will never be a complete set of test programs to check software exhaustively for all bugs for a given input sequence.
3. *Ease of programming*: The fact that software programming is easy to learn encourages many people with little formal training and education in the field to start developing programs, but many are not knowledgeable about good programming practices or able to check for errors.
4. *Misunderstanding of basic design specifications*: This affects the subsequent design phases including coding, documenting, and testing. It also results in improper and ambiguous specifications of major components of the software and in ill-chosen and poorly defined internal program structures.

As we already discussed in Section 8.1.4, the environment in which a software product is produced and tested has a great bearing on its safety.

8.3   Risk

The first step in understanding the nature of software is to study the concept of risk, software risk in particular. However, before we define risk, let us define *hazard*. A hazard is a state or set of conditions of a system or an object that, together with other conditions in the environment of the system, or object, will lead inevitably to an accident [7]. According to Leveson, hazard has two components; severity and likelihood of occurrence. These two form the hazard level. Risk is a hazard level together with the likelihood of an accident to occur and the severity of the potential consequences [7]. Risk can also be defined in simpler terms as the potential or possibility of suffering harm or loss; danger, in short. Peter Neumann defines risk as a potential problem, with causes and effects [4]. Risk can be both voluntary, with activities that we knowingly decide to undertake, or involuntary with activities that happen to us without our prior consent or knowledge as a result of nature's actions such as lightning, fires, floods, tornados, and snow storms. Since our focus here is on the big picture of the dangers of software in particular and computer systems in general, we will leave the details of the definitions at that.

How does risk play in software? Because we have defined risk as a potential problem with causes and effects, software risks, therefore, have causes and effects. Among the causes of software risks are poor software design, a mismatch of hardware software interfaces, poor support, and maintenance. Others include [11]:

- Personnel shortfalls
- Unrealistic schedules and budgets
- Developing the wrong functions and properties
- Developing the wrong user interface
- Continuing stream of requirements changes
- Shortfalls in externally furnished components
- Shortfalls in externally performed tasks
- Real-time performance shortfalls
- Straining computer-science capabilities

Because computers are increasingly becoming a part of our lives, there are numerous ways computers and computer software in particular affect our lives. In many of these encounters, there is risk involved. For example, computers are used in medical care and delivery, in power generation and distribution, in emergency services, and in many other facets of life. So wherever we are, be it at work, on the way to or from work, or in our own homes, where there is direct or indirect use of computer software there is always a risk of an accident to occur.

For example, there is no way for a system manager to predict how and when a system failure or attack by hackers or viruses will occur. As our world become increasingly engulfed with computer and telecommunication networks, network-related threats by hackers, viruses, system overloads, and insider misuse are increasing to such a level that the risk involved is shaping the way we work. Appropriate and effective measures need to be taken to deal with risk. Let us look at some here.

8.3.1 Risk Assessment and Management

Risk management is a process to estimate the impact of risk. It is an approach for system managers to measure the system's assets and vulnerabilities, assessing the threat and monitoring security. For software, we look at risk management both during the design phase and during use. Risk is an important aspect of the design process. Because it is so important, two constituent components must be included. These are assessment and control. To implement these two components, there must be a requirement that no software project may be delivered or accepted until and unless a risk assessment or risk control evaluation has been carried out on it. There must be documentation of the probability and consequences of hazards and accidents to help figure out what the risks are and what to do about them.

The assessment aspects in the documentation should involve a list of all the potential dangers that are likely to affect the project, the probability of occurrence and potential loss of each item, and how each item ranks among all the listed items.

The control component in the documentation should consist of [11]:

- Techniques and strategies to mitigate the highest ordered risks
- Implementation of the strategies to resolve the high-order risks factors
- Monitoring the effectiveness of the strategies and the changing levels of risk throughout the design process

After the design process, when software is in use, risk management then involves the following phases: assessment, planning, implementation, and monitoring.

8.3.1.1   Assessment

This involves identifying the software's security vulnerabilities and may consist of a variety of techniques including question and answer, qualitative assessment, or methodology and calculation. A simple equation for calculating risk is:

$$\text{Risk} = \text{Assets} \times \text{Threats} \times \text{Vulnerabilities}$$

8.3.1.2   Planning

Planning involves outlining the policies for security management.

8.3.1.3   Implementation

A good implementation may seek to match the security needs of the system with all available security tools.

8.3.1.4   Monitoring

Risk management is an ongoing process that needs constant monitoring. This helps to determine the necessary changes and new security applications to the system. The monitoring tools must be chosen based on the nature and applications of the system being protected. For example, if the system being protected is a network, the tools may include a firewall as well as intrusion detection and network forensics software.

8.3.2   Risks and Hazards in Workplace Systems

The workplace is only second to our homes in the amount of time we spend there. For most people with nine to five work schedules, work comprises about 40 h of the 168-h week. When you figure in commuting to and from work and other work-related activities, we spend on the average 84 h a week at home. Because we spend so much time outside our homes and in close contact with people from all walks of life and most often work with workplace machinery and people, which we call workplace systems, there is always a high risk associated with these systems, as well as with the commute to and from work.

In a workplace environment accidents resulting from this three-faceted model of hardware, software, and humanware, are caused by the intertwining of the components whereby each part affects the others. According to Leveson [7], an accident is then a coincidence of factors related to one another through this intertwining. Each component's contribution to system accidents depends on the environment the system is in. Different environments may cause different types of accident. In some accidents, software may contribute more than the other two, while in others, humanware may contribute more, especially in cases where there is lack of effective training of the human component. There is a perception that humanware is more prone to errors in workplace systems than both hardware and software. According to Leveson, most workplace accidents are caused by what she calls a safety culture due to humanware—a general attitude and approach to safety consisting of overconfidence, complacency, placing low priority on safety, and accepting flawed resolutions of conflicting goals. To these we also add poor employee training and poor employee morale. In workplace systems where there is a transient human component, overlooking the human component for a critical-safety decision-making process may result in high-risk system safety.

This perception is enhanced by the credibility problem and the myth about computers. People still hold the computer dear, that it is more reliable and creates less risk, that software testing eliminates software errors, that increased software reliability automatically implies increased safety, and that reusing software increases its safety level. All these are myths. Software safety is as unpredictable as its counterpart, the humanware.

For those with such perception, there is good news. The development of intelligent computer technology and communication devices may lessen the human component in the workplace. However, this does not mean that workplace systems will be error free. It will, however, shift the burden on software since hardware errors are more readily predictable than those by humanware and software.

Hardware errors can easily be located and fixed. Software errors, on the other hand, may take many hours before they are found, and fixing them may take even longer. Yet software systems are becoming even more complex with complicated codes and tight delivery schedules.

8.3.3 Historic Examples of Software Risks

In the maiden days of the "Wonder Machine," risk and vulnerability of both the computer user and data were not a problem. Software was unknown, the way we know it today, because it was embedded. Also, the computing system consisted more of hardware than software, and projects were small. As systems became smaller and less dependant on hardware, software came out of the hardware, and projects became bigger, complex, and more dependent on software and human-ware. Then the problems of risk and vulnerabilities set in. Ever since then, major system mishaps in hardware, software, and humanware have been recorded that have given us a glimpse of the development of computer systems and the long road that system safety, vulnerability, and risk have taken.

In his book *Computer-Related Risks* [4], Peter G. Neumann, for many years the moderator of the on-line Internet group, "The Risk Forum," and contributor to ACM's "Inside Risk," has documented a wide collection of computer mishaps that address problems in reliability, safety, security, and privacy issues in day-to-day computer activities.

Numerous other authors have written about hundreds of incidents that have made headlines in their day. We cannot list them all. But we will look at the major history-making system safety incidents, a few among many, that have dotted the computing landscape.

8.3.3.1 The Therac-25

The Therac-25 is a computer-controlled electronic-accelerator radiation-therapy system developed by Atomic Energy of Canada, Ltd. (AECL). Between 1985 and 1987 the system was involved in a number of accidents, some resulting in deaths because of radiation overdose.

The machine works by creating a high-energy beam of electrons targeted to the cancerous tumor, leaving the healthy tissue surrounding the tumor unaffected. The Therac-25 was not supposed to malfunction, but like all systems, there are many pos-sibilities for errors. Therac-25 accidents did not occur until after 6 months of use, thus creating a high degree of confidence. And when malfunctions occurred they were very irregular and the system successfully worked on hundreds of patients in between malfunctions. Whenever malfunctions occurred, the Therac-25 could send through the patient readings in the range of 13,000 to 20,000 rads instead of the normal 200 rads. Anything over 500 rads can cause death. The Therac-25 used a software upgrade of the older model of the Therac-6. The manufacturers of the Therac-25, sure of the safety record of Therac-6, paid little attention to software. They were overconfident that it worked very well. So they simply upgraded it, adding in more parameters with few changes. In addition to endangering patients, the Therac-25 also endangered operators because of the stress that resulted from the situation. For the full account of the investigation into the Therac-25 accident, the reader is referred to the paper: "An Investigation of the Therac-25 Accident" by Nancy G. Leveson and Clark S. Turner. *Computer*, vol. 26, #7, July 1993, pp. 18–41.

8.3.3.2   The Space Shuttle Challenger

On January 28, 1986, the US National Aeronautical and Space Administration (NASA)'s flight of mission STS 51-L using the *Challenger* spaceship burst into flames 72 s after takeoff. Flight 51-L of the *Challenger* space-craft was scheduled originally to fly in July 1985, then it was postponed three other times until this fateful day. The accident left millions of people in shock, and it was a great setback for NASA and the prestige of the space program. The combination of these and other matters surrounding the accident, including problems within NASA, forced President Ronald Regan to appoint a commission of inquiry into the accident and the working of NASA so that future accidents like this could be avoided. The commission, chaired by William P. Rogers, former secretary of state under President Nixon (1969–1973) and attorney general under President Eisenhower (1957–1961), was to:

> (i) [R]eview the circumstances surrounding the accident to establish the probable cause or causes of the accident; and (ii) develop recommendations for corrective or other action based upon the commission's findings and determinations.

In its deliberations, the commission interviewed more than 160 individuals, held more than 35 formal panel investigative sessions, and examined more that 6,300 documents, totaling more than 122,000 pages, and hundreds of photographs.

On June 6, 1986, the commission handed their findings and recommendations to the president. In its executive summary report, the commission and other investigative agencies found that the loss of the *Challenger* was the result of a failure in the joint between the two lower segments of the right solid rocket motor. More specifically, the seals that prevent hot gases from leaking through the joint during the propellant burns of the rocket motor were destroyed, thus causing the joints to fail. Below is the commission's findings [21].

1. A combustion gas leak through the right Solid Rocket Motor aft field joint initiated at or shortly after ignition eventually weakened and/or penetrated the External Tank initiating vehicle structural breakup and loss of the Space Shuttle Challenger during STS Mission 51-L.
2. The evidence shows that no other STS 51-L Shuttle element or the pay-load contributed to the causes of the right Solid Rocket Motor aft field joint combustion gas leak. Sabotage was not a factor.
3. Evidence examined in the review of Space Shuttle material, manufacturing, assembly, quality control, and processing on non-conformance reports found no flight hardware shipped to the launch site that fell outside the limits of Shuttle design specifications.
4. Launch site activities, including assembly and preparation, from receipt of the flight hardware to launch were generally in accord with established procedures and were not considered a factor in the accident.

5. Launch site records show that the right Solid Rocket Motor segments were assembled using approved procedures. However, significant out-of-round conditions existed between the two segments joined at the right Solid Rocket Motor aft field joint (the joint that failed).

   (a) While the assembly conditions had the potential of generating debris or damage that could cause O-ring seal failure, these were not considered factors in this accident.
   (b) The diameters of the two Solid Rocket Motor segments had grown as a result of prior use.
   (c) The growth resulted in a condition at time of launch wherein the maximum gap between the tang and clevis in the region of the joint's O-rings was no more than 0.008 in. and the average gap would have been 0.004 in.
   (d) With a tang-to-clevis gap of 0.004 in., the O-ring in the joint would be compressed to the extent that it pressed against all three walls of the O-ring retaining channel.
   (e) The lack of roundness of the segments was such that the smallest tang-to-clevis clearance occurred at the initiation of the assembly operation at positions of 120° and 300° around the circumference of the aft field joint. It is uncertain if this tight condition and the resultant greater compression of the O-rings at these points persisted to the time of launch.

6. The ambient temperature at time of launch was 36°F, or 15° lower than the next coldest previous launch.

   (a) The temperature at the 300° position on the right aft field joint circumference was estimated to be 28° plus or minus 5°F. This was the coldest point on the joint.
   (b) Temperature on the opposite side of the right Solid Rocket Booster facing the sun was estimated to be about 50°F.

7. Other joints on the left and right Solid Rocket Boosters experienced similar combinations of tang-to-clevis gap clearance and temperature. It is not known whether these joints experienced distress during the flight of 51-L.

8. Experimental evidence indicates that due to several effects associated with the Solid Rocket Booster's ignition and combustion pressures and associated vehicle motions, the gap between the tang and the clevis will open as much as 0.017 and 0.029 in. at the secondary and primary O-rings, respectively.

   (a) This opening begins upon ignition, reaches its maximum rate of opening at about 200–300 ms, and is essentially complete at 600 ms when the Solid Rocket Booster reaches its operating pressure.
   (b) The External Tank and right Solid Rocket Booster are connected by several struts, including one at 310° near the aft field joint that failed. This strut's effect on the joint dynamics is to enhance the opening of the gap between the tang and clevis by about 10–20% in the region of 300–320°.

9. O-ring resiliency is directly related to its temperature.

(a) A warm O-ring that has been compressed will return to its original shape much quicker than will a cold O-ring when compression is relieved. Thus, a warm O-ring will follow the opening of the tang-to-clevis gap. A cold O-ring may not.

(b) A compressed O-ring at 75°F is five times more responsive in returning to its uncompressed shape than a cold O-ring at 30°F.

(c) As a result it is probable that the O-rings in the right solid booster aft field joint were not following the opening of the gap between the tang and cleavis at time of ignition.

10. Experiments indicate that the primary mechanism that actuates O-ring sealing is the application of gas pressure to the upstream (high-pressure) side of the O-ring as it sits in its groove or channel.

(a) For this pressure actuation to work most effectively, a space between the O-ring and its upstream channel wall should exist during pressurization.

(b) A tang-to-clevis gap of 0.004 in., as probably existed in the failed joint, would have initially compressed the O-ring to the degree that no clearance existed between the O-ring and its upstream channel wall and the other two surfaces of the channel.

(c) At the cold launch temperature experienced, the O-ring would be very slow in returning to its normal rounded shape. It would not follow the opening of the tang-to-clevis gap. It would remain in its compressed position in the O-ring channel and not provide a space between itself and the upstream channel wall. Thus, it is probable the O-ring would not be pressure actuated to seal the gap in time to preclude joint failure due to blow-by and erosion from hot combustion gases.

11. The sealing characteristics of the Solid Rocket Booster O-rings are enhanced by timely application of motor pressure.

(a) Ideally, motor pressure should be applied to actuate the O-ring and seal the joint prior to significant opening of the tang-to-clevis gap (100–200 ms after motor ignition).

(b) Experimental evidence indicates that temperature, humidity, and other variables in the putty compound used to seal the joint can delay pressure application to the joint by 500 ms or more.

(c) This delay in pressure could be a factor in initial joint failure.

12. Of 21 launches with ambient temperatures of 61°F or greater, only four showed signs of O-ring thermal distress; i.e., erosion or blow-by and soot. Each of the launches below 61°F resulted in one or more O-rings showing signs of thermal distress.

(a) Of these improper joint sealing actions, one-half occurred in the aft field joints, 20% in the center field joints, and 30% in the upper field joints. The division between left and right Solid Rocket Boosters was roughly equal.

(b) Each instance of thermal O-ring distress was accompanied by a leak path in the insulating putty. The leak path connects the rocket's combustion chamber with the O-ring region of the tang and clevis. Joints that actuated without incident may also have had these leak paths.

13. There is a possibility that there was water in the clevis of the STS 51-L joints since water was found in the STS-9 joints during a destack operation after exposure to less rainfall than STS 51-L. At time of launch, it was cold enough that water present in the joint would freeze. Tests show that ice in the joint can inhibit proper secondary seal performance.

14. A series of puffs of smoke were observed emanating from the 51-L aft field joint area of the right Solid Rocket Booster between 0.678 and 2.500 s after ignition of the Shuttle Solid Rocket Motors.

(a) The puffs appeared at a frequency of about three puffs per second. This roughly matches the natural structural frequency of the solids at lift off and is reflected in slight cyclic changes of the tang-to-clevis gap opening.

(b) The puffs were seen to be moving upward along the surface of the booster above the aft field joint.

(c) The smoke was estimated to originate at a circumferential position of between 270° and 315° on the booster aft field joint, emerging from the top of the joint.

15. This smoke from the aft field joint at Shuttle lift off was the first sign of the failure of the Solid Rocket Booster O-ring seals on STS 51-L.

16. The leak was again clearly evident as a flame at approximately 58 s into the flight. It is possible that the leak was continuous but unobservable or non-existent in portions of the intervening period. It is possible in either case that thrust vectoring and normal vehicle response to wind shear as well as planned maneuvers reinitiated or magnified the leakage from a degraded seal in the period preceding the observed flames. The estimated position of the flame, centered at a point 307° around the circumference of the aft field joint, was confirmed by the recovery of two fragments of the right Solid Rocket Booster.

(a) A small leak could have been present that may have grown to breach the joint in flame at a time on the order of 58–60 s after liftoff.

(b) Alternatively, the O-ring gap could have been resealed by deposition of a fragile buildup of aluminum oxide and other combustion debris. This resealed section of the joint could have been disturbed by thrust vectoring, Space Shuttle motion and flight loads inducted by changing winds aloft.

(c) The winds aloft caused control actions in the time interval of 32–62 s into the flight that were typical of the largest values experienced on previous missions.

In conclusion, the commission stressed that the *Challenger* accident was the result of failure of the pressure seals in the aft field joint of the right Solid Rocket Booster. The commission also concluded that the failure, therefore, was a result of a faulty design unacceptably sensitive to a number of factors that include temperature, physical dimensions, character of materials, the effects of reusability, processing, and the reaction of the joint to dynamic loading.

During the commission's hearing, information emerged indicating that engineers at Morton Thiokol, Inc., the Utah company that designed the Rocket Booster joints in the *Challenger*, warned management against the launch of the space shuttle because of the predicted low temperatures. They feared that the predicted low temperatures would stiffen the O-rings.

Against their company's guidelines to give "yes" or "no" answers to the commission's questions, three engineers, Allan McDonald, Arnold Thompson, and Roger Boisjoly, broke ranks with management to reveal the warning. The three, led by Roger Boisjoly, told the commission that they warned management that the temperature of 18°F (−8°C) predicted the morning of the launch may make the booster O-ring stiff, preventing them from sealing the gases properly. They presented evidence to the commission to show that at 53°F, in one of the past launches, one of the two redundant joints had not sealed. It was learned that although Morton Thiokol's management had not previously approved any launch at temperatures below 53°F, on this occasion, management changed their position under duress from NASA, after previously postponing the *Challenger* launch four times. NASA argued that there was never any such data on the booster joints' acceptable range of temperatures and they were therefore ready to go. Up to the last moment of launch, engineer Allen McDonald, the Morton Thiokol resident engineer at the Kennedy Space Flight Center, fought NASA to postpone the launch, but he did not succeed and the launch went ahead—at least for 27 s [20].

8.3.3.3 The Indian Bhopal Chemical Accident

The Union Carbide industrial accident in Bhopal, India, illustrates many of the elements of this safety culture. In December 1984, an accidental release of methyl isocyanate killed between 2,000 and 3,000 people and injured tens of thousands of others, many of them permanently. The accident was later blamed on human error. The official report stated that water was let into the storage tank of methyl isocyanate through an improperly cleaned pipe ([7], p. 40). According to Leveson, Union Carbide management, including scientists, believed that because of the modern technology they had at the plant, such an accident could not happen there. It did.

8.3.3.4 The Chernobyl Nuclear Power Accident

The 1986 Chernobyl nuclear power accident in northern Ukraine, then a republic of the USSR, was the worst nuclear accident that has ever occurred. For a number of days after the accident, the Soviet government kept the world guessing at what was happening. But when details started to spill out, it was discovered that things started going bad on April 26, 1986, when during an experiment to determine the length of time the turbine and the generator could supply the emergency cooling system with electricity if an accident were to occur, the experiment went haywire and the operators started to notice a decline in the power output.

On noticing the decline, the operators turned off two automatic systems which were supposed to activate the controller rods in an emergency. At the same time they pumped more water into the reactor tank. When the water in the reactor tank stopped boiling, they then decreased the fresh water flow into the reactor tank—a bad mistake.

This action resulted in an unprecedented power upsurge in a very short time when the water in the reactor tank started to boil again. This overwhelming power, generated in only a couple of seconds, overheated the nuclear fuel, and a third of the core exploded from the inside. The quick upsurge in power and the subsequent explosion resulted from the fact that the steam from the boiling reactor tank water reacted with the graphite in the reactor and formed carbon dioxide and hydrogen, generating high steam pressure which lifted the lid off the reactor tank and quickly reacted with the air outside to cause the huge explosion. Immediately after, radioactive emissions were blown by the wind and quickly covered the surrounding areas and threatened western Europe [19].

8.4 Consumer Protection

Asset purchasing is a game of wits played between the buyer and the seller. Any time you make a purchase, remember that you are starting at a disadvantage because unlike the seller you do not have all the cards to win the game; the seller does. He or she always has more information about the item for sale than you, the buyer. As the game progresses the seller picks and chooses the information to give to the buyer.

In the case of software purchases, the buyer needs to be even more careful because many software products do not always work as the seller claims they do, or at least as the buyer would like them to. Software products may not work as expected because the buyer has unrealistic expectations about the product, the environment in which the product is supposed to work is inadequate, the seller exaggerated the capacities of the software, or the software is simply faulty. So what can buyers do if the product just purchased does not live up to expectations? It usually depends on how much buyers know about their rights. Without claiming to be lawyers, let's begin this section by defining the legal jargon buyers need in order to press for their rights and to take legal action if nothing else works. Legal action should be the last resort, however, because once filed, a lawsuit takes on a life of its own in expense, time, and outcome.

8.4.1 Buyers' Rights

What are our rights as purchasers of a software product that does not live up to our expectations? The first step is to review the available options by contacting the developer of the product. If the developer is not the seller, then start with the vendor from whom you bought the product. Sometimes the vendor or seller may replace the product with a new one, depending on the elapsed time and warranties, or may refer you to the developer.

When talking to the developer, explain specifically and clearly what it is that you want, why you are not satisfied with the product, and what you want to accomplish. Although developers claim to help unsatisfied customers, computer software is more difficult to deal with once it has been opened, and you may have to do more than you would with a different kind of product to convince both the vendor and the developer that their product is not satisfactory. Developers typically have technical teams to help customers with problems, and most of the problems are solved at this level. However, if you are still not satisfied with the service, other options are open to you such as the following:

- *Product replacement*: You may demand a product replacement if you think it will solve the problem. Most developers usually do replace faulty products.
- *Product update*: When the product is found to have a fault that the provider was not aware of at the time of shipping the product to market, the producer may fix the fault by providing a patch or an upgrade of the product that can either be downloaded or shipped to all customers who report that fault (e.g., the Netscape case and the Intel Pentium chip debacle).

In the Netscape case, a serious flaw in the then just released Netscape Communications Corporation's browser was uncovered by a small Danish software company called Cabocomm. The bug made it possible for web site operators to read anything stored on the hard disk of a PC logged on the web site. Netscape acknowledged the error and offered to send upgrades to its customers [12].

The Intel Pentium chip situation was very much like that of Netscape, Inc., except that for Intel it was a hardware problem. A mathematics professor using a Pentium-based office PC found that at a high level of mathematical computation, the chip froze. He reported his discovery via e-mail to a colleague, and the word spread like wildfire. But unlike Netscape, Inc., which immediately admitted fault, Intel did not at first admit it until the giant IBM and other small PC companies threatened not to use the chip in their line of products. Intel then accepted responsibility and promised to send upgrades to all its customers [13].

If none of the options already discussed prove viable, the next and probably last step is legal action. A liability suit is filed in civil court against the producer of the product for damages. In some cases, if the product has resulted in a casualty, a criminal suit against the producer can also be filed if the customer believes there was criminal intent. If you decide to file a civil liability suit, two avenues are open to you—the contract and/or tort options (see Sections 8.4.3 and 8.4.4). For a successful outcome in a software case, you need to proceed with care to classify what was purchased either as a product or a service. The decision of the courts in a purchase lawsuit depends heavily on this classification.

8.4.2 Classification of Computer Software

As we explained earlier, computer software falls into three categories: product, service, and a mixture of both service and product.

8.4.2.1 What Is a Product?

A product must have two fundamental properties. First it must have a tangible form, and second it must have a built-in intrinsic value for the buyer. Let's look at a few examples. Consider a lottery ticket you have just bought for which the jackpot is $100 million. Suppose you paid $1 for your ticket. The ticket has a form that everyone can see and touch; it is tangible. Now suppose your grandmother, who is visiting with you, lives in a state with no lottery. She finds your ticket lying on the kitchen table. To her, although the ticket has a tangible form because she can see and touch it, it has no value to her. To you, however, the ticket not only has tangible form, it also has an intrinsic value worth millions of dollars.

For a second example, suppose you have a splitting headache, which your physician tells you can be cured by a certain tablet. For you this tablet has a tangible form because you can see and touch it, but it also has an intrinsic value because you believe it will cure your headache. To somebody else who does not have a headache, the tablet simply has a tangible form but no value beyond that. For software to be considered a product, it must have both a tangible form and an intrinsic value. Many software packages have these two properties and can therefore be considered as products. For example, when you buy a US tax preparation package and you live in the United States, to you the package has both a tangible form and an intrinsic value. But to somebody else living in another country, the package, although it has tangible form, does not have any intrinsic value at all.

8.4.2.2 What Is a Service?

A service, unlike a product, has intrinsic value, but it does not have a tangible form. Because it has no tangible form, whoever wants a service must describe it. A service most often involves a provider–client or provider–customer relationship: The provider in this equation is the person offering the service and the client is the person receiving the service. For professionals, the relationship is always provider–client, where there is an imbalance of power in favor of the provider (e.g., an attorney–client relationship or a doctor–patient relationship).

In nonprofessional situations, it is often a provider–customer relationship and the power play here is in favor of the customer because customers must always get what they want, and the customer must always be satisfied. What the provider and customer receive in this relationship, though, has no tangible form—but it does have intrinsic value. The customer gets satisfaction with the service and this satisfaction is the value of the service. The provider in turn gets paid, and again that is the value of the service.

8.4.2.3   Is Software a Product, a Service, or a Mixture?

Now that we have differentiated between a product and a service, let us tackle the problem of classification of computer software. According to Deborah Johnson [15], courts do not always equate products with what is tangible. If we accept this line of reasoning, then software with no tangible form can be considered a product and therefore can be protected by patent laws that protect products. But we have to be very careful with this line of argument not to conclude too hastily that software is going to be accepted as a product because there are items with no tangible forms that even the courts cannot accept as products.

If we define software as a set of instructions describing an algorithm to perform a task that has intrinsic value for the buyer, this definition classifies software as a service. For example, suppose you want a software item to perform a certain task for your company but you cannot find the appropriate type on the market. You describe what it is that you want done to a software developer, and the software developer comes up with what you want. What has been produced can be considered a service performed; it has intrinsic value for you, but no tangible form.

But suppose you want a program to do a task for you, and instead of describing it to a software developer, you decide to go to your discount store where you know such a software item is sold, and you buy a box containing that item. What you have just paid for is a product no different from that box of potato chips you picked up at the same store. Suppose further that when you open your potato chips you find them crushed to a powder, or suppose when you eat the potato chips they make you sick, and later you find they were contaminated. Legally you cannot sue the producer of the chips for malpractice or negligence, but you can sue for product liability. Similarly, then, you cannot sue for malpractice or negligence if the contents of a software box do not work properly. You should sue for product liability because in this case software seems to be an indisputable product.

There are interesting yet mixed views concerning the classification of software. Jim Price [14] defines three categories of software classes using the producer–market–customer relationship:

1. *Canned software*: Off-the-shelf software for a general market customer. Tax preparation software packages fall in this category.
2. *Customized software*: The software produced for a customer after the customer has described what he or she specifically needs to the software producer.
3. *Hybrid software*: Canned software that is customized to meet certain customer needs, but cannot be used to perform the whole task without focused modifications.

Price argues for a product classification of all software falling in category 1 on the basis of three principles:

1. The product was placed in mainstream commerce by the producer with the purpose of making a profit, and the producer therefore should be responsible for the implied safety of the product.
2. The producer has a better understanding of the product than the buyer, and therefore is in a better position to anticipate the risks.
3. The producer can easily spread the burden of the cost of product liabilities due to injuries over the entire range of product customers without the customers knowing, thus minimizing the costs and risks to him or her [15].

With software in category 1, strict liability for a bad product, including negligence, can be raised by the customer seeking benefits from the producer. For software in category 2, customers can seek benefits from the producer resulting from injuries by using malpractice laws because software in this category is a service.

With these two categories, the distinction between a product and a service is straightforward. But this is not the case with software in category 3. Some elements in this category belong to a product classification (e.g., placing the item in the mainstream of commerce in a tangible form).

Also, because the software can be changed to suit individual needs, the principle that the producer can spread the burden of the cost of product liability because of injuries over all product customers does not apply anymore. This is what Johnson calls a mixed classification case because it belongs in two categories: the canned category and the customized category. Johnson suggests that such software should be treated in the following way. If there is an error in the canned part, then it can be treated like a product. And if it develops an error in the customized part, then it should be handled as a service. The problem with this line of thinking, though, is that for an average software user it is almost impossible to tell in which part the error originated.

As technology advances, new categories will definitely emerge, and ideally new laws will be enacted to cover all these new categories. We cannot keep on relying on old laws to cope with the ever-changing technological scene.

When you have successfully classified your software, then you can pursue the two possible options open to you: contract or tort.

8.4.3 The Contract Option

Lawyers define a contract as a binding relationship between two or more parties. A contract need not be in a physical form like a document; it can be oral or implied. For a relationship to be a contract, it must satisfy several requirements including mutual consent. Mutual consent is a meeting of the minds on issues such as the price bargained or agreed upon, the amount paid or promised to be paid, and any agreement enforceable by law.

In contract laws, a producer/developer can be sued for breach of contract. Contract laws also cover express and implied warranties, third-party beneficial contracts, and disclaimers. Warranties are guarantees that the product or service will live up to its reasonable expectations. Some warranties are not specifically written down but are implied, whereas others are merely expressed either orally or in some other form.

8.4.3.1 Express Warranties

Express warranties are an affirmation of a fact, a promise, or a description of goods, a sample, or a model made by the seller to the buyer relating to the goods and as a basis for payment negotiations. Express warranties are entered into between the customer and the producer when a producer agrees to supply the product to the customer. They also involve promises made by the producer through sales representatives and written materials on packaging attesting to the quality of the product and guidelines buyers must follow to get detectable errors corrected by the producer. These warranties are also included in the US Uniform Commercial Code (UCC) and, unless specifically excluded by the seller, express warranties become enforceable immediately upon application of the UCC transaction.

Producers usually limit their liability on products by stipulating a time frame on warranties and contracts. But in most cases, time limits do not apply, especially in cases of express warranties because of advertising and description of the product capacity on or in packages [16].

8.4.3.2 Implied Warranties

Implied warranties are enforced by law according to established and accepted public policy. For example, in the nonideal world we live in, we cannot expect a contract to contain everything the buyer and producer may want. Remember that the process of buying and selling is a game in which there is a winner, a loser, or a draw. In this game, as we pointed out earlier, the seller has more cards than the buyer.

On the buyer's side are quite a number of things they do not have to negotiate because they do not know as much and need time to learn the product. The law protects buyers so they do not have to negotiate every small detail of the product conditions. Implied warranties make such conditions always part of the package agreement even if they are not specifically written down in the contract. An implied warranty guarantees that a product is of average quality and will perform no less than similar products and that it is fit for the intended use. For buyers to benefit from implied warranties, proof must be given that the contract did not exclude some features and there is no time limitation for reporting defects; some companies, however, stipulate a time frame in which defects must be reported. Implied warranties are advantageous to buyers because they enforce a degree of discipline on the producers and vendors to sell standard products for the intended purposes.

They are also useful to the producer and vendors because they create a degree of confidence and trust in buyers, hence increasing sales of products. However, there is a downside to implied warranties; they tend to make software expensive because the producer anticipates the cost of the lawsuits that might be generated and passes such costs on to the customers.

8.4.3.3 Third-Party Beneficiary Contracts

If a software product injures a user other than the buyer, under a third-party beneficiary contract the user may sue the producer for benefits due to injuries or loss of income resulting from the product. Third-party beneficiary contracts suits are not common because they are rarely found valid in courts.

8.4.3.4 Disclaimers

Producers try to control their liability losses by putting limits on warranties via disclaimers. Through disclaimers producers preempt lawsuits from buyers by telling buyers in writing on the contracts the limits of what is guaranteed.

Many users see disclaimers as a way producers try to avoid responsibility. Producers see them as a way of informing the users of the risks before they buy the product, and they also like them because they put the burden of proof and risk taking squarely on the buyers—caveat emptor (the buyer beware), so to speak. Whether these disclaimers are recognized in courts depends on a number of factors including the belief that the disclaimers were made in good faith.

8.4.3.5 Breach of Contract

A contract entered into between two or more parties and not performed as promised by either party can be considered breached by the party not in compliance. If the complaint is not very serious, the breach may not cause the termination of the contract, but the breaching party may be asked to pay some damages. However, if the breach is considered serious by one of the parties, it may cause the termination of the contract. In this case the offended party may demand damages from the breaching party in the contract upon satisfactory proof that there were indeed damages resulting from contract breaching.

8.4.4 The Tort Option

If a buyer cannot seek benefits from the producer through contracts laws, another avenue of legal action is through tort. A tort is a wrong committed upon a person or property in the absence of a contract. A tort may include negligence, malpractice, strict liability, and misrepresentation. Torts fall into two categories: intentional and unintentional. For example, if you are passing by a construction site and somebody pours concrete on you, this act may be interpreted as intentional if the worker who poured the concrete knew it was you passing; otherwise it is unintentional.

8.4.4.1 Negligence

Negligence can be used by the buyer to obtain benefits from the producer if there is provable evidence that the product lacked a certain degree of care, skill, and competence in the workmanship. Carelessness and a lack of competence may be proved from the design stage through the testing, installation, and user training stages of the product. For example, suppose that the buyer of a computer software product is a large hospital and the product is life-sustaining software. If it causes injury to a patient because the hospital personnel using the software were not adequately trained by the producer of the software, and this can be proved beyond a reasonable doubt, then the producer can be sued for negligence. In other words, negligence in this case is holding the software producer party liable for the injuries he or she did not intend and even tried to avoid while making the software. Negligence cases apply mainly to services rendered.

8.4.4.2 Malpractice

Malpractice is a type of negligence. It is also applicable in cases involving services. For example, if you visit the doctor for a simple eye surgery and he or she cuts off your ear, you can sue the doctor for malpractice. Malpractice lawsuits are common in professional services. In the case of software, if it is taken as a service, then malpractice applies.

8.4.4.3 Strict Liability

Strict liability is a tort involving products. Any product sold in a defective condition that ends up endangering a person creates a case of strict liability to the seller of such a product even if the buyer did not make a direct purchase from the seller. In strict liability lawsuits, the burden of proof of negligence is shifted to the producer, and the costs due to defects in the product are squarely in the hands of the producer. Under strict liability, it is the product itself that is on trial. The product is examined and if it is found to be defective and dangerous, the buyer is awarded benefits. Strict liability laws are harsh. They ignore efforts made by the producer of the product to make the product safe for the reason that the producer was in a better position to know the risks [17].

8.4.4.4   Misrepresentation

Most computer software and other computer products are no longer sold by their original producers and developers but by third-party sellers and vendors. Examples of such third-party sellers are mail-order computer hardware and hundreds of software companies and many big brand-name computer outlets. So very few original manufacturers and software developers are selling directly to the buyer. To the buyer of a computer product, this situation may add another layer of bureaucracy and more problems. The problems are not one-sided, though; indirect selling also causes additional problems for the producer. Many of the producer problems added by this layer actually come from misrepresentation of the product. Misrepresentation may be intentionally done by the sales representative to induce the buyer to buy the product or it may be just a genuine mistake. Consider car manufacturers, for example. Usually they buy back faulty new cars from customers when these cars have developed specific problems within a designated period of time. These cars are usually repaired and sent back to the dealers to be sold, not as new but as used products. Sometimes, however, car dealers sell these cars as new cars. Whether car manufacturers are aware of these sales practices or not, customers always end up suing the car manufacturers.

Before you sue the producer, however, determine first whether it was an intentional misrepresentation called fraudulent misrepresentation or not. To prove fraudulent misrepresentation, you need to prove that the vendor was aware the facts given were not true or that the vendor would have known the true facts but opted not to inform the buyer accordingly. You also need to show, and be believed, that you as a buyer relied on that information to buy the product. And finally you need to show that the product resulted in damage. If you can establish all these facts and be believed by the courts, then you have a case [15].

8.5   Improving Software Quality

The problem of software quality cannot be solved by courts alone. Software producers must themselves do more to ensure software quality and hence safety.

8.5.1   Techniques for Improving Software Quality

Reputable software standards, reliability of software, and software safety depend greatly on the quality of the software. If the quality is low, software is prone to errors, is therefore not reliable, and hence has poor standards. In Section 8.1.1, we stated that software can be enhanced by techniques such as developmental testing, V&V, and programming standards. But the quality of software cannot be assumed by looking at these factors only. According to Linger et al. [17], software cannot be made reliable by testing alone. Software quality can be improved through these innovative new review techniques:

- *Formal review*: Presentation of the software product by a person more familiar with the product to others with competent knowledge of that product so they can critique the product and offer informed suggestions.
- *Inspection*: Involves checking the known specific errors from past products and establishing additional facilities that may be missing in the product to bring the product up to acceptable standards.
- *Walk-through*: Requires code inspection line-by-line by a team of reviewers to detect potential errors. Each review session is followed by a discussion of the findings by the members of the review team, usually with the creators of the code present.
- *Phased inspection*: Technique developed by Jack C. Knight and Ann Mayers [18]. It is an enhanced method combining the previous three methods by putting emphasis on the limitations of those methods. It consists of a series of coordinated partial inspections called phases during which specific properties of the product are inspected.

If care is taken by the software developer to improve the development process of software by improving validation, verification, and the survivability of the software, the liability on their part will be minimized, and software safety will be greatly improved. If software developers paid more attention to software quality using many of the techniques cited here during development, there would be little need to discuss consumer protection.

8.6   Producer Protection

In Section 8.4 we outlined user rights and protection mechanisms in the case of substandard software. In this section we focus on the other side of the same coin: the software producer's rights and protection mechanisms. Software producers need to protect themselves against piracy, illegal copying, and fraudulent lawsuits. But because of the high costs, time, and the unpredictability of the outcome of lawsuits, it is not good business practice for software producers to sue a single person making a copy of the software. It only makes sense to go after big-time and large-scale illegal copying. Software producers should be prepared to seek protection from the courts to protect the software itself from illegal copying, piracy, and also from lawsuits from customers. In addition, producers should be prepared to protect themselves from lawsuits filed by consumers. For this kind of protection, producers are advised to use the courts as much as possible and ask for advice from lawyers and business colleagues. There is no one single magic bullet approach.

Exercises

1. Discuss the difficulties faced by software producers.
2. Discuss ways software customers can protect themselves from substandard software products.
3. Discuss how the following are used to protect a software customer:
   • Implied warranty
   • Express warranty
   • Disclaimer
   • Strict liability
4. It has been said that software's problems are a direct result of its differences from hardware. Discuss.
5. Discuss the elements of software quality. How can software quality be a solution to many of software's liability problems?
6. Do safe software systems imply reliable systems? Why or why not?
7. Software reliability, especially in critical systems, is vital. Discuss the necessary conditions for reliability.
8. With the development of scanning and snooping software, computer systems cannot be assured of security. Discuss what steps need to be taken to ensure system safety.
9. We discussed in this chapter that risk can be both voluntary and involuntary. Give examples in each case.
10. Why do we always take risk as a crucial design component? What two aspects must be considered?
11. In carrying out the risk assessment and control of a software product, what aspects must be considered and why?
12. Why is there a myth that computers (hardware and software) do not make errors?
13. Does the myth about computers complicate the safety issue?
14. How does humanware affect system safety?
15. If workplace systems were all automated, could this eliminate workplace system risks? Would it reduce it?
16. Why is software safety so difficult to attain? Can it be guaranteed?

References

1. Hamlet, Richard. "Special Section on Software Testing." *Communications of the ACM,* 31(6), 1988, pp. 662–667.
2. Parnas, David, John van Schouwen, and Shu Kwan. "Evolution of Safety-Critical Software." *Communications of the ACM,* 33(6), 1990, pp. 636–648.
3. Taylor, Jeff. "America's Loneliest Airport: Denver's Dreams Can't Fly." *Kansas City Star,* August 28, 1994. NewsBank, Transportation, 1994, fiche 43, grids D12–14.
4. Neumann, Peter. *Computer-Related Risks.* New York: ACM Press, 1995.
5. Neumann, Peter. "The Role of Software Engineering." *Communications of the ACM,* 36(5), 1993, p. 114.
6. Davis, Ahl. "Employee Computer Crime on the Rise." *Creative Computing,* June 1985, p. 6.
7. Leveson, Nancy. *Safeware: System Safety and Computers.* Reading, MA: Addison-Wesley, 1995.
8. Littlewood, Bev, and Lorenzo Strigini. "Validation of Ultrahigh Dependability for Software-Based Systems." *Communications of the ACM,* 36(11), 1993, pp. 69–80.
9. Ritchie, Davis. "Reflections on Trusting Trust." *Communications of the ACM,* 27(8), 1984, pp. 761–763.

10. Haag, Stephen, M.K. Raju, and L.L. Schkade. "Quality Function Deployment Usage in Software Development." *Communications of the ACM,* 39(1), 1996, pp. 41–49.
11. Boehm, Barry W. *Software Risk Management: Principles and Practices.* New York: IEEE Computer Society Press, 1989.
12. Young, Steven. "Netscape Bug Uncovered," CNNfn, June 12. http://cnnfn.com/digi-taljam/9706/netscape-pkg/
13. "Computer Stock Tumble Over Chip Flow." *New York Times,* December 4, 1994, section D.
14. Prince, Jim. "Negligence: Liability for Defective Software." *Oklahoma Law Review,* 33, 1980, pp. 848–855.
15. Johnson, Deborah. *Computer Ethics* (2nd ed.). Englewood Cliffs, NJ: Prentice Hall, 1994, p. 134.
16. Neitzke, Frederick. *A Software Law Primer.* New York: Reinhold, 1984.
17. Linger, C., H.D. Mills, and B. Witts. Structured Programming: Theory and Practice. Reading, MA: Addison-Wesley, 1979.
18. Knight, Jack, and Ann Mayers. "An Improved Inspection Technique." *Communications of the ACM,* 36(11), 1994, pp. 51–61.
19. "Nuclear Accidents" Swedish Nuclear Power Generation. http://www.thn.edu.stockholm.se/projekt/energi/kk/index.htm
20. Karen Fitzgerald. "Whistle-blowing: Not Always a Losing Game." *IEEE Spectrum,* 26(6), Dec. 1990, pp. 49–52.
21. "President's Commission on the *Challenger* Accident Report." http://science.ksc.nasa.gov/shuttle/missions/51-l/docs/rogers-commission/table-of-contents.html

Further Readings

Banker, Rajiv, Srikant Datar, Chris Kemerer, and Dani Zeneig. "Software Complexity and Maintenance Costs." *Communications of the ACM,* 36(11), 1993, pp. 81–94.
Fetzer, James. "Program Verification: The Very Idea." *Communications of the ACM,* 31(9), 1988, pp. 1048–1063.
Gelperin, David, and Bill Hetzel. "The Growth of Software Testing." *Communications of the ACM,* 31(6), 1988, pp. 687–690.
Grady, Roberts. "Practical Results from Measuring Software Quality." *Communications of the ACM,* 36(11), 1993, pp. 50–61.
Laprie, Jean-Claude, and Bev Littlewood. "Probablistic Assessment of Safety-Critical Software: Why and How?" *Communications of the ACM,* 35(2), 1992, pp. 13–21.
Leveson, Nancy. "Software Safety in Embedded Computer Systems." *Communications of the ACM,* 34(2), 1991, pp. 34–46.

Chapter 9
Computer Crimes

Learning Objectives

After reading this chapter, the reader should be able to:

1. Describe trends in computer crimes and protection against viruses and denial-of-service attacks.
2. Enumerate techniques to combat "cracker" attacks.
3. Discuss the history of computer crimes.
4. Describe several different cyber-attacker approaches and motivations.
5. Identify the professional's role in security and the tradeoffs involved.
6. Develop measures to be taken both by individuals themselves and by organizations (including government) to prevent identity theft.

Scenario 7

All in the Open, My Friend—Be Watchful for You Will Never Know the Hour!

Josephine Katu owns a company that manufactures women's cosmetics. She has loyal and dedicated employees, and each one of them works very hard. Josephine has been good to them too. She compliments them and rewards them handsomely when the occasion presents itself.

However, Josephine has become suspicious of some of the employees, without knowing which one(s) in particular. She is also not sure what it is that is not right, but she suspects something is going wrong somewhere in her company and she is not happy. So she decides to do something about it.

During the Christmas season, Josephine buys each of her 20 or so employees a laptop for his or her homes and she promises to pay for their online expenses. In addition, she also promises to take care of all system maintenance, using the company technician, if they ever need it. Josephine writes a virus that she occasionally and selectively uploads to her employees' home computers. The virus disables the machine and the employee is forced to call in the technician.

Josephine has instructed the technician that every time he goes to service any of her employee's home computers, the technician must make a copy of everything on the computer being serviced and bring it to her. The technician is never to reveal the plan to anyone. The plan is working very well and Josephine is getting plenty of information whenever the virus is released. She is even planning on bringing in the press and the FBI.

Discussion Questions

1. *Is Josephine right to release a virus on her employees' computers?*
2. *Do the computers belong to her or to her employees?*
3. *Are the employees' rights being violated? What rights?*
4. *What are the social and ethical implications of Josephine's little tricks?*

J.M. Kizza, *Ethical and Social Issues in the Information Age*, Texts in Computer Science, DOI 10.1007/978-1-84996-038-0_9, © Springer-Verlag London Limited 2010

9.1   Introduction

It is difficult to define a computer crime without getting tangled up in the legal terminology. We will try to make it simple for the rest of us nonlawyers. A computer crime is a crime like any other crime, except that in this case the illegal act must involve a computer system either as an object of a crime, an instrument used to commit a crime, or a repository of evidence related to a crime. With the Internet, the scope of computer crimes has widened to actually include crimes that would normally be associated with telecommunication facilities. Because of this, we want to expand our definition of a computer crime to be an illegal act that involves a computer system or computer-related system like a telephone, microwave, satellite, or other telecommunication systems that connect one or more computers or computer-related systems.

Acts using computers or computer-related technologies that fall within the limits that the legislature of a state or a nation has specified are considered illegal and may lead to forfeiture of certain civil rights of the perpetrator. In the United States, local, state, and federal legislatures have defined such acts to include the following and more:

- Intrusions of the Public Switched Network
- Intrusions into Public Packet Networks
- Network integrity violations
- Privacy violations
- Industrial espionage
- Pirated computer software
- Fraud
- Internet/email abuse
- Using computers or computer technology to commit murder, terrorism, pornography, and hacking.

Computer crimes target computer resources for a variety of reasons [1]:

- Hardwares such as computers, printers, scanners, servers, and communication media
- Software that includes application and special programs, system backups, diagnostic programs, and system programs such as operating systems and protocols
- Data in storage, transition, or undergoing modification
- People that include users, system administrators, and hardware and software manufacturers
- Documentation that includes user information for hardware and software, administrative procedures, and policy documents
- Supplies that include paper and printer cartridges

An attack on any one of these resources is considered a computer or computer-related attack. Some of these resources are more vulnerable than others and are, therefore, targeted more frequently by attackers. Most computer attacks on the resources above fall into the three categories below. Our focus in this chapter will be on the last category [1, 2]:

- Natural or inadvertent attack, which includes accidents originating from natural disasters such as fire, floods, windstorms, lightning, and earthquakes, and which usually occur very quickly without warning and are beyond human capacity, often causing serious damage to affected cyberspace resources.
- Human blunders, errors, and omissions that are usually caused by unintentional human actions. Unintended human actions are usually due to design problems. Such attacks are called *malfunctions*. Malfunctions, though occurring more frequently than natural disasters, are as unpredictable as natural disasters.
- Intentional threats that originate from humans caused by illegal or criminal acts from either insiders or outsiders, recreational hackers, and criminals. For the remainder of this chapter we are going to focus on this last category.

9.2 History of Computer Crimes

As we look at the history of computer crimes, we will focus on two aspects of such crimes: viruses and hacking. These have been the source of almost all computer attacks. Sometimes they become one when hackers use viruses to attack computer systems, as we will discuss below. As we saw in Section 1.4.1, the term *virus* is derived from a Latin word *virus* which means poison. Until recently, the term had remained mostly in medical circles, meaning a foreign agent injecting itself into a living body, feeding on it to grow, multiply, and spread. Meanwhile, the body weakens and loses its ability to fight foreign invaders and eventually succumbs to the virus if not treated.

Unlike a biological virus, however, a computer virus is a self-propagating computer program designed to alter or destroy a computer system's resources. Like its cousin, it follows almost the same pattern when attacking computer software. It attaches itself to software, grows, reproduces many times, and spreads in the new environment. It spreads by attacking major system resources including data and sometimes hardware, weakening the capacity of these resources to perform the needed functions and eventually bringing the system down.

We also noted in Section 1.4.1 that the word virus was first assigned a non-biological meaning in the 1972 science fiction stories about the G.O.D. machine, which were compiled in a book *When Harly Was One* by David Gerrod. Later, Fred Cohen, then a graduate student at the University of Southern California, associated the term with a real-world computer program he wrote for a class demonstration [3]. During the demonstration, each virus obtained full control of the system within an hour. That simple class experiment has led to a global phenomenon that has caused nightmares in system administrators, security personnel, and cyberspace users.

Hacking, as a computer attack technique, utilizes the internetworking between computers and communication devices. As long as computers are not interconnected in a network, hacking cannot take place. So the history of hacking begins with the invention of the telephone in 1876 by Alexander Graham Bell which has made internetworking possible. However, there was a long gap between the invention of the telephone and the first recorded hacking activity in 1971 when John Draper, commonly known as "Captain Crunch," discovered that a toy whistle from a cereal box could produce the precise tone of 2,600 Hz needed to make free long distance phone calls [4]. With this act, "Phreaking," a cousin of hacking, entered our language. With the starting of a limited national computer network by ARPANET, in the 1970s, a limited form of system break-in from outsiders started appearing. The movie "War Games," which appeared in 1983, glamorized and popularized hacking. It is believed by many that the movie gave rise to the hacking phenomena.

The first notable system penetration attack actually started in the mid-1980s with the San Francisco-based 414-Club. The 414-Club was the first national news-making hacker group. The group named their group 414 after the area code of San Francisco they were in. They started a series of computer intrusion attacks via a Stanford University computer which they used to spread the attack across the country [5]. From that small but history-making attack, other headline-making attacks from Australia, Germany, Argentina, and the United States followed.

In the United States, these activities, although at a low scale, started worrying law enforcement agencies so much so that in 1984 the Comprehensive Crime Control Act was enacted giving the Secret Service jurisdiction over computer fraud. Also at around this time, the hacker movement was starting to get active. In 1984, *2600: The Hacker Quarterly*, a hacker magazine, was launched and the following year the electronic hacking magazine *Phrack* was founded. As the Internet grew, hacker activities increased greatly. Then, in 1986, the US Congress passed the Computer Fraud and Abuse Act. Hacker activities that had only been in the United States started to spread worldwide. In 1987, the Italian hacker community launched *Decoder* magazine, similar to the United States's *2600: Hacker Quarterly* [4].

The first headline-making hacking incident involving a virus took place in 1988 when a Cornell graduate student created a computer virus that crashed 6,000 computers and effectively shut down the Internet for 2 days [5]. Robert Morris's action forced the US government to form the federal Computer Emergency Response Team to investigate similar and related attacks on the nation's computer networks. Law enforcement agencies started to actively follow the comings and goings of and sometimes eavesdrop on communication networks traffic. This did not sit well with some activists who in 1990 formed the Electronic Frontier Foundation to defend the rights of those investigated for alleged computer hacking.

The 1990s saw heightened hacking activities and serious computer network "near" meltdowns, including the 1991 expectation of the "Michelangelo" virus which was expected to crash computers on March 6, 1992, the artist's 517th birthday, but which passed without incident. In 1995, the notorious, self-styled hacker Kevin Mitnick was first arrested by the FBI on charges of computer fraud that involved the stealing of thousands of credit card numbers. In the second half of the 1990s, hacking activities increased considerably, including the 1998 Solar Sunrise, a series of attacks targeting Pentagon computers that led the Pentagon to establish round-the-clock, online guard duty at major military computer sites. Also, there was a coordinated attack on Pentagon computers by Ehud Tenebaum, an Israeli teenager known as "The Analyzer" and an American teen. The close of the twentieth century saw heightened anxiety in both the computing and computer user communities about both the millennium (Y2K) bug and the ever-rising rate of computer network break-ins. So in 1999, President Bill Clinton announced a $1.46 billion initiative to improve government computer security. The plan intended to establish a network of intrusion detection monitors for certain federal agencies and encourage the private sector to do the same [4]. The year 2000 probably saw the most costly and most powerful computer network attacks including "Mel-lisa," "Love Bug," "Killer Resume," and a number of devastating distributed denial of service attacks. The following year, 2001, the elusive "Code Red" virus was released. The future of viruses is as unpredictable as the types of viruses themselves.

As Table 1.1 shows, the period between 1980 and 2001 saw sharp growth in reported incidents of computer attacks. Two factors have contributed to this phenomenal growth: the growth of the Internet and the massive news coverage of virus incidents.

9.3   Computer Systems: Types of Attacks

A great number of computer attacks defined above fall into two categories: penetration and denial of service attacks.

9.3.1   Penetration

A penetration attack involves breaking into a system using known security vulnerabilities to gain access to a cyberspace resource. With full penetration, an intruder has full access to all that system's resources. Full penetration, therefore, allows an intruder to alter data files, change data, plant viruses, or install damaging Trojan horse programs into the system. It is also possible for intruders—especially if the victim computer is on a network—to use it as a launching pad to attack other network resources. Penetration attacks can be local, where the intruder gains access to a computer on a LAN on which the program is run, or global on a WAN like the Internet, where an attack can originate thousands of miles from the victim computer. Penetration attacks originate from many sources including:

(i) *Insider Threat.* For a long time, penetration attacks were limited to in-house employee-generated attacks to systems and theft of company property. In fact, disgruntled insiders are a major source of computer crimes because they do not need a great deal of knowledge about the victim computer system. In many cases, such insiders use the system everyday. This allows them to gain unrestricted access to the computer system, thus causing damage to the system and/ or data. The 1999 Computer Security Institute/FBI report notes that 55% of respondents reported malicious activity by insiders [6].

(ii) *Hackers.* Since the mid-1980s, computer network hacking has been on the rise mostly because of the wider use of the Internet. Hackers penetrate a computer system for a number of reasons, as we will discuss in the next section, including the thrill of the challenge, bragging rights in the hacker community, and for illicit financial gain or other malicious purposes. To penetrate the system, hackers use a variety of techniques. Using the skills they have, they download attack scripts and protocols from the Internet and launch them against victim sites.

(iii) *Criminal Groups.* While a number of penetration attacks come from insiders and hackers with youthful intents, there are a number of attacks that originate from criminal groups—for example, the "Phonemasters," a widespread international group of criminals who in February 1999 penetrated the computer systems of MCI, Sprint, AT&T, Equifax, and even the FBI's National Crime Information Center. A member of the group in the U.S., Calvin Cantrell downloaded thousands of Sprint calling card numbers. He later sold the numbers to a Canadian. From Canada, the numbers found their way back to America and on to Switzerland and eventually ended up in the hands of organized crime groups in Italy [6].

(iv) *Hactivism.* Demonstrations have taken place in Seattle, Washington DC, Prague, and Genoa by people with all sorts of causes, underlining the a new phenomena of activism that is being fueled by the Internet. This activism has not only been for good causes, but it has also resulted in what has been dubbed *hactivism*—motivated attacks on computer systems, usually web pages or email servers of selected institutions or groups by activists. A group with a cause overloads email servers and hacks into web sites with messages for their causes. The attacks so far have not been harmful, but they still cause damage to services. Such groups and attacks have included the "Electronic Disturbance Theater," which promotes civil disobedience on-line in support of the Zapatista movement in Mexico; supporters of Serbia, during the NATO bombing of Yugoslavia; electronically "ping" attacked NATO web servers; and supporters of Kevin Mitnick, the famed computer hacker while in federal prison, hacked into the Senate web page and defaced it [6].

9.3.2 Denial of Service

Denial of service attacks, commonly known as distributed denial of service (DDoS) attacks, are a new form of computer attacks. They are directed at computers connected to the Internet. They are not penetration attacks and, therefore, they do not change, alter, destroy, or modify system resources. However, they affect the system by diminishing the system's ability to function; hence, they are capable of bringing a system down without destroying its resources. They first appeared widely in the summer of 1999. The year 2000 saw this type of computer attack become a major new category of attack on the Internet. Headlines were made when a Canadian teen attacked Internet heavyweights Amazon, Ebay, E*Trade, and news leader CNN.

Unlike penetration attacks, DDoS attacks typically aim to exhaust the network bandwidth, its router processing capacity, or network stack resources, thus eventually breaking the network connectivity to the victims. This is achieved by the perpetrator breaking into weakly secured computers. The victim computers are found using freely available scan software on the Internet that pinpoints to well-known defects in standard network service protocols and common weak configurations in operating systems. Once the victims have been identified, the perpetrator breaks in and may perform additional steps that include the installation of software, known in the industry as a "rootkit," to conceal the break-in trail and make the tracing of subsequent activities impossible.

When the perpetrator has control of several victim machines under its control, the controlled machines are then used to mount attacks on other machines in the network, usually selected machines, by sending streams of packets, as projectiles, to the secondary line of victims. For some variants of attacks like the Smurf attack (which will be discussed shortly), the packets are aimed at other networks, where they provoke multiple echoes all aimed at the victim.

Like penetration electronic attacks (e-attacks), DDoS attacks can also be either local, where they can shut down LAN computers, or global, originating thousands of miles away on the Internet, as was the case in the Canadian-generated DDoS attacks. Attacks in this category include, among others, IP-spoofing, SYN-Flooding, Smurfing, Buffer Overflow, and Sequence Number Sniffing.

9.4 Motives of Attacks

Hacking has many dubious motives. More recently, however, we have seen more cases of hacking for illicit financial gain or other malicious purposes. It is difficult to exclusively discuss all the motives, but let us look at the following major categories [2]:

(i) *Political Activism.* There are many causes that lead to political activism, but all these causes are grouped under one burner—hactivism—as discussed in Section 9.3.1.

(ii) *Vendetta.* Most vendetta attacks are for mundane reasons as a promotion denied, a boyfriend or girlfriend taken, an ex-spouse given child custody, and other situations that may involve family and intimacy issues.

(iii) *Joke/Hoax.* Hoaxes are warnings that are actually scare alerts started by one or more malicious persons, and are passed on by innocent users who think that they are helping the community by spreading the warning. Most hoaxes are viruses although there are hoaxes that are computer-related folklore and urban legends. Virus hoaxes are often false reports about nonexistent viruses that cause panic, especially to the majority of users who do not know how viruses work. Some hoaxes can get extremely widespread as they are mistakenly distributed by individuals and companies with the best of intentions. Although many virus hoaxes are false scares, there are some that may have some truth about them, but which often become greatly exaggerated such as the "Good Times" and the "Great Salmon." Virus hoaxes infect mailing lists, bulletin boards, and Usenet newsgroups. Worried system administrators sometimes contribute to this scare by posting dire warnings to their employees, which become hoaxes themselves.

(iv) *The Hacker's Ethics.* This is a collection of motives that make up the hacker character. According to Steven Levy, hackers have motivation and ethics and beliefs that they live by, and he lists six as below [7].

- Free access to computers and other ICT resources—and anything that might teach you something about the way the world works—should be unlimited and total.
- All information should be free.
- Mistrust authority; promote decentralization.
- Hackers should be judged by their hacking, not bogus criteria such as degrees, age, race, or position.
- You can create art and beauty on a computer.
- Computers can change your life for the better.

If any of these beliefs is violated, a hacker will have a motive.

(v) *Terrorism/Extortion.* Our increasing dependence on computers and computer communication has opened up a can of worms we now know as electronic terrorism. Electronic terrorism that hits individuals by attacking the banking and military systems is committed by a new breed of hacker who no longer holds the view of cracking systems as an intellectual exercise but as a way of personally gaining from their actions. But cyber-terrorism is not only about obtaining information; it is also about instilling fear and doubt and compromising the integrity of the data, which leads to extortion. In many countries, financial institutions, such as banks, brokerage firms, and other large corporations, have paid large sums of extortion money to sophisticated international cyber terrorists.

(vi) *Political and Military Espionage.* For generations, countries have been competing for supremacy of one form or another. During the Cold War, countries competed for military dominance. At the end of the Cold War, the espionage tuft changed from military to gaining access to highly classified commercial information that would not only let them know what other countries are doing but might also give them either a military or commercial advantage without spending a lot of money on the effort. It is not surprising, therefore, that the spread of the Internet has given a boost and a new lease of life to a dying Cold War profession. Our high dependency on computers in the national military and commercial establishments has given espionage a new fertile ground. Electronic espionage has a lot of advantages over its old-fashioned, trench-coated, sun-glassed, and gloved Hitchcock-style cousin.

(vii) *Business and Industrial Espionage.* As businesses become global and world markets become one global bazaar, business competition for ideas and market strategies has become very intense. Economic and industrial espionage is on the rise around the world as businesses and countries try to outdo the other in the global arena. As countries and businesses try to position themselves and be a part of the impending global cut-throat competition, economic and industrial espionage is beginning to be taken seriously by company executives. The Internet has created fertile ground for cyber sleuthing, and corporate computer attacks are the most used business espionage technique. It usually involves physical system penetration for trophies like company policy, as well as management and marketing data. It may also involve sniffing, electronic surveillance of company executive electronic communications, and company employee chat rooms for information.

(viii) *Hate.* The growth of computer and telecommunication technology has unfortunately created a boom in all types of hate. There is growing concern about a growing rate of acts of violence and intimidation motivated by prejudice based on race, religion, sexual orientation, or ethnicity. Hate is being given a new and very effective and global forum.

(ix) *Personal Gain/Fame/Fun.* Personal gain motives are always driven by the selfishness of individuals who are not satisfied with what they have and are always wanting more, mostly financially.

9.5 Costs and Social Consequences

Are nations, businesses, and individuals prepared for computer attacks? Are they ready to pay the price? The answers to these questions at the moment are both probably no. It is not that we are not aware of it. It is not that we do not talk about it. And it is not that it has not happened before. It has. In fact, there have been heated and sometimes furious debates about it. There have been newspaper reports, and television and congressional discussions about the United States's preparedness for a national electronic attack. Yet not enough is being done beyond discussions. Since there is not enough data collection and analysis by US intelligence agencies, or business and financial communities that would have provided lead information, assessment, and preparedness of the nation for an electronic attack on the national information infrastructure, a good credible policy cannot be formulated. In fact, during 1996 Congressional hearings on "Intelligence and Security in Cyberspace," a senior member of the intelligence community in charge of collecting such data compared the efforts in place at the time to a "toddler soccer game where everyone just runs around trying to kick the ball somewhere" [8].

This is not a problem limited to the United States only; country after country around the globe is facing similar problems. Very few countries, if any, have assessed and analyzed any information on their information infrastructure, on how an electronic attack can not only affect their national security but also other essential infrastructures such as businesses, power grids, and financial and public institutions. There are various reasons to this lack of information including the following [2]:

- In nearly all countries there is no required reporting mechanism in government agencies, even the private sector, to detect intrusions and report such intrusions.
- In the private sector, there is very little interest in the reporting of any system-related intrusions. This is a result of the fear of marketplace forces that would expose the management's weaknesses to the shareholder community and competitors.

- There is no adequate enforcement of existing reporting mechanisms. In the United States, for example, there are legal requirements that require both public and private sectors to report system intrusions. Under these requirements banks must report unexplained shortages over $5,000 [9]. In addition the Federal Securities and Exchange Commission (SEC) requires all financial institutions, which include securities firms and publicly traded corporations, to report certain activities.
- The insider effect. There are various reports pointing to a blank picture about the effects of insider intruders on the overall detection and reporting of e-attacks. It is reported in some studies that a majority of all e-attacks are generated and started by inside employees. This makes the job of detection and reporting very murky. It is like having an arsonist working in the fire department.
- Many nations have no required and trained security agencies to fight e-attacks.

The danger is real; the ability to unleash harm and terrorize millions of people, thus causing widespread panic, is possessed by many. The arena to play the game is global, and there is no one who can claim a monopoly on such attacks. In the United States, and probably in other countries, most attacks originating from outside the country are directed, for the moment, toward military and commercial infrastructures, for obvious reasons. Although most reporting of attacks seem to come from government and public sources, there is a similar rate of attempt and probably success in the private sector. However, private industry has yet to become a partner with the public sector in reporting.

The universality of cyber attacks creates a new dimension to cyberspace security. In fact, it makes it very difficult to predict the source of the next big attack, let alone identify trouble spots, track and apprehend hackers, and put a price on the problem that is increasingly becoming a nightmare to computer systems administrators, the network community, and users in general.

Every computer crime and computer attack survey indicates a rising trend. There are several reasons that we can attribute to this rather strange growth of cyber crimes [2].

(i) *Rapid technology growth.* The unprecedented growth in both the computer and telecommunication industries has enabled access to the Internet to balloon into millions. Wireless and portable laptops and PDAs have made Internet access easier because people can now log on to the Internet anytime, anywhere. But this easy access has also made hiding places plentiful. From Alaska's snowcaps to the Sahara desert to the Amazon and Congo forests, cyber access is as good as in London, New York, or Tokyo, and the arena of possible cyber attacks is growing.

(ii) *Easy availability of hacker tools.* There are an estimated 30,000 hacker-oriented sites on the Internet advertising and giving away free hacker tools and hacking tips [9]. As the Manila-generated "Love Bug" has demonstrated, hacking prowess is no longer a question of affluence and intelligence but of time and patience. With time, one can go through a good number of hacker sites, picking tips and tools, and come out with a ready a payload to create mayhem in cyberspace.

(iii) *Anonymity.* The days when computer access was only available in busy, well-lit public and private areas are gone. Now as computers become smaller and people with these small Internet-able gizmos become more mobile, hacker tracing, and apprehension have become even more difficult than before.

(iv) *Cut-and-paste programming technology.* This has removed the most important impediment that prevented many would-be hackers from trying the trade. Historically, before anybody could develop a virus, one had to write a code for it. The code had to be written in a computer programming language, compiled, and made ready to go. This means, of course, that the hacker had to know or learn a programming language! Learning a programming language is known to be more than a 1-day job. It takes long hours of studying and practicing. Well, today this is no longer the case. We're in an age of *cut-and-paste programming*. The pieces and technical know-how are readily available from hacker sites. One only needs to have a motive and the time.

(v) *Communications speed.* With the latest developments in bandwidth, high volumes of data can be moved in the shortest time possible. This means that intruders can download the payload, usually developed by cut-and-paste offline, very quickly log off, and possibly leave before detection is possible.

(vi) *High degree of internetworking.* There is a computer network in almost every country on earth. Nearly all these networks are connected on the Internet. In many countries Internet access is readily available to a high percentage of the population. On a global scale, studies show that, on the average, currently up to 40% of developed countries and 4% of all developing countries have access to the Internet, and the numbers are growing daily [10]. As time passes, more and more will join the Internet bandwagon, creating the largest human community in the history of humanity. The size of this cybercommunity alone is likely to create many temptations.

(vii) *Increasing dependency on computers.* The ever increasing access to cyberspace, together with increasing capacity to store huge quantities of data, increasing bandwidth in communication networks to move huge quantities of data, increased computing power of computers, and plummeting prices on computer equipment have all created an environment of human dependency on computers. This, in turn, has created fertile ground for hackers.

9.5.1 Lack of Cost Estimate Model for Cyberspace Attacks

As computer prices plummet, computers and Internet devices become smaller, and computer ownership and Internet access skyrocket. Cost estimating computer attacks in this changing environment is becoming increasingly very difficult. Even in a good environment, estimates of computer crimes are difficult. The efforts to develop a good cost model is hindered by a number of problems including the following [2]:

(i) It is very difficult to quantify the actual number of attacks. Only a tiny fraction of what everyone believes is a huge number of incidents is detected, and even a far smaller number of that is reported. In fact, as we noted in the previous section, only one in 20% of all system intrusions is detected, and of those detected only one in 20% is reported [11].

(ii) Even with these small numbers reported, there has been no conclusive study to establish a valid figure that can at least give us an idea of what it is that we're dealing with. The only few known studies have been regional and sector based. For example, there have been studies in education, on defense, and in a selected number of industries and public government departments.

(iii) According to Terry Guiditis, of Global Integrity, 90% of all computer attacks both reported and unreported are done by insiders [12]. Insider attacks are rarely reported even if they are detected. As we reported in Chapter 9, companies are reluctant to report any type of cyber attacks, especially insider ones, for fear of diluting integrity and eroding investor confidence in the company.

(iv) Lack of cooperation between emergency and computer crime reporting centers worldwide. There are over 100 such centers worldwide, but they do not cooperate with one another because most are in commercial competition [12].

(v) Unpredictable types of attacks and viruses. Attackers can pick and choose when and where to attack. Also, the types of attacks and topography used in attacks cannot be predicted. Because of these factors, it is extremely difficult for system security chiefs to prepare for attacks and, therefore, reduce the costs of each attack, if it occurs.

(vi) Virus mutation is also another issue in the rising costs of cyber attacks. The recent "Love Bug" and "Code Red" email attacks are examples of a mutating virus. In each incident the viruses started mutating within a few hours after release. Such viruses put enormous strain on systems administrators to search and destroy all the various strains of the virus.

(vii) There are not enough trained system administrators and security chiefs in the latest network forensics technology who can quickly scan, spot, and remove or prevent any pending or reported attack and quickly detect system intrusions. When there is a lack of trained and knowledgeable personnel, it takes longer to respond when an attack occurs, and to clear the system from such an attack in the shortest period of time possible, thus reducing the costs. Also, failure to detect intrusion always results in huge losses to the organization.

(viii) Primitive monitoring technology. The computer industry as a whole and the network community in particular, have not achieved the degree of sophistication that would monitor a computer system continuously for foolproof detection and prevention of system penetration. The industry is always on the defensive, always responding *after* an attack has occurred and with inadequate measures. In fact, at least for the time being, it looks as if the attackers are setting the agenda for the rest of us. This kind of situation makes every attack very expensive.

The table below (Table 9.1) provides a part of the picture of possible costs in the different categories of computer crimes.

Table 9.1 Estimated costs of computer attacks

Category of crime	Possible crimes	Estimated costs
Fraudulent	Communications and bookkeeping theft, monitor law enforcement, extortion	Undisclosed huge sums of money are being given out to extortionists by financial institutions, such as banks, brokerage firms, and other large corporations.
Political activism	Press, communication, propaganda, theft, sabotage, disruption, information warfare	The rise in political activism using computer communication is resulting in possible e-crimes whose costs, though still difficult to quantify, are on the rise.
General crime	Eavesdropping, theft, sabotage, disruption, sabotage	The Computer Security Institute surveys of 1998 and 1999 report general computer crime loss estimates of $136 million and $265 million, respectively [13]. Consider that for every $1 million stolen electronically from a financial or investment institution, the recovery costs can exceed $100 million. That includes costs for forensic investigations, crisis management, litigation, and lost customers.
Organized crime	Communications, eavesdropping on law enforcement, extortion, theft	The Internet facilitates organized crime with estimate on society based on illicit drug, securities fraud, and telemarketing scams, money laundering, production and sale of counterfeit products, and illegal smuggling. Estimates of costs to prevent these are huge.
Hate/fringe groups	Press, communication, propaganda, theft, sabotage, disruption, information warfare	Still not huge costs but are on the rise. Estimates are based on law enforcement expenditure and victim losses.
Business and industrial espionage	Information theft, eavesdropping, sabotage, hacking	Actual dollar amount is in billions and heavily debated, but very few would argue it isn't significant. DataQuest estimates $13 billion in US business loses in 2000 [14].
Political/military espionage	Eavesdropping, data collection, information warfare, intelligence gathering, sabotage	Estimates are difficult but should include money for training of system users and risk assessors, assessing risks, protecting systems, responding to incidents, assessing damage, and updating systems.
Terrorism	Eavesdropping, information warfare, intelligence gathering, sabotage	Terrorists attacks are intent on disrupting national security. So far most of the major cybersecurity incidents have been at best nuisance attacks. Estimates are difficult and based on training, equipment, investigation, and recovery. Could run in billions of dollars.

(continued)

Table 9.1 (continued)

Category of crime	Possible crimes	Estimated costs
Joke/hoax	Communication, disruption	There are an estimated 1,000 e-attacks a day in the United States alone. Multiplying this with estimated costs of each results in huge costs [2].
Hacker's ethics	Information theft, eavesdropping, sabotage, hacking	There are indirect rising costs to hackers services. Estimates are low but on the rise.
Personal gain/fun	Information theft, eavesdropping, sabotage, extortion	The 2000/2001 DDoS attacks demonstrated the costs involved. For example Canadian-generated DDoS resulted in estimated $1 billion in losses, Melissa $80 million [14].

9.5.2 Social and Ethical Consequences

Although it is difficult to estimate the actual costs of e-attacks on physical system resources, we are making progress toward better estimates. What we cannot now do, and probably will never be able to do, is to put a cost estimate on e-attacks on individual members of society. This is difficult because of the following [2]:

(i) *Psychological effects.* These depend on the attack motive and may result in long psychological effects such as hate. Psychological effects may lead to individual reclusion and increasing isolation. Such trends may lead to dangerous and costly repercussions on the individual, corporations, and the society as a whole.

(ii) *Moral decay.* There is a moral imperative in all our actions. When human actions, whether bad or good, become so frequent, they create a level of familiarity that leads to acceptance as "normal." This type of acceptance of actions formerly viewed as immoral and bad by society is moral decay. There are numerous e-attacks that can cause moral decay. In fact, because of the recent spree of DDoS, and email attacks, one wonders whether people performing these acts seriously consider them as immoral and illegal anymore!

(iii) *Loss of privacy.* After the recent headline-making e-attacks on CNN, Ebay, E*Trade, and Amazon, and the email attacks that wreaked havoc on global computers, there is a resurgence in the need for quick solutions to the problem that seems to have hit home. Many businesses are responding with patches, filters, intrusion detection (ID) tools, and a whole list of other "solutions." Among these "solutions" are profile scanners and straight email scanners like Echlon. Echlon is high-tech US government spying software housed in England. It is capable of scanning millions of emails given specific keywords. Those emails that are trapped by it are further processed, and subsequent actions are taken as warranted. Profile scanners are a direct attack on individual privacy. This type of privacy invasion in the name of network security is a threat to all of us whose price we will never estimate and we are not ready to pay! The blanket branding of every Internet user as a potential computer attacker or a criminal—until proven otherwise—is perhaps the greatest challenge to personal freedom yet encountered by the world's societies.

(iv) *Trust.* Along with privacy lost, trust is lost. Individuals once attacked, lose trust in a person, group, company, or anything else believed to be the source of the attack or believed to be unable to stop the attack. E-attacks, together with draconian solutions cause us to lose trust in individuals, businesses, especially businesses hit either by e-attacks or trying to forcibly stop attacks. Such customer loss of trust in a business is disastrous for that business. Most importantly, it is a loss of the society's innocence.

9.6 Computer Crime Prevention Strategies

Preventing computer crime is not a simple thing to do because to do that one needs to understand how these crimes are committed and who is involved in these crimes. To prevent such crimes, therefore, we need to focus on three entities in the game and these are: the computer as a tool used to committee the crimes, the criminal who is the source of the crime, and the innocent victim of the crime. Our approach to prevention will therefore involve strategies from all three.

9.6.1 Protecting Your Computer

For better protection of your computer consider the following measures based on a list by the San Diego Police Department [15]. Similar measure can be found at many police departments in many countries.

9.6.1.1 Physical Protective Measures

Install surface locks, cable-locking devices, and fiber-optic loops prevent equipment theft.

- Locate the computer room and data storage library away from outside windows and walls to prevent damage from external events.
- Install strong doors and locks to the computer room to prevent equipment theft and tampering.
- Reinforce interior walls to prevent break-ins. Extend interior walls to the true ceiling.
- Restrict access to computer facilities to authorized personnel. Require personnel to wear distinct, color-coded security badges in the computer center. Allow access through a single entrance. Other doors should be alarmed and used only as emergency exits.

9.6.1.2   Procedural and Operational Protective Measures

- The computer as the main tool in the execution of the crime. Realizing this leads us to find those elements of the computer that are more susceptible to being the good conduit. The list of these items may include data, software, media, services, and hardware.
- Using this list, analyze the dangers to each item on the list. Buy and install protective software based on the value of each item on the list.
- Classify information into categories based on importance and confidentiality. Use labels such as "Confidential" and "Sensitive." Identify software, programs, and data files that need special access controls.
- Install software access control mechanisms. Require a unique, verifiable form of identification, such as a user code, or secret password for each user. Install special access controls, such as a call-back procedure, if you allow access through a dial-telephone line connection.
- Encrypt confidential data stored in computers or transmitted over communication networks. Use National Institute of Standards and Technology (NIST) data encryption standards.
- Design audit trails into your computer applications. Log all access to computer resources with unique user identification. Separate the duties of systems programmers, application programmers, and computer programmers.
- Establish procedures for recovering your operating system if it is destroyed. Store all back-up data offsite.
- Review automated audit information and control reports to determine if there have been repeated, unsuccessful attempts to log-on both from within and outside your facility. Look for unauthorized changes to programs and data files periodically.

9.6.1.3   Anti-virus Protection

The following measures can help protect your computer from viruses:

- Don't bring disks in from outside sources.
- Scan demo disks from vendors, shareware, or freeware sources for viruses.
- Restrict use of electronic bulletin boards.
- Scan downloaded files for viruses. Avoid downloading executable files.
- Make regular back-ups to aid in recovery.

9.6.2   The Computer Criminal

There are two measures that I would consider as appropriate for the computer criminal.

9.6.2.1   Pass Computer Crime Prevention Laws

Local and national governments should pass laws directed towards computer crimes including computer tempering, computer fraud, and other computer crimes so that if a person commits a computer crime offense, when knowingly and without the authorization of a computer's owner, or in excess of the authority granted that person, if found guilty, should serve a court sentence consumelete to the extend of his or her crime. An increasing number of countries now either have such laws or are in the process of enacting them.

9.6.2.2   Enforcement of Criminal Laws

We cannot fight computer crimes whether we have laws on the books or not unless those laws can be enforced. So one way of reducing computer crime is to aggressively enforce computer crime laws with just but stiff sentences that send a message to would-be criminals that they will pay the price if they perpetuate computer crimes.

9.6.2.3   Moral Education

Throughout this book, I have been advocating for computer ethics education. There is a need for computer ethics education that includes an ethical framework that may make the would-be criminal reflect on the pending act. Computer ethics education, just like all types of education, is a long-time investment especially in the youth to build not only their character but also to guide their actions throughout their lives.

9.6.3   The Innocent Victim

The following measures should be focused on the victims of the computer crimes [15].

9.6.3.1   Personnel Policies

- Monitor activities of employees who handle sensitive or confidential data. Watch for employees who work abnormally long hours, or who refuse to take time off. Many computer crime schemes require regular, periodic manipulation to avoid detection. Be aware of employees who collect material not necessary to their jobs, such as programming manuals, printouts for data, programs, and software manuals.
- Change security password codes to block further access by employees who leave or are fired. The latter become a high risk to your company for revenge or theft.

• Establish rules for computer use by employees, including removal of disks or printed output. All employees should sign and date a printed copy of these rules to indicate that he/she understands them.

9.6.3.2   Educating the Computer User

Just as we did with the computer criminal, we need to educate the user to be aware of possible sources of computer crime and what to do if and when one becomes a victim of a computer crime. This education can go a long way in reducing computer crimes if the users take crime preventive steps every time they use the computer and when owning a computer.

Exercises

1. List five types of computer attacks.
2. In a short essay, discuss the differences between a denial of service attack and a penetration attack.
3. Which attack type is more dangerous to a computer system, a penetration attack or a denial of service attack?
4. List and briefly discuss five attack motives.
5. Why do hackers devote substantial amount of time to their trade?
6. Discuss the challenges in tracking down cyber criminals.
7. Why is it so difficult to estimate the costs of business e-crimes both nationally and globally?
8. What is the best way to bring about full reporting of e-crimes, including costs?
9. Why do countries worldwide have very little information to help them combat cyber crimes?
10. Why are cyber crimes on the rise?
11. In addition to monetary costs, there are ethical and social costs of e-crimes; discuss these "hidden" costs.
12. Construct a table similar to Table 9.1 and add two or more attack motives giving cost estimates for each category added.

References

1. "Section A: The Nature and Definition of a Critical Infrastructure." http://www.nipc.gov/nipcfaq.html
2. Joseph M. Kizza. *Computer Network Security and Cyber Ethics.* McFarland, Jefferson, NC, 2001.
3. Karen Forchet. *Computer Security Management.* Boyd & Fraser, 1994, Danvers, MA.
4. Timeline of hacking. http://fyi.cnn.com/fyi/interactive/school.tools/timelines/1999/computer.hacking /frameset.exclude.html
5. Peter J. Denning. *Computers Under Attack: Intruders, Worms and Viruses.* New York: ACM Press, 1990.
6. Louis J. Freeh. "FBI Congressional Report on Cybercrime." http://www.fbi.gov/congress00/cyber021600.htm
7. Steven Levy. *Hackers: Heroes of the Computer Revolution.* Anchor Press/Doubleday, Garden City, NY, 1984.
8. Security in Cyberspace: U.S. Senate Permanent Subcommittee on Investigations. June 5, 1996.

9. John Christensen. "Bracing for Guerilla Warfare in Cyberspace," CNN Interactive, April 6, 1999.

10. Carnegie Mellon University. CERT Coordination Center. "CERT/CC Statistics 1998–1999." http://www.cert.org/stats/cert-stats.html

11. David S. Alberts. "Information Warfare and Deterrence—Appendix D: Defensive War: Problem Formation and Solution Approach." http://www.ndu.edu/inns/books/ind/appd.htm

12. "Hacker Sittings and News: Computer Attacks Spreading (11/19/99)." http://www.infowav.com/hacker/99/hack-11/1999-b.shtml

13. "Annual Cost of Computer Crime Rise Alarmingly," Computer Security Institute. http://www.gocsi.com/prela11.html

14. Trigaux, R., "Hidden Dangers," *St. Petersburg Times,* June 16, 1998.

15. San Diego Police Department. "Tips for Businesses: Computer Crime Prevention." http://www.sandiego.gov/police/prevention/computer.shtml

Further Readings

Anderson, K.E., "Criminal Threats to Business on the Internet: A White Paper," Global Technology Research, Inc., June 23, 1997. This is a discussion of the increasing trend of criminal activity against information systems, from the low-level, amateur intruder to organized crime, and industrial and international espionage.

Chaturvedi, A., et al., "Fighting the Wily Hacker: Modeling Information Security Issues for Online Financial Institutions Using the SEAS Environment." INET JAPAN 2000 Conference, July 18, 2000. The paper discusses proposed methods to analyze the online risks faced by the financial industry.

Computer Security Institute/Federal Bureau of Investigation, "Annual Cost of Computer Crime Rise Alarmingly: Organizations Report $136 Million in Losses," Press Release, Computer Security Institute, March 4, 1998. This is a summary of the 1998 survey on computer crime.

Counterintelligence Office of the Defense Investigative Service, "Industry CI Trends," OASD-PA/96-S-1287, December 26, 1996. This paper discusses threats and techniques used for low-level intelligence collecting by foreign companies and governments against U.S. DoD contractors.

General Accounting Office (GAO), "GAO Executive Report—B-266140," Report to the Committee on Governmental Affairs, U.S. Senate, May 22, 1996. This gives a detailed report on attacks to U.S. Department of Defense computer systems with recommendations for improved security.

Kapor, M., "Civil Liberties in Cyberspace: When Does Hacking Turn from an Exercise of Civil Liberties into Crime?" *Scientific American,* September 1991. This is a discussion of the various legal, social, and privacy-related issues within computer networks using the U.S. Secret Service's raid on Steve Jackson Games as a case study.

National Counterintelligence Center, "Annual Report to Congress on Foreign Economic Collection and Industrial Espionage," Annual Report to the U.S. Congress, 1998. This is a summary of the espionage threat to the United States Specific highlights include the interest in information security and information warfare.

Overill, R.E., "Computer Crime—An Historical Survey," Defence Systems International, 1998. This paper discusses the historical development of computer crime.

United Nations, "International Review of Criminal Policy—United Nations Manual on the Prevention and Control of Computer-Related Crime," *International Review of Criminal Policy,* No. 43 and 44, 1994. These are extensive documents reviewing all aspects of international computer crime.

U.S. Department of Justice. News Release, March 1, 1998. "Israel Citizen Arrested in Israel for Hacking U.S. and Israel Government Computers" http://www.usdoj.gov/opa/pr/1998/march/125.htm.html

"Section A: The Nature and Definition of Critical Infrastructure" http://www.nipc.gov/nipcfaq. htm

Andrew Grosso. "The Economic Espionage ACT: Touring the Minefields." *Communications of the ACM,* August 2000, 43(8), 15–18.

Grampp, F. and Morris, R. "Unix Operating System Security" *AT&T Bell Laboratories Tech J.* 63, 8, Part 2 (October 1984), 1649.

Peter G. Neumann. "Risks of Insiders." *Communications of the ACM,* December 1999, 42(12), p. 160.

Joseph M. Kizza. *Civilizing the Internet: Global Concerns and Efforts Toward Regulation.* McFarland, Jefferson, NC, 1999.

"Computer Attacks: What They Are and How to Defend Against Them," *ITL Bulletins,* May 1999. http://www.nist.gov/itl/lab/bulletins/may99.html

Chapter 10
New Frontiers for Computer Ethics

Artificial Intelligence, Cyberspace, and Virtual Reality

Learning Objectives

After reading this chapter, the reader should be able to:

1. Understand the value of ethics in automated decision making.
2. Identify and discuss the different forms of automated decision making.
3. Recognize the role ethics plays in artificial environments.
4. Identify and discuss credible safeguards to ensure privacy concerns and prevent run-away computation resulting from autonomous agents.
5. Understand the role of autonomous agents in our daily lives.
6. Recognize and discuss the responsibilities of users of virtual environments.

Scenario 8
One for the Road—Anyone?

> *Florence Yozefu is a brilliant scientist who heads a robotics research laboratory at one of the top ten research universities. Florence has been developing wearable robotics gear that can take over the driving functions of a vehicle from a human operator when it is worn by the driver. In laboratory tests, the robot, nicknamed Catchmenot, has performed successfully whenever Florence and her assistants have worn the robot. However, no real-life experiment has ever been conducted outside the lab. Florence has been meaning to try it out 1 day, but has not got a chance as yet to do so.*
>
> *For New Year's Eve, Florence has plans to visit her mother and sister, about 100 miles away. This was a good opportunity to show her mother and her sister what she has been up to these last few months. So she decides to take Catchmenot with her. She packs her car the evening before and on the morning of the trip, she passes by the lab to get her robot and put it in the car. She drives the 100 miles in a little under her usual time and arrives at her mother's house earlier than usual. In the evening, Florence bids her mother good-bye and passes by her sister's apartment as promised. But at her sister's apartment, she finds a few of her teen friends and they get right into a party mode.*
>
> *Florence drinks and dances and forgets about time. There are many stories to tell and to listen to. About 1:00 a.m., after the midnight champagne toast, she decides to leave and drive back to her apartment. She had promised to accompany her friend to a preplanned engagement. Although she is very drunk, and against her friend's advice and insistence that she should not drive, Florence puts on Catchmenot and in a few minutes she is off. Thirty minutes later, she is cruising at 70 mph and she is also sound asleep.*
>
> *She is awakened by a squirrel running all over her car at about 5:00 a.m. She is parked by the roadside in front of her apartment complex. She has made it home safely. She has no idea when and where she passed out and what happened along the way. She will never know. Although she is surprised, confused, and feels guilty, she is happy how well Catchmenot has worked. She decides to market it.*
>
> *How much should she charge for it, she wonders.*

J.M. Kizza, *Ethical and Social Issues in the Information Age*, Texts in Computer Science, 207
DOI 10.1007/978-1-84996-038-0_10, © Springer-Verlag London Limited 2010

Discussion Questions
1. *Why did Florence feel guilty?*
2. *Is Florence right to market Catchmenot?*
3. *If anything went wrong along the ride home, would Florence be responsible? Who should be?*
4. *Is it ethical to market Catchmenot?*
5. *Discuss the ethical implications of artificial intelligence based on Catchmenot.*

10.1 Introduction

Artificial intelligence (AI), cyberspace (CP), and virtual reality (VR) are all exciting technological frontiers offering novel environments with unlimited possibilities. The AI environment works with the possibilities of understanding and extending knowledge to create intelligent agents perhaps with a human-value base, intended to help solve human problems; the CP environment investigates the reality of the assumed presence of objects and peers: You know they are there, but you do not know where or who is "really" out there; and the VR environment simulates the reality of "other worlds" through modeling and creating better tools for understanding the complexities of our world, thus moving humanity closer to a better way of living.

Human beings are naturally curious and drawn to investigate new phenomena whenever possible. Thus, the frontiers we discuss in this chapter have drawn a number of people, some for the experience to participate in cyberspace, others to experience the thrills of virtual reality, and yet others to investigate the application of knowledge in areas yet unknown. Wherever and whenever they are drawn to these environments, human beings are participatory: They try out and get involved as they pursue individual social goals.

This chapter examines the effects of human actions in these environments. We analyze the difficulties encountered in passing judgment for responsibility of individual actions in and as a result of these environments. Responsibility is placed on two parties in each environment: the user and the creator.

10.2 Artificial Intelligence

Artificial intelligence (AI) is a field of learning that emulates human intelligence. The recent development of AI and its seemingly unbounded potential to solve real-life problems has broadened computer technology applications into exciting areas that were thought to require deep human intelligence. Because human intelligent behavior is so varied, ill defined, and difficult to predict, let alone understand, most artificial intelligence studies concentrate on a limited number of areas in which human abilities to think and reason are clear and the overall human intelligent behavior is well understood.

These areas exhibit those aspects of human intelligence that can be represented symbolically with first-order logic such as game playing and natural language understanding. Other areas that exhibit a high degree of human intelligence such as thought processes, pattern recognition, and concept formation are still abstract and scarcely understood. However, with the recent realization that most real-world problems that are usually not so difficult for human intelligence, but are still intractable for current machine intelligence, involve numerical computation, and the improvement in the computation power of new computers, AI research is slowly shifting from those areas that use symbolic manipulation to numerical computation. This is bringing diversification and practicability to AI and increasing the repertoire of AI techniques. But because of the lack of incorporation of common sense into AI techniques, progress in real terms has been slow except in areas such as robotics and machine learning in which there has been more excitement because of the practicability of the applications to our daily lives. However, the realization is opening new doors in AI research in areas such as neural networks and fuzzy logic theory, and it is causing scholars to take a new look at ways of achieving machine intelligence and at the same time start to study the social and ethical impact and where to place responsibility for such machines, if they ever come to be. In this section we look at the social and ethical implications in these active areas where AI techniques have made advances and are getting established.

10.2.1 Advances in Artificial Intelligence

Starting with Alan Turing in his 1950 machine intelligence experiments, in which he proposed a game played between a computer and a human being that could demonstrate whether a machine, in this case a computer, could think, there has been a steady growth of interest in building intelligent machines, commonly known as *autonomous agents*, in those areas of AI in which intelligence can be modeled easily such as in game playing, expert systems, natural language understanding, neural networks, and robots.

Autonomous agents are not new to AI. Since Turing, numerous scholars such as Marvin Minsky, Alan Key, and Rodney Brooks have at various times studied agents' behavior and sometimes constructed autonomous agents. An autonomous agent is a collective name encompassing both hardware and software intelligent agents. Autonomous agents can take different forms depending on the nature of the environment. For example, if the environment is real 3D, the agents are robots, whereas in 2D they are computer programs referred to as intelligent agents.

As progress is made in AI research, areas of application of autonomous agents are becoming more numerous. For example, robots have been used in a number of areas including surveillance, exploration, and in inaccessible and hazardous environments. More intelligent agent robots are being helped by better vision systems, sensors, and easier programming languages. The field of robotics is getting wider, involving areas such as perception, cognition, and manipulation in which success has been most apparent through industrial applications. For example, in perception, the development of autonomous vision-guided vehicles has made significant progress. Projects in this area include the Autonomous Land Research Project (ALV) for Advanced Research Project Agency (ARPA), and Unmanned Ground Vehicle (UGV), both in the United States, the Prometheus Project from Europe's Eureka Project, and the Personal Vehicle (PV) Project from Japan's MITI [1]. All these have been major AI robotics projects.

In addition to autonomous driven vehicles displayed in the projects just described, robots have also been used to handle hazardous materials and to reach remote areas where it is impossible for humans to go safely. Such robot projects include the Pathfinder rover named *Sojourner*, the remote-controlled Mars vehicle; the AMBLER project, a six-legged walker to traverse challenging terrain; and the DANTE project used to explore volcanic Mt. Erebus in the cold Antarctica [1]. Robots such as DANTE can also be used in undersea and extraterrestrial explorations.

Although all these projects involve large mechanical creatures, research has also miniaturized robotics. Microelectromechanical systems, or MEMS, are becoming popular. These miniature creatures depend more on mechanical than on electronic properties to operate. MEMS can easily change and control the space around them. Because they are small, they can be integrated or combined to perform many useful functions [1].

As technology improves and the techniques get more refined, robots will become common in our daily lives, and industrial and manufacturing processes will depend more on robots. Already in some sectors of manufacturing, robots are playing an ever-increasing role. For example, in personal computer assembly, use of robots is nearly total.

Meanwhile, software intelligent agents are being used in a variety of areas such as information filling and retrieval, mail management, meeting scheduling, and in selection of activities and items to engage and help all types of end users. Agents also assist users in other areas such as hiding the complexity of a task at hand, teaching and collaborating with the user on certain areas of the task, and monitoring the progress of the task at hand [2].

There are prototypes of intelligent agents in several areas including personal assistantships, meeting scheduling, email handling, filtering, and entertainment. For example, JULIA, an autonomous agent that lives in a text-based Multi-User Simulation Environment (MUSE), performs tasks such as holding discourse with players, overhearing conversations and gossiping about them later on, relaying messages between players, and helping players with navigation problems [3]. In personal assistance, PHIL, in John Scalley's "The Knowledge Navigator" by Apple, playing the role of a teacher, resource manager, and knowledge retrieval agent, is an example of a personal assistant intelligent agent. There is also ongoing research in other areas such as the ACDS project seeking to deploy agents relevant to the design process [4]. At the University of Washington, a project for a software robot called SOFTBOT is being developed to interact with a wide range of Internet resources such as FTP, TELNET, MAIL, and other file manipulation commands to provide an integrated and expressive interface to the Internet. In addition, it provides backtracks fluidly from one Internet facility to another based on information collected at runtime and chooses dynamically which facilities to invoke and in what sequence [5].

In the area of learning there are currently a number of personal assistants including CAP (Calendar APprentice), which learns its user's scheduling preferences from experiences from summaries up to 5 years [6], and COACH (Cognitive Adoptive Computer Help), which records user experience to create personalized user help. It learns by watching the user's moves to build an adoptive user model that selects appropriate advice [7]. M is another software agent that integrates multiple "reasoning agents" whose collaborative results serve to assist a user working together with other users in an electronic conference room [8].

10.2.2   Artificial Intelligence and Ethics

Human beings by nature strive to create a good life for themselves through the acquisition of knowledge and the creation of intelligent machines to do most of the jobs that we are either not able to do or do not like to do. But according to George Lugar and William Stubblefield [11], the notion of human efforts to gain knowledge as a transgression against the law of God is deeply rooted in us, and we still believe that the human quest for knowledge must eventually lead to disaster. This belief has not been affected by current philosophical and scientific advances, but instead has produced the Frankenstein monster syndrome of fear of new advances in intelligence, particularly machine intelligence. It is this fear that has been the source of controversy in the field of artificial intelligence and has the potential to hinder its development.

Fictional writers such as Isaac Asimov [12] and others have written about AI. The most positive has been Jack Williamson who, in "With Folded Hands" [13], portrayed a young scientist disillusioned by man's destructive nature who creates robots to follow the Asimovian Prime Directive [14]: "To serve and obey, and guard men from harm." In the story, robots replicate themselves and do all the jobs he wants them to do—until he realizes the mistake he has made. But it is too late. He has rendered himself useless. "Men sat with idle hands because there was nothing left for them to do." Science was forbidden because the laboratories were dangerous to man. There was no need to acquire knowledge because the robots could do anything and do it better. "Purpose and Hope were dead. No goal was left for existence." One would ask why the young scientist could not kill the robots. He tries, but they stop him because he is violating the Prime Directive. Meanwhile they multiply.

Philosophers too have long expressed this fear. According to Weizerburm [15], it is immoral to use a computer system to replace human functions involving interpersonal respect, understanding, and love. Floyd believes that computers should only be used if "there remains sufficient scope outside the computer application for other human faculties and forms of experience not to degenerate" [15].

Marvin Minsky likens it to an old paradox dealing with slave education: "If you keep them from learning too much you limit their usefulness; if you help them become smarter than you, then you may not be able to trust them to make better plans than they do for you" [16].

To us all, AI represents a social and ethical paradox. We want the machines to do those things we are not able to do because we are not good at them, yet we do not want them to get too good. We probably would have no reservations and certainly no objections if only we could be assured that they have, to put it in Hans Moravic's words, "our very own mind-children" [16]—that is, that they share our own values, truths, and virtues. As these autonomous agents achieve better intelligence and become more widely used and acceptable, they will be taking on more and more responsibility and autonomy that only humans have been known to have. This raises many questions about the future of these autonomous agents, their relationship with humans, their behavior, and emotions. Among such questions are the following:

- How will humans perceive these intelligent agents?
- How will the autonomous agents themselves feel about human beings?
- Will human beings let these intelligent "creatures" keep on getting more and more intelligent even though they are aware the ultimate end result would be to surpass human intelligence?
- How will they do what they are supposed to do?
- Will they do only what they are supposed to do?
- Who will be responsible for the actions of these agents?
- Will these agents outperform their owners?
- Will they eventually eliminate the need for human skills?
- And the most important of these questions is, how much power and autonomy should we give these creatures, and will these agents eventually take away human autonomy and consequently take control of human destiny?

According to Mitchell Waldrop [14], as these autonomous agents become more and more intelligent, we need a theory and practice of machine ethics that will embody a built-in code of ethics in these creatures in the spirit of Asimov's laws of robotics and Carbonell's hierarchy of goals [14, 17].

Isaac Asimov created his fictional robot characters with an implanted code of conduct he called the Laws of Robots:

1. A robot may not injure a human being or, through inaction, allow a human to come to harm.
2. A robot must obey the orders given to it by human beings except when such orders would conflict with the first law.
3. A robot must protect its own existence as long as such protection does not conflict with the first or second law [12].

According to Jim Carbonell [17], programs can be governed by a hierarchy of goals that act as a guide and a prescribed direction in the program's reasoning processing. This hierarchy should then be set up so that it inputs a code of ethics into the programs.

The question, though, is whether it will be followed by the intelligent programs and robots, and to what extend? Is there a possibility that they can vary the code, however much we try to stop them from doing so? Carbonell's concept is good, but it creates many questions that still need answers.

10.2.3 The Future Role of Autonomous Agents

Are AI's overblown expectations much ado about nothing? Since the Turing prediction [9] in the 1950s that we would create an intelligent machine by the year 2000, has AI done anything dramatic for human beings? According to people such as Toshinori Munakata, AI has made impressive progress in manufacturing, consumer products, finance, management, and medicine. Remarkable advances have also been made in knowledge engineering systems, perception, human language understanding, fuzzy systems, and modeling of the brain and evolution [10].

The current success stories in AI in areas such as machine vision, speech understanding, and knowledge processing do not incorporate common sense, thus progress in AI research as a realization of human intelligence has been dismal at best. Whether AI progress is seen as advanced computing that does not deal head on with the common sense problem or as an area of simulation of human intelligence that involves inclusion of common sense techniques, the future of AI is going to remain controversial. Two schools of thought have been forming according to what is perceived as good or bad about AI's contribution to humanity.

In one school are those who take a dark view of AI contributions, labeling all AI activities as research gone wrong, "mad scientist" research in the spirit of Mary Shelley's Frankenstein. They list the following as some of their concerns:

1. Lack of credible safeguards to ensure privacy concerns and prevent runaway computations.
2. The computer, shrouded in an armor of infallibility and regarded as the keeper of absolute truth, may intimidate a large number of the most vulnerable, and even the most intelligent may eventually reach a point beyond which their understanding fails.
3. When computers start to do most of the tasks in the workplace, people will begin to abdicate their responsibilities, saying, "The computer did this and that."
4. Digitizing information about individuals and entrusting it to a machine may disturb large numbers of the population who do not know how much information the computer has and what it can do with it.
5. If too much information is known about an individual by this superintelligent machine, what happens to that individual? Is the individual unknowingly a walking naked personality?
6. The agents' possession of everyone's total information may mean total control.

7. It is essential that people feel that they are in control of their daily activities, and experience has shown us that we accept automation with reluctance. For example, very few of us would like to be passengers on a plane with no real human pilot.
8. Those who expect AI to be a savior for humankind have overblown expectations. Part of this overexpectation of the agents' abilities is attributed to designers who try to create robots and agents that are very close and similar to human forms in likeness, responses, expressions, and intelligence.

In contrast to these naysayers, those in the other school see the future of AI as very beneficial to humanity. They see a fruitful partnership with the agents in which the agents are relieving us of all our dangerous and tedious tasks, making our lives a little easier and helping us reach our ultimate goal of the good life.

10.3 Cyberspace

Cyberspace is a concept of an environment made up of invisible information. This information can take different shapes. According to Mindy McAdams [18], cyberspace is a world made up of pure but invisible information that takes the shape of 3D visible objects. The environment including the objects is created by a global network of computers working together via agreed on protocols. The word *cyberspace* was first coined by fiction writer William Gibson [19] to describe the interaction between a network of computers and people using them.

To understand the effects and contributions of cyberspace to the study of computer ethics, we will look at the roles played by the two constituent parts of cyberspace—the Internet and the World Wide Web (WWW), or the Web. However, since in our introductory chapter we dealt in great detail with the development of both the Internet and the Web, and since Chapter 11 also deals exclusively with cyberspace and cyberethics, we will refer our discussion of the social and ethical implications there.

10.4 Virtual Reality

Virtual reality (VR) as a concept had its beginning in the 1960s. It is mostly credited to the work of scientists like Ian Sutherland and D.L. Vickers [20]. It is a simulation of a real or imaginary phenomena in a 3D environment. This simulated environment, believed to be real through feeling, is made of virtual objects created by animated and highly interactive computer graphics programs utilizing a graphic display, a transducer, and an image generator.

Graphic display devices present the total effects of the environment created. The displays can be audio, touch, or visual, and they come in different sizes from very small ones, which can be worn as goggles, to really big sizes in rooms. The most common of these are worn as headphones producing simulated sounds. Touch displays are usually gadgets that transmit the effects of touch through the tips of fingers, and then the user can visualize the object. The technology for touch gadgets is not very well developed, however. Transducers create a channel of communication between the person in the environment and the sources of the environment. The main task of the transducer is to map or transform an action by the occupant of the environment such as the movement of eyes, hands, brain activity, speech, and sometimes the movement of blood in veins into a computer-compatible form so the computer system can provide an appropriate response. An image generator is a creator of images to be displayed on the designated display device. Image generators create these images from computer systems' outputs in response to inputs from the transducers. The image produced can be visual, like the simulation of somebody traveling in the galaxies; it can also be in other forms such as audio, which can simulate sounds like a waterfall or a thunderstorm.

When all these components are working together, a highly graphic interactive computer-generated environment is produced. These three-dimensional computer-generated environments containing interactive sensor devices create experiences, not illusions, for the occupant of the environment because users interact with contents and objects, not pictures, and they are never physically in these created environments.

VR started as a science without applications and VR applications in real life were difficult to come across and develop, prompting many to label it a "solution in search of a problem" [21]. Today, however, VR applications are on the rise in several medical and scientific areas including visualization of scientific and simulation data. VR visualization maps high-volume multidimensional scientific research and simulated data into 3D displays that offer a more accurate and realistic approach to the representation of the original numeric data and thus help in a better understanding of the abstract phenomena under study [22]. Let us look at several VR projects.

In the entertainment domain for which VR is most known, there are a couple of interesting projects such as the Artificial Life Interactive Institute Video Environment (ALIVE) at the Massachusetts Institute of Technology (MIT) [3]. ALIVE creates a virtual environment that allows wireless free-body interaction between a human participant and a virtual world inhabited by animated autonomous agents. Through the interaction with the agents, the system learns the user's reactions and emotions, which it uses to create a plan for the next move in the game with the user. Besides entertainment, VR has been most useful in scientific visualization, in which VR turns the complex data structures in computation science, making them easy to understand and thus study. In medicine, VR is being used successfully and skillfully to bring volumes of data into 3D imaging through a combination of reflected stereoscopic display and a number of rotations through varying degrees of freedom. An illustrative example of this work is the John Hopkins University's Center for Information Enhanced Medicine (CIEMED) in collaboration with the center for Information Enhanced Medicine of the University of Singapore. The project simulated 3D medical images of the brain and heart during surgery [23].

Outside the world of medicine, scientific visualization, and simulation, VR is being used in several areas including driving and pilot training. The SIRCA (Simulador Reactivo de Conduccion de Automobiles) project at the LISITT (Laboratorio Integrado de Sistemas Intelligentes y Tecnologias de la Infor-mación en Tr áfico) of the University of Valencia, Spain, is a good illustration of the effects in this area of VR application. The SIRCA project is engaged in the development of small- and medium-size object-oriented driving simulations with the aim of training drivers [23].

Although VR started with humble beginnings and suffered jokes like the one about a science in search of applications, in recent years, it has seen significant general acceptance as it has found applications in diverse areas such as medicine, design, the arts, entertainment, visualization, simulation, and education, to name but a few, and its future is bright.

10.4.1 Ethics in Virtual Reality

As we stated earlier, VR is a new frontier. To many the image evoked by the word *frontier* rekindles a sense of free adventurism, unregulated and pure. The VR environment brings the user closer to this romantic vision. But illusion is illusion, and it brings forth two major social and ethical themes. One is the reactions and feelings of the occupant of the environment, and the other is the intention of the creator of the environment. Some of the factors and issues to consider include the following:

1. *The emotional relationship and the feeling of being in control*: This is a major psychological problem that confronts many VR users while in, and even sometimes after they leave, the environment. Although users get to interact with the agents inside the VR environment and enjoy the emotional highs generated by the agents, they also tend to develop an emotional relationship with the agents. This relationship may take the form of a deeper attachment to the agents, which gives the user a sense of being in control and later creates a sense of responsibility and trust on the part of the user. The relationship may also take the adversarial form, in which case the user feels out of control and may become hostile both inside and after he or she leaves the environment. In both cases, there is a possibility that the user may take the character of one of the agents and try to live it outside the environment. The immediate question that arises out of this situation is who should be held responsible for the outcome of the VR environment.

2. *Safety and security*: Besides the psychological and mental conditions that the user of the VR environment may develop, there is also the danger of security of the user while in the environment. With the ever-increasing intelligence of the agents in the VR environment, the agents may cause a feeling of, or the reality of, both bodily or mental harm to the user. The effects may be directly caused by the contacts of the user while in the environment or may be delayed for some time, perhaps weeks after the user has left the environment.

3. *Human–agent interaction*: The interaction between the user and the agents in the VR environment has many consequences including the nature of the interaction, the activities to be performed, and the reaction and emotions of the user and the agents. If the interaction is perceived as friendly by the user, it may not be problematic; otherwise, there might be an impression of superiority of the agents and the user may feel threatened because of the high level of intelligence associated with the agents. This may lead to the user going amok because of a loss of control and probable feelings of helplessness.

4. *The intentions of the creator*: These are always very difficult to predict and probably in this direction may lie the greatest danger for the user. One will never be sure whether these environments are doing what they are intended to do. There may be some malicious intent in which the environment is used, for example, to collect information on the user for the creator or agents of the creator without the user ever knowing about it. It may be that the environment is used secretly by some authority for mental and psychological transformation of the user.

Unfortunately, unlike AI intelligent agents where a good number of people are reluctant to surrender to them, in VR there is an unquestionable willingness to give it all up upon first being asked because people are looking for pleasure. Because VR is a very new science, there have been no comprehensive studies focused on VR environment users' behavior. It is worth research, and ideally as VR makes strides such studies may come. The question, though, is, What should we do if there are problems? We can fight any sinister creator intentions and user irresponsibility by making the VR environment operate in an implanted code of ethics both in the software and in the hardware as we discussed earlier in the spirit of Asimov. But as we pointed out earlier, there is no way to predict the outcomes of these VR agents with such embedded code. The question remains the same. Would the VR environment stick to the code or vary it? And to what extent? We will never know. So educating the users about responsible use of the VR environment can help in this regard.

This responsibility should be based on sound ethical and moral principles relating to VR. Collins Beardon [15] outlines three traditional principles by famous philosophers quite relevant to VR:

1. One should not do things with computers for which one should not accept responsibility without computers.
2. Continuous exposure to VR will impoverish those aspects of life that determine social development, interpersonal insights, and emotional judgment.
3. Computers should be used in applications where computation and symbol manipulation are adequate ways of dealing with reality.

To these let us also add deception, a Kantian ethical principle because a user can masquerade as somebody else and deceive others. For example, consider the following VR scenario: You are happily married; you are aware of the problems with extramarital affairs and you do not approve of them. You have a list of compelling reasons such as health (STDs such as AIDS, herpes, and syphilis), outcomes like unwanted and probably illegitimate children, moral sanctions against infidelity, and your own self-respect. But in your next encounter with VR, you are paired with a very beautiful sexual partner and you find yourself getting involved in illicit sexual acts you would not have in the real world. The VR environment has removed all your constraints about extramarital affairs; you can now justify your actions even using utilitarian ethical theory. Is this a confusion in the traditional ethical theories or a redefinition of these theories in the new realities of VR? This scenario reflects what Beardon has defined VR to be—a deep philosophical confusion [15].

Exercises

1. Discuss the implications of the common knowledge problem on advances in AI.
2. Is the "mad scientist" syndrome justifiable? Discuss.
3. Why was VR characterized as a science without applications?
4. Some people believe VR is the same as cyberspace. Support or reject the claim.
5. Discuss the social and ethical issues associated with VR.
6. Why is the study of AI limited to only small arrears? Will this not hinder the study of human behavior in other areas?
7. Will the study of AI make us better understand human behavior?
8. Can the understanding of AI, if this ever happens, help to understand and model human behavior, and hence develop better techniques for teaching computer ethics?
9. As AI applications increase like in the use of robotics, will the wider use of these "manlike" machines compromise our moral value system? Why or why not?
10. Is the Frankenstein Syndrome an exaggeration or it is real?
11. Is it possible to develop a robot with our own moral value system?
12. Will the development of more advanced intelligent systems improve the declining moral value?
13. Discuss the future of AI and its ethical implications
14. Which of the schools of AI do you belong to and why?
15. VR was discredited as a science in search of a solution. Was/is this a fair characterization? Why?
16. Research the current VR projects and suggest how they contribute to social and ethical values of your society.
17. Discuss the VR's deep philosophical confusion!
18. How do you reconcile this philosophical confusion?
19. Discus the future of computer ethics in the integrated environment of AI, VR, and cyberspace.

References

1. Kanade, Takeo, Michael Reed, and Lee Weiss. "New Technologies and Applications in Robots." *Communications of the ACM* 37(3), 1994, pp. 58–67.
2. Maes, Pattie. "Agents that Reduce Work and Information Overload." *Communications of the ACM* 37(7), 1994, pp. 30–40.
3. ——. "Artificial Life Meets Entertainment: Lifelike Automous Agents." *Communications of the ACM* 38(11), 1995, pp. 108–117.

4. Edmonds, Ernest, Linda Candy, Recheal Jonas, and Bassel Soufi. "Support for Collaborative Design: Agents and Emergence." *Communications of the ACM* 37(7), 1994, pp. 41–47.

5. Etzioni, Oren, and Daniel Weld. "A Softbolt-Based Interface to the Internet." *Communications of the ACM* 37(7), 1994, pp. 72–76.

6. Mitchell, Tom, Rich Caruana, Dyne Feritag, John McDermott, and David Zabowski. "Experience with a Learning Personal Assistant." *Communications of the ACM* 37(7), 1994, pp. 81–91.

7. Selker, Ted. "A Teaching Agent That Learns." *Communications of the ACM* 37(7), 1994, pp. 92–99.

8. Riecken, Doug. "M: An Architecture of Integrated Agents." *Communications of the ACM* 37(7), 1994, pp. 107–116.

9. Turing, A.M. "Computing Machinery and Intelligence" *Mind* 59, 1950, pp. 433–460.

10. Munakata, Joshironi. "Commercial and Industrial AI." *Communications of the ACM* 37(3), 1994, pp. 23–25.

11. Luger, George, and William Stubblefield. *Artificial Intelligence* (2nd ed.). Reading, MA: Benjamin Cummings, 1993.

12. Asimov, Isaac. *The Rest of the Robot.* New York: Doubleday, 1964.

13. Williamson, Jack. "With Folded Hands." In *The Best of Jack Williamson.* New York: Ballantine, 1978, pp. 154–206.

14. Waldrop, Mitchell. "A Question of Responsibility." In R. Dejoie, George Fowler, and David Paradice (eds.), *Ethical Issues in Information Systems.,* Boston, MA: Byrd & Fraser, 1991.

15. Beardon, Collins. "The Ethics of Virtual Reality." *Intelligent Tutoring Media* 3(1), 1992, pp. 22–28.

16. Minsky, Marvin, and Doug Riecken. "A Conversation with Marvin Minsky About Agents." *Communications of the ACM* 37(7), 1994, pp. 23–29.

17. Carbonell, Jaime. *Subjective Understanding: Computer Models of Belief Systems.* Ann Arbor, MI: University of Michigan Press, 1979.

18. McAdams, Mindy. "Cyberspace: Tw o Flavors" http://www.well.com/user/mmcadams/

19. Gibson, William. *Neuromancer.* New York: Ace Books, 1984.

20. Vickers, D.L. "Sorcerer's Apprentice: Head-Mounted Display and Wand." In J.A. Bist and H.L. Hast (eds.), *A Symposium on Visually Coupled Systems: Development and Applications.* AMD, TR 73–1, 1972.

21. Singh, Gurrinder, Steven Feiner, and Daniel Thalmann. "Virtual Reality: Software and Technology," *Communications of the ACM* 39(5), 1996, pp. 35–36.

22. Bryson, Steve. "Virtual Reality in Scientific Visualization." *Communications of the ACM* 39(5), 1996, pp. 62–71.

23. Bayani, Salvador, Marcos Fernandez, and Mariano Pevez. "Virtual Reality for Driving Simulation." *Communications of the ACM* 39(5), 1996, 72–76.

Further Readings

Barlow, John. "Electronic Frontier: Private Life in Cyberspace." *Communications of the ACM* 34(8), 1991, pp. 23–25.

Bates, Joseph. "The Role of Emotion in Believable Agents." *Communications of the ACM* 37(7), 1994, pp. 122–125.

Boden, Margaret. "Agents and Creativity." *Communications of the ACM* 37(7), 1994, pp. 117–121.

Cowie, Jim, and Wendy Lehner. "Information Extraction." *Communications. of the ACM* 39(1), 1996, pp. 80–91.

Green, Menlo, and Sean Halliday. "A Geometrical Modelling and Animation System for Virtual Reality." *Communications of the ACM* 39(5), 1996, pp. 46–53.

Hayes Roth, F., and Neil Jacobstein. "The State of Knowledge-Based Systems." *Communications of the ACM* 37(3), 1994, pp. 22–39.

Kanade, Takeo, Micheal Read, and Leve Weiss. "New Technologies and Application in Robots." *Communications of the ACM* 37(3), 1994, pp. 58–67.

Munakato, Toshimori, and Yashant Jani. "Fuzzy Systems: An Overview." *Communications of the ACM* 37(3), 1994, pp. 69–75.

Norman, Donald. "How Might People React with Agents?" *Communications of the ACM* 37(7), 1994, pp. 68–71.

Poston, Timothy, and Luis Serra. "Dextrous Virtual Work: Introduction." *Communications of the ACM* 39(5), 1996, pp. 37–45.

Riecken, Doug. "Intelligent Agents: Introduction." *Communications of the ACM* 37(7), 1994, pp. 18–21.

Schoppers, Marcel. "Real-Time Knowledge-Based Control Systems." *Communications of the ACM* 34(8), 1991, pp. 27–30.

Singh, G., Steven Fisher, and Daniel Thalmann. "Virtual Reality Software and Technology: Introduction." *Communications of the ACM* 39(5), 1996, pp. 35–36.

Webe, Janyce, Gracme Hirst, and Dianne Horton. "Language Use in Context." *Communications of the ACM* 39(1), 1996, pp. 102–111.

Wilkes, Maurice. "Artificial Intelligence as the Year 2000 Approaches." *Communications of the ACM* 35(8), 1992, pp. 17–20.

Wilkes, Yonick. "Natural Language Processing." *Communications of the ACM* 39(1), 1996, pp. 60–62.

Chapter 11
Cyberspace, Cyberethics, and Social Networking

Learning Objectives

After reading this chapter, the reader should be able to:

1. Understand cyberspace.
2. Learn how to safeguard cyberspace.
3. Understand the issues of cyberspace.
4. Learn the complexity of cyberspace issues.
5. Acquire knowledge and understand where in cyberspace ethics is essential.
6. Learn the ethical framework of cyberspace.
7. Learn how languages and culture are influenced by cyberspace.

Real-Life Experience
The Net Twins

"It is illegal, completely illegal, in this country for people to buy and sell babies or children, and that is entirely as it should be, because it is frankly a revolting idea."

Jack Straw
British Home Secretary

The twin girls Kiara and Keyara Wecker were born in St. Louis in June 2000 to Tranda and Aaron Wecker. But around the time of the birth of the twins, the parents split. The twins were then given up for adoption to a California couple, Richard and Vickie Allen of San Bernardino. The Allens had paid $6,000 to an Internet placement service called A Caring Heart. This would not have made news had Tranda Wecker, 28, the twins' birth mother, not changed her mind after only 2 months, and for unknown reasons, given the twins to another set of adoptive parents, a British couple, Judith and Alan Kilshaw of Wales.

It was later learned from court papers that the Kilshaws had paid the same Internet placement service $12,000. The Kilshaws made a quick swing through the American heartland that took them from San Diego, where they met with the birth mother, to St. Louis, to pick up birth certificates, and then to Arkansas to complete the adoption. In Little Rock, Arkansas, the judge granted them custody of the twins and the Kilshaws then drove to Chicago for the return flight to Britain.

After publicity of the twins' case, the Allens in California challenged the British adoption of the twins. A war of words continued across the Atlantic with the Allens accusing the Britons of kidnapping. The Allens further asked the FBI to help return the girls to the United States. Because of the circumstances surrounding the double adoption of the twins, the FBI set up a preliminary investigation to determine jurisdiction and possible wire-fraud violations and to find why the children were offered for adoption twice through an Internet service.

However, after Richard was accused of molesting two baby sitters, the Allens gave up the fight. The international publicity from the case caused a British court to order that the twins be placed in foster care in Britain pending a decision on custody. Because neither the Kilshaws

J.M. Kizza, *Ethical and Social Issues in the Information Age*, Texts in Computer Science,
DOI 10.1007/978-1-84996-038-0_11, © Springer-Verlag London Limited 2010

nor Tranda Wecker had ever lived in or established residency in Arkansas, the court in the state invalidated the adoption of the twins by the Kilshaws and they gave up their custody fight soon after. The twins were brought back to St. Louis [16].

Discussion Questions
1. *Was this an Internet fraud? Who is involved?*
2. *Do you think the Kilshaws were innocent? What about the Allens?*
3. *Should there be international laws on adoption of children?*
4. *What role did the Internet play in this saga?*

11.1 Introduction

When William Gibson first coined the word cyberspace in his novel Neuromancer, he was describing the vision of a three-dimensional space of pure information consisting of networks of computers linking people, machines, and other objects as information sources and sinks. This space offered a high degree of movement, enabling users to navigate cyberspace, or to surf, as it is now commonly referred to. A cyberspace user is described as a generator or recipient of a utility collection of packets of information that move in cyberspace.

From Gibson's conceptualization to the actual realization of cyberspace, we notice the dominant role of the Internet as the global network of computers. So throughout this chapter, we at times interchangeably use the word Internet in the place of cyberspace when we need to emphasize the role of the network. Cyberspace represents a frontier of technological development that brings with it a complex new environment with controversial ethical and social issues. In our journey from Chapter 1 to now, we have defined and discussed two types of ethics: traditional ethics and computer ethics. As we have followed a technological revolution, we have noticed with concern its effects on the traditional ethical issues in the new technological environment. A new definition of ethics is needed to reflect these changes. We now introduce a third type of ethics: cyber ethics. As we pointed out in Chapter 3 when we introduced computer ethics, cyber ethics is not new ethics. It is the traditional ethics in the new environment. So, many of the traditional issues such as privacy, security, anonymity, property rights, and the goodness of human actions are also seen in this new environment. In this chapter, we focus on some of the major issues in cyberspace including cyberspace safeguards, intellectual property rights, censorship, privacy, security, global ethics, language, global culture, and the social realities in the cyber café.

11.2 Cyberspace Safeguards

The detection and prevention of computer crimes in cyberspace is a daunting job that requires advanced techniques and prevention methods. Both the detection and prevention techniques are changing very fast. Because of this, what is discussed in this section is only current at the time of writing.

11.2.1   Detecting Computer Attacks

A detection system deployed around a computer system or a computer network is a 24-h monitoring system to alert the owner or system manager whenever something unusual – something with a non-normal pattern, different from the usual pattern of life in and around the system – occurs. The monitoring system is actually an alarm system that must continuously capture, analyze, and inform the system manager on the daily patterns of life in and around the computer system.

In capturing, analyzing, and reporting, several techniques are used including: network forensics, intrusion detection (ID), and vulnerability scanning. These techniques together offer early information to the system manager.

11.2.1.1   Network Forensics

Network forensics is an investigative process that studies the network environment to provide information on all issues of a healthy working network. It seeks to capture network information on:

(i) Network traffic and the changing traffic patterns
(ii) The trends of individual network packet traffic. For example, it gathers information on an individual network packet tracing its time of entry into the network, port number through which it entered, where it is in the network at a specific time, how long it stays in the network, and what resources it is using and in what quantities. All this information gathered from all network packets creates a sort of traffic pattern. Traffic patterns tend to follow a specific pattern for a normal operating network. Large swings in these patterns and large deviations from the norm usually signal an intrusion.
(iii) The density of traffic at specific times of the day as traffic patterns are traced; their sources and entry points in the network, must be noted.

Network forensics requires that programs be provided with historic traffic patterns, and the programs themselves have a degree of intelligence not only to capture, trace, and note traffic pattern variations, but most importantly analyze changes in the traffic patterns and intelligently report to the system administrators.

The greatest benefit of network forensics is that using the information provided, network administrators can target specific abnormal traffic patterns and use them to preempt intended intrusions. If network intrusions are accurately predicted and nipped while still in the bud, the benefits are many to the network community, ranging from completely preventing an attack to shortening an attack that had already started. In either case the process is cost-effective. Much of the information network forensics uses comes from port traffic, system logs, and packet information.

11.2.1.2 Intrusion Detection

Intrusion detection (ID) is a new technology based on the fact that software used in all cyber attacks often leaves a characteristic signature. This signature is used by the detection software, and the information gathered is used to determine the nature of the attack. At each different level of the network investigative work, there is a different technique of network traffic information gathering, analysis, and reporting. Intrusion detection operates on already gathered and processed network traffic data.

It is believed by designers of ID tools that the anomalies noticed from the analysis of this data would lead to distinguishing between an intruder and a legitimate user of the network. The anomalies resulting from the ID analyses are actually large and noticeable deviations from historical patterns of usage. ID systems are supposed to identify three categories of users: legitimate users, legitimate users performing unauthorized activities, and, of course, intruders who have illegally acquired the required identification and authentication.

As more research is done in ID and linkages are established between ID and artificial intelligence, newer ID tools with embedded extended rule bases that enable them to learn are being developed, and over time they will be able to make better analyses and, therefore, decisions. The debate is not what kind of rule base to put in the ID tools, but what type. Currently the rule bases have been those that teach the ID tools the patterns to look for in network traffic and learn those patterns. For example, if an application is not supported by the server that application's port number should never be active. However, the new movement differs from the traditional embedded rule bases. The focus now is actually to embed into these ID tools what Murcus Ronam calls "artificial ignorance" which embeds into the ID tools a rule base that teaches them of things not to look for [17]. People following this line of thought believe the rule base then will be simpler and the product more effective.

The scope of ID systems is also changing in another direction. For a while now it has been assumed, wrongly though, by management and many in the network community that ID systems protect network systems from outside intruders. But studies have shown that the majority of system intrusion actually is from insiders, so newer ID tools are focusing on this issue. Also, since the human mind is the most complicated and unpredictable machine ever, as new ID tools are being built to counter systems intrusion, new attack patterns are being developed to take this human behavior unpredictability into account. To keep abreast of all these changes, ID systems must be constantly changing.

As all these changes are taking place, the primary focus of ID systems has been on a network as a unit where they collect network packet data by watching network packet traffic and then analyzing it based on network protocol patterns "norms," "normal" network traffic signatures, and network traffic anomalies built in the rule base. But since networks are getting larger and traffic heavier, it is becoming more and more difficult for the ID system to "see" all traffic on a switched network like an Ethernet. This has led to a new approach to looking closer at the host. So, in general, ID systems fall into two categories: host-based and network-based. Tools in host-based ID focus on a network server to monitor specific user and application traffic handled by that server. They actually track log files and audit traffic in and out of this one machine. Besides tracking in and out traffic, they also check on the integrity of system files and watch the activities of all processes on the machine for abnormal process behavior. Host-based ID systems are indeed either personal firewalls, or agents. Personal firewalls, sometimes called wrappers, are configured to look at all network packets, connection attempts, and login attempts including dial-ins and non-network communications.

Network-based ID tools monitor the whole network traffic including traffic on the communication media and on servers looking for signatures of known attacks, anonymous behavior, and misuse patterns.

11.2.1.3 Vulnerability Scanning

System and network scanning for vulnerability is an automated process where a scanning program sends network traffic to all computers or selected computers in the network and expects receiving return traffic that will indicate whether those computers have known vulnerabilities. These vulnerabilities may include weaknesses in operating systems and application software and protocols.

According to Steve Jackson [18], vulnerability scanning has so far gone through three generations. The first generation required either code or script, usually downloaded from the Internet or fully distributed, to be compiled and executed for specific hardware or platforms. Because they were codes and scripts that were platform- and hardware-specific, they always needed updates to meet specific specifications for newer technologies.

These limitations led to the second generation which had more power and sophistication and provided more extensive and comprehensive reports. Tools were able to scan multiple platforms and hardware and to isolate checks for specific vulnerabilities. This was a great improvement. However, they were not extensive and thorough enough, and quite often they gave false positives and negatives.

The third generation was meant to reduce those false reports by incorporating a double and sometimes triple scans of the same network resources. It used data from the first scan to scan for additional and subsequent vulnerabilities. This was a great improvement because those additional scans usually revealed more datagram vulnerabilities, the so-called second-level vulnerabilities. Those second-level vulnerabilities if not found in time and plugged, are used effectively by hackers when data from less secure servers are used to attack more systems servers, thus creating cascade defects in the network.

11.2.2 System Survivability

In the new networked computer environments, system survivability is the ability of a computing system, whether networked or not, to provide essential services in the presence of attacks and failures and gracefully recover full services in a timely manner.

The emergence of computer systems and telecommunications services resulting in large communication computer networks has made the issue of system survivability after an attack into a new, very important discipline that combines computer security with risk management. The discipline focuses on the detection and prevention of computer attacks, to ensure that during the period of attack business goes on as usual to meet set goals with as little disturbances to the critical business functions as possible. A good system survivability policy must include the following [19]:

(i)   System survivability requirements that are based on distributed services should include the following:

   • Distributed logic
   • Distributed code
   • Distributed hardware
   • Shared communications
   • Routing infrastructure
   • Diminished trust
   • Lack of unified administrative control

(ii) Intrusion requirements to demonstrate the correct performance of essential and nonessential system services as well as the survivability of essential services during intrusion.
(iii) Development requirements to make sure that there are sound development and testing practices during the development of the system, especially software systems. Good development and testing practices prevent devastating errors from developing and hence increase the chances for system survivability and curtail opportunities for intruder exploitation.
(iv) Operations requirements to define channels of communicating survivability policies, monitoring system use, responding to intrusions, and evolving system functions as needed to ensure survivability as usage environments and intrusion patterns change over time.
(v)   Evolution requirements to be able to quickly respond to user requirements for new functions and be able to determine and counter increasing intruder knowledge of system behavior and structure.

For extended readings on system survivability, the reader is referred to a technical report by the Carnegie-Mellon University, Software Engineering Institute, entitled "Survivable Network Systems: An Emerging Discipline," which can be found at http://www.sei.cmu.edu/publications/documents/97.reports/97tr013/97tr013 abstract.html

11.3 Intellectual Property Rights in Cyberspace

In the last years of the twentieth century, we witnessed a boom in e-commerce and unprecedented growth of the Internet, driven mostly by this boom. As this was happening, tremendous changes in the social, financial, and legal underpinnings of societies were taking place, too. The old concept of property, context, and all other physical attributes of society are in flux, and many do not apply in cyberspace. We noted in Chapter 6 that intellectual property rights are protected by a body of laws and statues, namely copyrights, patents, trademarks, and trade secrets. Historically, as technology advances, laws and statutes are revised to bring them up to date and relevant to the technology of the day.

In Chapter 6 we discussed intellectual property rights laws and what can be protected. However, those rights and laws were developed during the pre-Internet period when it was easier to control distribution of protected items. The media, players, and culprits were all easily identifiable. This is no longer the case in cyberspace. By its very nature, cyberspace fosters the distribution of information on intangible goods to the far reaches of the globe with no solid street addresses. Intellectual property works such as text, art, music, photographs, and computer software can all be easily digitized and distributed quickly and widely.

This is good because this allows creators, developers, and producers to greatly reduce the costs of production and distribution, which cuts down or totally eliminates costs on manufacturers, distributors, packaging, storage, and retailers. This is also a bonanza to copyright and other intellectual property right holders to bring their products to the consumer faster and cheaper. As Al Teller of MCA Music predicts, digital delivery of music and movies will soon surpass retail outlets to meet consumer demand [22].

However, cyberspace has problems that lawmakers, artists, producers, and others interested in intellectual property rights have to deal with:

1. *Anonymity.* The rapid advances in computer and telecommunication technology make it easy for a typical computer user to digitize video, music, photographs, computer software, or text and distribute it in any amount to any location on the globe in the shortest time possible. This is of course a nightmare for intellectual property owners. They are unable to identify, let alone track down, the infringers of the property rights in the vastness of cyberspace.
2. *Internet Paradox.* What has come out of this is a muddle of conflicting ideas and concepts – an Internet paradox. The nature of the Internet technology requires fast access, maximum compatibility of information between servers, and low-cost services. With these in place, information exchange is easy and rapid. In a sense, Internet technology fosters open borders and quick and massive movements of information. But mass access begets competition. So we can say that the Internet technology is a medium that fosters competition. However, what is moved on the Internet, that is, the content of the Internet, most often represents products, works, discoveries, and inventions that have a strong base in intellectual property. The Internet paradox, therefore, lies in the opposing philosophies of what it is and what it carries.

This paradox is rooted in the antitrust–intellectual property axis. Antitrust because by nature the Internet fosters competition, and yet intellectual property – because of the content of the Internet – requires monopoly protection. This axis of conflict is going to worsen as more and more businesses gain access to the

Internet and yet fight for monopoly and dominance of their services by use of copyrights, patents, trademarks, trade secrets, and personal identity laws and statutes. Later we will see how this conflict plays out in each of the components of the intellectual property rights.

3. *Browsing Rights.* The nature of the WWW requires that website materials, especially rich hypertext materials, first be copied onto a client computer disk before they can be viewed by the client because of caching. Web browsers work this way. The old copyright law recognizes browsing as fair use. For example one can walk into a bookstore and browse through the entire bookstore, book to book, and still be within the current copyright laws concerning fair use. The difference is in caching. Cyberspace browsing requires caching of the content at the local mass storage. Although caching does not save materials on the client disk permanently, the client may want to save the material for later viewing for which the image was intended. Caching is very important to the client computer and Internet traffic because it keeps the traffic on the electronic highways low, but it makes a muddle of the copyright law. Because Internet materials on the web get an automatic, implied copyright, can this kind of saving of the web materials for later personal use and the purpose the materials were intended to be used for be considered as fair use or is it an infringement on the implied Internet copyright? Of course, the matter is clearer if the client saves the materials for future commercial value. But if the saving is for purely personal use, the matter is less clear because it is more difficult to judge whether it is fair use or infringement.

In Section 6.4.5 we discussed what comprises the fair use doctrine, but fair use is difficult to judge. The list given in Chapter 6 by itself is not comprehensive enough to guarantee fair use of any copyrighted work; the fair use doctrine is still in a gray area even to the best copyright lawyers. For example, for works copied and sold, the decline in commercial value can be measured in the drop of earnings of the work as experienced by the owner of the copyright. But by the nature of the web, this becomes another very difficult issue. Does making a copy of the web page make it any less valuable or decrease its value for whatever the purpose? Also, does a personal web page have any commercial value to the owner? This raises two issues that again need discussion: the author's role and the hidden nature of the process.

Does the author have any control on the way the image is used? Can the author prevent the downloading of the image he or she intended to be viewed, knowing full well that it cannot be viewed unless it is downloaded at least for caching purposes? The answers to these questions are probably all no. So does the author's inability to control the situation make the copying process an infringement on the author's copyright? Even if the author had the know-how and the technology to control the copying, the large number of users on the Internet and the lack of knowledge of who, where, and when they will download the image make enforcing the copyright law a daunting task.

Note that during the caching process, the user of the material from the website is not aware that the material in question is being cached on the user's machine because the whole process of caching is hidden from the user. If the user decides to save the material for later viewing, for example, he or she saves that material from the cache. So the question here is whether the copying process is effectively done from the website or from the cache. If it is done from the cached material, which is legal given the nature of the Internet process, is this downloading or reproduction?

4. *Lack of Control on Cyberspace Services.* FTP (file transfer protocol) is a means to move files across servers to one's own computer. When a file is put on an anonymous FTP server or submitted to a discussion group, it is difficult to know who will use it and how it will be used. The problem is even more complex because millions of files are changing servers every minute. How can the copyright law be enforceable in this situation?

5. *Distributed Liability.* If a copyrighted work or piece of information or a patented work is distributed on the Internet, who should bear responsibility? Should it be the distributor, the ISP, the server owner, or the user?

11.3.1 *Copyrights*

In Chapter 6 we discussed a representative list of what is and is not copyrightable in the United States according to US statutory law. The key elements in the copyright law are fixation, originality, and expression. Any work for which copyright protection is sought must be original, expressive, that is, artistic, and must be fixed in a tangible medium such as print, recording, picture, or electronic transformation. Are these works patentable now in cyberspace? The answer to this question is yes. The digitizing of these works does not and should not take them out of the protection domain of the copyright laws. But there is disagreements in some countries on the definition of digitization and what needs to be included in the "new" Copyright Acts for the future. The disagreement, in some countries, is rooted in the fact that the definition of digitization as extended to current copyright laws is not broad enough, and in others that it is too broad. The Canadian Association of Photographers and Illustrators in Communications, for example, are demanding that digital works be defined to refer to creation, storage, manipulation, reproduction, or distribution of any work by means of electronic, computer, or digital recording equipment [20].

On the other hand, the newly approved US Digital Millennium Copyright Act (DMCA) is considered too broad. There is rising opposition to the DMCA, especially from academia, because of the likelihood of misinterpretation of its circumvention provisions. There is fear in the scientific and academic community that DMCA's definition as outlined in subsection 1201(a)3 (see Appendix A), and in particular subsection 1201(a)3, parts A and B, is likely to criminalize technologies and technological devices that have a potential to be used in the circumvention of protected works. As pointed out in the ACM declaration filed with the US federal court regarding the legal challenge in *Felten v. RIAA* (see Barbara Simons's viewpoint: The ACM declaration in *Felten v. RIAA*, Communication of the ACM,

Vol. 44, No. 10. pp 23–26), there is fear in the scientific community regarding subsection 1201(a)3 of DMCA that:

- The broad prohibition on dissemination of information and technology may restrict freedom of speech as protected by the US Constitution's First Amendment.
- There is a likely harm to research, publication, and sponsorship of professional conferences where scientific papers assessing the strength and weaknesses of technologies and other works are discussed, as in the case of *Felten v. RIAA*.
- Because of the non-requirement of DMCA's "intent to circumvent" in the finding one in violation of the law, many individuals making one or fewer copies of a copyrighted work to be used only to understand the working of the work could be charged under DMCA.
- DMCA could criminalize many university courses and research in information technology [22].

If we follow the new DMCA in its broad definition of digitization of copyrightable works, all pre-DMCA works and more are copyrightable. According to Matt Rosenberg [1], copyright merely "subsits," meaning that every person who produces an original work on the Internet automatically has a copyright for that work in the extended definition of digitization. As per the copyright law, therefore, prior permission must be sought in order to copy, distribute, edit, manipulate, and resell the work. For example, downloading a picture of your favorite movie actor from a website, archiving a discussion group's e-mails, and copying a musical composition off the Internet are all cases of copyright infringement unless such copies, graphics, and musical pieces are explicitly allowed by the website owner as fair use or they are allowed by implied licenses [2]. On the practical side, however, this rarely applies to works on the Internet where millions of data bits are routinely copied, downloaded, and repackaged without ever seeking author permission. This is made possible not because users want to circumvent the copyright law but because of the nature of the Internet. But the Internet is changing daily.

11.3.2   Patents

Because cyberspace is primarily a medium of information, the patent law does not directly affect much of the contents of cyberspace. As we stated in Chapter 6, the patent law only affects original and nonobvious inventions.

11.3.3   Trade Secrets

By its very nature, cyberspace is a mass access medium, as we pointed out earlier. With the expansion of Internet use, many companies are becoming heavy users because there are many advantages, especially for research personnel. Many Internet users are in a scavenger hunt for leaking information.

Two types of information can leak in cyberspace: (1) information on devices, designs, processes, software designs, and many other industrial processes and (2) information on individual employee's life possessions –employee accumulated knowledge and experience. When an employee is hired by a company, he or she usually signs a contract with the new employer against disclosure of information "acquired in the course of the employment." But by the nature of cyberspace, an employee can live by this contract and yet disclose as much information, most times unknowingly, into cyberspace community. What is passed is considered "soft" information, and it is disclosed not once, but over a period of time, without both the employee and the employer realizing what is happening. However, as the information leaks in cyberspace, the employee also gains from information leaking from others.

For the employer, this information from cyberspace is free and would have otherwise probably taken years of research and millions of dollars to compile, a plus to the company's bottom line. Companies not only obtain vital and essential information free from cyberspace; they also obtain other resources free or almost free. For example, companies can get free or very inexpensive consultancy in cyberspace that would have required them to hire an expert for a lot more money.

Individual employees also gain tremendously from the Internet, mostly through interaction with peers. Through peers and colleagues on the Internet, employees can pose serious professional questions and get answers or consultancy free and quickly. In fact, it is these personal and professional contacts that are credited with the rapid development of the Internet because since its early days, the Internet has been mainly used by researchers in both educational and research institutions exchanging information and research data. In the process of getting these benefits, however, companies and individuals may find themselves releasing a lot more of their own information than they are actually obtaining from cyberspace. For the information sleuths, cyberspace is a fertile source of information. Most of the rudimentary sources of information one is looking for can be found in cyberspace. It is like a leaking vessel for trade secrets.

With the worldwide scope of cyberspace, global markets are opening up for trade and commerce, thus accelerating the globalization of economies. This will lead to increased global competition in the exchange of goods and services among nations. Cyberspace will provide a background and a backbone for this competition. Workers, especially skilled ones, will start to move in search of greener pastures and better living conditions. Because most trade secrets cases begin with departures of skilled employees to either competitors or self-employment, cyberspace is going to speed up this process.

11.3.4 Trademarks

As we discussed in Chapter 6, in the United States trademark ownership does not require registration unless it is part of "commerce that Congress may regulate," that is, if it crosses state, national, or territorial lines. Trademark rights within the country are based on use. A person or a company may own a trademark and claim infringement without ever knowing the location of the US copyright and patent registration office as long as they have the trademark in use. We explained earlier that any word, phrase, symbol, design, sound, or distinctive color is a trademark once it fulfills a set of criteria.

Trademark laws that apply to products and services in the real world – the non-cyberspace world – also apply very well to products and services in cyberspace. But in particular, and because of the nature of cyberspace, there are currently two areas of contention in which trademarks disputes have started to emerge. One is the area of network domain names, and the other is cyberspace advertising and sales. A domain name is a unique server-identifying name that makes server identity easy to remember instead of long Internet IP decimal addresses. Because these names, which can be simple words such as "me.com" or "redhead.net" or phrases such as "mynode. com" or "smartpants. net" are popping up daily around the globe, cases and disputes have already started arising in which such names and phrases used as domain names have been claimed to be already in use by other people either in the real world or in cyberspace. In the United States, a number of cases referred to as domain name sitting have already been filed in courts for trademark infringements (see scenario 4).

Another area of contention in which trademark infringement is becoming controversial is cyberspace advertising and sales. With the help of WWW graphics, many company logos, symbols, and marks are beginning to appear on the Internet as more and more companies stake their presence in cyberspace. As this happens, the usual fight for trademark infringement and protection is beginning to surface as thousands of companies and individual symbols, marks, and phrases are being added to cyberspace daily from around the world.

This area of trademark infringement seems to present intractable problems for a number of reasons including court jurisdictions on a global scale and different laws for registering trademarks and enforcing trademark laws. Historically, trademarks have been used based on geographical and physical boundaries. Even in one country, similar symbols can still be used without great confusion as long as those symbols are in different geographical regions and in different domains.

A number of small businesses, for example, have been known to use similar names of restaurants as long as those businesses are in remotely separated areas. On a global level, suppose a company or an individual is using a trademark symbol or a phrase in China, legally registered in China, and another company in the United States is also using a similar logo, also registered. Of the two companies, which company has the legal right to the symbol? What court jurisdiction will a case like this go to and what enforcement, if any, will be used? All these are still unanswered questions. As cyberspace technology advances, other areas of friction will certainly arise.

11.3.5 Personal Identity

In Chapter 6 we identified personal identity as a right, a crucial right. Nothing is more fundamental to an individual than personal identity. The ability to control the use of personal information and personal attributes is undeniably a personal right. One needs to be able to keep one's anonymity without interference from others. If I want to eat chili for dinner, for example, I want to do it without the whole world knowing. This is personal information and should remain so because it is nobody's business. I should be able and have the means to control personal information.

The nightmare that can befall a person who loses his or her personal identity is highlighted in the film The Net, produced and directed by Irwin Winkler [3]. The main character, Angela Bernett, lives in an electronic society working as a systems analyst, creating computer games and fighting system viruses. As a member of the electronic society, her life is literally on the net, computerized and sheltered. She never pays attention to it until she finds herself in the middle of a world she least expected to be in: one involving murder, corruption, and conspiracy. It is in this world that she loses her identity when her computerized life is altered and her identity is given to somebody else. She struggles to regain her identity. Although this is fiction, it can have many real-life parallels. Cases abound in the press that parallel the dilemmas of this fictional character, except these are real.

11.4 Regulating and Censoring Cyberspace

The bombing in Atlanta, Georgia, on the night of July 26, 1996, during the height of the Olympics Games reignited the debate and soul searching in Western capitals about the availability in cyberspace of materials believed to be how-to manuals for bomb-making. Although many people do not believe this, nevertheless the easy availability of offensive materials on the Internet and the easy access to such materials in today's world is a growing concern. Although the West is reacting slowly, other cultures are not waiting. They are cautiously instituting cyberspace censorship measures in varying degrees.

Terrorism is not the only reason why many governments are using cyberspace censorship. Depending on the country, the rationales for censorship have varied from historical, social, political, and economic to cultural grounds. In Singapore, for example, known for its use of cyberspace to censor materials entering the country, historical and sociopolitical reasons are cited. The Singapore government and indeed many Singaporeans believe that uninhibited reporting can incite multiracial and multireligious unrest [4]. Other reasons to justify censorship include protection of the young and of religious communities by targeting specified evils such as language use, graphic images, and video or audio.

But cyberspace censorship is proving to be both difficult and very expensive for those trying, and many governments and censorship bureaus are fighting a losing battle because of the exponential growth of the Internet. For governments and censorship bureaus to keep pace with this growth, they have to be continually hiring censors, which is very expensive.

In addition to the explosive growth, Internet content is becoming highly specialized and richer in graphics, which requires very expensive equipment and highly trained people to keep pace. Also, cyberspace's one-fits-all role of telecommunication, broadcast, and computer services is making censorship very difficult and expensive. Effective censorship calls for a better focus on at least one of these because not all three media carry the same materials. Censors may concentrate on materials of a broadcast nature like web pages, assuming that the content they are looking for is more likely to be in this kind of medium, but may find this is not the case. Contents of materials also change in nature and focus from time to time and from medium to medium.

Cyberzens in general are ready to fight any moves to curb their freedom by mostly changing tactics and venues. Although cyberspace's three major media – communication for e-mail, broadcast for web pages, and computer services for services like FTP – are clearly defined, it is still highly disorganized when it comes to searching for specific "content" that one has no prior idea about. Furthermore, cyberspace presents a legal situation in which the laws are chasing technology, always behind, inadequate, and with unfit modifications and clarifications of laws originally meant for old technologies such as print and radio.

And finally, applying geographically defined court jurisdictions in cyberspace, a physical boundary-less entity, is proving to be futile at best. Any attempt to enforce the law in one country means enforcing the same law in a lot more than one. Case in point was the German government's action to block certain sexually oriented user groups from US-based CompuServe online services in Germany. Following a Bavarian police investigation, a court prosecutor in Munich, Germany, made charges, and German officials pressured CompuServe to block access to those objectionable areas because they violated German laws. But because CompuServe did not have the technology and software to block country by country, they ended up facing a global blocking [5].

Many cyberspace problems that lead to censorship have been brought about by the transient nature of membership in cyberspace communities. Users rarely stay in the same community with the same peers for long. These transitions are brought about by a number of factors including changing interests, job changes, changing lifestyles, and a host of others. Each cybercommunity is a moving target community. Transients do not have allegiance and, therefore, no responsibility and accountability.

If the ideal situation is to be realized for every community user worldwide, cyberspace needs to be a place of comfort and entertainment where one can be satisfied and one's curiosity and dreams fulfilled. It needs to be a decent place where children can log on without sparking fear in their parents that their offspring will stumble onto inappropriate material. How this wished-for security can be achieved in cyberspace is the focus of many governments and civic organizations around the globe. The question is how, without total censorship of cyberspace, can these governments and civic organizations do it? As pressure builds for some kind of action, governments have started formulating policies for cyberspace use, some of which is ending up as censorship. An array of measures is being debated in legislatures and government board rooms around the globe. Such measures include the following:

- Guidelines, usually issued by a government body, outlining the dos and don'ts for cyberspace users. For example, China and Singapore have issued guidelines requiring existing providers to use government-provided channels for on-ramp access to cyberspace. Intended providers must apply for approval from the State Council [4].
- Some governments are encouraging the filtering process – picking certain domains and specific names they deem suggestive of what they are looking for. This kind of filtering is usually delegated to system administrators and system operators.
- States are setting up cyberspace on-ramp services and, through low user fees, are encouraging users to opt for these instead of private services. They also urge all educational and research institutions to use these services for free.
- Other governments are encouraging cyberspace user groups to "self-censor" through appeals to patriotism and nationalism and asking users to refrain from using or downloading what they deem offensive materials and sometimes to even report whenever they see objectionable materials [4].
- The use of blocking gadgets is also on the table. An industry for these gadgets is emerging. The blocking software programs work by blocking unwanted cyberspace materials [7]. But blockers have a serious drawback: They can be very easily circumvented by smart programmers.
- Another method is the web rating system. First initiated in the United States, the Platform for Internet Content Selection, or PICS, is a movie-like rating system for Internet content. PICS will offer voluntary technical standards of codes embedded in browsers to be set by individuals, groups, and government agencies in charge of cyberspace access.
- And finally, some governments are either enacting laws or are amending existing laws. For example, European countries spearheaded by France are drafting what they call international rules for cyberspace.

In the US Congress, over the course of several years now, lawmakers have been trying to come up with ways to regulate indecent activities on the Internet. Such efforts have of course yielded a series of acts and bills with the majority of them in 1995 and 1996, the 2 years that encompassed the widely debated Telecommunications Bill of 1996. This bill contained the controversial Communications Decency Act, now defeated in court, whose purpose was to provide protection to citizens, especially minors, against harassment, obscenity, and indecency by means of telecommunication devices such as computers. This was not the first legislative measure to censor the Internet. Other legislation includes the Protection of Children from Computer Pornography Act of 1995, the Comprehensive Terrorism Prevention Act of 1995, the Digital Millennium Copyright Act (2001), the Children Online Protection Act (1998), and the Children Online's Privacy Act (1998).

The intent of these efforts has always been to protect the helpless, like children, from indecent and illicit activities on the Internet. But because of the borderless nature of cyberspace and the rapid growth of the technology these efforts are meant to fight, they have had little or no impact on their intended targets, and there are always new cries for more control. Individual governments' efforts are also complicated by other factors. Chief among them is the realization that because of the differences in political, social, cultural, and religious systems around the globe, what is considered politically offensive in one locale may not be so in another and whatever is considered tolerable in one culture may not be so tolerated in another.

11.5   The Social Value of Cyberspace

The totality of cyberspace is in reality a borderless self-regulating and decentralized mosaic of communities with a variety of cultural, political, and religious agendas. Although this is the way it is, with no central governance, it still works fine. It is a functioning anarchy, but it works. It is also value-ridden. Individuals, communities, and countries have drawn value out of it. To many, cyberspace has provided a way to form new relationships. There have been many marriages that started with simple cyberspace encounters. Many lost families and friends have been reunited because of cyberspace, and of course many lost life companions, like animals, have been found and reunited with their owners. In the September 11, 2001, terrorist attack on the United States, cyberspace provided means for friends and families to comfort one another, check on their loved ones, and grim as it was, check on the list of missing and dead as it was continuously provided by the many emergency centers. For those not directly affected, cyberspace provided a space for discussions, chat, news, and instant messaging so much so that people from around the world felt as one family. Through cyberspace people touched by the incident donated blood and financial help and offered prayers.

Not so long ago, cyberspace provided the same space for those involved in the Tiananmen Square uprising in China and others in the Eastern European freedom movements. To these, cyberspace provided a voice to those who were voiceless. Cyberspace has leveled the playing field for many in need. The dramatic changes in the status quo have not gone unnoticed by many individuals and governments who have started to look for appropriate powers of control, some with the interests of the governed in mind and without limiting human freedoms, and others with total disregard for human freedoms. It is unlikely, however, that such controls through acts, bills, statutes, and other similar instruments will solve the problems.

11.6   Privacy in Cyberspace

On March 10, 1996, the Chattanooga Free Press carried a story by Elizabeth Weise of the Associated Press in which Weise described an ordeal by John Kaufman, a writer in San Francisco. Kaufman, a subscriber to the Internet Usenet, a global bulletin board, was being stalked over the Internet by a female admirer. Every letter he typed was downloaded by her to a point of almost building up his life's profile. This kind of scary search and compilation of scattered information, which in the days of the typewriter cut and paste would have taken probably years, is done in seconds by the powerful cyberspace search engines now being introduced almost every day.

In Chapter 5 we described a scenario in which Citizen X no longer has privacy. In fact, many have been questioning the very concept of personal privacy – whether it still exists at all.

According to recent studies, personal privacy is becoming the number-one social and ethical issue of concern for the information age. Advances in technology have brought with them gadgetry that have diminished individual private spaces through electronic surveillance and monitoring, transmission, scanning, tapping, and fast and more efficient means of collecting, categorizing, and sorting data. Among the current issues of concern are the following:

1. Transmission, scanning, and tapping using computers and cellular phones. Areas most prone to tapping and monitoring are the workplace, telecommunications, and the home.
2. Information gathering as a result of better software and equipment. In this category cyberspace is proving to be a fertile ground because of its powerful search engines and the volume and speed of data. Information gathering, especially from an individual, is now the most threatening and worrisome form of invasion of privacy because of its ever-increasing commercial value. With the right tools at the right time, one can gather all forms of information one needs about a subject in a matter of hours from sources that include county offices, auto registration offices, credit card bureaus, utility companies, postal records, telephones, and satellites. In a day's work one can build an individual profile that in the past would have taken years, if not outright impossible.
3. Individual tracking through mobile and paging devices and computers. Many carrier companies are now using employee tracking to get up-to-the-minute information on what the employee is doing at any given moment.
4. Private investigators (PIs) have found a new partner in cyberspace using satellites; PIs can track and report on any individual with alarming details.
5. Information-gathering abuses by established information-gathering agencies. Governments and government agencies such as the National Security Agency (NSA), the Federal Bureau of Investigations (FBI), the Central Intelligence Agency (CIA), all in the United States; MI5 in Britain; and the Federal Information Agency in Russia, all gather information in the name of national security and crime fighting. In such cases information is gathered on an individual before even an arrest is made. The biggest threat from these established information-gathering agencies is that if not properly focused and supervised, they have the capacity and means to do whatever they like with individual freedoms. This brings us to the privacy paradox that too much individual privacy is very dangerous. According to Daniel Braudt [6], society consists of individuals; if each individual has total privacy, then society as a whole has zero security. Of course, no government can allow this to happen. Because no government can exist without security, somebody's privacy has to be sacrificed.

11.6.1 Privacy Protection

As a cyberspace community member, or cyberzen, you have to be proactive in protecting your privacy. This can be done through information control, property control, and use of anonymity. You are in control of your privacy and you decide on how much to give up. Individual privacy is threatened whenever you voluntarily surrender information through online transactions such as paying bills with credit cards, filling out survey forms, making phone calls, or posting correspondence. Make sure you surrender personal information only when you must and as minimally as possible. Controlling access and information about your personal property (e.g., car, house, or computer) can also help safeguard your privacy.

11.7 Online Social Networks

11.7.1 The Growth of Online Social Networks

Social Networking is the grouping of individuals into groups based on specific interests that members of the group may share. The concept of social networking is not new. In fact it is prehistoric. From prehistoric man through to the current generation, we have been grouping ourselves for different interests ranging from security, food availability to modern easy access to resources. Online social networking unlike other forms of social networking, involves online groupings based on a website that offers specific services desired by the members of the group. The appeal of all online social networks is to offer forums for keeping in contact with old acquaintances and meeting new ones. Users of these networks upon joining, create their own web pages on which they can post unprecedented details about themselves. Until recently, there seemed to be no limit on what they could post about themselves including pornographic images of themselves and sometimes others. What has been even more attractive, especially to young people, is the ability to link to friends on the same site, whose photos, names, and perhaps a brief description, also appear on the linking page. There many online social network groups that have become established and household names like Facebook, Myspace, Friendster, YouTube, Flickr, and LinkedIn.

11.7.2 Social Networking Types

Users of social networking are grouped into tribes based on their interests while online. The tribes are:

- Socializing – usually called "essentialists"
- Business networking

- Getting back in touch
- Dating

Every social network does offer some all or of these services but some offer then better than others.

Discussion Issues: List all social networks you can find and put them into the tribes above based on the services they offer.

11.7.3   Security and Privacy in Social Networks

As the growth of online social networks skyrocketed, so did privacy and other social concerns for the user and other innocent bystanders. The problems of online social networking have been made worse by the growing number of youth flocking into these online social networks without or paying little attention to privacy issues for themselves or others. If you have been following the online social networking trend, you probably know by now that there has been growing concern over breaches in privacy caused by social networking services. Many users feel that their personal details are being circulated far more widely than they intended it to be. For example, take Facebook's 2006 News Feed and Mini Feed features designed to change what Founder and CEO Mark Zuckerberg called Facebook's old "Encyclopedic interface," where pages mostly just list off information about people, to a stream of fresh news and attention content about not only the user but also the user's friends and their activities [23]. The first, News Feed, brought to the user's home page all new activities on all friends and associate links including new photos posted by friends, relationship status changes, people joining groups, and many others, thus enabling the user to get an abundance of information from every friend's site every day.

Although these features adhered to Facebook's privacy settings, meaning that only people a user allowed to view the data were able to see it, it still generated a firestone from users across the world. Over 700,000 users signed an online petition demanding the company discontinue the feature, stating that this compromised their privacy [24]. Much of the criticism of The News Feed was that it gave out too much individual information.

Since online social networks, just like their predecessor cyberspace communities are bringing together with no physical presence to engage in all human acts that traditionally have taken place in a physical environment that would naturally limit the size of the audience and the amount of information given at a time. As these cyber-communities are brought and bound together by a sense of belonging, worthiness, and the feeling that they are valued by members of the network, they create a mental family based on trust, the kind of trust you would find in a loving family. However, because these networks are boundaryless, international in nature, they are forming not along well-known and traditional identifiers such as nationalities, beliefs, authority, and the like, but by common purpose and need with no legal jurisdiction and no central power to enforce community standards and norms.

What is happening in these communities is no longer the traditional epicenter of authority with everyone obeying the center with a shared sense of responsibility by all members. This type of community governance with no central command, but an equally shared authority and responsibility, is new, and a mechanism needs to be in place and must be followed to safeguard every member of the community. But these mechanisms are not yet defined, and where they are being defined, it is still too early to say whether they are effective. The complexity, unpredictability, and lack of central authority is further enhanced by:

- *Virtual personality*: You know their names, their likes and dislikes. You know them so well that you can even bet on what they are thinking, yet you do not know them at all. You cannot meet them and recognize them in a crowd.
- *Anonymity*: You work with them almost every day. They are even your friends; you are on a first-name basis, yet you will never know them. They will forever remain anonymous to you and you to them.
- *Multiple personality*: You think you know them, but you do not because they are capable of changing and mutating into other personalities. They can change into as many personalities as there are issues being discussed. You will never know which personality you are going to deal with next.

These three characteristics are at the core of the social and ethical problems in online social networks in particular and cyberspace in general; the larger and more numerous these communities become, the more urgent the ethical concerns become.

What is happening in these online social networks is a reflection of what is happening in large cyber communities. Numerous social and ethical problems are arising in these online communities because of and directly as a result of user behavior or lack of moral character. Shrouded in cyberspace, users have gambled, participated in cyber pornography, embezzled, settled vendettas, vandalized, victimized, and committed many other evil acts under the cover of cyberspace. They have done all these with impunity because they know that they are out of reach of the law, at least at the moment. For a long time, they are likely to remain in the shadows of the law because [15]:

- There is limited reporting of such illegal acts. Many employees who would like to report such crimes do not because of both the economic and psychological impact such news might have on both the shareholders' confidence and the overall name of the company. Lack of customer confidence is a competitor's advantage and it may spell financial ruin to the company. So, companies are reluctant to report any form of computer attacks on their systems for fear that others, including shareholders, will perceive company management as weak with poor security policies.

- Little to no interest in reporting.
- The law enforcement agencies, especially the FBI, do not have highly special-ized personnel to effectively track down the intruders. Even those few are over-worked and underpaid.
- Companies and businesses hit by cyber vandalism have little faith in law enforcement agencies, especially the FBI, because they think such agencies can do little. The burden to catch and apprehend cyber criminals is still on the FBI. This explains why there has been slow progress in apprehending recent perpetrators. Source: Chattanooga Times/Free Press, Sunday, Jan 20, 2000 section H4.
- The FBI's problems are perpetuated by the fact that the laws that would help the FBI speed up the search and apprehension processes have not kept up with technology. For example, the FBI cannot quickly and readily share evidence of viruses and attack programs they might stumble on with private companies that have the capacity and technical know-how. By the time private computer industry, with the technical know-how, gets hold of such evidential samples, according to Federal Grand Jury evidence rules, the tracks left by the intruders have become cold.

11.8   Global Cyberethics

Hans Kung [8] defines global ethics as a minimal fundamental consensus concern-ing binding values, irrevocable standards, and fundamental moral attitudes. Chikuro Hiroike defines supreme morality as a global superclass of all morality advanced by the sages [21]. The question is can Kung's and Hiroike's requirements be used as a basis for formulating global cyberethics? For the sake of argument, let us assume that these standards can be developed, compiled, and distributed by a global committee of experts in the relevant fields. But there is still a possibility because of geopolitics that someone somewhere is bound to reject them on the grounds that they were compiled under the influence of political, religious, or cultural agents to advance such peoples' ideologies. As human beings acquire wealth, they tend to become more individualistic and shy away from organized standards that they believe are threatening their way of life and do not protect and/or advance their agendas.

Ideally, as communities, which for years have been separated by languages, culture, history, politics, religion, and geography, come together, Kung's and Hiroike's minimal fundamental consensus of binding values, standards, and fun-damental moral attitudes will begin to emerge in cyberspace. Indeed, cases of such emergence have already started to appear in many cyberspace communities as the etiquettes of cyberspace. Starting small among cyberspace communities, these etiquettes will eventually amalgamate, mutate, and spread into global cyberethics.

11.9   Cyberspace Lingua Franca

Because the cyberspace community, at least at the moment, is overwhelmingly English-speaking, it is appropriate to say that English is its unofficial language. However, English did not assume this role because the global community of users voted it in; the reason for its dominance is basically economic, although the Internet was also born in the United States, an English-speaking country. According to Anatoly Votonov, director of Glasnet, a Russian Internet provider, the level of English in cyberspace makes cyberspace the "ultimate act of intellectual colonialism" [9].

Contrary to popular belief, cyberspace may be a household word, but very few households own Internet connections globally because they are still too expensive. In the United States, for example, not everyone has Internet connections. According to the NTIA 2000 report, 41.8% have Internet connections [10]. Consequently, those who have cyberspace access are from predominantly rich, technologically advanced countries, and except for Japan, France, and Germany, these countries are overwhelmingly English-speaking. For the same economic reasons, more business transactions are done in English than in any other language. As the Internet experiences phenomenal growth, more and more businesses are discovering that cyberspace is a fertile ground for them and are making their posting and advertising in the self-declared language of cyberspace: English.

With the rapid global spread of the Internet, however, English is no longer English as we know it. It is becoming "cyberspace English" which is an amalgam of various versions of regional and national English variants such as American (United States), Canadian, Caribbean, Australian, and South African English.

Although cyberspace English has been unceremoniously accepted by most of cyberspace community, it is not likely to ever be accepted as the official lingua franca of cyberspace. There are various reasons for this. Widespread as this English may be, it is not spoken by every person capable of buying a computer and acquiring Internet access. As the Internet engulfs the globe, other languages will gain prominence.

In order for any language to be an official language to any group of people, it must be learned by the members of that group either by force or voluntarily because of its apparent benefits. Historically, imperialism and colonialism were successful means by which traditional languages were forced on people. For example, Latin and Greek were spread by and during the Roman Empire, Spanish through Spanish conquests, and French and English through French and British imperialism and colonialism. Given the current state of human development, however, the advances in technology made so far, and, most important, the nature of cyberspace technology, which is decentralized, this method of language growth is not viable.

Many languages have been learned voluntarily because of their appeal to the learners, and in English's case, this voluntary approach is viable because of English's economic clout. But English carries negative connotations because of its beginnings. It is still considered a colonial language by many. Others see it as either an imperial or neo-imperial language and as a political and economic tool for affluent English-speaking countries like the United States.

The colonial past, imperialistic stealth, and the emergence of other language blocs in cyberspace as it grows will minimize in due time the preeminence of English as the de facto language of cyberspace. Christian Huitema [9], a member of the board of the Internet Society, says it takes about two million customers to establish a workable market in any language, so as the Internet grows, the body of other people speaking other languages will grow as well, and English will be just another cyberspace language. As more and more people with varying views and preferences join cyberspace, and as technology develops, cyberspace may construct its own language. Such a language inevitably will contain phrases of English because of its clout in cyberspace, but it will also contain a lot of inputs from other languages and new technology-supplied terms. If the Internet maintains its rate of growth, this is likely to happen sooner rather than later. Already a small skeleton of such a constructed language is beginning to appear, although it is still symbolic. These symbols are universal and from no known language, yet they are able to express feelings and emotions, as exemplified by the smiling face symbol ("smiley").

Korpela [11] foresees another alternative to "cyberspace English" and a constructed language. He predicts the development of better language machine translation algorithms. Such algorithms will result in efficient and sufficient quality language translators, and there will be no need for a lingua franca. If this happens, then cyberspace will truly become a global infrastructure. There are other proposals on the horizon. A number of programming languages now in use in cyberspace are using unicode standard, a language code system that incorporate all the characters of the world's languages into one huge standard code. Some people are drumming up support for the adoption of ASCII as the de facto code. They argue that because ASCII is already on the way to becoming a de facto character code standard, there is no need to reinvent the wheel [12].

11.10   Global Cyber Culture

New developments in telecommunications have brought nations closer than ever before. The process picked up momentum in the last half-century with the development of mass communications technology such as radio and television. Jet engine technology increased human mobility, thus facilitating cultural

"FRANKLY, I MISS THE OLD DAYS OF JOHN DILLINGER AND AL CAPONE."

exchanges. People who were born in one culture found themselves growing up in a different culture. In particular, the advent of the Internet has moved us into a new age that is affecting human life on a global scale in economics, languages, politics, and entertainment. Cyberspace has accelerated this process and has made it even more personal, an achievement both television and radio communication did not make. According to Micheal Hauben [13] of the Usenet news, the web, e-mail, and other Internet services have facilitated the growth of global interactive communities. As new interactive communities flourish in cyberspacet, increasing numbers of global cultures are joining those cybercommunities. As they do, it raises the question of whether the whole process will end as an amalgam of a global cyber culture that will be a hybrid of many global cultures, or as one de facto culture that has in effect swallowed up all the other cultures.

There are now hundreds of these cybercommunities with interests ranging from gardening to space exploration. What is common to all these cybercommunities is the bond of an interest in a particular topic. To stay as cybercommunities, members follow certain community etiquettes and they share their reactions and emotions. As the interaction between these cybercommunities continues, a new common language is slowly forming. As we already mentioned, there are already symbols like "smiley" that are understood by every cybercommunity member. Many other new terms are already widely used such as URL, WWW, HTTP, FTP, e-mail, and Telnet, and many others are yet to come. These terms are used in the new "superstructural society," which according to Tim North [14] spans the mainstream cultures represented in these interactive communities and depends on them for its existence. The new cyber language and culture developing are not a reflection of purely one culture. According to North, the new culture incorporates cultural elements from many nations and cultures.

Exercises

1. From your point of view, discuss the social implications of cyberspace.
2. Is there a likelihood of a global civil society?
3. Discuss the issues involved in cyberspace access, including risks and threats.
4. Some people have hailed cyberspace for giving the voiceless a needed voice. Discuss.
5. Comment on the right of passage to cyberspace.
6. Comment on the growth of a lingua franca of cyberspace.
7. Rapid changes in cyberspace have made most intellectual property laws obsolete. Discuss.
8. Suggest the best ways to deal with property issues on a changing landscape of cyberspace.
9. What is an Internet paradox?
10. What is the best way to deal with this axis of conflict?
11. Why are copyrights and trademarks difficult to protect in cyberspace?
12. Suggest ways to protect all intellectual property rights in cyberspace.
13. Suggest ways to protect personal identity.
14. List ways identity thieves use to acquire personal identity.
15. Why is personal identity so important?
16. What is giving rise to cyberspace censorship?
17. Why is it so difficult to censor cyberspace?
18. Suggest reasons why cyberspace should not be censored.
19. List the steps taken by governments to curb cyberspace ills.
20. Discuss the merits and demerits of censorship measures.
21. Discuss the civic roles of cyberspace.
22. Comment on the statement that when citizens have total privacy, society has zero security.
23. Discuss the weaknesses of the TCP/IP protocol suite.
24. Suggest the best ways to safeguard server security.
25. Discuss the need for a universal cyberspace language.
26. Do you believe in a "new" cyberspace culture? Why or why not?
27. Why is it so difficult to apprehend cyber criminals?
28. Discuss the three characteristics of cyber communities. How do these contribute to the difficult of policing cyberspace?
29. What are the best ways to policy cyberspace? Is it possible?
30. Discuss the governance of cyberspace.
31. Can law enforcement structures such as Interpol work in cyberspace?
32. Discuss the privacy issues in online social networks. Was Facebook's user revolt the beginning of user interest in upholding privacy issues, user good behavior in online social networks?

References

1. Rosenberg, Matt. "Copyrights Law Meets the World Wide Web." Crossroads, 2(2), 1995. http://info.acm.org/crossroads/
2. Leesing, Larry, David Post, and Eugene Vololch. "Copyright Law in Cyberspace, Cyberspace Law Institute for Non-Lawyers." http://www.counsel.com/cyberspace/
3. The Net [motion picture]. http://www.spe.sony.com/pictures/sonymovies/
4. Lewis, Peter. "Limiting a Medium Without Boundaries." New York Times, January 15, 1996, D1.
5. Ang, Deng, and Balinda Nadarajan. "Censorship and the Internet: A Singapore Perspective." Communications of the ACM, 39(6), 1996, pp. 72–78.
6. Brandt, Daniel. "Cyberspace Wars: Microproceesing vs. Big Brother." NameBase NewsLine 2, July–August 1993. http://ursula.btythe.org/NameBase/NewsLine.02/
7. Bhimani, Anish. "Securing the Commercial Internet." Communications of the ACM, 39(6), 1996, pp. 29–35.
8. Kung, Hans. "Declaration Towards a Global Ethic." http://rain.org/~origin/genetic.html

9. "Internet as 'Intellectual Colonialism'" The Council Chronicle, June 1996, p. 6.
10. National Telecommunications and Information Administration, Technical Report 2000 (NTIA 2000). "Falling Through the Net: Toward Digital Inclusion." http://www.ntia.doc.gov.ntia-home/ftfn00/front00.htm
11. Korpela, Jukka. "English: The Universal Language on the Internet?" http://www.hut.fi/jkor-pela/lingua-franca.html
12. Engst, Adam. "Need to Know: The Electronic Lingua Franca." http://etext.archive.umich.edu/zines/
13. Hauben, Micheal. "Culture and Communication: Interplay in the New Public Commons—Usenet and Community Networks." http://www.columbia.edu/~hauben/project-book.html
14. North, Tim. "The Internet and Usenet Global Networks: An Investigation of Their Culture and Its Effects on New Users [on-line]." http://foo.curtin.edu.au/Thesis/
15. Kizza, Joseph M. Computer Network Security and CyberEthics. McFarland: Jefferson, NC 2002.
16. Joe Stance. "Net twins' in Missouri, but home still unclear." The Associated Press. http://www.inlandempireonline.com/de/adoption/adopt042001.shtml
17. Ranum, Marcus. "Network Forensics: Network Traffic Monitoring." http://www.nfr.net/publications/
18. Jackson, Steve. "ESM NetRecon: Ultrascan Technology." http://www.si.com.au/Appendix/NetRecon%20Ultranscan%20.Technology.html
19. Carnegie Mellon University, Software Engineering Institute "Survivable Network Systems: An Emerging Discipline." http://www.sei.cmu.edu/publications/documents/97.reports/97tr013/97tr013abstract.html
20. Rosenblum, Robert. "Sorting Through the Confusion: Interpreting Recording Agreement Provisions of the Digital Era." The Entertainment Law Reporter. November 1999.
21. Chikuro Hiroike. Towards Supreme Morality. The Institute of Moralogy. Japan. 2002.
22. Barbara Simons. "The ACM Declaration in Felten v. RIAA," Communication of the ACM, 44(10), pp. 23–26.
23. Michael Arrington. "New Facebook Redesign More Than Aesthetic" TechCrunch, September 5, 2006.
24. Brian Colgan. "Facebook News Feed feature inspires student ire". The Wesleyan Argus, Sept. 12, 2006, Vol. CXLI, No. 2.

Further Readings

Borestein, Nathaniel. "Perils and Pitfalls of Practical Cybercommerce." Communications of the ACM, 39(6), 1996, pp. 36–44.
CNN Headline News, January 15, 1996. http://www.cnn.com/
Denning, D., and Dannis K. Branstad. "A Taxonomy for Key Escrow Encryption Systems." Communications of the ACM, 39(3), 1996, pp. 34–39.
Dornin, Rusty. "The Internet: Will It Last or Fade into the Past?" CNN Interactive. http://www.cnn.com/
Kung, Hans. "The Principle of a Global Ethic." http://rain.org/~origin/genetic.html
Levy, Steven, "Prophet of Privacy." Wired, November 1994, p. 126.
Maher, David. "Crypto Backup and Kew Escrow." Communications of the ACM, 39(3), 1996, pp. 48–53.
Pyle, Raymond. "Electronic Commerce and the Internet." Communications of the ACM, 39(6), 1996, p. 23.
Samuelson, Pamela. "Intellectual Property Rights and the Global Information Economy." Communications of the ACM, 39(1), 1996, pp. 23–28.
Sterling, Bruce. "History of the Internet." http://gopher.iso.org:70/internet/history/
Walker, Stephen, Steven Lipner, Carl Ellison, and David Balenson. "Commercial Key Recovery." Communications of the ACM, 39(3), 1996, pp. 41–47.
Weiser, Mark. "Whatever Happened to the Next-Generation Internet?" Communication of the ACM, 44(9), pp. 61–68.

Chapter 12
Computer Networks and Online Crimes

Learning Objectives

After reading this chapter, the reader should be able to:

1. Describe the evolution and types of computer networks.
2. Understand networking fundamentals, including network services and transmission media.
3. Understand network software and hardware, including media access control, network topologies, and protocols, as well as connectivity hardware for both local area and wide area networks.
4. Understand how the network infrastructure helps to perpetuate online crimes.
5. Recognize the difficulties faced in fighting online crime.

12.1 Introduction to Computer Networks

A *computer network* is a distributed system consisting of loosely coupled computing elements and other devices. In this configuration, any two of these devices can communicate with each other through a communications medium. The medium may be wired or wireless. To be considered a communicating network, the distributed system must communicate based on a set of communicating rules called *protocols*. Each communicating device in the network must then follow these rules to communicate with others. A standard wired computer network would look like the network in Fig. 12.1.

Individually, network elements may own resources that are local or global. Such resources may be either software-based or hardware-based. If software, it may consist of all application programs and network protocols that are used to synchronize, coordinate, and bring about the sharing and exchange of data among the network elements. Network software also makes the sharing of expensive resources in the network possible. The hardware components of a computer network consist of a collection of nodes that include the end systems commonly called *hosts* and intermediate switching elements that include hubs, bridges, routers, and gateways.

12.1.1 Computer Network Models

Several network configuration models are used in the design of computer networks, but the most common are two: the centralized and distributed models shown in

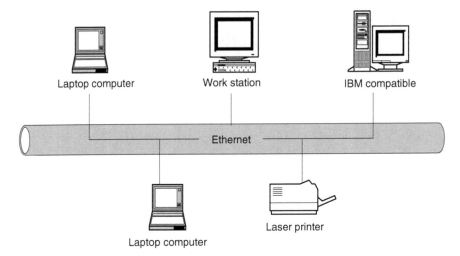

Fig. 12.1 A computer network

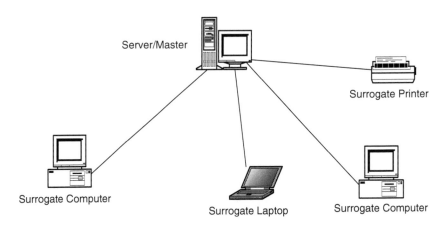

Fig. 12.2 A centralized network model

Figs. 12.2 and 12.3. In a centralized model, all computers and devices in the network are connected directly to a central computer, through which they can interconnect to each other. This central computer, commonly called the master, must receive and forward all correspondence between any two or more communicating computers and devices. All other computers in the network are correspondingly called dependent or surrogate computers. These surrogates may have reduced local resources, such as memory, and shareable global resources are controlled by the master at the center. The configurations are different, however, in the distributed network model. This consists of loosely coupled computers interconnected by a communication network consisting

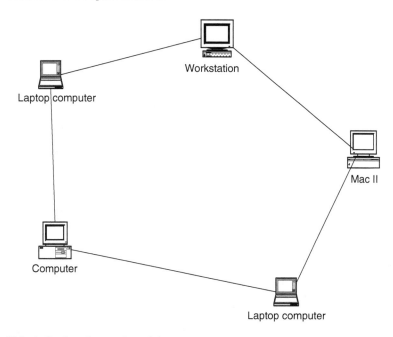

Fig. 12.3 A distributed network model

of connecting elements and communication channels. However, unlike in the centralized model, here the computers themselves may own their own resources locally or may request resources from a remote computer. Computers in this model are known by a string of names, including host, client, or node.

12.1.2 Computer Network Types

Computer networks, in any configuration centralized or distributed, come in different sizes depending on the number of computers and other devices the network has. The number of devices, computers or otherwise, in a network and the geographical area covered by the network determine the network type. There are, in general, three main network types: the local area network (LAN), a wide area network (WAN), and metropolitan area network (MAN).

12.1.2.1   Local Area Network

A LAN is a computer network with two or more computers or clusters of network and their resources connected by a communication medium sharing communication protocols and confined in a small geographical area such as a building floor, a building, or a few adjacent buildings. In a LAN, all network elements are in close proximity, which makes the communication links maintain a higher speed and quality of data movement. Figure 12.4 shows a LAN.

12.1.2.2   Wide Area Network

A WAN is a computer network made up of one or more clusters of network elements and their resources but unlike in the LAN, here, the configuration is not confined to a small geographical area. It can spread over a wide geographical area like a region of a country, or across the whole country, several countries, or the entire globe like the Internet for example, which helps in distributing network services and resources to a wider community. Figure 12.5 shows a WAN.

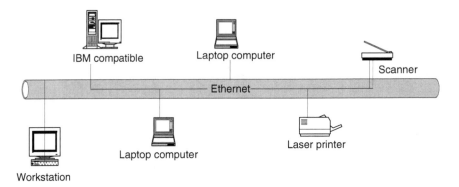

Fig. 12.4 A LAN network

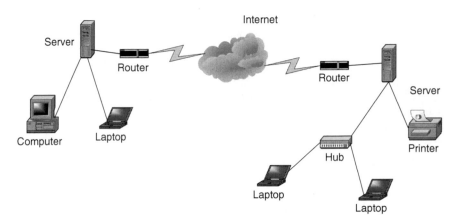

Fig. 12.5 A WAN network

12.1.2.3   Metropolitan Area Network

A metropolitan area network (MAN) is an unusual and less used type of a network that falls between a LAN on the one side and a WAN on the other. It covers a slightly wider area than the LAN but not so wide as to be considered a WAN. Civic networks that cover a city or part of a city are a good example of a MAN.

12.2   Online Crimes

Although currently most computer-related crimes are online crimes, it was never like this. Before the advent of the Internet and the widespread use of computers in businesses, schools, and homes, computer crimes were simple, stand-alone computer-related like making computer-aided forgeries. The Internetworking and wide use of computers have created fertile ground for online crimes. All said and done, online crimes come in many different forms including viruses and worms, hacking and phreaking, identity theft, denial of services, online pornography and pedophilia, and many others. In Chapter 9, we discuss all computer crime both online and offline. We also give the history of computer crimes. Further in Table 9.1 we discuss many of the online computer crimes. The interested reader is referred back to Chapter 9.

Online crimes, in tandem with the growth of computing technology, are one of the fastest growing types of crimes and they pose the greatest danger to online activities, e-commerce, and the general public in general. An *online crime* is a crime like any other crime, except that in this case, the illegal act must involve a connected computing system either as an object of a crime, an instrument used to commit a crime, or a repository of evidence related to a crime. Also online crimes are acts of unauthorized intervention into the working of the telecommunication networks and/or the sanctioning of authorized access to the resources of the computing elements in a network that lead to a threat to the system's infrastructure or cause a significant property loss. The International Convention of Cyber Crimes and the European Convention on Cyber Crimes both list the following crimes as online crime [1]:

- Unlawful access to information
- Illegal interception of information
- Unlawful use of telecommunication equipment
- Forgery with use of computer measures
- Intrusions of the Public Switched and Packet Network
- Network integrity violations
- Privacy violations
- Industrial espionage
- Pirated computer software
- Fraud using a computing system
- Internet/e-mail abuse
- Using computers or computer technology to commit murder, terrorism, pornography, and hacking

12.2.1 Beware of Ways to Perpetuate Online Crimes

As we pointed out in Chapter 9, if we have to fight online crimes, we have to first learn how they are perpetuated. Earlier, we noted that online crimes are defined in a variety of ways. This reflects the many different ways these crimes are perpetuated. Some of the most common ways are through: system penetration and denial of service attacks.

12.2.1.1 System Penetration

System penetration is the most widely used approach to committing online crimes. A system penetration is a process of gaining unauthorized access to a protected system's resources, the system may be automated or not. Penetration attacks always compromise the integrity of the resources of a system. Most penetration attacks are not accidental; they are preplanned and proceed with a coordinated reconnaissance. The goal of the reconnaissance is to acquire the following lead information on the targeted system:

- IP addresses of all hosts or selected hosts in the victim network
- Accessible UDP and TCP port numbers
- The type of operating system(s) used on all hosts or selected hosts in the network

There are two types of reconnaissance: passive and active. In a *passive reconnaissance*, the attacker gathers freely available system information mostly from open source. A typical passive reconnaissance can include physical observation of buildings housing the system, dumpster diving near the target system collecting discarded papers and system computer equipment in an attempt to find equipment or data that may include personal identifying data like username and passwords that will lead them to gain access to the company system. It also includes using other information gathering techniques like eavesdropping on employee conversations, social engineering, packet sniffing, and others. Some common sources and tools used when looking for open source information legally include [2]:

- A company website
- Electronic data gathering, analysis, and retrieval (EDGAR) filings (for publicly traded companies)
- Network news transfer protocol (NNTP) USENET newsgroups
- User group meetings
- Business partners
- Dumpster diving
- Social engineering

Active reconnaissance on the other hand involves collecting information about a target system by probing that system or neighboring systems. A typical active reconnaissance involves port scanning to discover vulnerable ports through which to enter the system, probing firewalls and system routers to find ways around them, and others. Some of the tools used in active host reconnaissance include:

- NSLookup/Whois/Dig lookups
- SamSpade
- Visual Route/Cheops
- Pinger/WS_Ping_Pro

12.2.1.2 Distributed Denial of Service

Another approach perpetuators of online crimes use is the *denial of service*. This is an interruption of service of the target system. This interruption of service occurs when the target system is made either unavailable to users through disabling or destruction of it. Denial of service can also be caused by intentional degradation or blocking of computer or network resources. These denial of service attacks are commonly known as *distributed denial of service* (DDoS) attacks because they attack hosts in a network.

Like penetration attacks (e-attacks), DDoS attacks can also be either local, where they can shut down LAN computers, or global, originating thousands of miles away on the Internet. Attacks in this category include [1]:

- *IP spoofing*. A forging of an IP packet address such as the source address, which causes the responses from the destination host to be misdirected, thus creating problems in the network. Many network attacks are a result of IP spoofing.
- *SYN flooding*. Using a three-way handshake protocol to initiate connections between a malicious (spoofed) source nodes and flood the target node with so many connection requests thus overwhelming it and bringing it down.
- *Smurf attack*. In which the intruder sends a large number of spoofed ICMP Echo requests to broadcast IP addresses. Hosts on the broadcast multicast IP network then respond to these bogus requests with reply ICMP Echo significantly multi-plying the number of reply ICMP Echos to the hosts with spoofed addresses.
- *Buffer overflow*. In which the attacker floods a carefully chosen field such as an address field with more characters than it can accommodate. These excessive characters, usually executable malicious code, when executed may cause havoc in the system, effectively giving the attacker control of the system.
- *Ping of death*. In which the attacker sends IP packets that are larger than the 65,536 bytes allowed by the IP protocol knowing that many network operating systems cannot handle, leading to the possible freezing or eventual system crash.
- *Land.c attack*. In which the land.c program sends TCP SYN packets whose source and destination IP addresses and port numbers are those of the victims.
- *Teardrop.c*. In which the attacker causes a fragmentation of TCP packets in order to exploit the reassembling process that may lead to the victim to crash or hang.
- *Sequence number sniffing*. In which the intruder takes advantage of the pre-dictability of sequence numbers used in TCP implementations to sniff the next sequence number to establish legitimacy.

12.3   Defense Against Online Crimes

Although there are systems which are randomly attacked, most victim systems, however, are preselected for attack. Because of this, we can defend systems against online attacks. An effective defense plan consists of prevention, detection, and analysis and response.

12.3.1   Prevention

Prevention is perhaps the oldest and probably the best defense mechanism against online crimes. However, prevention can only work if there is a strict security discipline that is effectively enforced and must include the following:

- A security policy
- Risk management
- Vulnerability assessment
- Use of strong cryptographic algorithms
- Penetration testing
- Regular audits
- Use of proven security protocols
- Legislation
- Self-regulation
- Mass education

Let us discuss some of these. More details on some of these may be found in Sections 5.3 and 8.3.

12.3.1.1   A Security Policy

A security policy is a critical and central document in an organization security efforts that spells out in great details how the organization manages risk, controls access to key assets and resources, and implements policies, procedures, and practices for a safe and secure environment [3]. A security policy usually also spells out what resources need to be protected and how organization can protect such resources. It is a living document and sometimes controversial. There are as many opinions on the usefulness of security policies in the overall system security picture as there are security experts. However, security policies are still important in establishing an organization's security guidelines like:

- *Hardware and software acquisition and installations in the organization.* For example, if a functioning firewall is to be configured, its rule-base must be based on a sound security policy.
- *User discipline.* All users in the organization who connect to a network, such as the Internet, must do so in conformity to the security policy.

A security policy is unique for each organization and covers a wide variety of topics and serves several important purposes in the organization's security cycle. Because of this, the following carefully chosen set of basic steps must be established and carefully followed in the construction of a viable implementable and useful security policy:

- Determining the resources that must be protected and for each resource drawing a profile of its characteristics
- Determining, for each identified resource, from whom the resource must be protected
- Determining, for each identifiable resource, the type of threat and the likelihood of occurrence of such a threat
- Determining, for each identifiable resource, what measures are needed to give it the best protection
- Determining what needs to be audited
- Determining and defining acceptable use of system resources such as e-mail, News, and Web
- Considering how to implement and deploy security protocols such as encryption, access control, key creation, and distributions and wireless devices that connect on the organization's network
- Providing for remote access to accommodate workers on the road and those working from home, and also business partners who may need to connect to the organization's network via a VPN

12.3.1.2   Vulnerability Assessment

Like risk assessment, vulnerability assessment is the process of identifying and quantifying vulnerabilities in a system. A *vulnerability* in a system is an exploitable weakness in the system. As we saw in Section 8.3, this is a two-part process; we need to first identify all system vulnerabilities and then develop strategies to mitigate the effects of these vulnerabilities. The rest of the steps usually taken are similar to those in Section 8.3.

12.3.1.3   Use of Strong Cryptographic Algorithms

Cryptography is a Greek word meaning "secret writing." It was used to describe the art of secret communication. As shown in Figs. 5.1 and 12.6, cryptographic system consists of four essential components [1]:

- Plaintext – the original message to be sent
- A cipher – consisting of mathematical encryption and decryption algorithms
- Ciphertext – the result of applying an encryption algorithm to the original message before it is sent to the recipient
- Key – a string of bits used by the two mathematical algorithms in encrypting and decrypting processes

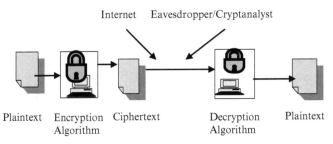

Internet   Eavesdropper/Cryptanalyst

Plaintext   Encryption   Ciphertext   Decryption   Plaintext
            Algorithm   Algorithm

Fig. 12.6 Symmetric encryption

Table 12.1 Modern cryptographic security services

Security services	Cryptographic mechanism to achieve the service
Confidentiality	Symmetric encryption
Authentication	Digital signatures and digital certificates
Integrity	
Decryption of digital signature with a public key to obtain the message digest. The message is hashed to create a second digest. If the digests are identical, the message is authentic and the signer's identity is proven	
Nonrepudiation	
Digital signatures of a hashed message then encrypting the result with the private key of the sender, thus binding the digital signature to the message being sent	
Nonreplay	Encryption, hashing, and digital signature

Cryptographic technologies are today being used increasingly to fight off massive invasion of individual privacy and security, to guarantee data integrity and confidentiality, and to bring trust in global e-commerce. In fact, cryptography has become the main tool for providing the needed digital security in the modern digital communication medium. Its popularity is a result of its ability to guarantee authorization, authentication, integrity, confidentiality, and nonrepudiation in all communications and data exchanges in the new information society. Table 12.1 shows how cryptography guarantees these security services through five basic mechanisms that include symmetric and public key encryption, hashing, digital signatures, and certificates.

The main components of the cryptography are the cipher and the key. A *cipher* or a cryptosystem is a pair of invertible functions; one for encrypting or enciphering, the other for decryption or deciphering. The word *cipher* has its origin in an Arabic word *sifr*, meaning *empty* or *zero*. The encryption process uses the cryptographic algorithm, known as the *encryption algorithm*, and a selected key to transform the plaintext data into an encrypted form called *ciphertext*, usually unintelligible form. The ciphertext can then be transmitted across the communication channels to the intended destination. There are two encryption techniques: symmetric and asymmetric.

Symmetric encryption. Symmetric encryption as defined in Section 5.3 uses a common key and the same cryptographic algorithm to scramble and unscramble the message so that eavesdroppers and cryptanalysts with no knowledge of the key are unable to read the message (see Fig. 12.6). However, this presents a problem in a number of ways because of the need to safeguard the integrity of the key. This problem gets worse in a distributed environment with large number of users.

In addition to the sharing of the single key, symmetric encryption also suffers from a size problem – the size of the communication space. Because, again in a large distributed environment with a large number of players who can carry on communication in a many-to-one, one-to-many, and many-to-many, the secret key cryptography, if strictly used, requires billions of secret keys pairs to be created, shared, and stored. This can be a nightmare eventually leading to system failures. There are also other problems including the following [4]:

- The integrity of data can be compromised because the receiver cannot verify that the message has not been altered before receipt.
- It is possible for the sender to repudiate the message because there are no mechanisms for the receiver to make sure that the message has been sent by the claimed sender.
- The method does not give a way to ensure secrecy even if the encryption process is compromised.
- The secret key may not be changed frequently enough to ensure confidentiality.

Asymmetric (public key) encryption. As we discussed in Section 5.3, unlike the symmetric encryption *asymmetric (public key) encryption* uses two different keys, a public key known by all and a private key. This ensures data confidentiality and integrity because for data to be modified by an attacker, it requires the attacker to have a private key. Data confidentiality and integrity in public key encryption are also guaranteed.

Using a double asymmetric encryption as shown in Fig. 12.7, guarantees all four aspects of security namely confidentiality, integrity, authentication, and nonrepudiation.

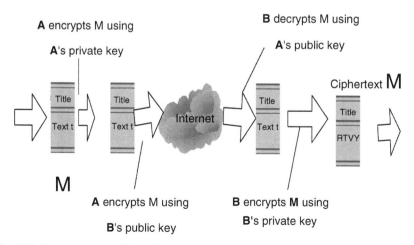

Fig. 12.7 Ensuring data confidentiality and integrity and user authentication and nonrepudiation

One big advantage of public key encryption over its older sister, the symmetric encryption, is that no secret key is passed between two communicating parties. This means that this approach can support all communication topologies including one-to-one, one-to-many, many-to-many, and many-to-one and along with it several to thousands of people can communicate with one party without exchange of keys. This makes it suitable for Internet communication and e-commerce applications. Its other advantage is that it solves the chronic repudiation problem experienced by symmetric encryption. This problem is solved, especially in large groups, by the use of digital signatures and certificates.

12.3.1.4 Penetration Testing

One of the core security techniques for safeguarding the security of an organization's system is to periodically do a penetration test of the system. The test may be outsourced for it to be more authentic or it could be carried out in-house as long as one has competent personnel to do it. The process of penetration testing actively evaluates an organization's system resources and information in real time looking for design weaknesses, technical flaws, and vulnerabilities in the system. This can be done on a regular basis or after a schedule time frame. The possible outcomes of the test vary depending on the focus of the test.

Penetration testing may also focus on the security of information on the organization network by doing tests like document grinding, privacy of information review, and intelligence scouting among others. If the organization supports wireless technology, this component must also be tested. No penetration testing can be complete without testing social engineering, communication within and outside the organization, and the physical security within the organization. Finally physical testing may require testing access to the facilities, monitor the perimeter and alarm systems, and an environment review.

12.3.1.5 Regular Security Audits

While a penetration testing of an organization system is a focused look at the security holes in the system's resources such as firewalls and servers, a security audit is a systematic, measurable, and quantifiable technical assessment of the organization security and the security of its system. Management usually requests for security audits in order to gain knowledge and understand the security status of the organization's system. From the audit report, management may decide to upgrade the system through acquisition of new hardware and software. In "Conducting a Security Audit: An Introductory Overview," Bill Hayes suggests that a security audit should answer the following questions [4]:

- Are passwords difficult to crack?
- Are there access control lists (ACLs) in place on network devices to control who has access to shared data?

- Are there audit logs to record who accesses data?
- Are the audit logs reviewed?
- Are the security settings for operating systems in accordance with accepted industry security practices?
- Have all unnecessary applications and computer services been eliminated for each system?
- Are these operating systems and commercial applications patched to current levels?
- How is backup media stored? Who has access to it? Is it up-to-date?
- Is there a disaster recovery plan? Have the participants and stakeholders ever rehearsed the disaster recovery plan?
- Are there adequate cryptographic tools in place to govern data encryption, and have these tools been properly configured?
- Have custom-built applications been written with security in mind?
- How have these custom applications been tested for security flaws?
- How are configuration and code changes documented at every level? How are these records reviewed and who conducts the review?

If genuine and trustful answers are given to many of these questions, a realistic security status of the organization's system emerges.

12.4 Proven Security Protocols and Best Practices

There are hundreds of security protocols to meet the needs of organizations trying to improve their systems' security. There are so many of them, some are open source and others are not, that they pose a problem to security professionals to choose a really good product. The security personnel must strive to come up with a list of the best protocols and best practices to suit the system. Some of these protocols include the following.

12.4.1 Authentication

Authentication is the process of validating the identity of someone or something. It uses information provided to the authenticator to determine whether someone or something is in fact who or what it is declared to be. The process usually requires one to present credentials or items of value to the authenticating agent in order to prove the claim of who one really is. The items of value or credential are based on several unique factors that show something you know, something you have, or something you are [1]:

- *Something you know.* It may be something you mentally possess like a password, a secret word known by the user and the authenticator. This technique of authentication is cheap but has weaknesses like memory lapses.

- *Something you have.* It may be any form of issued or acquired self-identification such as SecurID, Activcard, or any other forms of cards and tags. This authentication technique is slightly safer.
- *Something you are.* These are individual physical characteristics such as voice, fingerprint, iris pattern, and other biometrics. Biometric authentication as we are going to see in Chapter 14 is the safest form of authentication.

Besides these, there are other forms of authentication using a variety of authentication algorithms. These authentication methods can be combined or used separately, depending on the level of functionality and security needed. Among such methods are password authentication, public key authentication, anonymous authentication, remote and certificate-based authentication.

12.4.2 Access Control

Access control is a process of determining how access to the system's potential resources can be provided to each of the system users. Because a system, especially a network system, may have thousands of users and resources, the management of access rights for every user per every object may become complex. Several control techniques and technologies have been developed to deal with this problem; they include access control matrix, capability tables, access control lists, role-based access control, rule-based access control, restricted interfaces, content-dependent access control, and biometrics.

12.4.3 Legislation

Ever since the start of noticeable computer technology misuse, governments and national legislatures around the world have been enacting laws intended to curb the growth of these crimes. The report card on these legislations has been mixed. In some cases, legislation as a form of deterrent has worked and it has been a failure in others. However, we should not lose hope. Enforceable laws can be productive.

12.4.4 Self-Regulation

Perhaps one of the most successful forms of deterrence has been self-regulation. A number of organizations have formed to advocate parents and teachers to find a way to regulate objectionable material from reaching the children. Also families and individuals, sometimes based on their morals and sometimes based on their religion, have made self-regulation a cornerstone of their efforts to stop the growing rate of online crimes.

12.4.5   Detection

While it is easy to develop mechanisms for preventing online crimes, it is not so easy to develop similar or effective techniques and best practices to detect online crimes. Detecting online crimes constitutes a 24-h monitoring system to alert security personnel whenever something unusual (something with a non-normal pattern, different from the usual pattern of traffic in and around the system) occurs. Detection systems must continuously capture, analyze, and report on the daily happenings in and around the network. In capturing, analyzing, and reporting, several techniques are used including intrusion detection, vulnerability scanning, virus detection, and other ad hoc methods.

12.4.6   Recovery

Recovery is a process preceded by a process of analysis, which involves taking as much data as possible gathered during the last intrusion and analyzing it for patterns that can be used in future for a response, for detection in future, and for prevention. Recovery requires the use of all available resources to first mitigate the problem in progress, then recover whatever can be recovered and use it to build on new data in place of or to replace the destroyed data.

Exercises

1. Discuss five modern online crimes.
2. Discuss strategies that can be used to effectively eliminate online crimes?
3. If you were to write a framework to prevent cyber crimes what would be in it.
4. Is cryptography all we need to secure computer network and protect information?
5. Why is cryptography failing to protect digital systems and information? What do we need to do?

References

1. Kizza, Joseph M. *Computer Network Security*. New York, NY: Springer, 2005.
2. Newman, Daniel and Andrew Whitaker. "Penetration Testing and Network Defense: Performing Host Reconnaissance." http://www.ciscopress.com/articles/ article. asp?p=469623&seqNum=1&rl=1
3. Tittel, Ed. "Understanding Security Policies." http://www.informit.com/articles/ article. asp?p=25041&rl=1
4. Hayes, Bill. "Conducting a Security Audit: An Introductory Overview." http://www. securityfocus. com/infocus/1697

Chapter 13
Computer Crime Investigations – Computer Forensics

Learning Objectives

After reading this chapter, the reader should be able to:

1. Understand the science of digital crime investigation.
2. Understand the fundamental steps in digital crime investigation.
3. Understand digital evidence.
4. Learn to handle digital evidence.
5. Acquire the techniques required in digital crime investigation.
6. Recognize the difficulties encountered during digital crime investigation.

13.1   Introduction

In both Chapters 9 and 12, we have discussed computer crimes in depth. In Chapter 12, we confined ourselves to looking at online crimes and what needs to be done not only to protect the enterprising network, but also to mitigate the rate of their growth. Following the discussion in the preface to this edition, this chapter provides a three-pronged approach to a number of techniques, solutions, and best practices to address the problem of security or lack of it in this information age. First, we need to teach morality and ethics to our young people. Second, we need to define, develop, and build the best security protocols possible both hardware-based and software-based. And third, we need to follow through with prosecution of those responsible for committing any form of computer crime. For this we need to develop a strong and enforceable legal framework to meet the growing challenge.

This chapter focuses on the third challenge. Computer crime investigation or computer forensics, as it is increasingly becoming to be known, is the application of forensic science investigative techniques to computer-based material used as evidence. The search technique helps to reconstruct a sequence of activities that happened. The investigation process will involve the extraction, documentation, examination, preservation, analysis, evaluation, and interpretation of computer-based material to provide relevant and valid information as evidence in civil, criminal, administrative, and other cases. In the hunt for digital evidence, we will look at different

J.M. Kizza, *Ethical and Social Issues in the Information Age*, Texts in Computer Science,   263
DOI 10.1007/978-1-84996-038-0_13, © Springer-Verlag London Limited 2010

parts of the computer where digital evidence can be hidden and also at how to extract it from such areas. Our search for digital evidence will also go beyond a stand-alone computer to encompass an entire network and all points in the network where evidence can either be hidden or extracted from. In the search, the computer plays several roles: first, as a tool in the crime, where it is merely a role player, for example, as a communication tool, if the crime is committed using a computer network; second, as a storage facility, where the bounty is stored on computer files; third, as a victim where the computer is now the target of the attack and it becomes the focus of the forensic investigation. In either one of these cases the computer is central to the investigations because nearly all forensic cases will involve extracting and investigating data that are retrieved from the disks of the computer, both fixed and movable, and all its parts.

13.2   Digital Evidence

Evidence is something tangible and needed to prove a fact. For example, if you need to establish the fact that Johnson Jones is a thief, you have to provide something tangible to that effect to establish the claim. If evidence provided is accepted then the claim becomes a fact. Evidence is what is presented in courts of law to judges and juries to establish whether the accused is guilty or not. Also evidence may be used in civil disputes and in human resource management. In these cases, evidence establishes a claim as valid or not. Tangible evidence to prove a claim or an assertion can be from one of following sources:

- From an eye witness who provides a testimony
- From physical evidence as traces of the sequence of activities leading to the claim or assertion
- Digital evidence as digital footprints of the digital sequence of activities leading to the claim or assertion

The digital footprints left after every digital activity form a cybertrail and this is our focus in this chapter.

13.2.1   Looking for Digital Evidence

The only sure thinking when dealing with digital evidence is that every electronic activity leaves a sequence of footprints. So knowing that this sequence is there makes the task of looking for digital evidence a lot easier. However, because of the volume of these footprints for every digital activity, looking for the specific evidence is difficult and is comparable to searching for bits of evidence data from a haystack. The evidence usually sought includes binary data fixed in any medium such as on CDs, memory, and floppies, residues of things used in the committing of a crime and physical materials such as folders, letters, and scraps of papers.

At the start of the investigation, the examiner must decide on things to work with like written and technical policies, permissions, billing statements, and system application and device logs. Also decide early on what to monitor, if this is needed. This may include employer and employee computing activities, Internet e-mail, and chat rooms.

Serious work and attention must be given to appreciate the environment of the case, the nature of the case, specifics of the case, types of evidence to look for, types of operating systems in use at the time of the incident, known disk formats at the time of the incident, and location of evidence both physical and electronic.

Once this information is collected, the investigation may start creating the profile of the culprit. At this point you need to decide whether to let the suspect systems identified above run for a normal day, run periodically, or be pulled altogether if such actions will help the evidence gathering stage. Pulling the plug means that you will have to make copies of the computer content and work with the copies while keeping the original intact. Make sure that the system is disconnected and that all that may be affected by the disconnection of such volatile data is preserved before the disconnection.

13.2.2 Digital Evidence: Previewing and Acquisition

Dealing with digital evidence requires a lot of care because it is very volatile. The two processes previewing and acquiring of data may disturb the data evidence to a point of changing its status, thus creating doubt to its credibility. To make sure that this does not happen, a strict sequence of steps must be followed in handling the evidence.

13.2.2.1 Handling Evidence

Since the integrity of the evidence builds the validity of such evidence which consequently wins or loses a case under investigation, it is very important and instructive that extreme care must be taken when handling digital evidence. The cornerstone of this care is the establishment of a chain-of-custody. The *chain-of-custody* is the ability to maintain, with documentation, a chronological history of the activities that involve the evidence in order to guarantee the identity and integrity of the evidence. The documented chronology names all individuals collecting and handling the evidence, the time and place the evidence was handled and subsequently what was done on the evidence. The chain-of-custody gives us a logical map of the journey of evidence from the extraction to the court room. This sequence of events is traceable if one answers the following questions:

- Who extracted the evidence, how, and when?
- Who packaged it and when?

- Who stored it, how, when, and where?
- Who transported it, where and when?

This information may be filled in a form called the *chain-of-evidence* form.

13.2.2.2   Previewing Image Files

Before a target evidence image is copied, the process we are going to discuss, it is always better to take a preview. The preview allows the investigator to view the evidence media in order to determine if a full investigation is warranted. If so then the acquisition followed by the analysis is planned. Previewing has advantages because the investigator does not have to wait for hours of acquisition before doing a quick preliminary examination of the evidence. As an added advantage, while previewing, the investigator can, given the capabilities of some forensics tools, carry out keyword searches and even create bookmarks. These can then be saved in a case file for later use.

13.2.2.3   Evidence Acquisition

The process of evidence extraction can be easy or complicated depending on the nature of the incident and the type of computer or network upon which the incident took place. The million dollar question in evidence extraction is: What do I extract and what do I leave behind? The rule of thumb in evidence extraction is extract and collect as much as you can so that the return trip is never needed. What are the candidates for evidence extraction? There are many including hardware such as computers, printers, scanners, and network connectors such as modems, routers, and hubs. Software items include systems programs and logs, application software, and special user software. Documentation such as scrap paper and anything printed within the vicinity are also candidates and so are materials such as backup tapes and disks, CDs, cassettes, floppy and hard disks, and all types of logs.

Before the acquisition process begins, the discipline of acquisition must be followed to the letter beginning with the naming convention. In the naming convention, the source disk is the suspect hard disk from which evidence will be extracted. It is the disk that needs to be analyzed or copied. The destination disk is the target disk for the imaging operation. It is the disk that will receive the image of the evidence disk. Finally, the forensic computer is the investigator's computer that contains the forensics tools.

Evidence acquisition can be done in two ways. One is to acquire evidence from a computer that is not connected live on a network. Evidence can also be acquired from a computer that is live on the network. Acquisition of evidence from a stand-alone computer is easier than from a live computer. On stand-alone computers it is good to "freeze" the computer, meaning leaving it unplugged. One advantage of pulling the plug is to freeze the evidence and prevent it from being contaminated with either new use or modifications or alterations. Also freezing the system prevents errors committed after the reported incident and before a full investigation is completed. However, freezing the system may result in several problems including the destruction of any evidence of any ongoing processes.

Live systems present challenges to the investigator, the biggest of which is the dynamic nature of evidence. Evidence may change as time passes. For example, the intruder may anticipate that he or she is being tracked and he or she may alter the evidence well ahead of the investigator, thus compromising the validity of the evidence.

Other things to look out for before the acquisition are: always let the size of the disk, the duration you have to keep the disk, and the time you have for data acquisition determine which extraction method to use. Imaged copies of large original source disks may need to be compressed. There are two types of compression of computer forensics evidence: *lossless* compression which does not discard data when it compresses a file and *lossy* compression which loses data but keeps the quality of the data upon recovery. Use only acceptable lossless compression tools such as WinZip, PKZip, EnCase, and SafeBack. As data are compressed, a consistency code like MD5, SHA-1 hash, or cyclic redundancy check (CRC) must be done before and after compression of data is done for security and also after storage and transportation.

Make sure that you are as thorough as possible. This may involve possible recording of every activity done with or on every item of the evidence extracted. Where possible, video tape or take pictures of the whole process including individual items. This creates an additional copy of the evidence. Assign a unique identification number for every evidence item and write a brief description of what you think it is and where it was recovered from, carefully indicating the date and time it was extracted and by whom.

Sometimes, it may be necessary to seize evidence items. In this case, care must be taken to make sure that evidence is not destroyed. Also it may require the investigator, for some reasons, to dismantle the evidence object perhaps for security or easy moving. In this case it is instructive that the object is reconstructed at the destination site in a similar manner.

Be prepared also to arrive at the evidence scene and find all or some of the evidence encrypted. To deal with this problem, start by finding what encrypted algorithm was used. If it is known and by luck it is weak, software tools can be found to break such encryptions. However, if the encryption algorithm is of a strong class, look for known encryption products to help you with this problem, for example, if the encrypted evidence is an e-mail use PGP or SMIME.

13.3 Preserving Evidence

One of the cornerstones of crime investigation is the preservation of evidence. Given that digital evidence is very fluid, in that it can disappear or change so fast, extra care must be taken in preserving digital evidence. The techniques to preserve evidence depend on what is planned to be done on the evidence. The techniques used if evidence is to be moved are different from those used if evidence is to be left in one place. In either case, however, avoid excessive force in handling, folding, and also avoid crumpling containers of evidence because this may cause deterioration of the evidence. Make sure that there is no any evidence examination that would cause any damage, defacement, or modification unless it is part of the authorized analysis.

One way of preserving evidence is to strictly follow the following procedures:

- Secure the evidence scene from all parties that have no relevancy to it. This is to avoid contamination usually from deposit of hairs, fibers or trace material from clothing, footwear, or fingerprints.
- Secure catalog and package evidence in strong antistatic, well-padded, and labeled evidence bags.
- Image all suspected media as evidence to create a backup. Try to make several copies of each evidence item.
- Make a checksums of the original evidence disk before and after each copy. After imaging, the two checksums must agree.
- Institute a good security access control system to make sure that those handling the evidence are the only ones authorized to handle the evidence.
- Secure the evidence by encryption, where and if possible. Encryption ensures the confidentiality of the evidence.

13.4   Analysis of Digital Evidence

Of all the tasks in digital forensics investigation, perhaps evidence analysis is the most difficult and demanding. Data extraction does sound demanding but the degree of difficulty in extracting data really depends on the technology used to store them and the type of the medium in which they are stored. However, most forensics tools extract evidence easily because the technology used to store the evidence is well-known. Beside this phase being the most difficult and most opinionated, it is also the most important and most time-consuming. It is painstakingly slow and should be thorough. The process of analyzing evidence is done to support or reject a fact based on identified patterns of activities, file signature anomalies, unusual behaviors, file transfers, and several other trends in the evidence. According to Kruse and Heiser [1] the following tasks must each be thoroughly done:

- Examine shortcuts, Internet, Recycle Bins, and the Registry.
- Review the latest release of the system software with an eye on new methods of data hiding.
- Check every data tape, floppy disk, CD-ROM, DVD, and Flash Memory found during evidence extraction.
- Look in books, manuals, under keyboards, on the monitor, and everywhere where people usually hide passwords and other pertinent information.

- Double-check the analysis.
- Reexamine every file and folder, logfiles, and print spool.
- Recover any encrypted or archived file.

13.4.1 Analyzing Data Files

File analysis involves focusing on the structure and nature of files in order to understand the data in the file. Knowing certain attributes of files can tell us a lot about the data contained therein. We, therefore, need to focus on file directory structures, patterns, metadata, content, application, user configuration, and operating system types used to create the file.

13.4.1.1 File Directory Structure

Files are stored based on the type of operating system used. If you know the way files in a particular operating system are stored and there are deviations from this norm, this is enough to create suspicion which may result into a fruitful lead. Check all folders in each directory.

13.4.1.2 File Patterns

Investigation is more fruitful and easier if it follows a lead in a form of a pattern. Patterns can reveal a lot about the intentions of the suspect. Try to find a pattern in the files. The pattern could be in the way files are named, dating of files, arrangement of files, and so on.

13.4.1.3 Metadata

Metadata is higher information about data, giving us information about data embedded within files. For example, a title in your text is metadata of the data in the text. Its use helps in enriching the search process.

13.4.1.4 Content

Perhaps this is the most obvious start point in the investigation. Focus on the content of the file that best point to the case in point. Look for those files that have a content closest to what you are looking for. Check for file names that best reflect the content you want. File content types can tell us more about the suspect.

13.4.1.5 Application

The application of a file can give us information of the file use. File use helps to relate to the duties performed on this particular computer. For example, a file of unusual application is found on a machine; its use can raise suspicion that may lead to uncover new evidence or a new lead.

13.4.1.6 User Configuration

System users normally customize their systems to suit their day-to-day use of the system. For an investigator this is a trove of information that must not be overlooked. Based on information from the user configuration file, further investigative steps may be necessary.

13.4.2 Analysis Based on Operating Systems

Each operating system has its own way of creating and storing files. This kind of information is useful in the investigation. Knowing the type of files created by different operating systems, usually through file extensions, makes it easy to know of an existence of other operating systems on a computer. For example, if you are on a system running Windows and you come across a file with a strange extension that is not common to Windows-based systems, then you can very easily suspect the existence of another operating system on the computer in question.

Because operating systems play an important role in the overall function of computer system, most forensic analysis tools are developed to fit and work with particular platforms. Because of this, many forensic investigators have competency and prefer to work on specific platforms than on others. There are basically three classes of platform-based forensics tools: those based on Microsoft platform, those based on Unix-like platforms, and those based on Macintosh platform. Let us briefly look at forensic analysis based on these platforms.

13.4.2.1 Microsoft-Based File Systems

Because of the current extensive use of Windows-based system, most computer forensic tools so far are developed for Microsoft file systems, we will start with that. Microsoft-based file systems include the following file systems: the DOS-based FAT8 and FAT16, the more modern Windows-based FAT 32 and VFAT, and the modern NTFS. Analyzing evidence with tools based on these file system, the investigator must, according to Nelson et al. [2], do the following:

- Run an antivirus program scan for all files on the forensic workstation before connecting for a disk-to-disk bit-stream imaging.

- Run an antivirus scan again after connecting the copied disk-to-disk bit-stream image disk to all drives including the copied drive unless the copied volumes were imaged by EnCase.
- Examine fully the copied suspect disk noting all boot files in the root.
- Recover all deleted files, saving them to a specified secure location.
- Acquire evidence from FAT, VFAT, or NTFS.
- Process and analyze all recovered evidence.

13.4.2.2 UNIX and LINUX File Systems

Although forensic tools for Linux are still few, the recent surge in Linux use has led to the development of new tools including some freeware such as TCT, CTCUTILs, and TASK. These tools and most GUI tools can also analyze Unix. These include EnCase, FTK, and iLook. Because most Unix and Linux systems are used as servers, investigators, according to Nelson et al., must handle them as live systems. This saves the state of all running processes including those running in the background. These activities include [2]:

- Console messages
- Running processes
- Network connections
- System memories
- Swap space

13.4.2.3 Macintosh File System

Apple and Macintosh operating system have gone through a revolution. As a result, forensics tools that run on Mac platform fall into two categories: those systems running Mac OS 9X or later versions use the same forensic tools used on Unix, Linux, and Windows platform and those older ones before Mac OS 9X use tools like Expert Witness, EnCase, and iLook.

13.4.3 Analysis Based on Digital Media

Perhaps one of the trickiest forms of forensics analysis is one involving digital storage media. The analysis you do here, in either finding hidden evidence or not, may make or break a case. The first thing to look for when working with storage media is hidden data. Data can be hidden in a number of places so it is the duty of the investigator to find those places. There are many ways data can be hidden in a file system including in deleted files, in hidden files, in slack spaces both file and RAM, in spaces on the storage media designated as bad sectors, and by using steganographic utilities.

13.4.3.1   Deleted Files

Deleted files can be recovered manually using hex editor. When a file on a Windows platform is deleted, the first character of the directory entry is changed to a sigma (σ) character – hex value of E5. The operating system takes this sigma to indicate that the entry should not be displayed because the file has been deleted. The entry in the file allocation table (FAT) is also changed to zero, indicating unused sectors and, therefore, available to the operating system for allocation.

However, Windows platforms do not remove data in clusters of files declared as deleted. They merely mark them as available for reallocation. It is, therefore, quite possible to recover a file that has been deleted provided the clusters of the file have not been overwritten. DOS programs such as UNERASE and UNDELETE try to recover such files. But Norton Disk Editor is more effective.

13.4.3.2   Hidden Files

Data hiding is one of the most challenging aspects of forensic analysis. With special software, it is possible to mark a partition "hidden" such that the operating system will no longer access it. Other hidden areas can be created by setting partition tables to start at head 0, sector 1 of a cylinder, and the first sector of the partition proper – the boot record, to start at head 1, sector 1 of the cylinder. The consequence of this is that there will invariably be a number of unused sectors at the beginning of each partition, between the partition table sector and the boot record sector [3].

Operating systems also hide files and filenames from users, especially system files, because we want the users not to be able to access those files. Every operating system has a way of hiding and displaying these hidden files. For example, Linux has a very simple way of "hiding" a file. Creating a file with an added period to the front of the filename which defines to Linux that the filename is "hidden" makes it hidden. To display Linux hidden files add the **-a** flag (display all filenames) to the **ls** (list) command like "ls-a." This displays all of files in the current directory whether hidden or not. Similarly UNIX and Windows do not display any files or directories that begin with the dot (.) character. Such files can be displayed by either the Show Hidden Files option or the -a switch of the ls command.

Because of these cases, it is, therefore, always prudent to assume that the suspect system has hidden files and data. Hidden data are always a clue for investigators to dig deeper. There are a number of ways to hide data including encryption, compression, codes, steganography, and using invisible names, obscure names, and misleading names.

13.4.3.3   Slack Space

This is an allocated but unused space in a disk cluster. Both DOS and Windows file systems use fixed-size clusters. During space allocation, even if the actual data being stored requires less storage than the cluster size, an entire cluster is reserved for the file.

Sometimes this leaves large swats of allocated but unused space called *slack space*. When a file is copied, its slack space is not copied. It is not possible to eliminate all slack space without changing the partition size of the hard disk or without deleting or compressing many small files into one larger one. Short of eliminating these wasted spaces, it is good to have software tools to examine this slack space, find out how big it is, and what is hidden in it. If this is not done, there is a risk of slack space containing remnants of hostile code or hidden confidential files.

13.4.3.4 Bad Blocks

A bad track is an area of the hard disk that is not reliable for data storage. It is possible to map a number of disk tracks as "bad tracks." These tracks are then put into a bad track table that lists any areas of the hard disk that should not be used. These "bad tracks" listed on the table are then aliased to good tracks. This makes the operating system avoid the areas of the disk that cannot be read or written. An area that has been marked as "bad" by the controller may well be good and could store hidden data. Or a good sector could be used to store incriminating data and then be marked as bad. A lot of data can be hidden this way in the bad sectors by the suspect. Before formatting a disk always explore all the bad blocks because it may contain data hidden in "bad" sectors before you get to it.

13.4.3.5 Steganography Utilities

Steganography is the art of hiding information in ways that prevent its detection. Steganography, an ancient craft, has seen a rebirth with the onset of computer technology with computer-based steganographic techniques that embed information in the form of text, binary files, or images by putting a message within a larger one in such a way that others cannot detect the presence or contents of the hidden message. Steganography avoids drawing suspicion to the transmission of a hidden message. Forensic analysts pay special attention to this kind of hidden data. Steganalysis uses utilities that discover and render useless such covert messages.

13.4.3.6 Compressed and Coded Files

Sometimes data may be hidden through compression and coding. There are two techniques of coding and compressing data. *Coding* is a technique where characters of the data are systematically substituted by other characters. This technique can be used by system users to hide vital or malicious data. *Data compression* on the other hand is a way of reducing the size of data object like a file. This technique is also increasingly being used by suspects to hide data. Since vital evidence can be and is increasingly being hidden this way, forensic investigators must find a way to decipher coded or compressed evidence by either uncoding coded data or uncompressing compressed data. There are forensics tools on the market to do this.

13.4.3.7 Encrypted Files

Another way of indirectly hiding data is to encrypt it; a process which changes the original data to a point where it is unreadable unless there is a tool to reverse the process by decrypting it. Encryption is always used by unscrupulous people to hide information from others. For investigators to go round this problem, tools must be found to decrypt encrypted data. The tools may be simple mathematical tools which one can easily get from the Internet if you are lucky or very hard to find tools for hard encryptions.

13.4.3.8 Password-Protected Files

Many times data in files are protected by making a file or files unreachable unless one is in possession of a password. The only way around this problem for forensic investigators is to find password crackers. There are many of these on the Internet. However, it may be difficult to find the right tools.

13.5 Relevance and Validity of Digital Evidence

Once the existence of the digital evidence has been established through the existence of a cybertrail, we need to ask ourselves the question of relevancy of the evidence just established. The relevancy of the digital evidence depends on the requesting agency, nature of the request, and the type of the case in question. The question of validity of data is tied up with the relevance of data. It is also based on the process of authentication of that data.

13.6 Writing Investigative Reports

The last phase of a forensics criminal investigation process is report writing. The report is a summary of all findings of the investigation and it comes from all the documentation that has been made throughout the investigation. Remember, we said that based on the chain-of-custody all details of activities of everything done had to be recorded. It is this information that is reworked into a final report. According to Volonino et al. [4] the final report should include the following documents:

- All notes taken during meetings and contacts that led to the investigation
- All forms used in the investigation including the chain-of-custody forms
- Copies of search warrants and legal authority notes granting permission to conduct searches
- Notes, video recordings, and pictures taken at the incident scene describing the scene

- Notes and any documentation made to describe the computer components including description of peripherals and all devices
- Documentation and notes describing the networking of suspect's devices
- Notes made on what was discovered including passwords, pass phrases, encryption, and any data hiding
- Any changes to the suspect's scene configuration authorized or not
- Names of everyone at the suspect's scene
- Procedures used to deal with the scene including acquisition, extraction, and analysis of evidence
- Any observed or suspected irregularities including those outside the scope of the techniques in use

If you are using standard forensics tools like FTK and EnCase, most of these details would be bookmarked as the analysis process continues.

The main and critical part of the report is not to list and describe the suspect's scene but to analyze and summarize your findings which include your professional opinion. This means that the body of the report tends to be built up of documentations, findings, summaries, and conclusions drawn from the findings. It is possible for your conclusions to be based more on your professional experience than on the evidence present because you are an expert witness. This must be made clear in the report. Make sure that the report is easy to read, does not contain unnecessary jargons, and is written in a plain language that will be understood by a majority of people that will read it.

Finally, make the conclusion to the report short and precise. Because computer forensics is a technical discipline, and it is sometimes inevitable to use technical terms that may not be in common use by the general public, it may also be advisable to include a glossary of terms in your report as part of the supporting materials.

Exercises

1. Discuss the basic steps in digital crime investigation.
2. List and discuss the standard software tools for digital crime investigation.
3. Give reasons why the chain of custody is so important in a digital crime investigation.
4. Differentiate between an online and digital crime?
5. What is digital evidence? What are the characteristics of digital evidence?
6. Discuss why it is so important to handle digital evidence with care
7. Why is cryptography a problem in digital crime investigation? What do you need to do to solve this problem?
8. Who is an expert witness? What must an expert witness have that will make what he/she says believable?
9. What role does ethics play during a digital crime investigation?
10. Discuss ways to prevent digital crimes.
11. Discuss the future of digital crimes.
12. Discuss the future of digital crime investigation.
13. What makes digital crime investigation so expensive?
14. Discuss an incident you have heard or witnessed that you would consider to have digital evidence.
15. List and discuss cases both criminal and civil in which digital evidence might be involved.

References

1. Kruse II, Warren and Jay G. Heiser. *Computer Forensics: Incident Response Essentials.* Boston, MA: Addison-Wesley, 2002.
2. Nelson, Bill, Amelia Phillips, Frank Enfinger, and Chis Steuart. *Guide to Computer Forensics and Investigations* (2nd ed.). Boston, MA: Course Technology, 2006.
3. Sammes, Tony and Brian Jenkinson. *Forensic Computing: A Practitioner's Guide.* London: Springer, 2000.
4. Volonino, Linda, Reynaldo Anzaldua, and Jana Godwin. *Computer Forensics: Principles and Practices.* Upper Saddle River, NJ: Prentice Hall, 2007, p. 13.

Chapter 14
Biometrics

Learning Objectives

After reading this chapter, the reader should be able to:

1. Understand biometric science.
2. Learn to use biometric data in access control.
3. Understand how biometric data are used to fight crimes.
4. Learn where and when biometric data can be used.
5. Acquire the techniques required in biometric data acquisition.
6. Recognize the difficulties encountered in handling some biometric data in access control.

14.1   Introduction and Definitions

In the previous chapters, we have discussed the various types of computer crimes and how they are perpetuated. In Chapters 12 and 13, we have discussed the latest technologies to fight these crimes. In this chapter, we look at one of the latest and fastest growing technologies to fight computer crimes. *Biometric* technology, based on human attributes, is perhaps one of the safest, most reliable, and most secure forms of access control so far in use. Access control technologies are among the top known and widely used security solutions and best practices. These technologies, as we have seen in Section 12.4.1, are based on three axioms:

- Something you know – which includes all passwords and pass phrases.
- Something you have – which includes all physical security passes such as pass cards and all sorts of access cards.
- Something you are – which includes all human attributes. This is the group in which biometrics falls.

A biometric itself is a physical or psychological trait that can be measured, recorded, and quantified. Such traits are abundant in the human body, and in access control, they are used to do a biometric enrollment and stored in a database. The stored traits can then be used to compare with future traits collected from the same individual to confirm with a degree of certainty that this person is the same person, whose traits are in the database.

J.M. Kizza, *Ethical and Social Issues in the Information Age*, Texts in Computer Science,   277
DOI 10.1007/978-1-84996-038-0_14, © Springer-Verlag London Limited 2010

Biometric technologies confirm a person's identity by scanning physical characteristics such as a fingerprint, voice, eye movement, facial recognition, and others. A typical biometric system operates in two distinct stages: the enrollment stage and the authentication stage. During enrollment, the physical traits of the subject are extracted, analyzed, and put in a digital form called a *template* and stored in a database. To authenticate a user, the biometric data are once again acquired and processed, and a new template is created. The new template is matched against the template(s) stored in the database to identify a previously enrolled individual or to validate a claimed identity. Unlike other access control technologies, biometrics cannot be forgotten or stolen. Passwords are easily forgotten, keys and cards can easily be lost or forcibly taken away from us.

14.1.1   Definitions

Before we proceed, let us give the basic definitions of the terms we are going to use throughout the chapter:

- *Enrollment* is the recording of biometric traits resulting in the creation of a template.
- A *template* is a digital representation of a physical trait. It is a long string of alphanumeric characters that describe, based on a biometric algorithm, characteristics or features of a physical trait. It is generated from the preprocessed data (features).
- A *biometric algorithm* is a mathematical formula for turning the physical traits into a digital representation to form a template. It is also used in the matching of an enrolled template with a new template just created for verification or identification.
- The first template created at enrollment is referred to as a *stored template,* and templates created for recognition and identification processes are called *live templates*.
- When a stored and a live template are compared, the system calculates how closely they match. If the match is close enough, the person is *verified or identified*.
- During verification and identification processes, two templates are compared. If two templates of two different individuals were to match, this is classified as *false acceptance*.
- The probability of this happening is referred to as *false acceptance rate* (FAR).
- If the live template fails to match an enrolled template for an individual, this is referred to as a *false rejection*. The probability of this happening is the *false rejection rate* (FRR).
- Finally if an enrolled person fails to enroll to a biometric system, this is called *failure to enroll* (FTE).

Although there is a new interest in biometrics especially after September 11, 2001, biometrics use is as old as humanity itself. People have been identifying others like friends and adversaries for years using looks – facial, eyes and eye color, and fingerprints from medieval times. However, during the past several years and with heightened security, biometric technology has become increasingly popular. The technology, which can be used to permit access to a network or a building, has become an increasingly reliable, convenient, and cost-effective means of security.

Biometric technologies of the past, however, were very difficult, extremely intrusive, and not cost-effective. However, this has changed dramatically as advances in current technologies have made these technologies far less intrusive, highly invasive, and certainly cost-effective. This has made biometric access control much more practical than it has ever been in the past. Now a new generation of low-cost yet accurate fingerprint readers is available for most mobile applications so that screening stations can be put up in a few minutes. Although biometrics is one of those security control techniques that have been in use the longest, it does not have standards as yet. There is an array of services on the market for biometric devices to fit every form of security access control. Technological advances have resulted in smaller, high-quality, more accurate, and more reliable devices. Improvements in biometrics are essential because bad biometric security can lull system and network administrators into a false sense of safety. In addition, it can also lock out a legitimate user and admit an intruder. So, care must be taken when procuring biometric devices.

14.2 The Biometrics Authentication Process

Before a biometric technique can be used as an access control technique for the system, first an enrollment process is initiated for each user to have his or her biometric data scanned by a biometric reader, processed to extract critical features, and then those features stored in a database as the user's template. When a user requests access to a system resource, the user must be authenticated; the biometric readers verify customers' identities by again scanning their physical attributes, such as fingerprints, again. A match is sought by checking them against prints of the same attributes previously registered and stored in the database.

The key steps for this biometric authentication process are:

- Image capture – using a biometric reader or scanner
- Image recognition – based on a standard biometric algorithm
- Template creation – again using a standard biometric algorithm and extracted features
- Matching of the templates – both the live and the stored templates of the individual are compared for a match using a standard biometric algorithm

A standard biometric authentication used in the above phases usually comprises the following functional units:

- *Sensor device*: a reader or scanner to acquire the biometric raw data from the individual. The reader or scanner can capture images from a fingerprint, a face, an iris, or a sound from a microphone. Readers or scanners at this stage may do some limited preprocessing without introducing foreign information or creating redundancy.

- *Feature extraction*: to extract traits used in the creation of the template
- *Matcher*: to compare the live template with the stored reference template
- *Reference archive*: for storing the biometric reference templates

One of the advantages that have made biometrics increasingly popular is that while other methods of access control such as firewalls and encryption are crucial to network security and provide a secure way to exchange information, they are still expensive and difficult to design for a comprehensive security system. Other access control techniques such as passwords, while inexpensive to implement, are easy to forget and easy to guess by unauthorized people if they are simple, and too complex to be of any use if they are complex.

14.3   Biometric System Components

To function properly and perform those four functions above, all components of a biometric system must work in unison. These components are data acquisition, enrollment, signal processing, and decision policy.

14.3.1   Data Acquisition

The data acquisition component, the first of the biometric system components, captures the biometric traits presented to the system via a reader or a scanner. It then, as part of preprocessing, digitizes the raw data just captured. This process may be followed by data compression and parameterization, if needed. Finally, especially if data is to be moved over public communication channels, encryption of the data for added security is done.

14.3.2   Enrollments

If this is the first time a user's biometric traits are presented to the biometric system for any reason, the enrollment process must be done first. As already indicated, this produces the stored template which will be used in all future matching for future biometric authentication. During this stage, the user submits data for template/model creation. A number of issues must be dealt with at this stage including the quality of the scans, the settings of the reader or scanner to account for the types of devices used, the environment, the types of users to be enrolled, and sometimes a parentage threshold for the failure to enroll rate, as well as the need for training before completing the enrollment.

14.3.3   Signal Processing

This is the stage where raw data just acquired are worked on to extract relevant and needed features that form a template. This is done by processing the data to remove noise and extract only that information that carries the needed features. Several other functions including normalization, segmentation, and quality assessment may be performed on the data as well.

14.3.4   Decision Policy

This final component performs matching functions that help in decision making. A choice must be made whether the decision will lead to verification or identification. Also both FAR and FRR must be noted and compared because they influence the final decision. Finally, the crossover rate must also be taken and the equal error rate (EER) is taken noting its threshold. It is no good if it is high.

14.4   Types of Biometric Technologies

As we have pointed out, biometric technologies confirm a person's identity by scanning physical characteristics. These are technologies that vary depending on the traits used. There are a number of these traits including fingerprint, voice, eye movement, facial recognition, and others.

14.4.1   Finger Biometrics

Finger biometrics involves taking an individual's fingerprints. The authentication process using fingerprints is referred to as *fingerprint recognition*. During the process, a user places his or her finger on a scanner or fingerprint reader. The reader captures a number of images of the finger imprint, usually the center of the finger. The center usually is the area with the richest unique features known as the *minutiae*. Fingerprints contain many of these unique minutiae forming "ridges" and "valleys." These ridges and valleys form the basis for the loops, arches, and swirls that are characteristics of any fingerprint. From these minutiae, unique features are located and determined. There are two types of minutiae:

* Ridge endings – the location where the ridge actually ends
* Bifurcations – the location where a single ridge becomes two ridges

From these two types the following subtypes emerge:

* Bifurcation
* Bridge

- Double bifurcation
- Dot
- Opposed bifurcation
- Island (short-ridge)
- Hook (spur)
- Lake (enclosure)
- Ridge crossing
- Ridge ending
- Trifurcation
- Opposed bifurcation (ridge ending)

Figure 14.1 shows a fingerprint and Fig. 14.2(a–l) shows many of these biometrics features.

The next stage in fingerprint capture is template creation. The unique features of the minutiae going into the template are extracted and identified. Along with these unique features of the minutiae, the location, position, as well as the type and quality of each minutia are also taken into consideration in the template creation stage. Finally after the template has been created, it is then stored. Upon presentation of a second template, the live template from an individual, the stored template is retrieved and matched to the live one. This is referred to as *template matching*. During this process the system tries to either verify or identify an individual whose template was presented. There are two categories of fingerprint matching techniques: minutiae-based and correlation-based.

- In minutiae-based technique, the first minutiae points are found and then they are mapped relative to their placement on the finger. This approach, however, has problems in matching different sized (unregistered) minutiae patterns. Part of the problem is that the method does not take into account the global variations of people's pattern of ridges and furrows.
- Correlation-based technique tries to overcome some of these difficulties. However, correlation-based processing has its own problems including requiring a precise location of a registration point and it is also affected by image translation and rotation.

Fig. 14.1 Fingerprint basics

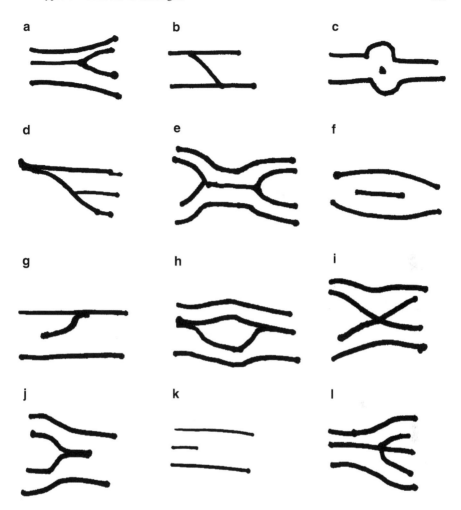

Fig. 14.2 (**a**) Bifurcation, (**b**) Bridge, (**c**) Dot, (**d**) Double bifurcation, (**e**) Opposed bifurcation, (**f**) Island (short bridge), (**g**) Hook (spur), (**h**) Lake (enclosure), (**i**) Ridge crossing, (**j**) Opposed bifurcation, (**k**) Ridge ending, (**l**) Trifurcation (New South Wales Police Service. http://www.policensw.com/info/fingerprints/finger08.html)

Modern, more reliable fingerprint processing techniques require sophisticated algorithms for reliable processing of the fingerprint image to eliminate noise, extract minutiae, be rotation and translation-tolerant, and be as fast as possible for comfortable use in applications with large number of users.

Fingerprint recognition technology is perhaps one of the oldest biometric technologies. Fingerprint readers have been around for probably hundreds of years. These readers fall into two categories: mice with embedded sensors and stand-alone units. Although fingerprint technology is improving with current technology, making it possible to make a positive identification in a few seconds, fingerprint identification is susceptible to precision problems. Many fingerprints can result in false positives due to oil and skin problems on the subject's finger. Also many of the latest fingerprint readers can be defeated by photos of fingerprints and 3D fingers from latent prints such as prints left on glass and other objects [1].

14.4.2   Hand Geometry

Hand geometry is an authentication technology that uses the geometric shape of the hand to identify a user. The technique works by measuring and then analyzing the shape and physical features of a user's hand, such as finger length and width and palm width. Like fingerprints, this technique also uses a reader. To initiate the device, all users' hands are read and measured and the statistics are stored in a database for future recognition. To activate the system the user places the palm of his or her hand on the surface of the reader. Readers usually have features that guide the user's hand on the surface. Once on the surface, the hand, guided by the guiding features, is properly aligned for the reader to read off the hand's attributes. The reader is hooked to a computer, usually a server, with an application that provides a live visual feedback of the top view and the side view of the hand. Hand features are extracted and taken as the defining feature vector of the user's hand, and then used to create a template. This template is then compared with the stored template created from the user's hand at enrollment.

As human hands are not unique, individual hand features are not descriptive enough for proper identification; hence, hand biometrics technology is not a very good technique for authentication without combining it with other techniques.

14.4.3   Face Biometrics

Like other human biometrics, facial biometrics are feature extraction, creating a template and then later creating another template of the subject whenever authentication of the subject is desired and then comparing the two templates. Facial biometric authentication utilizes the distinctive features of the subject's face. These features are sometimes microfeatures that include:

• Mouth
• Nose
• Eye
• Cheekbones
• Chin
• Lips
• Forehead
• Ears

Additional features include upper outlines of the eye sockets, the areas surrounding the cheekbones, the sides of the mouth, and the location of the nose and eyes, as well as the distance between the eyes, the length of the nose, and the angle of the jaw. Typical sources of facial images include video recording and fixed cameras like digital camera. Once the image has been captured, the biometric algorithm is then used to create a template. The algorithm uses specific features, called *eigenface*, and special technologies including local feature analysis, neural networks, and automatic face processing.

An *eigenface* is a characteristic feature of a face which is literally an "average face" derived from statistical analysis of many pictures of the face [2]. The algorithm then takes these eigenface features and produces a unique file called a template. To authenticate an individual, the algorithm uses a newly created template from a recently captured facial image and compares that template with the stored template created from the image of the subject at enrollment. Face physical traits can be captured by either live scans or through use of photograph or videos. Like in hand biometrics, facial biometrics suffers from limitations including the fact that photo and video recording destroy the concept of depth. Because of this, some algorithms do not use them without an additional high-quality scanner or an additional biometrics.

14.4.4   Voice Biometrics

Very often we recognize friends and colleagues from their voices without having a visual of them first. This is the case because each individual has individual voice components called *phonemes*. Each phoneme has three unique parts: a pitch, a cadence, and an inflection. These then give each one of us a unique voice sound. This uniqueness in voice holds for different people although there are some seemingly close likenesses of voices from people who share cultural and regional identities. This closeness of sound is a result of form of accents.

During speech, referred to as phonating, an individual's vocal folds produce a complex sound spectrum made up of a range of frequencies and overtones. As the spectrum travels through the various-sized areas in the vocal track, some of the frequencies resonate more than others. Larger spaces resonate at lower frequencies while smaller ones at much higher frequencies. The throat and the mouth, the two largest spaces in the vocal track produce the two lowest resonant frequencies called *formants*. These are resonant frequencies of the vocal tract produced when vowels are pronounced.

Linguists classify speech by looking at the characteristic formants in the spectrogram or frequency response of the speech. During speech, the human vocal track frequently opens and closes which causes changes in energy in all frequencies. In adult female the rate of repeated opening and closing can be high giving the sensation of a pitch in their speech.

Voice is captured by devices like a microphone or telephone. The quality of the captured voice depends on the recording device and the environment under which the recording is being done. After voice is captured, the voice algorithm being used by the voice biometrics then reduces each spoken word to segments composed of several dominant frequencies, the *formants*. The tones in each segment are then put into a digital format. The tones are then put into a template and stored. These tones in the template are collectively used to identify the subject's unique voiceprint. Upon subsequent capture of a subject's voice, another template is created and compared with the stored template created at enrollment for a match.

Voice recognition has been around for years; however, its real-life application has been slow because of the difficulties in deployment. Voice recognition is not a safe authentication technique because it can be fooled by recording types.

14.4.5   Handwriting Analysis

Another biometric that has been used for sometime is the handwriting analysis. Handwriting analysis can tell a lot about the personality of the subject. *Graphology* or handwriting analysis is a science of interpreting a person's character from his/ her personal handwriting. It is a scientific system of identifying and assessing the character and personality of a subject through a study of the subject's handwriting. The techniques use well-defined and standardized methods to identify strokes and slants and relate them to specific personality traits. Further evaluation of and analysis of the strokes and slants along with psychology and knowledge of inner human behavior can lead to secrets about the hidden behavior of the subject. It can also lead to discovery of inner personal conflicts in the life of the subject.

14.4.6   Iris Biometrics

Perhaps the most outstanding and the most secure form of biometrics are *iris* and *retina*. An *iris* is that area of the eye where the pigmented or colored circle rings the dark pupil of the eye. The iris contains lots of interesting features including ligaments, furrows, ridges, crypts, rings, corona, freckles, and a zigzag collarette. According to Panko, iris authentication is the gold standard of all biometric authentications [1]. Iris technology uses either regular, small, high-quality cameras or infrared light into the eye of the user to scan and capture the features that exist in the colored tissue surrounding the pupil of the subject's eye. This process takes only 1–2 s and provides the details of the iris that are mapped. Once the image is captured, the iris' elastic connective tissue, the trabecular meshwork, is analyzed, processed into an optical "fingerprint," and translated into a digital form and is stored as a template.

Whenever a user wants access to a secure system, he or she looks in an iris reader. Modern iris readers can read a user's eye up to 2 ft away. Verification time is short and it is getting shorter. Like in other eye scans, precautions must be taken to prevent a wrong person's eyes from fooling the system. This is done by varying the light shone into the eye and then pupil dilations are recorded.

The use of iris scans for authentication is becoming popular, although it is a young technology. Its potential application areas include law enforcement agencies, border patrol and airports, and the financial sector, especially in banking.

14.4.7   Retina

Retina is a thin layer of cells at the back of the eyeball. It is the part of the eye responsible for converting light into nervous signals. Because of this, it contains photoreceptor cells which receive the light that it passes to the neural cell which produces neural signals. The signals are later processed by other neurons in the subsequent processes. The retina is also characterized by an abundance of unique patterns of the blood vessels. Every eye has its own totally unique pattern of blood vessels with distinctive traits including the eyes of identical twins. Because of this fact, retina biometrics is considered to be the best. The technology works by directing a low-intensity infrared light to capture the unique retina characteristics consisting of patterns of blood vessels on the thin nerve on the back of the eyeball that processes light entering through the pupil. These captured characteristics are then digitized and put into a template and stored, if it is the first time to capture the subject's retina. The retina biometric technology is one of the smallest of all the biometric technologies and it is one of the most accurate and most reliable of the biometric technologies. However, the amount of effort and cooperation required of users has made it one of the least deployed of all the biometric technologies. Also the retina is small, internal, and difficult to measure makes capturing its image more difficult than most biometric technologies. So despite "retina" accuracy, it is still often thought to be inconvenient and intrusive.

14.5   The Future of Biometrics

The current biometric technologies are all characterized by three or four processes: the image capture, feature extraction, template creation, and the comparison. These processes are used in the biometrics quest for authentication. The biometrics authentication system itself consists of two phases: enrollment and matching. In the enrollment phase, a subject interacts with the biometrics system where one or more of the subject's selected physical characteristics are captured by the system. The characteristic features captured are then processed by a numerical algorithm, and entered into a database. To create an entry into the database, the algorithm creates a template, a digital representation of the obtained biometric.

On subsequent subject encounter with the system, the process of acquiring the biometrics and digitizing it is again performed. And a template is again created.

But instead of storing the new template of the subject, it is compared with the subject's stored template for authentication. The comparison process employs a Hamming distance measure, a mathematical technique which measures how similar two-bit strings are.

The measure of performance of a biometric is based on three concepts which we referred to earlier as FAR, *false nonmatch or reject rate* (FRR), and *failure to enroll rate* (FTE or FER). Biometric performance is commonly the rate at which both accept and reject errors are equal. This rate is referred to as the EER. We want EER to be as low as possible for a good biometric algorithm. Advances in technology and the great security awareness that we are currently experiencing are driving the use of biometric technologies to new heights. With increasing miniaturization, price reduction, ease of use, less intrusiveness, and more invasiveness, the future of biometric technology seems brighter than ever before.

However good the biometrics are, they can still fall victim of identity theft for example, when one gets access and modifies or changes the stored template. Also privacy concerns on the personal information collected from the subjects which may diminish personal liberties. Finally as the popularity of the technologies increases, more private concerns are on the rise that these technologies may cause physical harm to users.

Biometrics Discussion Questions

Biometrics: A Grand Challenge

A Discussion

To prepare for the discussion, read the following paper before coming to class. Biometrics: A Grand Challenge found at: http://biometric.cse.msu. edu/biometricchallane.pdf

The paper discusses several problems facing the biometric technology including:

(1) How to accurately and efficiently represent and recognize biometric patterns?
(2) How to guarantee that the sensed measurements are not fraudulent?
(3) How to make sure that the application is indeed exclusively using pattern recognition for the expressed purpose?
(4) How to acquire repeatable and distinctive patterns from a broad population?

Unless all these questions are satisfactorily answered, the future of biometrics is not going to take off as many currently believe.

Divide the class into groups. Within your group, discuss and take notes to present to the full class on the question assigned to your group. The questions are assigned as follows:

Group 1. How to accurately and efficiently represent and recognize biometric patterns?

Group 2. How to guarantee that the sensed measurements are not fraudulent?

Group 3. How to make sure that the application is indeed exclusively using pattern recognition for the expressed purpose?

Group 4. How to acquire repeatable and distinctive patterns from a broad population?

Exercises

1. What is a biometric? List the different characteristics for a chosen biometric.
2. Discuss the basic steps in correcting biometric data.
3. List and discuss the standard techniques and tools used in biometric data gathering.
4. List the different types of biometric data.
5. Differentiate between online and digital biometric data?
6. Discuss why it is so important to handle some types of biometric data with care.
7. Grade and list the different biometrics listed above in ascending order of trust.
8. Why are some biometrics more trustworthy than others?
9. What role does ethics play during biometrics data collection and use in access control.
10. Discuss the following statement "Fingerprints as biometrics data are the most widely used, yet, they are the least trusted."
11. Discuss the future of biometrics in access control.
12. What role does biometrics play in fighting crime? Discuss how this is done.
13. Discuss the future of biometrics in crime investigation.
14. Discuss the following statement: "The most trusted biometrics are the most expensive to extract."
15. Discuss an incident you have heard or witnessed in which biometric data for either access control or as evidence.
16. List and discuss cases both criminal and civil in which biometric evidence might be involved.

References

1. Panko, Raymond. R. *Corporate Computer and Network Security*. Upper Saddle River, NJ: Prentice-Hall, 2004.
2. Wikipedia – http://www.wikipedia.org/

Appendix A
The Digital Millennium Copyright Act[1]

Sec. 1201. Circumvention of Copyright Protection Systems

(a) Violations Regarding Circumvention of Technological Measures.

(1)

(A) No person shall circumvent a technological measure that effectively controls access to a work protected under this title. The prohibition contained in the preceding sentence shall take effect at the end of the 2-year period beginning on the date of the enactment of this chapter.

(B) The prohibition contained in subparagraph (A) shall not apply to persons who are users of a copyrighted work which is in a particular class of works, if such persons are, or are likely to be in the succeeding 3-year period, adversely affected by virtue of such prohibition in their ability to make noninfringing uses of that particular class of works under this title, as determined under subparagraph (C).

(C) During the 2-year period described in subparagraph (A), and during each succeeding 3-year period, the Librarian of Congress, upon the recommendation of the Register of Copyrights, who shall consult with the Assistant Secretary for Communications and Information of the Department of Commerce and report and comment on his or her views in making such recommendation, shall make the determination in a rulemaking proceeding on the record for purposes of subparagraph (B) of whether persons who are users of a copyrighted work are, or are likely to be in the succeeding 3-year period, adversely affected by the prohibition under subparagraph (A) in their ability to make noninfringing uses under this title of a particular class of copyrighted works. In conducting such rulemaking, the Librarian shall examine—

(i) the availability for use of copyrighted works;

(ii) the availability for use of works for nonprofit archival, preservation, and educational purposes;

---

[1] http://eon.law.harvard.edu/openlaw/DVD/1201.html

(iii) the impact that the prohibition on the circumvention of technological measures applied to copyrighted works has on criticism, comment, news reporting, teaching, scholarship, or
research;

(iv) the effect of circumvention of technological measures on the market
for or value of copyrighted works; and

(v) such other factors as the Librarian considers appropriate.

(D) The Librarian shall publish any class of copyrighted works for which
the Librarian has determined, pursuant to the rulemaking conducted
under subparagraph (C), that noninfringing uses by persons who are
users of a copyrighted work are, or are likely to be, adversely affected,
and the prohibition contained in subparagraph (A) shall not apply to
such users with respect to such class of works for the ensuing 3-year
period.

(E) Neither the exception under subparagraph (B) from the applicability
of the prohibition contained in subparagraph (A), nor any determination made in a rulemaking conducted under subparagraph (C), may be
used as a defense in any action to enforce any provision of this title
other than this paragraph.

(2) No person shall manufacture, import, offer to the public, provide, or otherwise traffic in any technology, product, service, device, component, or part
thereof, that—

(A) is primarily designed or produced for the purpose of circumventing
a technological measure that effectively controls access to a work protected under this title;

(B) has only limited commercially significant purpose or use other than
to circumvent a technological measure that effectively controls access to
a work protected under this title; or

(C) is marketed by that person or another acting in concert with that person with that person's knowledge for use in circumventing a technological measure that effectively controls access to a work protected
under this title.

(3) As used in this subsection—

(A) to "circumvent a technological measure" means to descramble a
scrambled work, to decrypt an encrypted work, or otherwise to avoid,
bypass, remove, deactivate, or impair a technological measure, without
the authority of the copyright owner; and

(B) a technological measure "effectively controls access to a work" if the
measure, in the ordinary course of its operation, requires the application
of information, or a process or a treatment, with the authority of the
copyright owner, to gain access to the work.

(b) Additional Violations.

  (1) No person shall manufacture, import, offer to the public, provide, or otherwise traffic in any technology, product, service, device, component, or part thereof, that—

    (A) is primarily designed or produced for the purpose of circumventing protection afforded by a technological measure that effectively protects a right of a copyright owner under this title in a work or a portion thereof;

    (B) has only limited commercially significant purpose or use other than to circumvent protection afforded by a technological measure that effectively protects a right of a copyright owner under this title in a work or a portion thereof; or

    (C) is marketed by that person or another acting in concert with that person with that person's knowledge for use in circumventing protection afforded by a technological measure that effectively protects a right of a copyright owner under this title in a work or a portion thereof.

  (2) As used in this subsection—

    (A) to "circumvent protection afforded by a technological measure" means avoiding, bypassing, removing, deactivating, or otherwise impairing a technological measure; and

    (B) a technological measure "effectively protects a right of a copyright owner under this title" if the measure, in the ordinary course of its operation, prevents, restricts, or otherwise limits the exercise of a right of a copyright owner under this title.

(c) Other Rights, Etc., Not Affected.

  (1) Nothing in this section shall affect rights, remedies, limitations, or defenses to copyright infringement, including fair use, under this title.

  (2) Nothing in this section shall enlarge or diminish vicarious or contributory liability for copyright infringement in connection with any technology, product, service, device, component, or part thereof.

  (3) Nothing in this section shall require that the design of, or design and selection of parts and components for, a consumer electronics, telecommunications, or computing product provide for a response to any particular technological measure, so long as such part or component, or the product in which such part or component is integrated, does not otherwise fall within the prohibitions of subsection (a)(2) or (b)(1).

  (4) Nothing in this section shall enlarge or diminish any rights of free speech or the press for activities using consumer electronics, telecommunications, or computing products.

(d) Exemption for Nonprofit Libraries, Archives, and Educational Institutions.

(1) A nonprofit library, archives, or educational institution which gains access to a commercially exploited copyrighted work solely in order to make a good faith determination of whether to acquire a copy of that work for the sole purpose of engaging in conduct permitted under this title shall not be in violation of subsection (a)(1)(A). A copy of a work to which access has been gained under this paragraph—

(A) may not be retained longer than necessary to make such good faith determination; and

(B) may not be used for any other purpose.

(2) The exemption made available under paragraph (1) shall only apply with respect to a work when an identical copy of that work is not reasonably available in another form.

(3) A nonprofit library, archives, or educational institution that willfully for the purpose of commercial advantage or financial gain violates paragraph (1)—

(A) shall, for the first offense, be subject to the civil remedies under section 1203; and

(B) shall, for repeated or subsequent offenses, in addition to the civil remedies under section 1203, forfeit the exemption provided under paragraph (1).

(4) This subsection may not be used as a defense to a claim under subsection (a)(2) or (b), nor may this subsection permit a nonprofit library, archives, or educational institution to manufacture, import, offer to the public, provide, or otherwise traffic in any technology, product, service, component, or part thereof, which circumvents a technological measure.

(5) In order for a library or archives to qualify for the exemption under this subsection, the collections of that library or archives shall be—

(A) open to the public; or

(B) available not only to researchers affiliated with the library or archives or with the institution of which it is a part, but also to other persons doing research in a specialized field.

(e) Law Enforcement, Intelligence, and Other Government Activities.

This section does not prohibit any lawfully authorized investigative, protective, information security, or intelligence activity of an officer, agent, or employee of the United States, a State, or a political subdivision of a State, or a person acting pursuant to a contract with the United States, a State, or a political subdivision of a State. For purposes of this subsection, the term "information security" means activities carried out in order to identify and address the vulnerabilities of a government computer, computer system, or computer network.

(f) Reverse Engineering.

(1) Notwithstanding the provisions of subsection (a)(1)(A), a person who has lawfully obtained the right to use a copy of a computer program may circumvent a technological measure that effectively controls access to a particular portion of that program for the sole purpose of identifying and analyzing those elements of the program that are necessary to achieve interoperability of an independently created computer program with other programs, and that have not previously been readily available to the person engaging in the circumvention, to the extent any such acts of identification and analysis do not constitute infringement under this title.

(2) Notwithstanding the provisions of subsections (a)(2) and (b), a person may develop and employ technological means to circumvent a technological measure, or to circumvent protection afforded by a technological measure, in order to enable the identification and analysis under paragraph (1), or for the purpose of enabling interoperability of an independently created computer program with other programs, if such means are necessary to achieve such interoperability, to the extent that doing so does not constitute infringement under this title.

(3) The information acquired through the acts permitted under paragraph (1), and the means permitted under paragraph (2), may be made available to others if the person referred to in paragraph (1) or (2), as the case may be, provides such information or means solely for the purpose of enabling interoperability of an independently created computer program with other programs, and to the extent that doing so does not constitute infringement under this title or violate applicable law other than this section.

(4) For purposes of this subsection, the term "interoperability" means the ability of computer programs to exchange information, and of such programs mutually to use the information which has been exchanged.

(g) Encryption Research.

(1) Definitions. For purposes of this subsection—

(A) the term "encryption research" means activities necessary to identify and analyze flaws and vulnerabilities of encryption technologies applied to copyrighted works, if these activities are conducted to advance the state of knowledge in the field of encryption technology or to assist in the development of encryption products; and

(B) the term "encryption technology" means the scrambling and descrambling of information using mathematical formulas or algorithms.

(2) Permissible acts of encryption research. Notwithstanding the provisions of subsection (a)(1)(A), it is not a violation of that subsection for a person to circumvent a technological measure as applied to a copy, phonorecord,

performance, or display of a published work in the course of an act of good faith encryption research if—

(A) the person lawfully obtained the encrypted copy, phonorecord, performance, or display of the published work;
(B) such act is necessary to conduct such encryption research;
(C) the person made a good faith effort to obtain authorization before the circumvention; and (D) such act does not constitute infringement under this title or a violation of applicable law other than this section, including section 1030 of title 18 and those provisions of title 18 amended by the Computer Fraud and Abuse Act of 1986.

(3) Factors in determining exemption. In determining whether a person qualifies for the exemption under paragraph (2), the factors to be considered shall include—

(A) whether the information derived from the encryption research was disseminated, and if so, whether it was disseminated in a manner reasonably calculated to advance the state of knowledge or development of encryption technology, versus whether it was disseminated in a manner that facilitates infringement under this title or a violation of applicable law other than this section, including a violation of privacy or breach of security;
(B) whether the person is engaged in a legitimate course of study, is employed, or is appropriately trained or experienced, in the field of encryption technology; and
(C) whether the person provides the copyright owner of the work to which the technological measure is applied with notice of the findings and documentation of the research, and the time when such notice is provided.

(4) Use of technological means for research activities. Notwithstanding the provisions of subsection (a)(2), it is not a violation of that subsection for a person to—

(A) develop and employ technological means to circumvent a technological measure for the sole purpose of that person performing the acts of good faith encryption research described in paragraph (2); and
(B) provide the technological means to another person with whom he or she is working collaboratively for the purpose of conducting the acts of good faith encryption research described in paragraph (2) or for the purpose of having that other person verify his or her acts of good faith encryption research described in paragraph (2).

(5) Report to Congress. Not later than 1 year after the date of the enactment of this chapter, the Register of Copyrights and the Assistant Secretary for

Communications and Information of the Department of Commerce shall jointly report to the Congress on the effect this subsection has had on—

(A) encryption research and the development of encryption technology;

(B) the adequacy and effectiveness of technological measures designed to protect copyrighted works; and

(C) protection of copyright owners against the unauthorized access to their encrypted copyrighted works. The report shall include legislative recommendations, if any.

(h) Exceptions Regarding Minors.

In applying subsection (a) to a component or part, the court may consider the necessity for its intended and actual incorporation in a technology, product, service, or device, which—

(1) does not itself violate the provisions of this title; and

(2) has the sole purpose to prevent the access of minors to material on the Internet.

(i) Protection of Personally Identifying Information.

(1) Circumvention permitted. Notwithstanding the provisions of subsection (a) (1)(A), it is not a violation of that subsection for a person to circumvent a technological measure that effectively controls access to a work protected under this title, if—

(A) the technological measure, or the work it protects, contains the capability of collecting or disseminating personally identifying information reflecting the online activities of a natural person who seeks to gain access to the work protected;

(B) in the normal course of its operation, the technological measure, or the work it protects, collects or disseminates personally identifying information about the person who seeks to gain access to the work protected, without providing conspicuous notice of such collection or dissemination to such person, and without providing such person with the capability to prevent or restrict such collection or dissemination;

(C) the act of circumvention has the sole effect of identifying and disabling the capability described in subparagraph (A), and has no other effect on the ability of any person to gain access to any work; and

(D) the act of circumvention is carried out solely for the purpose of preventing the collection or dissemination of personally identifying information about a natural person who seeks to gain access to the work protected, and is not in violation of any other law.

(2) Inapplicability to certain technological measures. This subsection does not apply to a technological measure, or a work it protects, that does not collect or disseminate personally identifying information and that is disclosed to a user as not having or using such capability.

(j) Security Testing.

(1) Definition. For purposes of this subsection, the term "security testing" means accessing a computer, computer system, or computer network, solely for the purpose of good faith testing, investigating, or correcting, a security flaw or vulnerability, with the authorization of the owner or operator of such computer, computer system, or computer network.

(2) Permissible acts of security testing. Notwithstanding the provisions of subsection (a)(1)(A), it is not a violation of that subsection for a person to engage in an act of security testing, if such act does not constitute infringement under this title or a violation of applicable law other than this section, including section 1030 of title 18 and those provisions of title 18 amended by the Computer Fraud and Abuse Act of 1986.

(3) Factors in determining exemption. In determining whether a person qualifies the exemption under paragraph (2), the factors to be considered shall include—

(A) whether the information derived from the security testing was used solely to promote the security of the owner or operator of such computer, computer system or computer network, or shared directly with the developer of such computer, computer system, or computer network; and

(B) whether the information derived from the security testing was used or maintained in a manner that does not facilitate infringement under this title or a violation of applicable law other than this section, including a violation of privacy or breach of security.

(4) Use of technological means for security testing. Notwithstanding the provisions of subsection (a)(2), it is not a violation of that subsection for a person to develop, produce, distribute, or employ technological means for the sole purpose of performing the acts of security testing described in subsection (2), [1] provided such technological means does not otherwise violate section [2](a)(2).

(k) Certain Analog Devices and Certain Technological Measures.

(1) Certain analog devices.

(A) Effective 18 months after the date of the enactment of this chapter, no person shall manufacture, import, offer to the public, provide, or otherwise traffic in any—

(i) VHS format analog video cassette recorder unless such recorder conforms to the automatic gain control copy control technology;

(ii) 8mm format analog video cassette camcorder unless such camcorder conforms to the automatic gain control technology;

(iii) Beta format analog video cassette recorder, unless such recorder conforms to the automatic gain control copy control technology, except that this requirement shall not apply until there are 1,000 Beta format analog video cassette recorders sold in the United

States in any one calendar year after the date of the enactment of this chapter;

(iv) 8mm format analog video cassette recorder that is not an analog video cassette camcorder, unless such recorder conforms to the automatic gain control copy control technology, except that this requirement shall not apply until there are 20,000 such recorders sold in the United States in any one calendar year after the date of the enactment of this chapter; or

(v) analog video cassette recorder that records using an NTSC format video input and that is not otherwise covered under clauses (i) through (iv), unless such device conforms to the automatic gain control copy control technology.

(B) Effective on the date of the enactment of this chapter, no person shall manufacture, import, offer to the public, provide or otherwise traffic in—

(i) any VHS format analog video cassette recorder or any 8mm format analog video cassette recorder if the design of the model of such recorder has been modified after such date of enactment so that a model of recorder that previously conformed to the automatic gain control copy control technology no longer conforms to such technology; or

(ii) any VHS format analog video cassette recorder, or any 8mm format analog video cassette recorder that is not an 8mm analog video cassette camcorder, if the design of the model of such recorder has been modified after such date of enactment so that a model of recorder that previously conformed to the four-line colorstripe copy control technology no longer conforms to such technology. Manufacturers that have not previously manufactured or sold a VHS format analog video cassette recorder, or an 8mm format analog cassette recorder, shall be required to conform to the four-line colorstripe copy control technology in the initial model of any such recorder manufactured after the date of the enactment of this chapter, and thereafter to continue conforming to the four-line colorstripe copy control technology. For purposes of this subparagraph, an analog video cassette recorder "conforms to" the four-line colorstripe copy control technology if it records a signal that, when played back by the playback function of that recorder in the normal viewing mode, exhibits, on a reference display device, a display containing distracting visible lines through portions of the viewable picture.

(2) Certain encoding restrictions. No person shall apply the automatic gain control copy control technology or colorstripe copy control technology to prevent or limit consumer copying except such copying—

 (A) of a single transmission, or specified group of transmissions, of live events or of audiovisual works for which a member of the public has exercised choice in selecting the transmissions, including the content of the transmissions or the time of receipt of such transmissions, or both, and as to which such member is charged a separate fee for each such transmission or specified group of transmissions;

 (B) from a copy of a transmission of a live event or an audiovisual work if such transmission is provided by a channel or service where payment is made by a member of the public for such channel or service in the form of a subscription fee that entitles the member of the public to receive all of the programming contained in such channel or service;

 (C) from a physical medium containing one or more prerecorded audiovisual works; or

 (D) from a copy of a transmission described in subparagraph (A) or from a copy made from a physical medium described in subparagraph (C). In the event that a transmission meets both the conditions set forth in subparagraph (A) and those set forth in subparagraph (B), the transmission shall be treated as a transmission described in subparagraph (A).

(3) Inapplicability. This subsection shall not—

 (A) require any analog video cassette camcorder to conform to the automatic gain control copy control technology with respect to any video signal received through a camera lens;

 (B) apply to the manufacture, importation, offer for sale, provision of, or other trafficking in, any professional analog video cassette recorder; or

 (C) apply to the offer for sale or provision of, or other trafficking in, any previously owned analog video cassette recorder, if such recorder was legally manufactured and sold when new and not subsequently modified in violation of paragraph (1)(B).

(4) Definitions. For purposes of this subsection:

 (A) An "analog video cassette recorder" means a device that records, or a device that includes a function that records, on electromagnetic tape in an analog format the electronic impulses produced by the video and audio portions of a television program, motion picture, or other form of audiovisual work.

 (B) An "analog video cassette camcorder" means an analog video cassette recorder that contains a recording function that operates through a camera lens and through a video input that may be connected with a television or other video playback device.

(C) An analog video cassette recorder "conforms" to the automatic gain control copy control technology if it—

    (i) detects one or more of the elements of such technology and does not record the motion picture or transmission protected by such technology; or

    (ii) records a signal that, when played back, exhibits a meaningfully distorted or degraded display.

(D) The term "professional analog video cassette recorder" means an analog video cassette recorder that is designed, manufactured, marketed, and intended for use by a person who regularly employs such a device for a lawful business or industrial use, including making, performing, displaying, distributing, or transmitting copies of motion pictures on a commercial scale.

(E) The terms "VHS format," "8mm format," "Beta format," "automatic gain control copy control technology," "colorstripe copy control technology," "four-line version of the colorstripe copy control technology," and "NTSC" have the meanings that are commonly understood in the consumer electronics and motion picture industries as of the date of the enactment of this chapter.

(5) Violations. Any violation of paragraph (1) of this subsection shall be treated as a violation of subsection (b)(1) of this section. Any violation of paragraph (2) of this subsection shall be deemed an "act of circumvention" for the purposes of section 1203(c)(3)(A) of this chapter.

Appendix B
The Federal False Claims Act[1]

Title 31. Money and Finance

Subtitle III. Financial Management

Chapter 37. Claims

Subchapter III. Claims Against the United States Government

§3729. False claims

(a) Liability for certain acts. Any person who—

    (1) knowingly presents, or causes to be presented, to an officer or employee of the United States Government or a member of the Armed Forces of the United States a false or fraudulent claim for payment or approval;

    (2) knowingly makes, uses, or causes to be made or used, a false record or statement to get a false or fraudulent claim paid or approved by the Government;

    (3) conspires to defraud the Government by getting a false or fraudulent claim allowed or paid;

    (4) has possession, custody, or control of property or money used, or to be used, by the Government and, intending to defraud the Government or willfully to conceal the property, delivers, or causes to be delivered, less property than the amount for which the person receives a certificate or receipt;

    (5) authorized to make or deliver a document certifying receipt of property used, or to be used, by the Government and, intending to defraud the Government, makes or delivers the receipt without completely knowing that the information on the receipt is true;

[1]Government Accountability Project: Federal Employee Protection, http://www.whistleblower.org/www/laws.htm

(6) knowingly buys, or receives as a pledge of an obligation or debt, public property from an officer or employee of the Government, or a member of the Armed Forces, who lawfully may not sell or pledge the property; or

(7) knowingly makes, uses, or causes to be made or used, a false record or statement to conceal, avoid, or decrease an obligation to pay or transmit money or property to the Government, is liable to the United States Government for a civil penalty of not less than $ 5,000 and not more than $10,000, plus 3 times the amount of damages which the Government sustains because of the act of that person, except that if the court finds that—

   (A) the person committing the violation of this subsection furnished officials of the United States responsible for investigating false claims violations with all information known to such person about the violation within 30 days after the date on which the defendant first obtained the information;

   (B) such person fully cooperated with any Government investigation of such violation; and

   (C) at the time such person furnished the United States with the information about the violation, no criminal prosecution, civil action, or administrative action had commenced under this title with respect to such violation, and the person did not have actual knowledge of the existence of an investigation into such violation; the court may assess not less than 2 times the amount of damages which the Government sustains because of the act of the person. A person violating this subsection shall also be liable to the United States Government for the costs of a civil action brought to recover any such penalty or damages.

(b) Knowing and knowingly defined. For purposes of this section, the terms "knowing" and "knowingly" mean that a person, with respect to information—

   (1) has actual knowledge of the information;

   (2) acts in deliberate ignorance of the truth or falsity of the information; or

   (3) acts in reckless disregard of the truth or falsity of the information, and no proof of specific intent to defraud is required.

(c) Claim defined. For purposes of this section, "claim" includes any request or demand, whether under a contract or otherwise, for money or property which is made to a contractor, grantee, or other recipient if the United States Government provides any portion of the money or property which is requested or demanded, or if the Government will reimburse such contractor, grantee, or other recipient for any portion of the money or property which is requested or demanded.

(d) Exemption from disclosure. Any information furnished pursuant to subparagraphs (A) through (C) of subsection (a) shall be exempt from disclosure under section 552 of title 5.

(e) Exclusion. This section does not apply to claims, records, or statements made under the Internal Revenue Code of 1986 [Title 26, USCS].

Title 31. Money and Finance

Subtitle III. Financial Management

Chapter 37. Claims

Subchapter III. Claims Against the United States

Government 31 USCS §3730 (1994)

§3730. Civil actions for false claims

(a) Responsibilities of the Attorney General. The Attorney General diligently shall investigate a violation under section 3729. If the Attorney General finds that a person has violated or is violating section 3729, the Attorney General may bring a civil action under this section against the person.

(b) Actions by private persons.

    (1) A person may bring a civil action for a violation of section 3729 for the person and for the United States Government. The action shall be brought in the name of the Government. The action may be dismissed only if the court and the Attorney General give written consent to the dismissal and their reasons for consenting.

    (2) A copy of the complaint and written disclosure of substantially all material evidence and information the person possesses shall be served on the Government pursuant to Rule 4(d)(4) of the Federal Rules of Civil Procedure. The complaint shall be filed in camera, shall remain under seal for at least 60 days, and shall not be served on the defendant until the court so orders. The Government may elect to intervene and proceed with the action within 60 days after it receives both the complaint and the material evidence and information.

    (3) The Government may, for good cause shown, move the court for extensions of the time during which the complaint remains under seal under paragraph (2). Any such motions may be supported by affidavits or other submissions in camera. The defendant shall not be required to respond to any complaint filed under this section until 20 days after the complaint is unsealed and served upon the defendant pursuant to Rule 4 of the Federal Rules of Civil Procedure.

    (4) Before the expiration of the 60-day period or any extensions obtained under paragraph (3), the Government shall—

        (A) proceed with the action, in which case the action shall be conducted by the Government; or (B) notify the court that it declines to take over the action, in which case the person bringing the action shall have the right to conduct the action.

(5) When a person brings an action under this subsection, no person other than the Government may intervene or bring a related action based on the facts underlying the pending action.

(c) Rights of the parties to qui tam actions.

(1) If the Government proceeds with the action, it shall have the primary responsibility for prosecuting the action, and shall not be bound by an act of the person bringing the action. Such person shall have the right to continue as a party to the action, subject to the limitations set forth in paragraph (2).

(2)

(A) The Government may dismiss the action notwithstanding the objections of the person initiating the action if the person has been notified by the Government of the filing of the motion and the court has provided the person with an opportunity for a hearing on the motion.

(B) The Government may settle the action with the defendant notwithstanding the objections of the person initiating the action if the court determines, after a hearing, that the proposed settlement is fair, adequate, and reasonable under all the circumstances. Upon a showing of good cause, such hearing may be held in camera.

(C) Upon a showing by the Government that unrestricted participation during the course of the litigation by the person initiating the action would interfere with or unduly delay the Government's prosecution of the case, or would be repetitious, irrelevant, or for purposes of harassment, the court may, in its discretion, impose limitations on the person's participation, such as—

(i) limiting the number of witnesses the person may call;
(ii) limiting the length of the testimony of such witnesses;
(iii) limiting the person's cross-examination of witnesses; or
(iv) otherwise limiting the participation by the person in the litigation.

(D) Upon a showing by the defendant that unrestricted participation during the course of the litigation by the person initiating the action would be for purposes of harassment or would cause the defendant undue burden or unnecessary expense, the court may limit the participation by the person in the litigation.

(3) If the Government elects not to proceed with the action, the person who initiated the action shall have the right to conduct the action. If the Government so requests, it shall be served with copies of all pleadings filed in the action and shall be supplied with copies of all deposition transcripts (at the Government's expense). When a person proceeds with the action, the court, without limiting the status and rights of the person initiating the action, may nevertheless permit the Government to intervene at a later date upon a showing of good cause.

(4) Whether or not the Government proceeds with the action, upon a showing by the Government that certain actions of discovery by the person initiating the action would interfere with the Government's investigation or prosecution of a criminal or civil matter arising out of the same facts, the court may stay such discovery for a period of not more than 60 days. Such a showing shall be conducted in camera. The court may extend the 60-day period upon a further showing in camera that the Government has pursued the criminal or civil investigation or proceedings with reasonable diligence and any proposed discovery in the civil action will interfere with the ongoing criminal or civil investigation or proceedings.

(5) Notwithstanding subsection (b), the Government may elect to pursue its claim through any alternate remedy available to the Government, including any administrative proceeding to determine a civil money penalty. If any such alternate remedy is pursued in another proceeding, the person initiating the action shall have the same rights in such proceeding as such person would have had if the action had continued under this section. Any finding of fact or conclusion of law made in such other proceeding that has become final shall be conclusive on all parties to an action under this section. For purposes of the preceding sentence, a finding or conclusion is final if it has been finally determined on appeal to the appropriate court of the United States, if all time for filing such an appeal with respect to the finding or conclusion has expired, or if the finding or conclusion is not subject to judicial review.

(d) Award to qui tam plaintiff.

(1) If the Government proceeds with an action brought by a person under subsection (b), such person shall, subject to the second sentence of this paragraph, receive at least 15 percent but not more than 25 percent of the proceeds of the action or settlement of the claim, depending upon the extent to which the person substantially contributed to the prosecution of the action. Where the action is one which the court finds to be based primarily on disclosures of specific information (other than information provided by the person bringing the action) relating to allegations or transactions in a criminal, civil, or administrative hearing, in a congressional, administrative, or Government Accounting Office report, hearing, audit, or investigation, or from the news media, the court may award such sums as it considers appropriate, but in no case more than 10 percent of the proceeds, taking into account the significance of the information and the role of the person bringing the action in advancing the case to litigation. Any payment to a person under the first or second sentence of this paragraph shall be made from the proceeds. Any such person shall also receive an amount for reasonable expenses which the court finds to have been necessarily incurred, plus reasonable attorneys' fees and costs. All such expenses, fees, and costs shall be awarded against the defendant.

(2) If the Government does not proceed with an action under this section, the person bringing the action or settling the claim shall receive an amount which the court decides is reasonable for collecting the civil penalty and damages. The amount shall be not less than 25 percent and not more than 30 percent of the proceeds of the action or settlement and shall be paid out of such proceeds. Such person shall also receive an amount for reasonable expenses which the court finds to have been necessarily incurred, plus reasonable attorneys' fees and costs. All such expenses, fees, and costs shall be awarded against the defendant.

(3) Whether or not the Government proceeds with the action, if the court finds that the action was brought by a person who planned and initiated the violation of section 3729 upon which the action was brought, then the court may, to the extent the court considers appropriate, reduce the share of the proceeds of the action which the person would otherwise receive under paragraph (1) or (2) of this subsection, taking into account the role of that person in advancing the case to litigation and any relevant circumstances pertaining to the violation. If the person bringing the action is convicted of criminal conduct arising from his or her role in the violation of section 3729, that person shall be dismissed from the civil action and shall not receive any share of the proceeds of the action. Such dismissal shall not prejudice the right of the United States to continue the action, represented by the Department of Justice.

(4) If the Government does not proceed with the action and the person bringing the action conducts the action, the court may award to the defendant its reasonable attorneys' fees and expenses if the defendant prevails in the action and the court finds that the claim of the person bringing the action was clearly frivolous, clearly vexatious, or brought primarily for purposes of harassment.

(e) Certain actions barred.

(1) No court shall have jurisdiction over an action brought by a former or present member of the armed forces under subsection (b) of this section against a member of the armed forces arising out of such person's service in the armed forces.

(2)

(A) No court shall have jurisdiction over an action brought under subsection (b) against a Member of Congress, a member of the judiciary, or a senior executive branch official if the action is based on evidence or information known to the Government when the action was brought.

(B) For purposes of this paragraph, "senior executive branch official" means any officer or employee listed in paragraphs (1) through (8) of section 101(f) of the Ethics in Government Act of 1978 (5 U.S.C. App.).

(3) In no event may a person bring an action under subsection (b) which is based upon allegations or transactions which are the subject of a civil suit or an

administrative civil money penalty proceeding in which the Government is already a party.

(4)

    (A) No court shall have jurisdiction over an action under this section based upon the public disclosure of allegations or transactions in a criminal, civil, or administrative hearing, in a congressional, administrative, or Government Accounting Office report, hearing, audit, or investigation, or from the news media, unless the action is brought by the Attorney General or the person bringing the action is an original source of the information.

    (B) For purposes of this paragraph, "original source" means an individual who has direct and independent knowledge of the information on which the allegations are based and has voluntarily provided the information to the Government before filing an action under this section which is based on the information.

(f) Government not liable for certain expenses. The Government is not liable for expenses which a person incurs in bringing an action under this section.

(g) Fees and expenses to prevailing defendant. In civil actions brought under this section by the United States, the provisions of section 2412(d) of title 28 shall apply.

(h) Any employee who is discharged, demoted, suspended, threatened, harassed, or in any other manner discriminated against in the terms and conditions of employment by his or her employer because of lawful acts done by the employee on behalf of the employee or others in furtherance of an action under this section, including investigation for, initiation of, testimony for, or assistance in an action filed or to be filed under this section, shall be entitled to all relief necessary to make the employee whole. Such relief shall include reinstatement with the same seniority status such employee would have had but for the discrimination, 2 times the amount of back pay, interest on the back pay, and compensation for any special damages sustained as a result of the discrimination, including litigation costs and reasonable attorneys' fees. An employee may bring an action in the appropriate district court of the United States for the relief provided in this subsection.

Title 31. Money and Finance

Subtitle III. Financial Management

Chapter 37. Claims

Subchapter III. Claims Against the United States

Government 31 USCS §3731 (1994)

§3731. False claims procedure

(a) A subpoena requiring the attendance of a witness at a trial or hearing conducted under section 3730 of this title [31 USCS §3730] may be served at any place in the United States.

(b) A civil action under section 3730 may not be brought—

   (1) more than 6 years after the date on which the violation of section 3729 is committed, or

   (2) more than 3 years after the date when facts material to the right of action are known or reasonably should have been known by the official of the United States charged with responsibility to act in the circumstances, but in no event more than 10 years after the date on which the violation is committed, whichever occurs last.

(c) In any action brought under section 3730, the United States shall be required to prove all essential elements of the cause of action, including damages, by a preponderance of the evidence.

(d) Notwithstanding any other provision of law, the Federal Rules of Criminal Procedure, or the Federal Rules of Evidence, a final judgment rendered in favor of the United States in any criminal proceeding charging fraud or false statements, whether upon a verdict after trial or upon a plea of guilty or nolo contendere, shall estop the defendant from denying the essential elements of the offense in any action which involves the same transaction as in the criminal proceeding and which is brought under subsection (a) or (b) of section 3730.

Title 31. Money and Finance

Subtitle III. Financial Management Chapter 37. Claims

Subchapter III. Claims Against the United States

Government 31 USCS §3732 (1994)

§3732. False claims jurisdiction

(a) Actions under section 3730. Any action under section 3730 may be brought in any judicial district in which the defendant or, in the case of multiple defendants, any one defendant can be found, resides, transacts business, or in which any act proscribed by section 3729 occurred. A summons as required by the Federal Rules of Civil Procedure shall be issued by the appropriate district court and served at any place within or outside the United States.

(b) Claims under state law. The district courts shall have jurisdiction over any action brought under the laws of any State for the recovery of funds paid by a State or local government if the action arises from the same transaction or occurrence as an action brought under section 3730.

Title 31. Money and Finance

Subtitle III. Financial Management

Chapter 37. Claims

Subchapter III. Claims Against the United States

Government 31 USCS §3733 (1994)

§3733. Civil investigative demands

(a) In general.

    (1) Issuance and service. Whenever the Attorney General has reason to believe that any person may be in possession, custody, or control of any documentary material or information relevant to a false claims law investigation, the

Attorney General may, before commencing a civil proceeding under section 3730 or other false claims law, issue in writing and cause to be served upon such person, a civil investigative demand requiring such person—

(A) to produce such documentary material for inspection and copying,

(B) to answer in writing written interrogatories with respect to such documentary material or information,

(C) to give oral testimony concerning such documentary material or information, or

(D) to furnish any combination of such material, answers, or testimony. The Attorney General may not delegate the authority to issue civil investigative demands under this subsection. Whenever a civil investigative demand is an express demand for any product of discovery, the Attorney General, the Deputy Attorney General, or an Assistant Attorney General shall cause to be served, in any manner authorized by this section, a copy of such demand upon the person from whom the discovery was obtained and shall notify the person to whom such demand is issued of the date on which such copy was served.

(2) Contents and deadlines.

(A) Each civil investigative demand issued under paragraph (1) shall state the nature of the conduct constituting the alleged violation of a false claims law which is under investigation, and the applicable provision of law alleged to be violated.

(B) If such demand is for the production of documentary material, the demand shall—

(i) describe each class of documentary material to be produced with such definiteness and certainty as to permit such material to be fairly identified;

(ii) prescribe a return date for each such class which will provide a reasonable period of time within which the material so demanded may be assembled and made available for inspection and copying; and

(iii) identify the false claims law investigator to whom such material shall be made available.

(C) If such demand is for answers to written interrogatories, the demand shall—

(i) set forth with specificity the written interrogatories to be answered;

(ii) prescribe dates at which time answers to written interrogatories shall be submitted; and

(iii) identify the false claims law investigator to whom such answers shall be submitted.

     (D) If such demand is for the giving of oral testimony, the demand shall—

        (i) prescribe a date, time, and place at which oral testimony shall be commenced;

        (ii) identify a false claims law investigator who shall conduct the examination and the custodian to whom the transcript of such examination shall be submitted;

        (iii) specify that such attendance and testimony are necessary to the conduct of the investigation;

        (iv) notify the person receiving the demand of the right to be accompanied by an attorney and any other representative; and

        (v) describe the general purpose for which the demand is being issued and the general nature of the testimony, including the primary areas of inquiry, which will be taken pursuant to the demand.

     (E) Any civil investigative demand issued under this section which is an express demand for any product of discovery shall not be returned or returnable until 20 days after a copy of such demand has been served upon the person from whom the discovery was obtained.

     (F) The date prescribed for the commencement of oral testimony pursuant to a civil investigative demand issued under this section shall be a date which is not less than seven days after the date on which demand is received, unless the Attorney General or an Assistant Attorney General designated by the Attorney General determines that exceptional circumstances are present which warrant the commencement of such testimony within a lesser period of time.

     (G) The Attorney General shall not authorize the issuance under this section of more than one civil investigative demand for oral testimony by the same person unless the person requests otherwise or unless the Attorney General, after investigation, notifies that person in writing that an additional demand for oral testimony is necessary. The Attorney General may not, notwithstanding section 510 of title 28, authorize the performance, by any other officer, employee, or agency, of any function vested in the Attorney General under this subparagraph.

(b) Protected material or information.

    (1) In general. A civil investigative demand issued under subsection (a) may not require the production of any documentary material, the submission of any answers to written interrogatories, or the giving of any oral testimony if such material, answers, or testimony would be protected from disclosure under—

     (A) the standards applicable to subpoenas or subpoenas duces tecum issued by a court of the United States to aid in a grand jury investigation; or

     (B) the standards applicable to discovery requests under the Federal Rules of Civil Procedure, to the extent that the application of such standards to any such demand is appropriate and consistent with the provisions and purposes of this section.

(2) Effect on other orders, rules, and laws. Any such demand which is an express demand for any product of discovery supersedes any inconsistent order, rule, or provision of law (other than this section) preventing or restraining disclosure of such product of discovery to any person. Disclosure of any product of discovery pursuant to any such express demand does not constitute a waiver of any right or privilege which the person making such disclosure may be entitled to invoke to resist discovery of trial preparation materials.

(c) Service; jurisdiction.

(1) By whom served. Any civil investigative demand issued under subsection (a) may be served by a false claims law investigator, or by a United States marshal or a deputy marshal, at any place within the territorial jurisdiction of any court of the United States.

(2) Service in foreign countries. Any such demand or any petition filed under subsection (j) may be served upon any person who is not found within the territorial jurisdiction of any court of the United States in such manner as the Federal Rules of Civil Procedure prescribe for service in a foreign country. To the extent that the courts of the United States can assert jurisdiction over any such person consistent with due process, the United States District Court for the District of Columbia shall have the same jurisdiction to take any action respecting compliance with this section by any such person that such court would have if such person were personally within the jurisdiction of such court.

(d) Service upon legal entities and natural persons.

(1) Legal entities. Service of any civil investigative demand issued under subsection (a) or of any petition filed under subsection (j) may be made upon a partnership, corporation, association, or other legal entity by—

(A) delivering an executed copy of such demand or petition to any partner, executive officer, managing agent, or general agent of the partnership, corporation, association, or entity, or to any agent authorized by appointment or by law to receive service of process on behalf of such partnership, corporation, association, or entity;

(B) delivering an executed copy of such demand or petition to the principal office or place of business of the partnership, corporation, association, or entity; or

(C) depositing an executed copy of such demand or petition in the United States mails by registered or certified mail, with a return receipt requested, addressed to such partnership, corporation, association, or entity at its principal office or place of business.

(2) Natural persons. Service of any such demand or petition may be made upon any natural person by—

(A) delivering an executed copy of such demand or petition to the person; or

(B) depositing an executed copy of such demand or petition in the United States mails by registered or certified mail, with a return receipt requested, addressed to the person at the person's residence or principal office or place of business.

(e) Proof of service. A verified return by the individual serving any civil investigative demand issued under subsection (a) or any petition filed under subsection (j) setting forth the manner of such service shall be proof of such service. In the case of service by registered or certified mail, such return shall be accompanied by the return post office receipt of delivery of such demand.

(f) Documentary material.

(1) Sworn certificates. The production of documentary material in response to a civil investigative demand served under this section shall be made under a sworn certificate, in such form as the demand designates, by—

(A) in the case of a natural person, the person to whom the demand is directed, or

(B) in the case of a person other than a natural person, a person having knowledge of the facts and circumstances relating to such production and authorized to act on behalf of such person. The certificate shall state that all of the documentary material required by the demand and in the possession, custody, or control of the person to whom the demand is directed has been produced and made available to the false claims law investigator identified in the demand.

(2) Production of materials. Any person upon whom any civil investigative demand for the production of documentary material has been served under this section shall make such material available for inspection and copying to the false claims law investigator identified in such demand at the principal place of business of such person, or at such other place as the false claims law investigator and the person thereafter may agree and prescribe in writing, or as the court may direct under subsection (j)(1). Such material shall be made so available on the return date specified in such demand, or on such later date as the false claims law investigator may prescribe in writing. Such person may, upon written agreement between the person and the false claims law investigator, substitute copies for originals of all or any part of such material.

(g) Interrogatories. Each interrogatory in a civil investigative demand served under this section shall be answered separately and fully in writing under oath and shall be submitted under a sworn certificate, in such form as the demand designates, by—

(1) in the case of a natural person, the person to whom the demand is directed, or

(2) in the case of a person other than a natural person, the person or persons responsible for answering each interrogatory. If any interrogatory is objected to, the reasons for the objection shall be stated in the certificate instead of an answer. The certificate shall state that all information required by the demand and in the possession, custody, control, or knowledge of the person to whom the demand is directed has been submitted. To the extent that any information is not furnished, the information shall be identified and reasons set forth with particularity regarding the reasons why the information was not furnished.

(h) Oral examinations.

(1) Procedures. The examination of any person pursuant to a civil investigative demand for oral testimony served under this section shall be taken before an officer authorized to administer oaths and affirmations by the laws of the United States or of the place where the examination is held. The officer before whom the testimony is to be taken shall put the witness on oath or affirmation and shall, personally or by someone acting under the direction of the officer and in the officer's presence, record the testimony of the witness. The testimony shall be taken stenographically and shall be transcribed. When the testimony is fully transcribed, the officer before whom the testimony is taken shall promptly transmit a copy of the transcript of the testimony to the custodian. This subsection shall not preclude the taking of testimony by any means authorized by, and in a manner consistent with, the Federal Rules of Civil Procedure.

(2) Persons present. The false claims law investigator conducting the examination shall exclude from the place where the examination is held all persons except the person giving the testimony, the attorney for and any other representative of the person giving the testimony, the attorney for the Government, any person who may be agreed upon by the attorney for the Government and the person giving the testimony, the officer before whom the testimony is to be taken, and any stenographer taking such testimony.

(3) Where testimony taken. The oral testimony of any person taken pursuant to a civil investigative demand served under this section shall be taken in the judicial district of the United States within which such person resides, is found, or transacts business, or in such other place as may be agreed upon by the false claims law investigator conducting the examination and such person.

(4) Transcript of testimony. When the testimony is fully transcribed, the false claims law investigator or the officer before whom the testimony is taken shall afford the witness, who may be accompanied by counsel, a reasonable opportunity to examine and read the transcript, unless such examination and reading are waived by the witness. Any changes in form or substance which the witness desires to make shall be entered and identified upon the transcript by the officer or the false claims law investigator, with a statement of the reasons given by the witness for making such changes. The transcript shall then be signed by the witness, unless the witness in writing waives the signing, is ill, cannot be found, or refuses to sign.

If the transcript is not signed by the witness within 30 days after being afforded a reasonable opportunity to examine it, the officer or the false claims law investigator shall sign it and state on the record the fact of the waiver, illness, absence of the witness, or the refusal to sign, together with the reasons, if any, given therefore.

(5) Certification and delivery to custodian. The officer before whom the testimony is taken shall certify on the transcript that the witness was sworn by the officer and that the transcript is a true record of the testimony given by the witness, and the officer or false claims law investigator shall promptly deliver the transcript, or send the transcript by registered or certified mail, to the custodian.

(6) Furnishing or inspection of transcript by witness. Upon payment of reasonable charges therefor, the false claims law investigator shall furnish a copy of the transcript to the witness only, except that the Attorney General, the Deputy Attorney General, or an Assistant Attorney General may, for good cause, limit such witness to inspection of the official transcript of the witness' testimony.

(7) Conduct of oral testimony.

(A) Any person compelled to appear for oral testimony under a civil investigative demand issued under subsection (a) may be accompanied, represented, and advised by counsel. Counsel may advise such person, in confidence, with respect to any question asked of such person. Such person or counsel may object on the record to any question, in whole or in part, and shall briefly state for the record the reason for the objection. An objection may be made, received, and entered upon the record when it is claimed that such person is entitled to refuse to answer the question on the grounds of any constitutional or other legal right or privilege, including the privilege against self-incrimination. Such person may not otherwise object to or refuse to answer any question, and may not directly or through counsel otherwise interrupt the oral examination. If such person refuses to answer any question, a petition may be filed in the district court of the United States under subsection (j)(1) for an order compelling such person to answer such question.

(B) If such person refuses to answer any question on the grounds of the privilege against self-incrimination, the testimony of such person may be compelled in accordance with the provisions of part V of title 18.

(8) Witness fees and allowances. Any person appearing for oral testimony under a civil investigative demand issued under subsection (a) shall be entitled to the same fees and allowances which are paid to witnesses in the district courts of the United States.

(i) Custodians of documents, answers, and transcripts.

(1) Designation. The Attorney General shall designate a false claims law investigator to serve as custodian of documentary material, answers to interrogatories, and transcripts of oral testimony received under this section, and

shall designate such additional false claims law investigators as the Attorney General determines from time to time to be necessary to serve as deputies to the custodian.

(2) Responsibility for materials; disclosure.

(A) A false claims law investigator who receives any documentary material, answers to interrogatories, or transcripts of oral testimony under this section shall transmit them to the custodian. The custodian shall take physical possession of such material, answers, or transcripts and shall be responsible for the use made of them and for the return of documentary material under paragraph (4).

(B) The custodian may cause the preparation of such copies of such documentary material, answers to interrogatories, or transcripts of oral testimony as may be required for official use by any false claims law investigator, or other officer or employee of the Department of Justice, who is authorized for such use under regulations which the Attorney General shall issue. Such material, answers, and transcripts may be used by any such authorized false claims law investigator or other officer or employee in connection with the taking of oral testimony under this section.

(C) Except as otherwise provided in this subsection, no documentary material, answers to interrogatories, or transcripts of oral testimony, or copies thereof, while in the possession of the custodian, shall be available for examination by any individual other than a false claims law investigator or other officer or employee of the Department of Justice authorized under subparagraph (B). The prohibition in the preceding sentence on the availability of material, answers, or transcripts shall not apply if consent is given by the person who produced such material, answers, or transcripts, or, in the case of any product of discovery produced pursuant to an express demand for such material, consent is given by the person from whom the discovery was obtained. Nothing in this subparagraph is intended to prevent disclosure to the Congress, including any committee or subcommittee of the Congress, or to any other agency of the United States for use by such agency in furtherance of its statutory responsibilities. Disclosure of information to any such other agency shall be allowed only upon application, made by the Attorney General to a United States district court, showing substantial need for the use of the information by such agency in furtherance of its statutory responsibilities.

(D) While in the possession of the custodian and under such reasonable terms and conditions as the Attorney General shall prescribe—

(i) documentary material and answers to interrogatories shall be available for examination by the person who produced such material or answers, or by a representative of that person authorized by that person to examine such material and answers; and

(ii) transcripts of oral testimony shall be available for examination by the person who produced such testimony, or by a representative of that person authorized by that person to examine such transcripts.

(3) Use of material, answers, or transcripts in other proceedings. Whenever any attorney of the Department of Justice has been designated to appear before any court, grand jury, or Federal agency in any case or proceeding, the custodian of any documentary material, answers to interrogatories, or transcripts of oral testimony received under this section may deliver to such attorney such material, answers, or transcripts for official use in connection with any such case or proceeding as such attorney determines to be required. Upon the completion of any such case or proceeding, such attorney shall return to the custodian any such material, answers, or transcripts so delivered which have not passed into the control of such court, grand jury, or agency through introduction into the record of such case or proceeding.

(4) Conditions for return of material. If any documentary material has been produced by any person in the course of any false claims law investigation pursuant to a civil investigative demand under this section, and—

(A) any case or proceeding before the court or grand jury arising out of such investigation, or any proceeding before any Federal agency involving such material, has been completed, or

(B) no case or proceeding in which such material may be used has been commenced within a reasonable time after completion of the examination and analysis of all documentary material and other information assembled in the course of such investigation, the custodian shall, upon written request of the person who produced such material, return to such person any such material (other than copies furnished to the false claims law investigator under subsection (f)(2) or made for the Department of Justice under paragraph (2)(B)) which has not passed into the control of any court, grand jury, or agency through introduction into the record of such case or proceeding.

(5) Appointment of successor custodians. In the event of the death, disability, or separation from service in the Department of Justice of the custodian of any documentary material, answers to interrogatories, or transcripts of oral testimony produced pursuant to a civil investigative demand under this section, or in the event of the official relief of such custodian from responsibility for the custody and control of such material, answers, or transcripts, the Attorney General shall promptly—

(A) designate another false claims law investigator to serve as custodian of such material, answers, or transcripts, and

(B) transmit in writing to the person who produced such material, answers, or testimony notice of the identity and address of the successor so designated. Any person who is designated to be a successor under this paragraph shall have, with regard to such material, answers, or transcripts, the same duties and responsibilities as were imposed by this section upon that person's predecessor in office, except that the successor shall not be held responsible for any default or dereliction which occurred before that designation.

(j) Judicial proceedings.

(1) Petition for enforcement. Whenever any person fails to comply with any civil investigative demand issued under subsection (a), or whenever satisfactory copying or reproduction of any material requested in such demand cannot be done and such person refuses to surrender such material, the Attorney General may file, in the district court of the United States for any judicial district in which such person resides, is found, or transacts business, and serve upon such person a petition for an order of such court for the enforcement of the civil investigative demand.

(2) Petition to modify or set aside demand.

(A) Any person who has received a civil investigative demand issued under subsection (a) may file, in the district court of the United States for the judicial district within which such person resides, is found, or transacts business, and serve upon the false claims law investigator identified in such demand a petition for an order of the court to modify or set aside such demand. In the case of a petition addressed to an express demand for any product of discovery, a petition to modify or set aside such demand may be brought only in the district court of the United States for the judicial district in which the proceeding in which such discovery was obtained is or was last pending. Any petition under this subparagraph must be filed—

(i) within 20 days after the date of service of the civil investigative demand, or at any time before the return date specified in the demand, whichever date is earlier, or

(ii) within such longer period as may be prescribed in writing by any false claims law investigator identified in the demand.

(B) The petition shall specify each ground upon which the petitioner relies in seeking relief under subparagraph (A), and may be based upon any failure of the demand to comply with the provisions of this section or upon any constitutional or other legal right or privilege of such person. During the pendency of the petition in the court, the court may stay, as it deems proper, the running of the time allowed for compliance with the demand, in whole or in part, except that the person filing the petition shall comply with any portions of the demand not sought to be modified or set aside.

(3) Petition to modify or set aside demand for product of discovery.

   (A) In the case of any civil investigative demand issued under subsection (a) which is an express demand for any product of discovery, the person from whom such discovery was obtained may file, in the district court of the United States for the judicial district in which the proceeding in which such discovery was obtained is or was last pending, and serve upon any false claims law investigator identified in the demand and upon the recipient of the demand, a petition for an order of such court to modify or set aside those portions of the demand requiring production of any such product of discovery. Any petition under this subparagraph must be filed—

   (i) within 20 days after the date of service of the civil investigative demand, or at any time before the return date specified in the demand, whichever date is earlier, or

   (ii) within such longer period as may be prescribed in writing by any false claims law investigator identified in the demand.

   (B) The petition shall specify each ground upon which the petitioner relies in seeking relief under subparagraph (A), and may be based upon any failure of the portions of the demand from which relief is sought to comply with the provisions of this section, or upon any constitutional or other legal right or privilege of the petitioner. During the pendency of the petition, the court may stay, as it deems proper, compliance with the demand and the running of the time allowed for compliance with the demand.

(4) Petition to require performance by custodian of duties. At any time during which any custodian is in custody or control of any documentary material or answers to interrogatories produced, or transcripts of oral testimony given, by any person in compliance with any civil investigative demand issued under subsection (a), such person, and in the case of an express demand for any product of discovery, the person from whom such discovery was obtained, may file, in the district court of the United States for the judicial district within which the office of such custodian is situated, and serve upon such custodian, a petition for an order of such court to require the performance by the custodian of any duty imposed upon the custodian by this section.

(5) Jurisdiction. Whenever any petition is filed in any district court of the United States under this subsection, such court shall have jurisdiction to hear and determine the matter so presented, and to enter such order or orders as may be required to carry out the provisions of this section. Any final order so entered shall be subject to appeal under section 1291 of title 28. Any disobedience of any final order entered under this section by any court shall be punished as a contempt of the court.

(6) Applicability of Federal Rules of Civil Procedure. The Federal Rules of Civil Procedure shall apply to any petition under this subsection, to the extent that such rules are not inconsistent with the provisions of this section.

(k) Disclosure exemption. Any documentary material, answers to written interrogatories, or oral testimony provided under any civil investigative demand issued under subsection (a) shall be exempt from disclosure under section 552 of title 5.

(l) Definitions. For purposes of this section—

(1) the term "false claims law" means—

(A) this section and sections 3729 through 3732; and

(B) any Act of Congress enacted after the date of the enactment of this section [enacted Oct. 27, 1986] which prohibits, or makes available to the United States in any court of the United States any civil remedy with respect to, any false claim against, bribery of, or corruption of any officer or employee of the United States;

(2) the term "false claims law investigation" means any inquiry conducted by any false claims law investigator for the purpose of ascertaining whether any person is or has been engaged in any violation of a false claims law;

(3) the term "false claims law investigator" means any attorney or investigator employed by the Department of Justice who is charged with the duty of enforcing or carrying into effect any false claims law, or any officer or employee of the United States acting under the direction and supervision of such attorney or investigator in connection with a false claims law investigation;

(4) the term "person" means any natural person, partnership, corporation, association, or other legal entity, including any State or political subdivision of a State;

(5) the term "documentary material" includes the original or any copy of any book, record, report, memorandum, paper, communication, tabulation, chart, or other document, or data compilations stored in or accessible through computer or other information retrieval systems, together with instructions and all other materials necessary to use or interpret such data compilations, and any product of discovery;

(6) the term "custodian" means the custodian, or any deputy custodian, designated by the Attorney General under subsection (i)(1); and (7) the term "product of discovery" includes—

(A) the original or duplicate of any deposition, interrogatory, document, thing, result of the inspection of land or other property, examination, or admission, which is obtained by any method of discovery in any judicial or administrative proceeding of an adversarial nature;

(B) any digest, analysis, selection, compilation, or derivation of any item listed in subparagraph (A); and

(C) any index or other manner of access to any item listed in subparagraph (A).

Appendix C
Projects

1. Morality and the law. In his article "Cultural Relativism and Cultural Values," Melville Hertskovits [1] argues that morality has no absolute identity and that it is a social and cultural phenomenon. Others disagree with this view. Read Chapter 2 and write an essay either in support of Hertskovits's view or your own.
2. Study the figure in Scenario 1 on page 19. Using the drawing as a starting point, research the issue and write an informed essay arguing the position taken in the drawing.
3. In "Sticks and Stones," John Arthur [1] states that hate speech is extremely disagreeable and causes offense. There are those who take a different view of hate speeches arguing that the principle of freedom of speech applies to hate speech as well. From our discussion in Chapter 11, research the topic and write an essay about the subject.
4. The development in technology and recent pronouncements by scientists that they intend to start human cloning, has ignited anew the debate about the value of human life and the need for finding a cure from diseases that afflict the human body. There are arguments and counterarguments to the value of human life; some argue that cloning will devalue the dignity and sanctity of human life, while others see it as a way to preserve human life through the discovery of new medicines and the manufacturing of human parts if not the whole body. Consider and write an essay about human cloning. You may choose any views as long as you support them.
5. Many religious leaders and scholars have taken the view that euthanasia violates the very core of the sanctity of human life, and therefore should never be legalized. Yet there are others, as we saw in Chapter 4, who take a humane view that those who are willing to try it have terminal illnesses and if in pain should be allowed to end their own lives. Suppose you are a programmer working for a company that develops technologies that measure the degree of pain and the longevity of life, and taking these two factors a system administers the lethal dose. You have just discovered this company's secret. What would be your reaction? Write as essay expressing your feelings about the whole issue.

6. Pornography has not only thrived in cyberspace, but it has also grown in leaps and bounds, becoming a multimillion dollar industry, usually out of reach of most national legal jurisdictions. There have been proposals to work from within the international law framework to overcome the mosaic of national jurisdictions and, therefore, curb it. However, some people see no need to do this arguing that people (adults) do have a right to pornography. Write an essay stressing the Internet's role in the wildfire-type spread of pornography.

7. Internet gambling has experienced a huge resurgence thanks to offshore gambling sites. Such sites are out of reach of many national legal and tax systems. Many have sought governments crackdown on the industry and others are calling for legalization. Write an essay on one of these views or your own.

8. Internet regulation has been a hot issue as concerned parents and civic leaders argue that lawmakers should control Internet content that many have objections to and see as out of control, evil, corrupting, and a source of many societal problems. Write an essay on Internet regulation and its enforcement.

9. Ever since the National Science Foundation (NSF) relinquished control of the Internet, it has been a free-for-all with big businesses wrestling one another for control. A loose international structure known as ICAAN has now been put in place to oversee the day-to-day management of the Internet. Study the structure and management styles of ICAAN and write an essay stating your own opinion on its effectives.

10. Cyberspace censorship has been justified by those doing it with many different reasons, including religious tolerance, cultural harmony, political stability, and citizenship, to name but a few. Write an essay for or against cyberspace censorship.

11. Statistics show that identity theft is the fastest growing crime today. Cyberspace and new technologies have enabled and made possible easy ways for criminals to steal targeted personal identities. Study the ways identity theft is done and how to prevent it. Stress your personal preference and why.

12. Many people have argued that cybercrimes are not a new breed of crimes, but are only different because of the different means of carrying them out. Write an essay in support of the argument. If you do not agree, argue otherwise.

13. One of the reasons the fight against cybercrimes has been so dismal is the fact that many people, especially businesses, are not reporting crimes directed against them. Those who report are usually underreporting. Study the problem and the rate of reporting and write an essay outlining the steps needed to be taken to bring about full reporting, if possible.

14. Many of those who oppose cyberspace regulation have suggested self-regulation, arguing that it gives the level of control according to individual needs. Those in support of strong regulation argue that, especially in public facilities such as schools and libraries, self-regulation does not work, therefore, strong collective measures are needed. Research and write an essay in support of one of the two arguments.

15. One of the resulting consequences of the September 11, 2001, terrorist attack on the United States has been the rise in employee background checks. Many

employers are requesting for more research to be done on workers, even those who have already been screened before. Others want more detailed information gathered about the employees, especially job applicants. In addition to employee background checks, monitoring of employee activities using high technology gadgets is up. Write an essay on the merits or dangers of these actions.

16. Many have expressed concern with the diminishing state of personal privacy. Others have in fact observed and publicly declared the demise of personal privacy, saying that privacy in today's cyberspace life is dead and we should forget it and move on with our lives. Write an essay in support of or against the observation.

17. ACM filed a declaration with the federal court regarding the case of *Felton* v. *RIAA* in which ACM expressed fear that its goal of supporting conference presentations and publications of scholars will be curtailed by subsection 1201(a)3 of the Digital Millennium Copyright Act (DMCA). Study section 1201(a)3 in Appendix A and write an essay in support of either ACM or RIAA.

18. Common morality runs across different cultures and embraces the standards of ethics and morality in respective cultures. Basic human rights and duties are good examples that form the basis of the standard of all types of ethics and morality. Discuss common morality in cyberspace.

Reference

1. Satris, Stephen (ed.). *Taking Sides: Clashing Views on Controversial Moral Issues*. New York: McGraw-Hill, 2000.

Index